AN ANALYTICAL PHILOSOPHY
OF RELIGION

AN ANALYTICAL PHILOSOPHY OF RELIGION

Willem F. Zuurdeeg

ABINGDON PRESS
NEW YORK NASHVILLE

AN ANALYTICAL PHILOSOPHY OF RELIGION

Library of Congress Catalog Card Number: 58-9527

Chapter VIII, pages 282-306, is based on an article entitled "Hermeneutics," by Willem F. Zuurdeeg, in *Nederlands Theologisch Tijdschrift*, October, 1951.

SET UP, PRINTED, AND BOUND BY THE PARTHENON PRESS, AT NASHVILLE, TENNESSEE, UNITED STATES OF AMERICA

TO

My Wife and Children

PREFACE

THIS BOOK IS WRITTEN WITH A THREEFOLD PURPOSE. FIRST, IT IS planned as a textbook in philosophy of religion. It is meant for students in philosophy who are well acquainted with modern analytical and empirical philosophy and who wonder what can be said about religion from the point of view of this philosophy. It is intended also for theological students who are well acquainted with modern theology and who wonder about the implications of contemporary philosophy for theological thinking.

The second purpose of the book is more ambitious. I hope that it will encourage a fruitful discussion between philosophers and theologians, between those who respect Carnap and Feigl and have read some of Sartre, and those who admire Barth, Nygren, and the Niebuhrs. Yet by means of this second intention also the volume addresses itself to students. By students are meant persons who do not "know," and who therefore want to discuss and to learn. They differ from another type of person, people who "know," who are quite certain and who therefore are no more in need of learning, namely, the "professors!"

The world of philosophers and theologians is full of professors. We have all met theologians who "know" that logical empiricism is "unspiritual," that it does not take into account "the deeper aspects of reality," and therefore cannot be of any use to a religious man. And who does not know those professors of philosophy who are quite certain that religion is a "cultural lag," and who suggest that a cultivated man who claims to be a Christian is lacking either in moral integrity or in intellectual keenness? I myself have not yet reached the maturity and certainty of such professors; my thinking is too full of question marks and doubts, as well in regard to "religion," as in matters of philosophy. I hope to find readers who suffer from similar doubts and questions, and who share my interest in an encounter of theological and philosophical thinking. It is not impossible that one can learn a great deal in this way.

The third purpose of the book is to try to defend a particular thesis. It is possible to discuss matters of faith in a more or less impartial way. It is possible to try to understand the deepest motivations of our own and of others' beliefs without immediately becoming defensive or aggressive. One can analyze these beliefs while being on guard as to one's own convictions and prejudices, lest they cloud one's vision and make an increase in understanding impossible. It is not easy, but it is sometimes possible to check one's inclination to preach, and to become a philosopher.

Furthermore, the world shows us so many theologians and metaphysicians who are full of their convictions (that is to say, full of themselves) that it is a relief to realize that an activity exists, philosophy, which takes a certain distance to these cherished and important convictions (or selves). Philosophy is not to be condoned as an attempt (a bit Utopian) to think impartially; it is to be hailed as a healthy counterbalance against a too anxious concern with our convictions.

I have not aimed at completeness. Certain pertinent problems have been selected, but not all the relevant issues have been brought into discussion. I have chosen some important authors, but not everyone who truly merits study has here received attention. It has seemed more important to show what can be done by the analytical approach in philosophy of religion than to pursue a completeness which could not easily be attained by a single man. Left out are such important problems as symbol, nondiscursive communication, demythologizing, and philosophers such as Kierkegaard, Wittgenstein, and Russell.

The reader may wonder why I do not refer to Kierkegaard and Buber, since my approach is akin to the basic position of these two men. The answer is, partly, that the full meaning of their ideas (especially in respect to Kierkegaard) still largely escapes my understanding; partly, that discussion of Kierkegaard and Buber is not strictly necessary, because the approach set forth in this essay has not been influenced (directly) by the methods of these scholars.

I regret that Ian T. Ramsey's *Religious Language*[1] was published after this manuscript was finished. Also, John Hick's *Faith and Knowledge*[2] and Walter F. Otto's *Die Gestalt und das Sein*[3] reached me after the manuscript was completed.

Perhaps the reader will feel that some of the thinkers discussed did not receive their due. I want to state emphatically that I have not intended either a full approval or a denunciation of the person or the work of any writer. I disclaim the ability and the right to such total appraisals

[1] *Religious Language: An Empirical Placing of Theological Phrases* (London: SCM Press, 1957).

[2] *Faith and Knowledge: A Modern Introduction to the Problem of Religious Knowledge* (Ithaca, N.Y.: Cornell University Press, 1957).

[3] Düsseldorf: Diederichs, 1955.

of men so eminent as Tillich or Whitehead. It could be suggested that in regard to some specific problems these men seem to be in the wrong. Opinions like this should not be interpreted in any specific case as an easy dismissal of the achievements of such major thinkers of our time.

The term "analysis" in the title of the book does not mean that I am convinced of having given a "pure," "neutral" analysis. I believe that a completely neutral analysis in matters of conviction is unattainable, even that the notion of such an analysis implies an ideal of questionable value. On the other hand, I believe that it is important to strive for an analysis which is as unbiased as is humanly possible.

Yet even such an unbiased analysis has not been fully realized in this book. First, I am limited in my understanding. It seems beyond doubt that an analytical philosopher should try to analyze only those convictions of which he possesses a more or less intimate knowledge. In this case I am acquainted with the ideas of what is called Reconstructed Liberalism, Neo-Reformation theology, a certain type of humanism, Marxism, Nazism, and to a small extent the ancient and primitive religions. Examples and illustrations are chosen from these convictions only, and the most from the convictions which I know most intimately, those of the churches united in the Ecumenical Movement.

Therefore, the fact that the last chapter deals only with some Protestant convictions does not mean that I consider these convictions to be the "best," the "highest," or the ones "most acceptable to a philosopher" (whatever that might mean). This fact simply shows that I do not know contemporary Judaism, Roman Catholicism, or naturalism well enough to discuss them in this chapter.

Second, I am not only limited in my understanding of contemporary convictions, but my analysis is inevitably informed by the convictions which I share. Sometimes such "information" will be a help (it can assist the author in seeing specific things); at other times it will be a hindrance (it can prevent him from seeing other things).

We could rise above both limitations if other analytical philosophers whose thinking is informed by other convictions, and who possess an intimate knowledge of a wider range of beliefs, would enter into the discussion of convictional language.

These remarks hope to make clear that this book is intended as more than the defense of a specific theology with philosophical means. I am interested not in defense but in understanding. I wish to understand convictional language—that is, man-who-speaks—not to defend a specific conviction, and have tried to make the understanding offered as unbiased as possible, in spite of the unavoidable limitations.

I am very grateful to Mrs. Esther C. Swenson, M.A., for her great help and constructive criticism. Mrs. Swenson has carefully reviewed the whole manuscript, and there is scarcely a chapter or section for which she has not made valuable suggestions. President Arthur R. McKay of McCormick Theological Seminary, Professors Tyler Thompson and William H. Poteat, and Professor K. A. H. Hidding of the University of Leiden have obliged me greatly by their helpful advice for the first chapters. Several former students of McCormick Theological Seminary, especially G. W. Bowen and A. D. Clark, have made valuable contributions in their discussion of some central concepts.

Several friends have been so gracious as to suggest improvements in the English diction of the manuscript. Mrs. Helena Carus subjected its language to a careful scrutiny; and the president of McCormick Theological Seminary, several of the members of the faculty, and two of the students, Henry W. Pilgram and Albert G. Ossentjuk, each read a part or the whole of the manuscript and proposed changes of diction.

Quotations from the works of W. B. Kristensen, K. A. H. Hidding, G. Gusdorf, M. Pradines, M. Eliade, M. Heidegger, and L. Binswanger are of my own translation.

WILLEM F. ZUURDEEG

CONTENTS

INTRODUCTION
Analysis and Language

1. The function of philosophy

a) There exist several and conflicting conceptions of the function of philosophy. In this book the conception of modern analytical philosophy is followed: it is the function of philosophy to analyze languages. This is not to say that other conceptions are held to be "wrong" or invalid. I am not competent to make such sweeping statements and condemnations. My purpose is different. Innumerable philosophies of religion have been written on the tacit or explicit assumption that the idealist conception of the function of philosophy is the obvious or even the self-evident method in philosophy of religion. I wish to dissociate myself from that position. I want, rather, to see how far one can go in philosophy of religion by following the approach of the analytical movement. Does it work? What does it help us see? What are its strong and weak points? Must qualifications be made, and how?

b) There are very good reasons to assume that the analytical conception of the function of philosophy is a fruitful approach in philosophy; it follows a method which complies with what we can observe about people. We know that we who belong to the Western civilization of the twentieth century speak a considerable number of languages, such as those of mathematics, of empirical science, of morals, of poetry, and of various religions. It makes very good sense to consider it the proper task of philosophy to analyze the structures of each of these and of other languages. Questions to be asked are the following: What is communicated by means of the language under consideration? Who is the communicator? What is the type of truth of the communication?

c) This approach implies the assertion that it is *not* the function of philosophy to establish, by the use of reason, the true meaning of life, the real value of things, the intrinsic nature of the universe, the Absolute, or God.

(1) Philosophy is not *a "higher" way* which grants us access to a "higher" world, as over against the ordinary, the "lower" way of science which offers us access merely to the ordinary, visible, tangible world.

(2) Philosophy does not *preach,* it does not call people to a "way of life," nor does it present itself as a guide to life and its values.

(3) Philosophy cannot ascertain *the "real" nature of good and evil,* of justice and injustice.

(4) Philosophy does not disclose, by harmonizing the "experiences" of science, morals, the arts, and the religions, *the "real" structure of the universe.*

2. The function of philosophy of religion

a) The conception of philosophy as analysis of languages implies the interpretation of philosophy of religion as analysis of religious language. This means that philosophy of religion is simply a branch of philosophy in general. Religious language is one of the languages which Western man of the twentieth century speaks. It must be analyzed lest the work of philosophy remain unfinished. To put this in a slightly different way: it may be questioned whether we can achieve a full understanding of the other languages, such as scientific and philosophical language, if we do not investigate religious language.

For reasons to be set forth later it seems useful to include in the work of philosophy of religion the analysis of several languages which are not strictly religious, namely, moral language and the languages of various *Weltanschauungen.* (The word "religion" is taken here to mean: overt religion, those phenomena which present themselves and are generally accepted as religions.)

b) This method implies the notion that it is *not* the task of philosophy of religion to defend a specific form of the Christian faith, or for that matter, of any religious conviction.

(1) Philosophy of religion is not a branch of theology, nor a preparation for systematic theology.

(2) Its task is not to broaden a faith which tends to be too much absorbed in itself, by means of a consideration of the "truths" of science, art, and philosophy.

3. The desire to preach

The desire to offer guidance to searching souls is deeply embedded in human nature. There is nothing illegitimate in the desire itself. It is not even, as some people are inclined to think, slightly ridiculous. However, it is not the task of philosophy to try to meet this desire. People should offer guidance by means of their faith, their morals, their world views, their novels, dramas, and poetry, but not via their philosophy. The rejection of the traditional conceptions of philosophy and philosophy of religion has therefore to be supplemented by the claim that questions and answers about the meaning of life and the nature of God are perfectly meaningful, but belong to a realm of meaning to be analyzed by philosophy and not to philosophy itself.

4. A philosophical revolution

a) We have to emphasize the revolutionary nature of the analytical conception of the function of philosophy. Actually, analytical philosophy has to be understood as a second revolution, following the principles brought to light by the first revolution, one which came about some centuries ago.

This first revolution has been described lately in the following way:

> Indeed it might almost be said that the history of philosophy in its relation to the sciences, consists, in part in the disentangling of those questions which are either empirical (and inductive), or formal (and deductive), from the mass of problems which fill the minds of men. . . . It is in this way that, for instance, astronomy, mathematics, psychology, biology, etc., became divorced from the general corpus of philosophy (of which they once formed a part).[1]

The second revolution, that of the twentieth century, consists in the consideration that there is another group of questions which have to be "disentangled" from philosophy, namely, questions of God, of the meaning of life. These problems, and also such as "What is really good?" and "What is the meaning of history?" cannot be answered (or for that matter, not even properly raised) by philosophy, but have to be left to the religions, the *Weltanschauungen,* the moral codes of those who ask these questions.

This radical difference between modern and traditional philosophy can be recognized much more clearly in analytical than in existentialist philosophy. The existentialists still raise questions about the meaning of life, but in spite of this fact, they are closer to modern than to traditional philosophy. Their discussion of the meaning of life is offered in the framework of an analysis of the human situation, and not (as is the case in traditional philosophy) as a part of the construction of a system intended to disclose the "real nature" of the All, to establish the existence of God, or to reveal the ultimate End of history.

b) It seems to be extraordinarily difficult to grasp the meaning of this philosophical revolution, and still to philosophize about religion in an analytical way.

We can discriminate between three groups of scholars who do not assume the task of philosophizing analytically about religion:

[1] *The Age of Enlightenment,* ed. Isaiah Berlin (New York: Mentor Books, 1956), p. 13.

(1) The large majority of analytical philosophers who are "not interested" in religion, and interpret the philosophical revolution to mean that philosophers, as philosophers, should not deal with religion.

(2) The philosophers of religion, who adhere to prerevolutionary philosophical methods, and who reject analytical philosophy because it does not offer them any help in defending or developing their faith.

(3) The new group of "language philosophers" which has developed in England, with Oxford as its center, and which moves not in the realm of analytical philosophy but in that of philosophical theology.

It is embarrassing for me to be obliged to dissociate myself from this Oxford group. These men deserve the warm interest of philosophers and theologians all over the globe for their efforts to establish communication between analytical philosophers and modern theologians. However, they have interpreted the challenge of analytical philosophy to mean that Christian (and non-Christian) "philosophers" should set forth and defend (or attack) the Christian claim in terms of the new philosophy.

I do not deny that the Oxford publications contain many valuable examples of genuine philosophical analysis, but I doubt whether the apologetic enterprise which is the major intention of these publications is compatible with the spirit of analytical philosophy. It is my understanding that analytical philosophy means an approach which can analyze and *only* analyze, and which *cannot* apologize, evaluate, prescribe, witness, persuade, convince, or preach. In other words, there exists an inner tension, if not a contradiction, between analytical philosophy and a philosophical theology which wants to render Christianity plausible (or implausible) by means of language philosophy.

We have to conclude that the philosophical revolution of our century has not yet touched the matter of religion. An analytical philosophy of religion does not yet exist. The present book is an attempt to enter upon this virgin field.

5. *Qualifications*

In the course of our investigation (How far does the analytical approach bring us in philosophy of religion?) we will find out that two of the main tenets of the analytical method in philosophy are especially fruitful for philosophy of religion: in addition to its conception of the function of philosophy, also its distrust of metaphysics and ontology. On the other hand, we will discover that the categories usually used by most language philosophers are insufficient in view of the matter to be investigated: the languages of religion, morals, and *Weltanschauungen*. Whereas in the case of, e.g., mathematics it is sufficient to analyze the language itself, in the case of religious language we have to concern ourselves with the person who speaks the language. For a full understanding of such a language it is further necessary to see the community in which the language functions, and to penetrate into the historical backgrounds, without which neither persons, nor their communities, nor their languages can be understood. In a word, in the case of such a language we have to analyze not only the language itself but also the *language situation.*

Hence we can formulate the central theme of this book in the form of two theses:

I. The analytical method is a most appropriate approach in philosophy of religion

a) in its conception of philosophy of religion as analysis of language, and

b) in its disqualification of metaphysics and ontology

II. The analytical approach to language, in the case of religious and similar languages, has to be qualified by an account of the language situation, to which belong:

a) the person who communicates

b) the community within which the language functions

c) the (subjectively) objective references of the languages

d) the "worlds" within which these elements are related

e) the historical backgrounds of these elements

The term "analysis," as used in this essay, therefore possesses various aspects of meaning:

1. The discussion starts with the meaning which the logical empiricists present, and which at this moment is generally accepted, that of *logical analysis.*

2. In the first chapter our discussion forces us to use "analysis" in the meaning of *situational analysis.*

3. At the end of Part I we will notice how a third aspect of meaning, that of a *distrust of lofty words,* is one of the underlying elements of both the first and the second aspect.

6. *Acknowledgment of gratitude*

The question might be raised as to whether the method expressed in these two theses is not strongly influenced by "existentialism," and should perhaps be labeled as an attempt to combine analytical and existentialist philosophy. This would be a misinterpretation. As was said earlier, I have tried out the analytical method, and when it seemed necessary, I have made qualifications. One can say that these qualifications brought me generally in the direction of "existentialism." "Analysis of the language situation" is pretty close to "analysis of the human situation," which last expression could count as a rendering of an important trend in the existentialist's thinking about the function of philosophy. It remains a fact, however, that I did *not* start with an attempt to combine these two philosophical schools. For one thing, it is not quite clear to me what "existentialism" is. Furthermore, there is a real difference between fullheartedly starting from an existentialist point of view, and in the course of an investigation approaching such a viewpoint, and that only in certain matters.

Finally, another factor plays a role. I received the stimulation to my philosophical thinking, not only from the logical positivists, but also from the approach of two Dutch philosophers of religion and ethics, Isaac J. de Bussy and Nicolaas Westendorp Boerma.[2] They represented an approach to philosophical ethics which was radically empirical, but which also shows a certain kinship to Kierkegaard. What may seem to an American reader a remark with existentialist flavor has sometimes been inspired by the work of these two thinkers.

7. *The concept of language*

The introduction has so far tried to clarify what the author means by analysis. A similar clarification should follow with regard to the term "language." If philosophy is analysis of language, what concept of language is held in our type of philosophy of religion?

In this book we are not interested in language and speech as possible objects of scientific research. The reader will find no references to the psychology of speech, to grammatics, lexicology, or phonetics.

It is not easy to say in a few words what it is that the reader *does* find in this book. As a preliminary idea of what is meant, a word of the eighteenth-century philosopher Lichtenberg may serve: "Our entire philosophy is a correction of our use of language." [3] "Language" here means something like this: the way in which human beings use words, expressions, exclamations, commandments, in order to find their place in the world.

In our attempt to say more clearly what we understand by language, we will follow the same method as in regard to the meaning of analysis. First, we will outline briefly the position taken by most analytical

[2] I. J. de Bussy, 1846-1920, professor in the theological faculty of the University of Amsterdam, 1892-1916. N. Westendorp Boerma, 1872-1952, professor in the same faculty, 1936-42. A reference to De Bussy's method is made in Chap. VII.

[3] *Unsere ganze Philosophie ist Berichtigung des Sprachgebrauchs,* quoted in R. von Mises, *Kleines Lehrbuch des Positivismus* (The Hague: Van Stockum, 1939), p. 1; English trans., *Positivism* (Cambridge: Harvard University Press, 1951).

philosophers. Second, we will indicate our own position by making some qualifications of this general analytical point of view.

I. The general analytical position asserts that language is a unity of word and thought and discriminates between:

a) "language as used in common life," "serving various functions," without distinguishing clearly between them

b) language as appropriately used in specific languages, such as mathematics and empirical science, each time serving one of these functions

c) language as inappropriately used in a "confusion" of the various functions, that is, in metaphysical language[4]

II. The qualification of this position is guided by the following considerations:

a) The general position omits a language which is not a specific language but the language which underlies both the language of common life and the specific languages, namely, convictional language.

b) Convictional language is not given full justice by terms such as "use" and "function"; it shows a unity of word, thought, and person; it *is* the person in his relationships to himself, to others, and to the "world."

c) We are analyzing not just words or sentences but languages in the sense of man-who-speaks.

d) "Language" is an ambiguous term, in that two aspects are always present:

(1) an individual, personal aspect, man-who-speaks

(2) a structural aspect; it is by means of language structures that man-who-speaks establishes his existence

e) Metaphysics is not merely a matter of the misuse of language and of confusion of its functions, but it is also a symptom of a particular relationship of the person to himself, to others, and the "world"; it is a specific way in which man-who-speaks establishes his existence.

[4] H. Feigl, "Logical Empiricism," in *Readings in Philosophical Analysis*, ed. H. Feigl and W. Sellars (New York: Appleton-Century-Crofts, 1949), p. 7.

PART ONE

Modern Man Is Homo Loquens, Homo Convictus

CHAPTER ONE

CONVICTION

Man-Who-Speaks Is Overcome by a Convictor

A. "CONVICTION" AS A TERM OF ANALYTICAL PHILOSOPHY

1. *The insufficiency of the term "emotive"*

a) If one adheres to the conception of philosophy as analysis of language, the first step to be taken is to distinguish between various realms of discourse. Feigl presents a diagram of such realms, the principle of which has been and still is the foundation of logical empiricism:

THE FUNCTIONS OF LANGUAGE, *or*	THE MEANINGS OF "MEANING"
Cognitive meanings (informational function)	*Non-cognitive meanings* (emotive expression and appeal function)
Purely formal	Pictorial (Imaginative)
Logico-arithmetical	Emotional (Affective)
Factual (Empirical)	Volitional-motivational (Directive)

Feigl begins his explanation with the following statement:

This table, correctly understood and properly used, is a powerful tool in the disentanglement of the traditional puzzles of philosophy. Many metaphysical "problems" and their "solutions" depend upon the erroneous presumption of the presence of factual meaning in expressions which have only emotive appeals and/or a formally correct grammatical structure. And many an epistemological question has been obscured by mistaking logico-mathematical for factual meanings. It is such confusion or erroneous pretense that is exposed to criticism on the basis of our table of meanings. No evaluation of the functions of language as such is implied. Emotive appeals are indispensable in the pursuits of practical life, in education, in propaganda (good or bad), in poetry, in literature, in religious edification and moral exhortation. Some of the highest refinements of our civilized existence depend upon the emotional overtones of spoken and written language.[1]

[1] From "Logical Empiricism," in *Readings in Philosophical Analysis*, p. 7. Used by permission of Philosophical Library, Inc.

b) While the attempt to distinguish between realms of discourse is indispensable, several aspects of Feigl's table are questionable. One objection will be raised here; others will follow later. Most of the terms in the column of noncognitive meanings are unsatisfactory, namely, "emotive," "emotional," "volitional," and "appeal function." These terms are meant to describe, among others, the languages of religion, morals, and propaganda. They are, however, insufficient to give account of a Communist's dedication to his cause, or a Moslem's loyalty to Allah. The language in which these men express themselves is not only emotional and volitional, though it is certainly that, but much more is involved. Not only do a Moslem's emotions, will, and persuasive intentions come into play, but so also does his intellect, and other aspects of his personality as well. That is to say: his whole person is involved, and it is not easy to say where the boundaries of "a whole person" are to be found. One cannot think of him apart from his wife, his children, his work, or his home. Emotions and will are part of the picture, but they are subordinate parts. We shall have to look for another term.

2. *The term "conviction" in general usage*

The term "conviction" seems a more appropriate one to use for the categories cited above. We will describe, first, its meaning in its Latin origins, and then the meaning of the English word itself with its equivalents in other modern languages. Finally, we will propose a specific usage of the term for philosophical analysis.

a) The English word "conviction" is derived from the Latin *convictio* and *convinco*. *Convinco* means: "to overcome, to conquer, to refute." *Convinco* is composed of *vinco,* meaning "to conquer," and of *cum* (*con*), meaning "with," and also "thoroughly." Though *vinco* was used in military language (see the word "victor"), *convinco* never was. This last verb seems to have been used in two ways: first, in legal language; second, in everyday language. In law it meant: proving someone guilty of an offense. If a criminal was convicted, that is, "convinced," this meant that he was thoroughly overcome by the power of evidence, or the testimony of a witness. One of the meanings in general usage was: to prove someone guilty of an error. He was then thoroughly overcome by an argument. Hence, *convinco* could also mean: to prove something incontestably, to show clearly, to demonstrate. It seems to be clear that the root meaning is: to overcome thoroughly.

b) The English word "conviction" has maintained this root meaning. A short survey of some dictionaries produces the following definitions:

(1) (purely intellectual) act of overcoming someone by argument, of "convicting" someone of error by means of proof or evidence

(2) (moral-religious) being "convicted" of sin, being "convicted" by one's conscience

(3) a certainty of a thorough kind; a strong persuasion or belief; intensity of a thorough conviction; a state of being fully persuaded (cf. "convincingly")

(4) a conscious act of the mind

(5) persuasions; beliefs which are settled, fixed

(6) an opinion which is merely probable, lacking sufficient evidence (also "belief" and "faith" are sometimes used in this weak sense)[2]

c) The same variety of meanings can be noticed in the French, German, and Dutch equivalents of "conviction." The dictionaries of these languages, however, add some features to the picture presented above. Lalande discusses a meaning of the French term which is most closely related to aspect (3): "a certitude which is strong and a sufficient ground for action, but which is not completely strict, either because it rests on a probability, be it a strong one, or because it rests on a mixture of intellectual reasons and strong sentiments." One speaks of *conviction intime,* an inner conviction.

The German and the Dutch are interesting because the roots of the words equivalent to "conviction" mean "witness." The German word is *Ueberzeugung,* from the root *zeug,* see *Zeuge,* witness. The Dutch word is *overtuiging,* from the root *tuig,* see *getuige,* witness. Kluge-Götze informs us that *überziugen, mit Zeugen überführen* (to overcome someone with the help of witnesses) has been used as a legal term since the thirteenth century. The dictionaries of the fifteenth and sixteenth centuries render its meaning always with *testibus evincere, coarguere* (to conquer, to prove someone's guilt with the help of witnesses). The present meaning, *mit Gründen zu einer Ansicht bekehren* (to persuade to a point of view on good grounds), which was derived from the medieval usage, was prepared for in the works of the theologians of the sixteenth century. It does not come into clear or common usage, however, before the eighteenth century.[3]

3. *Proposal for the philosophical usage of the term "conviction"*

It is necessary to state as clearly as possible the way in which we intend to use the term "conviction" in philosophical analysis.

[2] Harper's *Latin Dictionary* (New York: American Book Co., n.d.), *s.v. con-vinco;* Webster's *New International Dictionary* (Springfield, Mass.: G. & C. Merriam Co., 1928), *s.v.* "conviction"; Walter W. Skeat, *An Etymological Dictionary of the English Language* (3rd ed.; Oxford: Clarendon Press, 1897), *s.v.* "convince"; *Shorter Oxford English Dictionary* (2nd ed.; Oxford: Clarendon Press, 1936), *s.v.* "conviction," "convince."

[3] André Lalande, *Vocabulaire technique et critique de la philosophie* (6me ed.; Paris: Presses universitaires de France, 1951), *s.v. conviction;* F. Kluge und A. Götze, *Etymologisches Wörterbuch der Deutschen Sprache, s.v. Ueberzeugen.*

a) We take the term "conviction" to mean all persuasions concerning the meaning of life; concerning good and bad; concerning gods and devils; concerning representations of the ideal man, the ideal state, the ideal society; concerning the meaning of history, of nature, and of the All. We propose *not* to use the term in any purely intellectual realm of discourse. We will therefore not say that a scientist *is convinced* that a certain hypothesis is true, but that he takes it to be true. We will say, however, that a Nazi was convinced that the Aryan race was called to lead the world.

Of the meanings reported in No. 2*b* we will not use (1), (4), (5), and (6). Meaning (2) is revelant for us but this formulation is too narrow. Meaning (3) and Lalande's conception are closest to our usage.

b) The most valuable notions mentioned in No. 2 are *being overcome, witness,* and *certitude which is a sufficient ground for action.* "Being overcome" points to the somebody or something by whom a person is overcome. We should better write *somebody* or *something* because this element is of decisive importance in a conviction. It determines its content, form, intensity, depth—in a word, its whole character. Here we have to point out another weakness of Feigl's terminology. The use of the terms "emotive," "emotional," and "volitional" draws too much attention to the subjective aspect of the conviction. If Feigl's usage implies the assertion that there is no objective reference for one's convictions, we would have to accuse him of a confusion. It is certainly true that a philosopher cannot assert or prove the reality and value of such objective references. He is, however, not allowed to suggest their nonreality or lack of value either. The only thing which counts is whether the objective reference is a reality *for the believer*. It cannot be denied that Maat, Christ's kingdom, Allah, and the Communist *Heilstaat* are or were the really Real for ancient Egyptians, Christians, Moslems, and Communists, respectively.

Another remark must be added at this point. The influence of the overcoming element upon the conviction is so decisive that it determines almost exclusively the nature of the conviction. Christian faith is different from Moslem belief and Communist loyalty to such an extent that we should use the general term "conviction" with the greatest caution.

"Certitude which is a sufficient ground for action" is also a constitutive element of conviction. Here we touch upon an issue which is usually indicated by terms such as "risk," "adventure," "decision." We encounter here a very special kind of decision. Decisions are made in all types of languages. Hence no assertion in any type of language is completely "objective." The logical positivist Richard von Mises stresses this point and uses it in his argument for the relativity of scientific language.[4]

The formulation of Lalande (see *b*) does not sufficiently characterize the special kind of decision of convictional language. Some terms which he uses suggest that there is something lacking in the certitude upon which a convictional decision is made. These terms are: "probability, be it a strong one," "a mixture of intellectual reasons and strong sentiments." It is possible to read these expressions as meaning that if the probability could be replaced by certainty, or the intellectual reasons be freed from the sentiments, the certitude would be of such a character that it would present not merely a "sufficient" ground for action but an inescapable one.

The crucial point is that convictional certitude is something different in kind from scientific certitude, something *sui generis*. There is nothing lacking in the certitude of a Moslem that Allah is his God. If this kind of certitude can be fruitfully compared with scientific and with mathematical certitude at all, it should be said that convictional certitude is so overwhelming (notice the "being overcome" element) that the believer in many instances gives his life for his Cause. The whole person is involved, including his very existence, whereas mathematical and scientific certitude refers solely to the intellect. In short, a discussion of convictional certitude in terms of either probability or qualification of intellectual reasons by sentiment misses the point.

B. THE CONVICTIONAL SITUATION

We have to realize that the actual object of our discussion is "a convictional situation." Its structure should be made clear.

1. The convictor

The first element is that of the somebody or something which overcomes. We could call it: the convictor. Usual names for this element are: the gods, or the *summum bonum*. The most important characteristic of the convictor is its power. The following verbs suggest themselves: overawe, overlord, overpower, override, overshadow, overwhelm. Using these words as guides in Roget's *Thesaurus*, we are led to:

Success (731): mastery, victory, triumph, master of the situation, subdue, subjugate

Authority (737): prestige, prerogative, dominion, sovereignty, supremacy, control, hold, grasp, reign, rule, bend to one's will

[4] *Op. cit., passim.*

Master (745): lord, potentate, majesty, king, despot, tyrant

Influence (175): weight, pressure, preponderance, sway, magnetize, take hold, overbear, prevail

Repute (873): dignity, solemnity, grandeur, splendor, nobility, glory, honor, eminence, greatness

The last two groups of words remind us of the fact that the notion of power with regard to a god or a *summum bonum* is not a simple thing. A famous discussion of this issue is to be found in Rudolf Otto's *The Idea of the Holy*. He describes deity as the *mysterium tremendum et fascinosum,* the mystery which makes us tremble and also fascinates us. The convictor's power has both elements. It takes hold of us and overpowers us, but it also draws us irresistibly.

Connected with these two aspects of the convictor's power is the fact that he both threatens us and makes us promises. A Jew is convinced that he forfeits Yahweh's grace by disobedience. Loyalty to Hitler promised to a convinced Nazi participation in the glory and splendor of "the Third Reich."

2. *Convictus, witness, testimony, decision*

It is impossible to give a full discussion to all the elements of the convictional situation. Some of those which will receive only a brief treatment are dealt with in this section.

We will call the person who is overcome the *convictus*.[5] This term indicates what is usually called the "believer," but also the loyal Nazi, the dedicated Communist, and the nationalist who worships his country as his Highest Good.

The next element is the witness, or better, the *witnesses*. The importance of this element must be stressed because the mention of the convictor, the convictus, and the decision easily leads us to the erroneous opinion that being convinced is a relationship exclusively between the convictor and the convictus. This is not the case at all. Tradition and environment, parents, school, friends, the social groups to which we belong—all these influence deeply which convictions we shall entertain. We share the religious, moral, and political convictions of our group. We consider those persons to be reliable witnesses who are the bearers of authority in our group. For a Christian they include the patriarchs and the prophets of the Old Testament, the disciples of Christ, the church leaders and reformers, down to Schweitzer and

[5] I have derived the terms "convictor" and "convictus" from the Latin verb *convinco*. In classical Latin these two words were not used in this sense. The words did exist but had another meaning because they were derived from another verb, *convivo,* which has the same participle as *convinco,* viz., *convictum*. There is hardly a chance for confusion.

William Temple. For a Communist they include Marx, Lenin, and Stalin; and for an "enlightened" Frenchman, Voltaire, Pierre Bayle, Condillac, and Auguste Comte.

Another element is that of the *testimonies* given by the witnesses. For example, the Bible, the Koran, creeds, manifestoes (e.g., the Communist one), platforms, books (e.g., Plato's Dialogues, Spinoza's *Ethics*), religious and national anthems, and speeches (e.g., Hitler's political addresses).

The element now to be discussed is the *decision* made by the convictus. There are probably no decisions which do not possess an element of commitment, even in the case of scientific language. If a scientist decides in favor of a certain hypothesis, his act is not unrelated to a commitment to the value of truth, or better, to the value of the scientific enterprise. In the case of a convictional decision this commitment character plays a more important role. Such a decision is a dedication of the whole person to the convictor, because something of overwhelming importance is at stake: a cause has to be defended, a precious value protected, or a god is to be served. The convictus "decides" to give himself to this task.

The use of the term "decision" does not suggest the opinion that the act to which we refer is one which exclusively rises out of the depth of the convictus' existence. The power of the convictor, of the witnesses, of the testimonies, is much too real for this. It is, furthermore, impossible to estimate the relationship between the contributions of each of these elements. Goethe's dictum may serve as a guide: "*Halb sank er hin, halb zog sie ihn.*" [6]

3. *The act of assent*

The notion of "witness" possesses an implication which we have not yet considered. Is the testimony of a witness the ground for our assent to a specific conviction? There are several grounds for acts of assent. For example, in the case of the language of mathematics we have logical demonstration; in the case of scientific language, factual demonstration, factual evidence, and experiment. We must now ask, What is the nature of the ground of assent in convictional language? Why does one adhere to a specific conviction?

a) It is not on the basis of empirical evidence. This is not to say that evidence does not play any role at all, or that convictions are adhered to arbitrarily. Rather, the evidence in the meaning of empirical, factual evidence is not decisive for one's convictions. Many times people

[6] From the poem "Der Fischer." It refers to a fisherman who is drawn irresistibly by a mermaid, down into the deep. Half of it was that he sank down; half of it that she pulled him.

are convinced in spite of the so-called facts, "in the teeth of" the evidence. Christians are convinced that the crucified Christ is the revelation of a powerful God. This conviction was a stumbling block and a foolishness in the eyes of the Jews and the Greeks who entertained other convictions. The Christian conviction is not the only one which is independent of "evidence." Those who are convinced that man is a rational being, and those who believe that the world is *essentially* a well-ordered cosmos, speak "in the teeth of" a great deal of evidence that seems to be opposed to their beliefs. The very term "essential" points out that we are dealing with a conviction which is not at all plausible; one has to see more deeply, to penetrate to what is invisible, to the "essence," before one can detect the well-ordered harmony which is belied by the evidence which is before our very eyes. Of a similar nature are the communist convictions about an ideal society in which man will do good spontaneously, the Western belief in progress, and the Nazi convictions about the superior quality of the Aryan race.

b) The answer to the question why people adhere to their specific convictions begins with the convictor. People are convinced because a Good, a Cause, or a God has taken hold of them. They cannot help themselves; for they are drawn irresistibly, they are fascinated. The convictor is always a *Fascinans*. This means, if we use the term "ground for assent" at all in regard to convictional language, that these grounds have to be looked for both outside of and within the convictus. It seems that several kinds of "grounds" are at work in the convictus' assents to certain convictions: first, the convictor, a power which *for him* comes to him from the world outside himself; second, the witnesses, who by means of their testimonies have influenced this decision; third, the "goods" which are at stake—himself, his world, his whole way of living; fourth, the threat to these "goods" by hostile powers; fifth, the promise of a new life waiting for him who shares these convictions and who follows the convictor. This is to say that the whole convictional situation comes into the picture. The assent is given by *man in his convictional situation,* in his relationship to its various elements.

c) We may now turn to the discussion of the question as to whether the term "grounds for an act of assent" makes sense with regard to convictional language. The term "ground" suggests an attitude which is entirely compatible with the process of scientific or mathematical thinking, but which does not play a role in the convictional life, namely, the attitude of detached deliberation. A scholar can coolly consider various possibilities, weigh the evidence at his disposal, and analyze the grounds on which he will make his decision, without his own existence being involved at all. His very being and the grounds for assent are two different things. In the case of convictions, these two elements are so closely connected that one cannot make a distinction. It seems better to drop the term "grounds" and to say that the act of assent is an expression of the person.

d) Something more needs to be said about the difference between "assenting to a scientific hypothesis" and "becoming convinced." In the first case the situation is comparatively simple, because there is a stable point, namely, the person who is going to give his assent. In the case of "becoming convinced" this event actually implies a change in the person himself. A man who really has "become convinced that" is no longer the same man. Many times a person is convinced, not only "in spite of" the facts, but even "in spite of" himself. Saul kicks against the pricks (Acts 9:5). After his conversion he receives another name (Paul); that is to say, he has become another man. Conversion is a very strong, clear, outspoken form of becoming convinced. Conversion is here understood to mean, not exclusively the change from unbelief to belief, but more generally the change from one conviction to another. One can be converted from naturalism to Protestantism, from idealism to Catholicism, from democratic Western convictions to Communism, but also vice versa in each instance. Nobody can live totally without convictions. It is possible, however, for a person to live a long time without powerful convictions guiding his life in a clear way, and then at a given moment in a specific situation be overcome by another convictor. Everything in his own life, including other persons and the meaning of life, will appear in a new light emanating from the new convictor. We can call this event a conversion. "Conversion" is derived from the Latin verb *converto,* to turn around completely. What has been turned around here—that is, changed completely—is everything which a man values in life. He has a new convictor. The world appears in a new light. This implies that he himself has become another man.

Now it becomes evident why we should be careful with the term "grounds" in the case of convictional language. This term fits scientific language, in which we can give a full account of the grounds of our assent to a certain theory, but this full account is impossible in the case of convictions. Nobody understands himself well enough to account for his convictions, that is, for himself, as well as for the convictor who is the center of his life.[7] We can give as little account of the "grounds"

[7] A similar idea has been formulated by A. K. Saran in a discussion of David Bidney's *Theoretical Anthropology,* in *Ethics,* LXVI, No. 3 (April, 1956), 202: "It is hardly possible to exaggerate the importance of realizing that man is not fully self-reflective and that it is impossible *in principle* for man to know himself completely as an object."

for loving our wives as we can account for our trust in Christ, or for our following of Buddha. In this regard we always remain a mystery to ourselves and to other people.

Sometimes, however, people claim to be able to give a full account of their convictions. It seems plausible that in such cases we are dealing with rationalizations. Impressive systems of a philosophical or theological kind are offered to us, ontologies or metaphysics, but the analytical philosopher suspects that the real "why" of these convictions (it is better to avoid terms such as "grounds" or "reasons") is hidden from the system builder.

That is not to say that we always walk in utter darkness. Sometimes it happens that, after a "conversion," part of the veil is lifted, as in the case of Paul. But the "grounds" revealed in such a way are actually pronouncements of the glory and majesty of the new convictor.

On the other hand, we have to admit that it also happens that people do not have any idea of the "why" of their convictions during their whole lifetime. We meet this situation when specific convictions have been shared by so many people for so long a time that they seem self-evident, and that most of their adherents are not aware at all of their specific character. Before they were challenged by Nazis and Communists, most people of the Western countries were not aware that they entertained particular convictions at all; whereas their lives were actually informed by very definite Enlightenment convictions about the nature and destiny of man, about the meaning of history, and the like. The phrase "grounds for an act of assent" does not make any sense here at all.

4. *The confessional group*

The function of the confessional group has to be discussed in connection with the problem of the change of language. All languages change. The change sometimes occurs spontaneously, as in everyday language; sometimes it is planned, as in scientific vocabulary. The changes in convictional language are of both types.

a) Referring to the language of Christian faith, the Dutch philosopher of religion, Hendrik T. de Graaf, asserted that this language functions within a specific group, which he called the confessional group.[8] De Graaf further distinguished the theological vanguard of the confessional group whose task it is to propose changes in the group's language (confessional language) in order to improve and enrich it.

[8] De Graaf, 1875-1930, taught at Leiden University from 1926 to 1930. The remarks referred to were never published.

The following discussions are nothing more than an elaboration of De Graaf's ideas.

b) In his lectures De Graaf had in mind his own confessional group, that of the liberal Protestants, but there is no reason not to widen this concept. In a certain sense each religion is a confessional group. Furthermore, it makes sense to speak of confessional groups *within* a religion, such as the Mahayana and the Hinayana in Buddhism, or the Orthodox, the Romans, the Anglicans, and the Protestants in Christianity. In all these cases the group is bound together by common convictions which are articulated in creeds or confessions.

c) We can express the same thing by claiming that each group speaks its own confessional language. Here are some of its aspects:

(1) It expresses the common convictions in the sense of formulating them clearly and articulating them in a way which no single member of the group could ever achieve.

(2) It is the natural language used by the members and by the group itself when they speak about the meaning of life. It is natural for a Jew on such occasions to use terms like "prophet," "chosen nation," or "children of Abraham." These words come naturally, spontaneously, and there is a certain joy in their use.

(3) It has the luster of a gladly accepted authority.

(4) It is established and fixed in creeds, holy books, and anthems—in short, in the "testimonies" referred to above.

(5) Not in all cases but frequently deviations from the confessional language are decried. (See the heresy procedures in several Christian groups and in Soviet Communism.)

(6) It is a means of recognition for the members of the group. Fascists all over the world recognize each other by the way they speak about creeping socialism, and the healthy cleaning up of Spain by the morally sound rule of Franco. One of the traditional terms used in the Christian church for a creed is "symbol." This word is then used in one of its root meanings: "a means of recognition."

d) It is the task of the theological vanguard to give guidance to the process of change to which each language must submit. De Graaf expressed this for his own confessional group in these words:

> At the origin of the theological enterprise lies the conviction that the current language of one's group is shamefully insufficient in referring to the august, lofty reality held in mind. This language has to be corrected and enriched, in order that the members of the group may praise their Lord in a more appropriate language.[9]

[9] Quoted from memory.

This analysis applies equally well to other confessional groups. A theological vanguard functions in each of them.

This is not to deny that differences exist in this connection. These, however, have to do with the *interpretation* of the change of language occurring in the group to which one belongs. In De Graaf's group, that of liberal Protestantism, people are well aware of this procedure of changing language, and they admit its value, its legitimacy, and its inevitability. Other confessional groups do not recognize the problem as such, or they offer distorted explanations. Where the conviction prevails (as is the case in several Christian and Moslem communities) that "the Truth" has been expressed once for all in a completely satisfying and authoritative way, the renewing activity of theology *cannot* be admitted. Instead, new formulations will be read back into older ones; that is, they will not be acknowledged as new ones, but will be considered as eternally valid truths which have always been accepted and which merely require a stronger emphasis in the present.

These differences of self-interpretation should not blind us to the fact that in all confessional groups theological vanguards are at work, and in one way or another encourage or hinder certain changes, authorize or condemn them. Some examples of the vanguard activity may help to clarify the issue. In many churches currently connected with the World Council of Churches, Christ used to be spoken of as the "best man who ever lived." The vanguard proposed to change this language to "the Son of God" or "*Christus Victor*." In several American confessional groups the theological vanguard has proposed to drop words such as "those niggers" and to replace them by "our colored fellow citizens," or "our brethren in Christ who belong to another race." Stalin was active in the theological vanguard of his confessional group when he changed the slogan "Socialism can succeed only as a worldwide revolution" to the phrase "Socialism [is possible] in one country."

Theological activity clearly discloses the strong intellectual element in convictional language. Theology is inspired and guided by convictions, but it is at the same time an intellectual activity. If we take as an example the theology in the major Protestant churches, we see that it implies an intellectual account of the Christian faith in view of modern Bible study, the history of religious and secular thought in our Western civilization, the interpretation of non-Christian religions, a study of political and social movements, psychology, and sociology. In Chap. VIII we shall give a detailed analysis of the various disciplines which contribute to this theological activity. Here we shall merely point out that the intellectual element is not confined to the work of a small number of professional theologians. In present-day churches, creeds and pronouncements play a subordinate role. They are not considered as final authorities which discourage individual thinking, but as guides for the thinking of every member. Members are encouraged to think for themselves, that is, to give account of their own lives with the help of the directives provided for them in the pronouncements and confessions of their church. "Being overcome" by a convictor is, therefore, an act in which the whole person, including the intellect, plays a role. It is an event which is not confined to one moment but which lasts as long as life itself and involves a continual accounting of one's convictions and their implications for individual and social living.

5. *Theology in a wider sense*

The examples of the preceding pages were not chosen exclusively from the Christian faith and other phenomena which are usually called religions. There were, for example, references to Nazism and Communism. Now we shall have to ask ourselves what is implied when we speak of theologies, confessional languages, and groups in connection with nonreligious phenomena. It is my contention that we find convictional language not only in religious and moral utterances but also in political and philosophical statements.

a) Let us take as an example the Communist Manifesto.[10] We notice here a mixture of languages.

(1) In the first place, there are scientific statements or propositions which can be verified, for example, those referring to freeman and slave, patrician and plebeian (page 9). We call this kind of language "indicative language." (See Sec. C-1.)

(2) In the second place, these pages are full of moral language. See on page 11 the following expressions: "pitilessly torn asunder"; "naked self-interest"; "callous cash payment"; "the icy water of egotistical calculation"; "naked, shameless, direct, brutal exploitation." This moral language is, however, not the only kind of convictional language to be noticed in the publication.

(3) Take the very first sentence of the Manifesto: "The history of all hitherto existing society is the history of class struggles." This is not indicative language. An indicative statement—for example, in historical discourse—would run something like this: "Much of the history of many societies is the history of conflicts between social groups." The Manifesto sentence does not, in the first place, aim at establishing facts, but at proclaiming the meaning of history, the meaning of man's historical existence. It is *convictional* language.

[10] Karl Marx and Friedrich Engels, *Manifesto of the Communist Party* (10th ed.; New York: International Publishers, 1948). The page numbers refer to this edition.

Furthermore, it is a *theology*. This sentence, and the whole Manifesto, offers reasoning inspired by convictions; it is an attempt to give an intelligible account of the meanings of life and history, guided by very specific evaluations, e.g., about the value of "classes," revolutions, labor, etc. This theology is furthermore a *theology of history*. Some theologies give an intelligible account of the meaning of life with the help of an orientation toward nature, such as the primitive, ancient, and Oriental religions. Other theologies are oriented toward history, such as the Moslem, the Jewish, the Christian religions, and also the belief in progress. The Manifesto theology clearly belongs to the latter group.

(4) Another convictional element can be found, in that eleven paragraphs in sec. 1 of the Manifesto begin with expressions such as the following: "The bourgeoisie . . . has put an end to all feudal . . . relations"; "The bourgeoisie has stripped of its halo every occupation hitherto honored . . ."; "The bourgeoisie has torn away from the family. . . ." The repetition of these accusations suggests a trial. The bourgeoisie is the accused, while Marx and Engels are the prosecutors. The condemnation is more than a legal or even a moral one. The trial takes place in the presence of all generations; indeed it has cosmic dimensions. I cannot escape the impression that Marx and Engels are convinced that the bourgeoisie has trespassed upon laws of cosmic stature.

(5) Another convictional element shows itself clearly on page 13. The first new paragraph on that page pictures the immense power of the bourgeoisie. "It batters down all Chinese walls. . . . It forces the barbarians' intensely obstinate hatred of foreigners to capitulate. It compels all nations to adopt the bourgeois mode of production." The paragraph ends: "In a word, it creates a world after its own image." This is a portrayal of a superhuman being, a devil. To create something "after one's own image" is the work of a god (Gen. 1:26). If this creation is evil, it must be an evil god who has produced it. Page 15 discloses the joy over the expected downfall of this devil: "The bourgeoisie has forged the weapons that bring death to itself, and has called into existence the men who are to wield these weapons." Many overt religions know this joy about the stupid devil who falls into his own trap.

The fact that a devil occupies such an important place in the Manifesto theology should make us ask the question whether we can observe any other major religious categories. Most of them are not difficult to find: a *savior*—namely, the proletariat—which fights the good fight in order to eradicate not only the oppression by the bourgeoisie, but oppression as such; the proletariat acts and makes sacrifices for the sake of all future generations.

Furthermore we find very strong *eschatological* elements. The aspect of a radical break with the past is indicated on page 29, where the Communist revolution is discussed in terms of "the most radical rupture" with the traditional property relations and traditional ideas. The last two paragraphs on page 31 are nothing but an eschatological song of praise, joy over the evil (class distinctions and political power) which will have been eradicated in the new world, delight in the good which will have been established for ever and ever ("an association, in which the free development of each is the condition for the free development of all").

(6) What right do we have to call these utterances religious? Marx himself certainly would not agree. He writes:

> The theoretical conclusions of the Communists are in no way based on ideas or principles that have been invented, or discovered, by this or that would-be universal reformer. They merely express, in general terms, actual relations springing from an existing class struggle, from a historical movement going on under our very eyes.[11]

This amounts to the claim of having written scientific, indicative language. We cannot say anything else than, first, that the convictional element appears to be very strong; second, that Marx and Engels were not aware of the fact that they were using it. In other words, their religion was a *cryptoreligion,* their theology *cryptotheology.*

b) The use of the term "crypto" should not surprise us at all. What human being, either as an individual or as a member of a group, is fully aware of all his convictions? What human being knows himself, that is, his convictions completely? For to a certain extent we *are* our convictions. Our preferences, our sympathies, how and to what extent we give ourselves to a convictor—these things make us what we really are. Nobody knows in all respects the convictor, the god who has overcome him. Some people do not know this god at all. Everybody has some cryptoconvictions. We commenced our discussion with some remarks on Christian theology, but what person is exclusively a "Christian"? During the last few decades we found that in Germany, in Russia, and elsewhere, many people who thought of themselves as "Christians" were overcome by Hitler or by the Communist cause. How many "Christians" worship, in the first place, their own nation, or social

[11] *Ibid.*, p. 23.

group, or race, and many times without realizing that what they call "God" is for them only a second-class convictor? We ought therefore to distinguish, not only for Marx and Engels, but for each man, between the religion, the convictions, the theology, which he sets forth explicitly, and the implicit convictions and theology which really determine his thinking and his acting, even his whole being. The explicit convictions and the accompanying theology always possess the character of a rationalization. It has to be admitted that one individual may have a much clearer conception of his deepest convictions—that is to say, of his convictor and of himself—than other people have.

c) In the preceding assertions an idea is implied which should be made clear. It is the notion that everybody possesses convictions, whether he is aware of the fact or not. If a person does not present his convictions in the form of religious or moral persuasions, we should do well to look for his convictions elsewhere. They can hide in his politics, his poetry, or his philosophy.

This notion implies the conception that people cannot live long in a convictional "vacuum." Nobody can be himself—or better, can *be*, can exist—without having convictions and without giving account of them in one way or another. In the church circles to which I belong it is claimed that we can understand the sudden, powerful rise of Nazism and Communism after the end of World War I as the surge of new convictions in nations where people had been left with a convictional vacuum. Both the Russian and the German nations had claimed to be Christian, but in both cases Christianity had not been able to inspire convictions strong enough to guide these nations through periods of catastrophe. The Nazi and Communist convictions thus jumped into the vacuum. This analysis appears to be philosophically sound. If a traditional convictor has become nearly powerless, a new convictor takes hold of the hearts and minds.

d) The foregoing analysis may help us to interpret the character of many philosophical systems. In the same way that Marx and Engels presented their convictions in terms of a political manifesto, in which they formed the framework for indicative language, so also philosophers set forth their convictions in the form of metaphysical, ethical, or epistemological treatises, in which the convictions provided a framework for philosophical analysis. In this chapter no detailed analysis of philosophical systems will be given. These systems are presented in later chapters. Therefore a full discussion of our characterization of philosophical systems has to wait. We present here, however, some brief remarks about the popular work of Sartre as an illustration of our thesis, and some general observations about the convictional character of the philosophical enterprise.

(1) Most philosophers seem to have lived in crucial times. They have been dissatisfied with the traditional convictions and theologies, and have offered new theologies which formulated new convictions. Their enthusiastic following proves the fact that many other people also felt unhappy with the traditional confessional groups. These followers formed themselves into new confessional groups, of which the philosophers were the theological vanguard. Spinoza was dissatisfied with the teachings of the synagogue and finally broke with it. The adherents of his new theology recognized him as their spiritual guide. There still exists in Holland a group of Spinoza followers, a small confessional group.

Kant's case belongs to another category; here there was no break with the traditional confessional group at all. Yet Kant found it necessary to give account to himself and his readers of the implications of the new science, Newtonian physics, for his whole interpretation of life, including morals and religion, because of the fact that the church did not take this science seriously enough. Of the three questions which motivated his philosophizing—What can I know? What should I do? What may I hope for?—two were clearly of a convictional character, whereas it may be argued that convictional elements were not absent even in his epistemology. For that matter, the fact that nearly every philosopher of rank occupied himself with ethics and metaphysics tends to strengthen our supposition that convictional problems made up a considerable part of their philosophy.

(2) A peculiar example of the convictional element in philosophy is found in the popular sections of the work of Jean Paul Sartre, to wit, his plays, novels, and the short essay *Existentialism*.[12] Although it may be true that Sartre wrote this material with his tongue in his cheek, more to satisfy the general public than to give account of his serious philosophizing, it seems improbable that the convictions presented in his popular works would differ from those which play a role in *Being and Nothingness*. Furthermore, the very fact that the general public asked emphatically for such guidance as Sartre offers them is of importance, as well as the fact that they expected the leadership from a philosopher. In these works Sartre preaches a heroism of despair, and it would seem that many people in Western Europe

[12] *L'Existentialisme est un humanisme* (Paris: Nagel, 1946); American trans., *Existentialism,* tr. Bernard Frechtman (New York: Philosophical Library, 1947); English trans., *Existentialism and Humanism,* tr. Philip Mairet (London: Methuen & Co., 1948). The references are to the English translation.

need that preaching. There is clearly a confessional group around him. He appeals to those men who can find no satisfaction in Roman Catholic or in Communist convictions about the meaning of life and the destiny of man. He wrote "Existentialism . . . is a doctrine that does render human life possible." Man "will be what he makes of himself." "Man is of a greater dignity than a stone or a table." "Our responsibility . . . concerns mankind as a whole." [13]

e) A word of caution must be given with reference to two terms. The words "religion" and "cryptoreligion" do not imply an evaluation of any kind. They do not suggest that religious might be better than nonreligious convictions. Nor does the fact that Communism and Fascism are called cryptoreligions convey the opinion that they are "not so bad after all."

6. *A plurality of convictors*

a) Thus far we have dealt with the convictional situation in such a way as to suggest that a human being has only one convictor. Actually each man has been overcome by several convictors. This is demonstrated by the fact that nobody belongs just to one and only one confessional group. For instance, Mr. A. belongs to a Congregational church, is a member of the Republican Party, and is an Elk. Mr. B. is a Roman Catholic, a Democrat, an assiduous labor union man, and a fervent participant in the N.A.A.C.P. Instead of speaking of "many convictors" we can refer to a man's "region of convictors." This region possesses a certain structure. The convictors form a hierarchy; one of them has more power than the others; this convictor determines more decisively a person's outlook and behavior, even his very being.

This hierarchical structure is not permanent. It changes continually as long as the person grows or deteriorates. Most of the time these changes are scarcely noticed by the person himself, though sometimes a man can be sharply aware of a decisive turn. This happens, for instance, in the case of conversion. If we take the term "conversion" in a wider sense than conversion to a specific form of Christian belief, it can be considered as a revolution in the region of convictors.[14]

[13] *Ibid.*, pp. 24, 28, 29.

[14] One of the groups which has persistently warned against the oversimplification of assuming that man has only one convictor is the movement of the liberal Protestants, especially in Holland. This warning is one of the main themes of the teaching of L. J. van Holk, professor of philosophy of religion and ethics at the University of Leiden. He points out that modern Christians follow the authority of culture and civilization as well as that of their faith. In a discussion of the problem of authority Van Holk offers a list of all those elements which *actually* have authority over modern Christians: to wit, God, Christ, the Bible, priests, prophets, witnesses, creeds, and various aspects of the realms of art, science, mores, and the

b) Many people are accustomed to believe that they have only one convictor. This belief is encouraged by the attitude of many Christian ministers, who not only proclaim that a Christian *should* have one convictor (Christ), but also suggest that the faithful churchgoer actually enjoys such a privileged mode of living. Suggestions such as these do not so much reveal an admirable naïveté as a misleading glossing over of a factual situation: man is a complicated and ambiguous being, not all of a piece, but full of contradictions and conflicting loyalties. The suspicion widely felt, that being a Christian requires a considerable amount of hypocrisy, is connected with the awareness that so many "Christians" share in the "naïve" denial of man's ambiguity.

c) Perhaps our discussion can throw some light on the question of how we are to understand fanaticism. Usually the fanatic is characterized as a person who is so completely convinced of the truth of his own ideas that he thinks that all means are permitted to persuade other people to submit to the same truth. This means that the usual understanding of the fanatic is couched in the terms of an interpretation of the fanatic's *relationship to others.* On the basis of the foregoing discussion, we must add that the fanatic is also to be understood in *relationship to his convictor.* A fanatic is a person who does not see that he is actually inspired by several convictors. He believes, or makes himself believe, that he adheres to one and only one convictor. It is important to realize that these two relationships are closely connected with a third one: the fanatic's *relationship to himself.* The fanatic denies part of his own convictions; that is to say, he ignores, hates, and rejects part of his own being. The passionate refusal to accept the complexity and ambiguity of his own existence seems to be one of the main roots of the fanatical way of living.[15]

It is remarkable that there is such a basic similarity in the ways in which seemingly opposite types of people, such as the fanatic and the average churchgoer, interpret their convictional situations. In both cases all three relationships are grossly oversimplified. But there is also a basic difference. The fervor and passion of the fanatic distinguish him from the benign churchgoer, whose kind, "naïve" ignorance of his actual, ambiguous existence is not so much a fanatical attitude as a laudable attempt to construct a respectable façade behind which he can live his

state. L. J. van Holk, *De Boodschap van het Vrijzinnig Christendom* (Amsterdam-Paris, 1939).

[15] The notion of these three relationships and their intimate connection is akin to similar conceptions of Gabriel Marcel, e.g., his *Homo Viator,* tr. Emma Craufurd (Chicago: Henry Regnery Co., 1951) and Reinhold Niebuhr, *The Self and the Dramas of History* (New York: Charles Scribner's Sons, 1955). Marcel and Niebuhr, however, discuss this issue within a framework which is largely convictional.

real life in peace. We churchgoers and "church"-goers are too kind as to be shaken by the tortured passion of the real fanatic.[16]

d) There is a third type of person who can be understood in terms of the refusal to admit that man has more than one convictor. This is the partisan in the fields of philosophy and theology. We can notice here the same oversimplification in the three relationships mentioned above. Again, it is insufficient to say that the partisan considers his own school of "thought" (read: conviction) to be the only "right" one; that it is therefore plausible that he has at his disposal a little list of "wrong" schools; that it is easy to see why he is suspicious of those who claim to see something valuable in competing schools. Such considerations take into account only the relationship of the partisan to others. The typical partisan has a particular relationship to his convictor, be it a god, a science, idealism, empiricism, or existentialism. The convictor is the only true one, and "we" "know" him, while the "others" do not know him and are therefore fundamentally in the wrong. This attitude implies also a typical relationship of the partisan to himself: it is a first-rate folly to allow doubts and criticism of your own convictor, or your own school of "thought," to receive real attention. By means of this partisan attitude a whole series of entities—the convictor, the group, its theology or cryptotheology, and the man's own person—is elevated above doubt and fundamental questioning. It is interesting to see that these entities together form the convictional situation. By absolutizing this situation, Christian partisans and empiricist partisans are "protecting" themselves against fruitful challenges by the other group.

e) Here a few words are in order on the subject of "doubt." The fanatic, the average "church"-goer, the partisan—all are people who want to silence doubts. The man, however, who admits the plurality of his convictors herewith acknowledges the reality of doubt in his own existence and the importance of its function. The following of one of a man's many convictors implies the doubtful authority of the other convictors. Since man's convictional life consists largely of a continual rearranging of the hierarchy of convictors, a continual comparison of one convictor over against another is taking place.

f) In this connection something can be said about the function of philosophical and theological systems. A system tends to become a closed system, if it has a sole convictor; that is, it tends to become monistic, monolithic. Such a system will overlook and minimize the com-

[16] Churchgoers possess first cousins in the "church"-goers, that is to say, people who oversimplify their convictional situation, not by assuming that Christ is their only convictor, but by believing that they are essentially (!) "good Americans," "good Democrats," or simply "good people."

plexity and ambiguity of man's convictional situation; any contradictions and conflicts are in danger of being neatly straightened out. Man is "essentially" one thing; he is *homo sapiens, animal rationale, homo faber,* or a sex-ridden animal. William James's pluralism seems to be inspired by a healthy protest against such a monistic interpretation of man and life.

g) Some phenomena, sometimes wrongly considered to be exclusively "psychological," can be understood partly in terms of the present analysis of the convictional situation. It seems plausible that one aspect of schizophrenia is a conflict, within the sufferer's person, between loyalties to two convictors. What we call a well-balanced person can be understood as a human being who has brought about a working agreement between these loyalties to various convictors. A more or less stable hierarchy has been formed in the region of convictors. The notion of balance is related to that of freedom. A person can be considered to be free only to the extent that he fully admits the complexity and ambiguity of his convictional situation.

h) In addition, some so-called political phenomena can be partly understood in terms of the present discussion. A revolution is not only, perhaps not even in the first place, a change in the political, legal, and social structures. It is certainly in a very important way a change in the hierarchy of the convictors of a nation. In prerevolutionary Russia the decisive elements in this region were: God, the Czar, Holy Mother Russia. In Communist Russia these elements are: the Communist party, Lenin, Marx, the (holy) Russian nation (closely related to the Holy Mother Russia), and perhaps the workers' class. Stalin has lately been eliminated from this lofty company.

i) In conclusion a warning must be sounded. What I have intended here is an analysis and not an evaluation. For instance, the question has not been raised as to whether the plurality of convictors or the complexity and ambiguity of man's life is a good or a bad thing. This plurality, complexity, and ambiguity are facts, and we observe these facts in our attempts to analyze man's convictional language. Our analysis brings us to the realization that there are types of people who do not admit these facts, and who therefore have a confused understanding of life and of themselves. It does not belong to the philosopher's province to pronounce judgment about any of these language facts which it is his task to analyze and describe. As philosophers we cannot take sides, neither with those who highly appreciate some of these facts (for instance, romanticists who enjoy the complexity of man's life for the enrichment it can bring), nor with those who deplore them (for instance, Christians and Moslems who claim that man is forced to admit that he serves many lords, but that he *should* worship only one master).

C. CONVICTIONAL AND INDICATIVE LANGUAGE

A crucial issue for our whole approach is the relationship between convictional language and other languages. The other languages which lie within our range of interest are: indicative language, tautological language, and analytical language.

1. *Indicative, tautological, and analytical language*

a) *Indicative* language is found (*a*) in a crude form in everyday language, (*b*) in a purified form in the language of empirical science. Scientific language begins by indicating things and observing them. It continues with description, comparison, and explanation. Another phase is the search for relationships and the attempt to place the phenomenon within its own system of relationships. Finally, scientific-indicative language returns to what is observable.

The purpose of this language is to know, not to evaluate, or to prescribe behavior. Because it refers to the visible, tangible world, which is a changing world, the "truth" of its statements is "relative," that is, dependent upon both the changing world and the specific position of the observer in space and time. This language, like convictional language, functions within a specific group. Indicative language, in its crude form of everyday language, is spoken by everybody belonging to the Western nations. In its refined form of scientific language, indicative language functions within the small groups of scientists, scholars, and technicians. Further discussion will be found in the last chapter.

b) *Analytical* language is the language of philosophy. It refers to the various languages spoken by human beings. One can argue that it is a part of indicative language, and indeed both have many traits in common. The difference is that analysis is not interested in facts but in meanings, namely, the meanings of the various languages in which human beings refer to facts, values, and "ideas." What has been said, in regard to indicative language, about understanding and not evaluating, and about relativity, holds true also for analytical language.

c) *Tautological* language is the language of logic and mathematics. The language of mathematics refers not to the tangible world but to mathematical ideas, such as the idea of a purely straight line. Its statements cannot be verified experimentally, but must be demonstrated to follow logically from the initial definition. Tautological statements do not add anything at all to the knowledge of the actual world; they develop the logical implications of the first definition. The truth of tautological statements is not relative but absolute, that is, independent of the changing world of the senses. If the statements are logically acceptable, they are completely true. The validity of tautological statements is, however, confined to the specific system built upon the original definition. As soon as a mathematician starts with another first definition, he arrives at a very different system of tautological statements, which, in their turn, are absolutely true.

2. *Convictional and indicative language in their relation to "reality"*

One of the most frequent misunderstandings about convictional language is the notion that it is arbitrary, outside the range of intelligent discussion. The people who make this objection place convictional language over against indicative language and claim that the latter is objective and public, whereas the first is subjective, and merely the expression of a personal preference. To be sure, it is not a simple matter to check the truth of convictional language. Before we enter into this, something else has to be said. In the above objection the suggestion is implied that indicative language refers to reality, whereas convictional language is a matter of fancy or imagination. Such a notion is not implied at all in the concept of convictional language as it is used in this book. Both convictional and indicative languages refer to "reality." Here lies a crucial problem. The assertion that both languages refer to "reality" does not imply any judgment on the part of the analytical philosopher about the nature of these "realities," for example, as to whether or not they are illusionary. It is not the analytical philosopher's business to decide whether the reality meant in a certain language is "really" there or not. The only thing he can do is to notice that if human beings speak either indicative or convictional language they refer to something which is "real" *for them.*

The "reality" meant is not the same in both cases. Anybody who speaks any convictional language has in mind all the reality there is, including the values and meanings involved. The modern scientist claims (in opposition to his predecessor of the nineteenth century) that his language does not refer to the "real" nature of the universe. He considers his theories as hypotheses which he uses to describe "facts," to explain them as fully as possible, and to predict future events. Some hypotheses may suffice to explain certain phenomena but not others. A different hypothesis has then to be introduced. In other words, theories are tools, instruments of explanation and prediction. They do not reveal anything to us about the "real nature" of "reality." Still, these theories have reality in mind, or better, a certain aspect of reality. That is to say that the scientist abstracts, from all other aspects of reality, those which are irrelevant for his work of prediction.

Likewise, a person who speaks convictional language has reality in mind, but in his case it is the totality of reality as he sees it in the light of his specific convictions. There is only one indicative language (we think of its purified form, science), but there are numerous convictional languages. These latter see reality in a different light. The philosopher has to abstain from attempts to declare that either science or a specific conviction discloses the "really Real."

3. *The historical character of these languages*

We may now turn to the relationship, not between indicative language and convictional language as such, but between the purified language of empirical science and some convictional languages of the Western civilization. Both are historical phenomena. We can say that the language of empirical science was emancipated from the Western convictional languages roughly around 1600. The fact that this emancipation was possible says something about these convictional languages. We will return to this issue later. Here we desire merely to emphasize the fact that this emancipation resulted in an enormous revolution. Up to that moment man had given account of things only in a convictional way. The empirical, indicative approach was not yet admitted as a valid, significant method with a right of its own. The planets had been considered as the spirits of the forefathers or as God's handiwork; the rainbow was a bridge to heaven, or the sign of the covenant between Yahweh and his people. From 1600 on, a new way of giving account arose. Planets are now considered as satellites of a sun, a rainbow as a prism effect of sunlight on raindrops. With a modicum of exaggeration we might say that now for the first time "things" appear. Water is now a thing, to be classified as H_2O, whereas it had been formerly the element of baptism, or the primeval ocean out of which life arises.

4. *Languages and situations*

The foregoing picture can be misleading if we interpret it to mean that indicative language has quite appropriately taken the place of convictional language. If we assume this (Comtean) position, we have left the realm of analytical discourse and entered that of a specific theology of history. As philosophers we are not allowed to evaluate this "emancipation" as though it meant a liberation from evil. We may employ this term only as a description of a historical process.

We will then notice that outside the domain of Western civilization, and within this domain before about 1600, one kind of language—

namely, convictional language—was spoken almost exclusively, whereas in the modern Western world people speak various languages in different situations. People of this civilization may be said to deem it appropriate to speak scientific language in a laboratory and in a library, legal language in court, religious language in church and at a funeral, aesthetic language when discussing the value of a piece of sculpture, moral language in regard to the use of narcotics, etc. Thus there is a plurality of languages, each with its own approach, its own concern, its own kind of truth, each of them considered appropriate for its specific occasion.

5. *Convictional elements in indicative language, or the problem of objectivity*

The preceding remarks offer the background necessary to deal with the question as to whether anything like indicative language actually exists. People are likely to point out that no indicative statement, not even one from the realm of so-called purified science, is completely free from convictional elements. Hence, they say, there is no such thing as indicative language.

a) In order to answer this objection, we have to consider the present *situation* in connection with the problem of objectivity. This situation is characterized by the existence of two groups of scholars.

The two preceding sentences need clarification. Their main idea is that "the problem of objectivity" does not exist. What really exists is a variety of groups of human beings who differ with regard to this problem. It is an unwarranted abstraction to detach the problem from these groups. The problem can be understood only in its relationship to the opinions, the convictions, the arrogances, and the fears of these groups. What we can discuss is therefore *not* the problem of objectivity, but the situation in regard to (or even, as revealed by) the problem of objectivity. We can call this the *problem situation.*

What is said here about the problem of objectivity is also true for other problems in the fields of philosophy, and for the fields of theology and the humanities. Perhaps it is only in the fields of mathematics and of some natural sciences that we can consider a problem without taking into account the problem situation.

Hence, as soon as we raise "the problem of objectivity," the first question is, Which groups are involved in the conflict indicated by the term "objectivity"? We notice that two groups play a role. Bloc A defends the thesis that the ideal of *voraussetzungslose Wissenschaft,* of a science which claims to be free from presuppositions and therefore may be considered neutral and objective, is not only old-fashioned and naïve, but even a dangerous, misleading interpretation of man's situation. The proof texts for this opinion are taken from existentialist philosophers. Kierkegaard is heralded as the man who has shown once for all that all knowledge is subjective. Heidegger is quoted: "Interpretation is never a 'neutral' grasping of a datum, a grasping which is free from presuppositions." [17] The strongest denunciation of the ideal of "unprejudiced" science is given by Van der Leeuw, who claims that "the attempt has a disastrous effect," and who equates "unprejudiced" with "unintelligent." [18] Bloc A is made up of continental theologians, philosophers who consider themselves existentialists, and American theologians who are influenced by continental theology or existentialism.

Bloc B claims that science has to be neutral and objective, under penalty of losing the rank of science. Many times the same claim is made for philosophy. All emotive elements, all biases, all prejudices have to be eliminated. Sometimes it is held that a complete purification is possible. At other times it is set forth that this purification can never be complete, but that science does not deserve its name if the scientist does not attempt to follow up the process of neutralization as far as is humanly possible. Usually members of the B bloc stand for a thesis which irks the members of the A bloc in a special way. This thesis is sometimes tacitly assumed, but at other times openly asserted. It is the notion that purified science (and philosophy) is the highest intellectual and cultural achievement of Western man, while religion is something of a lower order. Religion is then supposed to be naïve, based on bias and prejudice, and, furthermore, intolerant and guilty of arrogance.

Bloc B is made up of logical positivists and other empirical philosophers, and of most scientists who follow an empirical method.

b) The use of the term "bloc" in the foregoing is not an attempt to be facetious. It seeks to indicate a deplorable situation in the intellectual life of the Western nations. Positivist and empirical philosophers on the one hand, existentialists and theologians on the other, actually form closed blocs, which possess their own slogans, and the members of which take exceeding little trouble to try to understand what motivates the thinkers of the "enemy" bloc. Instead of attempts to open up some understanding, we notice disdain and ridicule for the "enemy." Anyone

[17] "Auslegung ist nie ein voraussetzungsloses Erfassen eines Vorgegebenen," Martin Heidegger, *Sein und Zeit* (6th ed.; Tübingen: Neomarius Verlag, 1949), p. 150. Heidegger goes on to say: "Wenn sich die besondere Konkretion der Auslegung im Sinne der exakten Textinterpretation gern auf das beruft, 'was dasteht,' so ist das was zunächst 'dasteht' nicht anderes als die selbstverständliche, undiskutierte Vormeinung des Auslegers, die notwendig in jedem Auslegungsansatz liegt als das, was mit Auslegung überhaupt schon 'gesetzt,' d.h. in Vorhabe, Vorsicht, Vorgriff vorgegeben ist."

[18] G. van der Leeuw, *Religion in Essence and Manifestation*, tr. J. E. Turner (London: Allen & Unwin, 1938), p. 645.

who does not religiously repeat the slogans of his own group is marked as an eccentric. Very few empiricist publications will accept an existentialist or a theologian as a worthy disputant. Theologians either ignore logical empiricism or link it with naturalism and materialism as the enemy of all spiritual life. One of the effects of this herd attitude is the fact that no progress is made in regard to the problem of "objectivity." We need ask the question as to what the intentions are which lie behind the usually stark pronouncements of both blocs. The intensity of the mutual disdain reveals that each side is "convinced" that important goods are at stake. What are these goods? What convictions lie behind the conflict?

It cannot be denied that there is much weight in what the protagonists of "objective" science have to say as to their aims. It is true that something like *voraussetzungslose Wissenschaft* does not exist, but the faithful repetition of this notion changes it into a dangerous truism. If we leave the field of abstract reasoning and give our attention to some concrete examples, we notice that the will to check our prejudices is a first demand for each science which values true progress. A real science of the history of religions is possible only if the scientist is continually suspicious of his own prejudices. W. B. Kristensen, a Norwegian-Dutch scholar, whose work and method will be discussed in Chap. V, has definitely shown to what extent the older history of religions has been marred by tacit and, for that very reason, more powerful convictions of modern Western scholars. They handled ancient religions with a set of concepts originating in their rationalist and Christian convictions, and in this way did violence to these religions. The same thing is true for the history of philosophy. A very strong bias in favor of idealism has blinded many scholars to the merits of the sophists, cynics, empiricists, and skeptics.

On the other hand, we have to recognize a partial truth in the ideas defended by the existentialist-theological bloc. No science or philosophy exists in which convictions do not play an important role. No one can voluntarily drop his convictions, just as *no one can cast off his own skin*. We cannot stop being ourselves, that is, being our convictions.

However, exactly what is the function of these convictional elements in indicative language? The answer is that they belong, not in the scientific language itself, but in its realm of presuppositions. All sciences are built upon some specific assumptions of a convictional character:

(1) The assumption that "reality" is rational, at least to such an extent that there is a possibility for human beings to gain a reliable picture of it, if they approach it with their intellect.

(2) The assumption that such reliable information is very valuable for human beings in arranging their lives.

(3) The demand that each scientist ought to aim at producing information which is as reliable as possible.

Only on the basis of such convictions can a scientific procedure be erected which itself is as free as possible from convictions. Even so, such a science should not be called "objective." The term "intersubjective" gives a better indication of the claims of the modern scientist. Mutual criticism by the whole body of first-class scientists is needed to weed out prejudices, and if this cannot be done completely, the effort can at least show up which biases are still at work in any particular scientific field.

Behind the empiricists' requirement of a "neutral" science lies an important insight which the members of the existentialist-theological bloc are likely to overlook, because of their strong emphasis upon the notion that nobody can cast off his own skin. If a scholar is not suspicious of the convictions which are prevalent in his circle, he will not find new insights, but will always rediscover his own precious convictions. He is so taken up with these ideas of his that he is not able to *see* anything which does not agree with them. Some examples will make this clear. The study of the Old and New Testaments did not make much progress as long as the scholars tacitly assumed that Amos and Paul must have entertained the same notions as the modern churchmen who studied them. Only when biblical scholars admitted the possibility, and even the probability, that men in biblical times adhered to quite different conceptions of the world than those of modern Jews and Christians, did scholarship attain the capacity to *see* some of the outstanding characteristics of the biblical way of thinking and believing. It was recognized that older scholars did not see certain points because they naïvely read their Lutheran or Calvinist theology into the prophetic and apostolic writings. The success of modern biblical scholarship is possible only on the basis of the willingness of scholars to put aside for the moment their own cherished theology, in order to see what was the theology of Amos.

In the same way the study of primitive man will produce valuable results only when the scholars become acutely aware of the danger of finding their own ways of thinking in civilization alien to their culture. In Chap. V we will discuss an example of a study of primitive man which is severely handicapped by its author's incapacity to recognize his own convictions.

This is to say that the notion that nobody can cast his own skin has to be offset by the one that *nobody can see anything who is not able to withdraw from the ivory tower of his convictions.* A real understanding of the convictions of people who hold beliefs other than our own is possible only if we possess the capacity of leaving our shell. A snail does not see anything when it remains closed up in its spiral. This ability of leaving our shell is, at one and the same time, something very wholesome and very difficult to accomplish. This shell, these cherished convictions are we ourselves, and we are not inclined to dissociate ourselves from ourselves.

It is not easy to find the right terms to characterize the scholarly attitude described in the preceding pages. Terms such as "objectivity" and "neutrality" seem to be insufficient, because they are immediately met by the objection (based upon a misunderstanding of what is meant) that "real" objectivity is impossible. Terms such as "fairness" and "impartiality" are not much better, because they are so vague that they do not arouse any disagreement.

c) A crucial aspect of the problem of objectivity has not yet been mentioned. Impartial science and philosophy are not finalities; they are not aims in themselves. "Reason" is always a servant. Impartial science and philosophy have to be understood as elements functioning within a larger framework which is convictional in character. Impartial science and philosophy are always set forth and defended by people who are *convinced* that such science and philosophy are indispensable for a way of life which in their eyes is good. Both Christians and non-Christians entertain these convictions. Civilization means for them a way of life wherein propaganda is not all-powerful, but where there is a place for a disinterested investigation of all human problems.

One of the major sources of the resistance of the existentialist-theological bloc to the notion of objectivity is the suspicion that the defenders of the neutrality of science do not admit this servant character of science and philosophy. Indeed, many empiricists claim that neutral science and philosophy should be and can be the arbiters of the great questions of life. If we want to know the right relationship between parents and children, we should ask the biologist, the psychologist, and the social scientist. They assert that churches can give only biased advice, which is further vitiated by lack of concrete knowledge.

Thus it seems that on this point the suspicions of the existentialist-theological group are fully justified. Scientists, in their function as scientists, can never issue prescriptions about how life *ought* to be lived. They can describe and predict, but not prescribe. If a parent decides that he will educate his children in a democratic and not in a fascistic way, he makes his decision, not on the basis of his sociology or psychology, but by virtue of his convictions. After he has made this basic, convictional decision, he will use the achievements of various sciences to work out an acceptable educational policy.

The empiricists who elevate neutral science and philosophy to the position of ultimate counselors of life seem therefore to have misunderstood the role of science and of their own convictions. Actually, it is these convictions, humanistic or naturalistic, which play the role of the final guide to their lives. In fact, although they do not seem to be aware of it, science functions as a servant of this guide. Implied in this misunderstanding is the idea that while Christians, Jews, or Hindus offer advice for living based upon prejudices, empiricists offer such advice based upon neutral and objective science. Actually, everyone's opinions about the right of way of life are "biased," or "prejudiced," if one may use either expression. However, the expressions are misleading because they suggest that an "unbiased," to wit, "objective" scientific opinion of the right way of life is possible. The term "conviction" is not open to such misconceptions and, being admitted, prevents us from considering convictions different from our own as being of a lower quality.

What we have been discussing is one of the most fundamental issues of the present Western civilization. Within this civilization we come across several confessional groups, each guided by its own theology. The issue at stake is that of the relationship between one's convictions and the impartial sciences and philosophies. We can discriminate roughly among three positions:

(1) Some theologies reject impartial science and philosophies. These theologies show more or less outspoken totalitarian tendencies. Examples: Communism, Nazism, some forms of Protestantism, the traditional Roman Catholic theology.

(2) Other theologies deny that impartial science and philosophy function within the frame of a set of convictions. They claim that impartial science can function as a guide to life. Examples: many of those who call themselves empiricists.

(3) Those theologies which claim that the nurture of and the respect for impartial science is a condition *sine qua non* of civilization, and who assert that the taking account of the achievements of impartial science and philosophy is a basic characteristic of their convictions. Examples: some forms of humanism and Protestantism.

d) *Summary*. The enterprise of science stands or falls with the will to take seriously the requirement of impartiality. The indicative language of such impartial science is, however, connected with convictions in two different ways. First, all science is based upon a set of presuppositions and assumptions which are convictional in nature. Second, impartial science is not an entity in itself, but has to be understood as functioning within the frame of several typical Western and modern convictional views of life.

6. Convictional language informs indicative language

People possessed by strong convictions may often observe something which has indicative meaning and which had been overlooked. When Marx refers to class struggles, calls them necessary, and declares them an indispensable means to reach the good society, he speaks convictional language, yet he has also indicated something. Also, those present-day sociologists and economists who do not adhere to any form of Marxism at all admit that conflicts between groups of the population form a significant fact with which their science has to reckon. This fact was scarcely noticed before Marx formulated his convictional world view. Marx not only evoked convictional, theological thinking about the class struggle, but also opened the eyes of scholars to facts which had not been recognized earlier.

Many times men deeply moved by their convictions have stimulated scientific thinking. Freud's treatment of sex is highly convictional. Sex assumes in his "psychology" a cosmic, metaphysical status. Sex is the ruler of life, despised, repressed, veiled, but therefore the more powerful, the prime mover of arts, morals, civilization. And yet Freud has drawn attention to several undeniable facts, the importance of which is not denied by those who do not share his mythology at all.

It appears that people who are in the grip of convictions which are considerably different from the generally accepted beliefs can often open our eyes. For example, people moved by a powerful love, an intense hatred, or people living in other ages or different continents and who belong to confessional groups basically different from our group. The saying goes that love blinds, but sometimes love (or hatred, or other strong convictions) can sharpen our sight.

What is disclosed in this way has indicative meaning. We should not say that because Marx spoke of class struggle in a convictional way, modern sociological references to group conflicts are convictional also. The role of Marx's convictional language was heuristic. There is not an intrinsic but a heuristic relationship between Marx's conviction about class struggle and the modern scholar's indicative discussion of group conflicts. Marx's convictional speaking was the occasion for the rise of a fruitful indicative line of thought.

The service rendered by convictional to indicative language can be described as the blasting away of an obstruction, which prevented people from seeing clearly in an indicative way. This barrier is frequently of a convictional nature. In Marx's case the barrier consisted in people's conviction that the world has always known rich and poor and that therefore it meant a rebellion against God (or the World Order) to assume that society could be changed by human interference. In Freud's case the resistance against clear thinking derived from Enlightenment convictions about the basic rationality, goodness, and orderliness of "human nature."

The disclosing service rendered by convictional to indicative language effects a liberation. The thinking in many scientific fields (such as biology, psychology, economics, sociology, history of religions) is the result of an emancipation of indicative thinking from the power of convictional authorities and traditions. It has to be noticed that the process of emancipation is not a simple one. Many times the conviction which has destroyed an old obstruction immediately puts up a new one. Marx's conviction offers therefore a good example. This fact should warn us against the temptation to assume that the modern science of the twentieth century is completely free from such mental blocks. It is highly probable that future generations will wonder why we could not free ourselves from what they will consider obvious obstructions.

7. *Indicative elements in convictional language*

a) People sometimes object to the validity of the distinction between convictional and indicative language by remarking that convictional language also indicates facts—for instance, the language of Christian faith. They say that it is of the essence of the Christian faith to *know* certain things. First, this faith implies the claim to deal with historical persons, nations, and events: Moses, the prophets, the kings; Jesus of Nazareth; the disciples, the church, the reformers. All these and more are historical facts, which can be known. Second, this faith implies the claim that God is acting in history, that he is not merely a beautiful idea, but that the signs of his gracious activity can be seen and known in the actual world of history. Third, faith in God does not merely imply knowledge, it *is* knowledge of God. The believer knows more after his faith than before. He is certain, whereas before he was uncertain. Faith is trust, love, reverence, but these aspects are not different from knowledge, they are implied in it.

We begin our discussion with the third objection. The "knowing" which is spoken of here is different in kind from the knowledge of indicative language. It is an understanding which is guided by specific convictions. In order to keep our terminology clear we shall confine the use of "knowledge" and "cognitive" to indicative language. Sometimes theologians resent such procedure, apparently because they fear that this might arise out of a disdain for the Christian faith and a desire to set it aside as being not quite up to the level of respectable science. This is not necessarily the case. The knowledge expressed in indicative language is hypothetical, provisional, more or less probable, dependent upon verification, and impersonal. These characteristics do not at all apply to the understanding which is implied in the faith of a Christian, or in any other belief for that matter. Such an understanding is not *lower* than scientific knowledge, but different in character. Hence, we should not say that we can "know" God or any other nonempirical reality, that is, know in indicative language.

The answer to the second objection is basically the same, though we are not dealing here with nonempirical realities but with so-called historical facts. If one asserts, however, that a certain historical event is the result of God's work in history, one is speaking convictional language. The people who make such assertions do not mean something hypothetical, more or less probable. Therefore it is not indicative knowledge.

b) The problem seems to be different in the case of the first objection. Claims as to the historical existence of Moses, the prophets, and Jesus seem to be both indicative and indispensable elements of the Hebrew and the Christian faiths. Paul L. Holmer defends a particular thesis in this respect.[19] His discussion can be summed up as follows:

(1) Religious sentences are not "cognitive of trans-empirical realities."

(2) Some religious sentences are "cognitive of historical events."

(3) Religious sentences can be "the occasion for the cognition of . . . a new . . . mode of life."

(4) To consider sentences of type (2) and (3) to be true is not "the religious act of faith"; faith is the passionate becoming of a new man.

(5) To consider sentences of type (2) and (3) to be true is, however, "a necessary condition for religious faith." [20]

I agree with theses (1) and (4). In regard to the other theses the question has to be raised as to whether religious language about Moses or Jesus is ever indicative at all. Probably the answer has to be negative. Chap. V will treat more fully the claim that such language is "narrative," and that this is a kind of convictional language.

Here a few things can be pointed out: (*a*) In biblical times convictional and indicative languages were not distinguished as they are now. (*b*) When twentieth-century scholars look back upon the language of biblical times, they can distinguish between a convictional and an indicative aspect. (*c*) It appears to us that what biblical people were really interested in was what we would call the convictional element; the

[19] "The Nature of Religious Propositions," *The Review of Religion*, March, 1955.
[20] *Ibid.*, pp. 148-49.

indicative element was held in the convictional framework. (*d*) The convictional language of biblical man had a specific form: it was a narrative. (*e*) It is doubtful that the statements which churches require their members to affirm can be called indicative statements. The requirement is probably the "repetition" of the old convictional narrative.

c) If it is denied that convictional language contains indicative elements, the question is raised as to whether this approach does not necessarily lead to the position that we as convictional people live in ivory towers. To a certain extent we have to accept this accusation. There are neither scientific nor philosophical proofs or arguments which can validate or invalidate any conviction. There is no public, objective court of reason which can decide who is wrong and who is right.

There is more to be said than this, however. Certainly communication takes place between people of different convictions, though this communication does not possess a scientific or philosophical character. We continually witness to each other. By means of our moral judgments, even more by means of our behavior, or better, by the way we are, and live, and meet persons and problems, we give testimonies as to what is our highest good. By living we "demonstrate" our most genuine convictions. By means of certain linguistic aspects of our living, we set forth our explicit views.

These demonstrations, both the implicit and the explicit, act as a challenge. They are invitations to other people to live, to think, to speak as we do. On the level of explicit communication the challenge can assume the form of an expression of the implications of the convictions held, and of a comparison with the presupposed implications of other views. Such a comparison never proves anything; the other person always needs to make an existential decision as to whether he will accept our challenge or not. The challenge on this level can take on all forms from an open attack of the other man's convictions, a condemnation on the basis of considering the view held by oneself as unquestionably true, to an entering into the other's view inspired by respect and made possible by empathy.

8. Is-language

a) The distinction between convictional language and indicative language can be clarified by reference to a characteristic of language which is generally accepted by analytical philosophers. They hold that the meaning of a language is equivalent to the rules of its correct use.

It seems to be right for other languages to connect the meaning with the use of the language, e.g., in the case of tautological language (mathematics), analytical language (philosophy), and indicative language (science). For instance, a physicist may ask himself which terminology he should use in a specific case, that of waves or that of corpuscles. The attitude of the physicist is detached, his real self is not involved, his existence is not at stake; in a detached way he can consider which use is in this case the most appropriate.

When people speak convictional language, they do not *use* this language in the way the physicist uses his terminology. If someone says in anger, "That is a dirty trick," or in faith, "Christ is my Lord," his attitude is not detached. His deepest self is involved; something of great importance is at stake. We can express this difference between indicative and convictional language by saying that whereas we *use* a scientific terminology, we *are* our convictions. It is difficult to determine the most appropriate terminology on this point. Should we say that convictional language reflects the person, or that it expresses the person? This, however, is certain: our whole person enters into our convictions.

What is being said is not new. My thesis is the presupposition of everyone in everyday life, as well as that of some philosophers of language. It is particularly so in the instances in which philosophers protest against certain forms of convictional language. This protest is raised when convictional language is *used* and because it is *merely used,* and does not express the deepest self. This "merely using" of convictional language happens either deliberately or unintentionally.

If someone deliberately uses convictional language for promoting his self-interest, such as a politician using pious talk to impress his churchgoing voters, we are suspicious, not only of his piety, but of the whole man. Please notice that we condemn not only the language, but the person *in* the language.

The unintentional *use* of convictional language has been exposed and condemned by Marx, by Freud, and by the logical empiricists.[21] When Marx speaks of ideology, he accuses the bourgeois class of *using* impressive, high-sounding moral and religious language in order to hide their real interests. Freud exposes moralists who *use* lofty and exalted language in order to conceal the not-so-exalted, but authentic person. Logical empiricists denounce metaphysicians who *use* solemn ideas and august, overarching concepts in order to silence deep-seated fears within themselves of an unfamiliar and hostile universe.

In all these cases, people do two things. First, they analyze not only language but persons. Their main tool is the contrast between a real, authentic self, and a mask. It is the masked person who *uses* convictional

[21] We do not claim that the following remarks offer an account of these men's explicit theories of language. It seems, however, that their accusations, related here, are implied in these theories.

language. Second, they utter a moral condemnation of this *mere usage* of convictional language; and moral disapproval always refers to the whole person, not only to his acts.

Summary. The notion of *use* refers to an instrument. It is quite appropriate to call scientific language a tool, and inappropriate to think of convictional language in this way. We do not *use* convictional language, because we do not use ourselves as instruments. If we actually *use* convictional language, everyone feels that something is out of order.

b) The concept of "is" language is related to kindred concepts of the following authors.

I owe the notion that "we *are* our convictions" to my teacher Nicolaas Westendorp Boerma, who mentioned it often but did not elaborate it.[22]

Heidegger's position is expressed in the thesis *Die Rede ist ein Existenzial*, language is a basic characteristic of human existence.[23]

Marcel advocates a position similar to my own, for instance, in *Man Against Mass Society* and in *The Philosophy of Existence*. In the first work Marcel discusses the man of "proper pride." [24] About him Marcel says: "His word is himself," and elucidates this by stating, "for between being and the word there does exist . . . an irrefragable unity." In the other work Marcel refers to the fact "that we are witnesses and that this is the expression of our mode of belonging to the world." This formulation occurs in an essay which distinguishes two languages, statemental language and the language of testimony, and the main part of which consists of an analysis of the language of testimony and of what we might call "the testimonial situation." In another essay in the same book, Marcel speaks of an "affirmation of being" and says about it "an affirmation which I *am* rather than an affirmation which I *utter*." [25]

In his *Voor God wil ik Belijden* the Dutch theologian G. J. Sirks offers an analysis of the nature of "confessing our Christian faith." He suggests that we should characterize man not as *homo sapiens, homo faber*, or *homo ludens*, but as *homo confessor*.[26]

It may be asked whether the notion of the unity of person and word has been influenced by Christian doctrine. This unity is asserted for God in the biblical conception of God's person. See, for instance, the last words of John 1:1, "and the Word was God." It is not impossible that

[22] N. Westendorp Boerma, 1872-1952, professor of philosophy of religion, University of Amsterdam, 1936-42.

[23] *Sein und Zeit*, pp. 160 ff.

[24] Tr. G. S. Fraser (Chicago: Henry Regnery Co., 1952), p. 190.

[25] *The Philosophy of Existence*, tr. Manya Harari (London: Harvill Press, 1948), p. 71.

[26] G. J. Sirks, b. 1887, professor at the Remonstrant Seminary since 1949: *Voor God wil ik Belijden* (Amsterdam: Ploegsma, 1949), p. 6.

this conception encouraged people to interpret also the human person as one very closely related to his word, his language.

The characterization of man as *homo convictus* has to be preferred to that as *homo confessor* or *homo testatus*. Both confessing and testifying are responses. What comes first is that man is "convinced," overcome by a convictor. Confessing and testifying are responses which can be understood only within the context of a convictional situation.

c) Another distinction must be added to the difference between *is*-language and *use*-language. The language of theology does not fit into either category. We propose to speak of man *employing* his theological language. We can now discriminate between three language situations:

(1) A man is his convictions, his word.

(2) A theologian employs his language to give account of life.

(3) A scientist uses a specific language, according to specified, strict rules, for definite purposes.

Employ-language is akin to is-language in that it is related to and tries to express the personality center in regard to matters of ultimate importance. Employ-language is akin to use-language in that it implies an element of distance, of reflection.

Employ-language differs from is-language because of this reflective element. "The theologian employs his language" means: he gives account of his convictions, criticizes them, checks and compares them with other convictions, which may be similar or contrasting. Employ-language differs from use-language in that it does not operate according to strict rules, which are prescribed by specific purposes (for instance, the rules of mathematical astronomy, necessitated by the purpose of predicting celestial events), but in that employ-language attempts to order convictions and to elaborate their implications—activities for which no strict rules can be given.

It makes some sense to say that is-language is spontaneous, and use-language artificial. Employ-language cannot be easily characterized in this way. The laborious work of a theologian is neither the spontaneous approval of an act of generosity; nor is theological language artificial in the way in which chemical terminology deserves that name. The "giving account of" which characterizes employ-language can be called "reflective," or "meditative."

9. *Man-who-speaks*

If it is granted that a man *is* his convictions, his word, it follows that when we speak of "language" we mean man himself, man-who-speaks, *homo loquens*. This insight is one of the basic ideas of Georges Gusdorf's *La Parole*.[27] It is also one of the central conceptions of the present book.

a) Language is not only a terminology, a grammar, *logos*—that is, a unity of word and speech—though language always implies these elements. It is misleading to concentrate in linguistic philosophy upon sentences or words. We should never lose sight of the man who speaks.

Sometimes it is legitimate to speak of *a* language, as a group of sentences which are compatible with one another, as an entity possessing a certain structure. This entity can be indicated. It is the sum of sentences to be found in a particular group of publications—for instance, those which deal with chemical subjects. Yet in the final analysis these sentences also are spoken by human beings. It is man-who-speaks who has decided to bracket his convictions, to speak artificially in the specific language of chemistry; it is man-who-speaks who has constructed such *a* language.

The danger of referring exclusively to words and sentences, that is, to *a* language, is that such a manner of expression suggests that language always is an object, a static thing, at our disposal, subject to analysis and manipulation. Actually, we are dealing with man-who-speaks, with a human being who acts. Both the English expression "man-who-speaks" and the Latin *homo loquens* (a participle form, meaning literally, man-speaking) suggest this act.

The acknowledgment of this situation will protect us against the error of supposing that we can *fully* understand language or completely explain its structure, meaning, and function. We can never achieve an exhaustive, intelligible account of any human being.

b) For this same reason the accompanying diagram may give a wrong impression, namely, that it offers a total, rounded-off, and full account of man. What is attempted here is merely an account of some ways in which man speaks.

It says, first, that man-who-speaks is always *homo convictus*. Not only man-who-hopes, man-who-swears, and man-who-theologizes, but also *homo sapiens* is fundamentally *homo convictus,* even at the very moment that he decides to put aside and bracket his convictions.

It stresses, further, the "occasional" character of man's speaking. Man-who-speaks speaks a certain language always on a certain occasion. This holds especially if man uses or employs language. Here the occasion is chosen intentionally. It also holds for man-who-speaks spontaneously; for man prays, sympathizes, and speaks with prejudice on specific occasions. Each moment anew man-who-speaks decides how

[27] (Paris: Presses universitaires de France, 1953), pp. 93 ff.

HOMO LOQUENS I

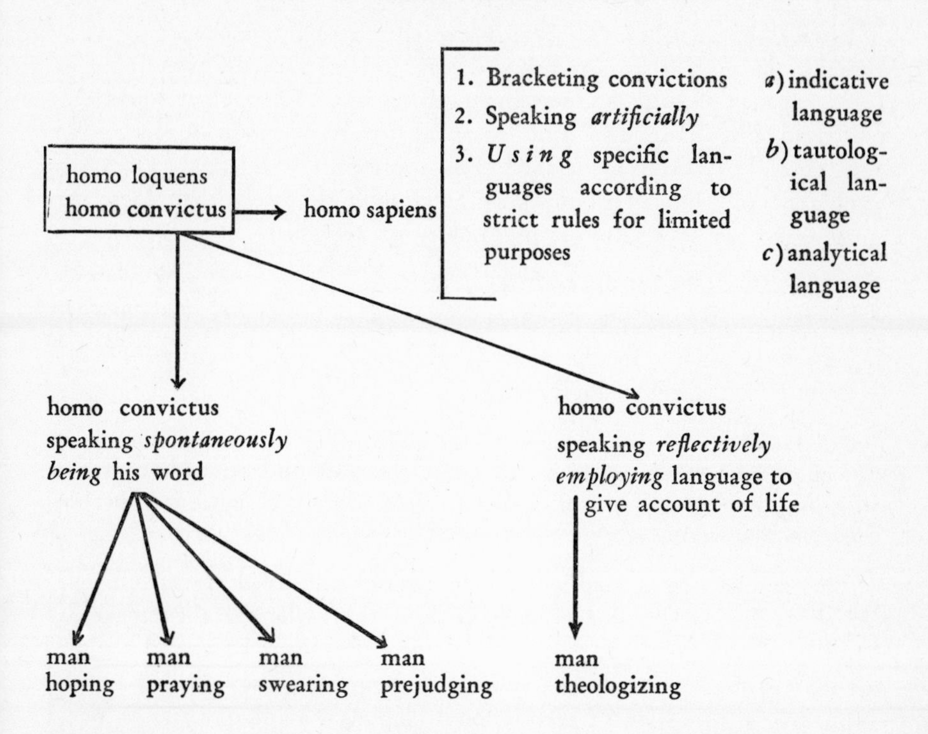

he is related or wishes to be related toward his fellows, his work, his convictor, and therefore decides which language he will speak.

Finally, the diagram does not say anything at all about the ways in which is-language, employ-language, and use-language influence each other. These influences are therefore neither asserted nor denied. Actually, they are very important. Employ-language, for instance, is nourished by is-language, but it sometimes also deeply influences the is-language. Man's hoping and praying are then prompted or inspired by his theologizing, or the theologizing of his group.

Employ-language is also influenced by use-language. There is scarcely any modern account of the meaning of life, for instance, in which there is no bearing of both the convictional aspects and the scientific findings of Freudianism.

These remarks about the mutual influences of is-, use-, and employ-language are very brief and sketchy. Some aspects of this problem will be more fully discussed in the chapters on metaphysics (IV), the Greek cosmos conviction (VI), and modern church languages (VIII).

D. CONVICTIONAL LANGUAGE AND LOGIC

In this chapter there has been no reference to the concepts of traditional logic, such as subject and predicate, nor to those of contemporary logic, such as proposition, statement, denotation. Except for some general terms like "language" and "meaning," only one more specific term, "emotive," has been mentioned, but immediately rejected. Does this avoidance of the accepted logical terminology mean that logic has nothing to say to analytical philosophy of religion?

1. *"Situational," not "logical" analysis*

a) It seems preferable, for the time being, to abstain from traditional logical terminology in the analysis of convictional language. Dewey, referring to traditional logic, writes:

> Observed facts . . . constitute what has traditionally been called the *subject.* The conceptual contents which . . . direct observational operations constitute what has traditionally been called the *predicate.* Their functional and operative correspondence with each other constitutes the *copula.*[28]

The crucial terms used in this discussion—observed, facts, observational, and correspondence—demonstrate that whereas the terms defined by them (subject, predicate, and copula) may be useful tools in discussing observational, i.e., indicative language, they should not be applied in a discussion of convictional language. If observation is not a main characteristic of convictional language, the use of "subject" and "predicate" may be misleading.

b) The same objection may be raised with reference to a more modern logical terminology. Hospers refers to sentences as "labels of situations or *states-of-affairs.*" [29] Beardsley discusses the concept of denotation with the help of an illustration, the class of widows. He specifies designation as the "list of characteristics that anything must have in order to be called a 'widow.' " [30] The words—labels, states-of-affairs, anything, widow, characteristics (in the way it is used here)—point clearly to indicative language.

c) We can say that both indicative language and its metalanguage—namely, the language of the philosophical analysis of indicative language—possess a "logical" structure. That is to say, indicative language conforms to the structure of logic, and therefore it makes sense to

[28] John Dewey, *Logic, the Theory of Inquiry* (New York: Henry Holt & Co., 1938), p. 124.

[29] John Hospers, *An Introduction to Philosophical Analysis* (New York: Prentice-Hall, 1953), p. 65.

[30] Monroe C. Beardsley, *Practical Logic* (New York: Prentice-Hall, 1950), p. 64.

discuss this language with the help of a language which possesses the same structure.

d) We should admit that convictional language does not possess this "logical" structure, and that therefore logic cannot serve as its metalanguage. That is to say that the metalanguage of convictional language must possess a nonlogical structure.

(1) A major implication of Hume's discussion of a priori and a posteriori reasoning in the Dialogues seems to consist in the acknowledgment that the logic which holds for indicative and tautological languages does not possess any validity for convictional language. When Hume discusses the question "What is God?" he warns us against "feeble conjectures," because the subject is "so remote from the sphere of our *observation*." [31] In regard to God we cannot infer "by custom," because the object is "single," individual, "without parallel." When Hume rejects reasoning a posteriori for such a convictional problem, he implicitly tells us not to use the type of logic which is oriented toward the indicative kind of reasoning.

(2) The Bible is full of language which clearly possesses a nonlogical structure. Matt. 25:31-46 relates a vision of Christ coming to judge the nations on the day of judgment. He addresses the righteous and says: "Come, O blessed of my Father . . . ; for I was hungry and you gave me food, I was thirsty and you gave me drink" (R.S.V.). The "I" who was hungry was "one of the least of these my brethren" but it was also Christ.

(3) We find the same structure just as well in nonbiblical convictional language. An example of long standing in ethnological literature is a South American tribe, the Botocudos, who claim to be red parrots. This does not mean that these Indians deny that they are human beings. What it means exactly is perhaps difficult to say, but probably it means more than that the parrots are "merely" a symbol of the tribe. According to these believers they *are* parrots, and this belief suggests something like the awareness of participating in a cosmic reality, a nonhuman reality of which the parrots are the representatives.

(4) The same nonlogical structure can be noticed in the language in which we make a philosophical analysis of convictional language. "Strictly" speaking—and "strictly" means here: according to the rules of a "logical" language—convictions and human beings are not identical. Still, in our analysis, we found that we could not under-

[31] *Selections*, ed. Charles W. Hendel (New York: Charles Scribner's Sons, 1927), pp. 310, 311. Italics mine.

stand the meaning of convictional language if we would not admit that human beings *are* their convictions.

(5) The inappropriateness of logical analysis for convictional language becomes the more conspicuous when we remember that it is especially for this language that our principle "language *is* man" holds. When we deal with language we deal with man-who-speaks. "Logical" analysis of man-who-speaks is a notion difficult to entertain. Although the language of empirical science is spoken by man-who-speaks, it is a different situation. Man-who-speaks has intentionally set up a specific situation, has decided to use language according to rules which conform to the demands of a logical system. Here logical analysis is appropriate.

e) Consequently, it seems necessary to drop the term "logical analysis" for the philosophical activity which deals with convictional language. This activity is certainly an analysis, but it should be qualified by a term other than "logical." We may call it situational analysis.

(1) The rejection of the term "logical" does not mean that situational analysis is illogical; it is nonlogical. It is not nonsensical, neither unreasonable, nor of a lower status than logical analysis. It is merely of another kind. It refers to another type of "sense."

(2) Situational analysis is still philosophical analysis. It would be arbitrary to confine philosophy to the analysis of only those realms of discourse for which the appropriate approach is that of logic. Our thesis is that it is the function of philosophy to analyze. Logical analysis is the proper method of analyzing some languages. For other languages another type of analysis is more appropriate, such as situational analysis for convictional language.

(3) We have chosen the name "situational" to characterize the nonlogical analysis for several reasons. Since people *are* their convictions, the analysis of convictional language immediately leads to a consideration of the person who speaks the language and of all the other elements of the *convictional situation,* such as the group, its historical setting, its "world," etc.

2. *The logical analysis of Ian T. Ramsey*

The rejection of "logical analysis" as a fruitful method in philosophy of religion will become clearer by comparing our approach to that of Ian T. Ramsey.[32]

a) The format of Ramsey's paper consists of: the development of a position; the discussion of examples which illustrate the position.

[32] We refer to an unpublished paper, "Theology and Language, Some Illustrative Examples," by Ian T. Ramsey, of Oriel College, Oxford.

The development of the position consists in stating two theses in the light of two purposes. The two purposes are: first, a suitable response by the Christian theologian to the challenge of contemporary philosophy; second, the development of a framework of theological language. The first of the two theses is that language consists of two elements. One is that of language-levels and the other is that of "lift (elevator)-words," or index-words. The second thesis runs that index-words have "objective references" because they are related to I-awareness, and this implies other-awareness.

In the elaboration of the first thesis Ramsey states that the various level-languages—e.g., those of the sciences—are logically isolated. They resemble a department store without stairs or elevator. When we mix levels we get absurdities. Language must have some sort of unity. Further, explanation cannot move on endlessly. There must be a special logical move which expresses a final option. We solve this problem by assuming that there is another kind of words which do not belong to one specific level but are used to supplement levels. These are the elevator- or index-words. Examples of index-words are: I, person, God. The word "God" assumes a special place. It is an apex word which is the keystone of the whole structure.

When elaborating the second thesis Ramsey states that level-languages possess "objective" references in the sense that they refer to what is seen, heard, touched, etc. The great question is whether index-words have a similar empirical anchorage. Ramsey claims they do. Index-words refer to something which is factual, namely, self-awareness, or I-awareness. I-awareness has to be distinguished from me-awareness, such as hand-awareness. I-awareness implies awareness of something other than I. This is to say that there is something factual in a second sense, namely, that to which I-awareness points. Hence the logical uniqueness of "I" and with it the logical oddness of "God" and "person." This second fact can never be described. It can be evoked, induced or shown. This happens in very many ways, e.g., on occasions of religious experience, or when we recognize moral obligation as a claim. This fact is also behind the existentialist effort to do justice to the "mystery" of our existence.

The elaboration of the two theses answers the first purpose, which is a theologian's response to the challenge of contemporary philosophy.

The second purpose, the development of a framework of theological language, is set forth in this way: the two theses suggest some things about the structure of theological language and about its empirical reference. The whole problem of the logical account of theological language is to elucidate, first, the index-words, second, the apex word

"God." This elucidation must take place with reference to straight level-language; otherwise we cannot talk *intelligibly* about it. It is, however, necessary to do justice to that *mystery* which eludes all objective language and which theology must emphasize. This is an *impropriety* from the point of view of level-language.

The discussion of examples which illustrate the position offers four groups of examples. They concern God and his attributes, Christian doctrine, Gospel narratives, and the language of worship, rite, and ceremony. We shall consider only the first two groups of examples.

The requirement of intelligibility is met by taking words from some level-languages which we use as models. Models can be philosophical (being, purpose, knowledge, creation), ethical (wise, good, powerful), scientific (mover, cause), and metaphorical (king, father, judge, tower). The requirement of preserving the mystery is met by means of "qualifiers." Their logical function is twofold. First, by their striking oddness—but their linguistic impropriety—they must indicate the special logical claim we are making for the word "God." Second, they must act as a mnemonic device by means of which the model gives rise to certain stories which evoke the self-other awareness. Examples of qualifiers are: infinite, supreme (fulfilling the first function), and holy, mysterious (fulfilling the mnemonic function).

In the second group of examples (Christian doctrine) the basic distinction is between natural theology and Christian theology. A natural theology is a language map with God as the apex. Christian theology starts with certain facts that commend an alternative apex. These facts are furnished by the Bible, the church, and the development of doctrine. They commend certain words, such as Father, Son, and Holy Spirit, and from them a triangular apex is constructed.

Father

Son Holy Spirit [33]

b) An appreciation of Ramsey's method should start with an acknowledgment of the originality of his thinking. Several philosophers in Britain have been discussing topics such as "the meaning of god-sentences," but most of them were outsiders in respect to the Christian faith, and therefore did not command a full understanding of the language they were discussing. It seems that Ramsey is the first theological leader of a Christian church who has done modern analytical

[33] Rather than using quotation marks, I have presented, in this section, Ramsey's thinking in words which are nearly exclusively his own.

philosophers the honor of taking their challenge seriously in order to *think with them* instead of dismissing or ignoring them. Therefore it should be emphasized that, in spite of the criticism of Ramsey's method (which will be set forth below), this disagreement does not demand that we discard Ramsey's approach. His method does not fit the philosophical approach in terms of convictions and situations. Even so, this does not mean that Ramsey's questions should not be asked. It is at this moment impossible to say what the implications of analytical philosophy for philosophy of religion are, because scarcely anyone has said anything on this issue. Furthermore, we should not only abstain from silencing Ramsey's questions because his is a *vox clamantis in deserto,* but also because his questions are significant in themselves. His basic concerns can be formulated in this way: "What is the logical function of the word 'God'?" "What is the logical status of natural theology? what of Christian theology?"

c) Ramsey's approach is incompatible with that followed in this book for several reasons.

(1) The simile of the department store with its levels and elevators is misleading. Languages are spoken by persons. The relationship between the languages is given with the person. The connecting element is not to be sought for in elevators, but in a larger unity of which the levels form a part. What Ramsey calls level-languages are *artificial languages,* that is, languages which are *depersonalized.* People in the Western civilization have seen that for the sake of specific purposes, such as the prediction of the weather, it is preferable to use the impersonal language of empirical science. It is only such artificial, depersonalized languages which show the "logical" structure. Other languages, which we could call *life-languages,* possess nonlogical structures. To these life-languages belong the convictional languages discussed in this book and also some other languages, such as the language of poetry. These life-languages form the larger frame within which the artificial languages must be placed. The logical "oddity" of such terms as "I" and "person" is, therefore, not so odd after all because these words belong in the life-languages and not in the logical, artificial languages.

(2) Another weakness of Ramsey's approach is related to his preoccupation with words rather than with sentences and languages. It is, strictly speaking, untrue that the word "God" is logically odd. For not only is this single word odd, but the sentence, or more accurately, the whole language of which it is a part. If Ramsey had thought in terms of languages instead of words, he would certainly have been led to ask for the positive characteristics of the language

which he now characterizes only in a negative way as logically odd or improper. This positive characterization (e.g., convictional) would have carried him across the boundary between logical and nonlogical languages, a boundary which is merely suggested in his present discussion. Had he crossed this boundary he would have been obliged to give up the idea that one can sensibly speak at all about God or person in logical terms. The terms "oddity" and "impropriety" are a clear indication that logical analysis is out of place in a discussion of God, I, and person.

(3) We can express our objection in again another way. The meaning of a sentence belonging to an artificial language is clear as soon as its logical status is clarified. The meaning of a sentence belonging to a life-language is clear only if we understand the person who speaks the sentence and the whole situation of which the person is a part.

(4) Applying these insights to Ramsey's paper, we see that an understanding of its ideas requires a situational analysis. First, the choice of "God," "person," and "I" as examples of index-words reveals the concern of a twentieth-century Christian, and more specifically an Anglican or a Protestant who has been influenced by existentialist philosophy. A Communist would be more interested in "we" than in "I." A Catholic would certainly not have left out the word "church." Second, Ramsey's work contains definite elements of philosophical analysis, but the over-all frame is decidedly convictional. What Ramsey actually offers is a theology, an apologetics for a modern form of the Anglican faith. It is a convictional activity which employs the means offered by analytical philosophy in order to express the Christian claim in terminology which sophisticated moderns can comprehend.

d) *Summary.* The method which I have followed is closer to that of Dewey than that of Ramsey. When Dewey, in his *Reconstruction in Philosophy,* discusses Plato's philosophy, he draws heavily upon what are usually called historical, sociological, and psychological backgrounds of this philosophy. It is better to say that he places this (convictional) philosophy in its (convictional) situation.

CHAPTER TWO

POWER

Man-Who-Speaks Establishes His Existence

INTRODUCTION

The point of view taken in Chap. I in respect to man-who-speaks, especially in regard to convictional language, is one-sided. Man is seen as the convictus, as a being who considers himself overpowered by a something or somebody, as one who is merely passive. Chap. II will emphasize another aspect of language. It will present man-who-speaks going forth out of himself into the world, and by means of his language bringing order into it. From this vantage point man-who-speaks is not passive but active. To speak is to exercise power. Man-who-speaks by means of his commands or laws can dominate other human beings, and by means of his science force nature to fulfill his wishes.

In this chapter we will discuss three ways in which human beings speak powerfully. The most conspicuous form of the exercise of power is the aggression by which one language encroaches upon the domain of another language: moral language intrudes into the realm of art, and vice versa; religious language and scientific language are likely to penetrate into each other's domains. We observe here something which has to be called imperialism, an imperialism of languages. There is another language phenomenon which can be considered from the point of view of power. We have touched upon it already in Chap. I, the claim made by a fanatical person. We will continue our analysis of this claim and show how it reveals strong imperialistic tendencies. Finally, we notice that power does not show itself exclusively in the excessive forms of imperialistic and fanatical language. All speaking is an exercise of power. It is by speaking that man arranges his life, establishes his existence.

A. IMPERIALISM OF LANGUAGES

1. *The problem*

a) We can observe that people living in countries belonging to the Western civilization speak various languages. The best way to distinguish one language from another is to notice the different judgments which they apply. People call some things "pretty" and other things "ugly." We say that people on this occasion speak aesthetic language. The judgments characterizing moral language are : "good" and "bad," or "kind" and "unkind," or "just" and "unjust." Besides moral and aesthetic language, we are accustomed to distinguish religious language (divine vs. demonic, holy vs. unholy, sacred vs. profane), and rational language (true vs. false, clear vs. confused, verifiable vs. nonverifiable). It seems that there are some other languages which play a large role in everyone's life but which are seldom discussed, namely, vital language and pragmatic language. Some judgments of vital language are: "healthy" and "unhealthy," "spontaneous" and "inhibited," "lively" and "apathetic," "young" and "old." Pragmatic judgments are "useful" and "useless," "skillful" and "clumsy."

These languages are all convictional languages. Still, they are *sui generis*. This does not mean that there are no relationships between them, but merely that we mean something different when we say, "That is a beautiful tree," than when we say, "That is a generous gift."

Languages are connected with values. When we speak a certain language—that is to say, when we give approval or disapproval—we have in mind certain goods. These goods have to be defended, promoted, expanded, for we cannot live without them. When we condemn adultery, we have in mind our families. Their existence is endangered by the disqualified behavior. When we are disgusted with a traitor, we think of our country, the existence of which is undermined by the actions which we morally condemn. Our moral language purports to defend and promote moral goods (family, nation, farm, church) without which we feel we cannot live.

The values meant in our languages are primarily concrete and not abstract values. Our claim is that moral language takes to heart, not "goodness," "kindness," or "tolerance," but our work, our schools, the communities in which we live and work. The values meant in rational language are, not "clearness" or "predictability," but empirical science, logic, mathematics. Vital values are, not spontaneity, charm, or youthfulness, but food, children, sports. Aesthetic values are, e.g., concerts, lakes, mountains. Pragmatic values are tools, clothes, houses. We live both for and from these concrete goods. They make life possible, and therefore we have to preserve and promote them. One of the ways of doing this is to speak the languages in which they are meant. Man-who-speaks-morally defends and cultivates the values which render life possible. (See diagram, page 71.)

b) Modern Western man seems to be a being who speaks several languages, each related to specific occasions. People consider it the right thing to speak legal language in a courtroom, the language of empirical science in a laboratory, religious language in a church and in a funeral parlor. Our present problem is the following: many times it happens that people speak a certain language which other people consider inappropriate for the occasion.

VALUES AND JUDGMENTS

Values	*Judgments*		
family school farm nation	good kind just	bad unkind unjust	moral
concerts woods lakes	pretty elegant tasteful	ugly ungraceful vulgar	aesthetic
church baptism prayer	divine holy sacred	demonic unholy profane	religious
empirical science mathematics logic	true clear verifiable	false confused nonverifiable	rational
food children sports	healthy spontaneous lively young	unhealthy inhibited apathetic old	vital
tools clothes houses	useful skillful	useless clumsy	pragmatic

There are instructors who not only teach in class, but sometimes preach, which in the opinion of other instructors is not the right thing to do. When somebody is seriously upset, without external circumstances sufficiently warranting his distress, one person thinks it fitting to speak scientific language (psychology), while another will prefer religious language. Probably each of these persons will deem the language of the other to be inappropriate.

It seems that we have to speak of an imperialism of languages. Each language seems to have the tendency to encroach upon the domain of the other. Not only the history of ideas, but also the entire history of Western man, is largely determined by fierce conflicts between scientific and religious languages, between political and moral languages, between aesthetic and moral languages. Perhaps also other civilizations show similar conflicts.

It is the purpose of this section to analyze such language conflicts, in order to achieve a better insight into the nature of language, and a better understanding of Western man who speaks these languages and who gets into language conflicts. We are not going to decide which languages *ought* to be spoken on specific occasions; neither are we going to tell the reader which actions we *should* call "good," which bodies "pretty," which institutions "sacred." We will merely try to understand man-speaking.

c) Let us scrutinize more closely one of these conflicts, namely, that between vital and moral language. We can distinguish between two aspects of the conflict: first, moral language assailing; second, vital language attacking. Let us consider two examples of each aspect.

Moral language intruding into the realm of vital values

(1) "All desires as such are bad."

(2) "Moral life includes the ability to say 'no' to things desired intensely."

Vital language encroaching upon the moral realm

(3) "Moral considerations are tampering unduly with the basic elements of life, namely, competition and strife."

(4) "True morality is not motivated primarily by the sense of duty but by a spontaneous love for a good."

The most important thing to notice here is the fact that many people will disagree with sentence (1) and agree with (2). The same goes for (3) and (4). This shows that we do not consider all imperialism of languages to be bad. Sometimes we think it wholesome, sometimes dangerous.

It should be noticed that the problem is not whether one agrees with the approvals and disapprovals which are assumed here. It is not the task of philosophy to decide whether such appraisals are valid. Philosophy merely wants to see what happens when human beings speak their languages. What we can see here is the fact that for everybody there are cases in which he will approve of moral language intruding into the vital realm, and other cases in which he will resent this intrusion. For different people the dividing line between approval and disapproval will have a different location, but there will always be such a line.

d) One possible way of indicating the task of philosophy is to say that it has to make an analysis of all languages which human beings speak and of all the conflicts between those languages. If we consider the six languages mentioned in the beginning of this chapter (moral, aesthetic, rational, religious, vital, and pragmatic), then there are fifteen fields of conflict. As there are many more languages, the number of fields of conflict increases considerably. A systematic analysis of these fields would offer an analysis of Western civilization.

e) It is perhaps possible to distinguish two types of imperialism of languages. We have discussed mainly the first type, but in our last remarks the second type has come into view. By the first type we could mean the intrusion of one language into the domain of another. By the second type we can understand the act by which one language usurps the place belonging to another language. This notion of usurpation presupposes the concept of a hierarchy of languages. It seems that in the view of many people one language is more important than the others. For adherents of a religion it is their religious language; for some humanists it is moral language.

In the eyes of most people convictional language possesses a higher rank than any other language. They will say that the language of science has its own legitimate domain, but that in our time such a subordinate language largely has usurped the place which belongs to commitment language. This accusation is given voice when people speak of scient*ism* and rational*ism,* the suffix "ism" connoting the blame.

On the other hand, there are people who see a great danger in the authoritarianism of many, perhaps all, convictional languages. They say that Communism, Nazism, and (certain forms of) Christianity rob scientific language of its precious independence.

2. *Attacks upon vital values*

a) One of the most interesting illustrations of imperialism of languages is the attack upon vital values made by moral, philosophical, and religious systems. There is a considerable group of philosophers who make it their main business to defend instincts, feelings, sex, the body, against religious or moral or philosophical aggression. For instance, Henri Bergson, Max Scheler, Sigmund Freud, and Gabriel Marcel. Some of these men belong to the philosophic trend called *Lebensphilosphie,* that is, philosophy of "life."

For instance, Freud claims that our sex life is of ultimate importance. He sets out to show that sex is so decisive for our lives and so much more powerful than our moral way of looking at the world and ourselves that we refuse to admit openly its importance and try to humble it. Further he says that we vindicate ourselves by giving sex a very low rank in our scheme of values, or even by considering it to be an enemy. And we achieve this aim by constructing impressive moral or religious language systems. For Freud, man-who-speaks is man who in speaking suppresses sex.

b) It is not only philosophers who are defenders of vital values who assert that moral and religious systems endanger nonspiritual values. Also quite different men, such as Marx, Heidegger, and the logical positivists, take positions like that of Freud. Marx's "materialism" wants to defend certain values against the aggression of religious, moral, and philosophical systems. These values are: economic life, that is to say, labor; the concern of a man for his family; his struggle with the powers of nature and of hostile groups in society.

In *The Origin of Russian Communism* Nicolas Berdyaev describes the convictions of a nineteenth-century revolutionary, Belinskij. Belinskij "rebels against an abstract idealism remote from concrete life, which sacrifices the individual to the general, the living human person to the world soul." [1]

Heidegger, in his *Sein und Zeit,* claims that the best avenue of access for the understanding of being is man. What Heidegger has in mind, however, is not man in his excellence—that is, artistic man, religious man, scientific man—but the ordinary man, man in his everyday life, in his relationships with tools, his work, and other human beings in their undistinguished existence.

Logical empiricists (and empiricists throughout the ages) deny that we can receive a better understanding of men and life by following the way of speculation, by setting up pretentious, lofty systems of seemingly deep ideas. We have to turn around and study assiduously the concrete, reliable things of life, the statements about which can be verified and purified from superstition and credulity.

c) We can express the affinity between the positions of the philosophers of life, on the one hand, and of Marx, Belinskij, Heidegger, and the empiricists, on the other, by saying that what they deem necessary

[1] (London: Geoffrey Bles, 1948), p. 39.

to defend against the arrogance of the systems of philosophy, morals, and religion is "life in its simplicity," or the *vital values.*[2] The values meant by Freud, Bergson, and others, we could call *vitality* values. It has to be understood that vitality values form one aspect of the larger group of the vital values.

d) It scarcely has to be mentioned that for the philosophers who point out the danger of overbearing religious, moral, and philosophical systems, their defense of vital values is connected with (1) the problem of understanding man, (2) the problem of salvation. They all claim that we can understand man only if we disregard the arrogant assertions of those systems and take into account an aspect of man's life which was covered up by them. In the same manner they claim that man can be *delivered* from his quandaries only if we take seriously the masked aspect of his life, be it sex, or labor, or the concrete, individual existence.

3. *The hostility between religious and moral language*

We want to avoid discussions of imperialistic conflicts which are obvious, such as that between religion and science. We choose instead the hostile relationship between religious and moral language, which remarkable relationship many times is overlooked. In our chapter on the nature of mythical language we will see how, according to the interpretation of W. B. Kristensen, the ancient nations were aware of the different nature of the religious and moral languages. In this section we will relate some of the discussions of a contemporary Christian, Maurice Pradines, who defends a similar theme for the Christian faith.[3] We should say, more accurately, that Pradines not only brings the contrast to light, but that at the same time he defends the nonmoral nature of the Christian faith against a moral misinterpretation. It is unnecessary to say that we are not interested in such a defense, but merely want to understand the mutual imperialism which formed the occasion for the defense.

a) Identity is claimed by morals and refused by faith. When Pradines refers to religion or faith, he means clearly the Christian faith, that is to say, this faith as understood in the Hebrew-Christian tradition. It is not at all clear what he means by morals. He probably has in mind the moral and social consciousness of certain modern Christians. Pradines presents the problem in the following way. It is generally assumed that religion offers a strong support to moral life. For a moral way of

[2] We use "vital" here in the meaning of "pertaining to life" (Latin *vita* means life), and disregard its meaning of "important."

[3] *Esprit de la religion* (Paris: Aubier, 1941), ch. xvii, "*Les conflits de la culture et de la foi*"; ch. xviii, "*Les compromis de la culture et de la foi.*"

thinking this supporting element is an aspect of faith itself, namely, "the belief in a divine power the very nature of which is to be morally good and wise." Religion refuses this identity; it claims to support moral life, but by an element which is not "good and wise" but "exterior to moral life itself." Religion and morality are heterogeneous entities, and "their principles are incompatible." [4]

b) According to Pradines "the proper object of religion . . . is the supernatural." Morality offers man "a natural way of living, that of virtue," whereas religion offers "a supernatural way, that of grace." Religion "grants us supernatural life, while redeeming us from natural life." It is a grave misunderstanding to say that it is a major function of religion to help man to live morally, for "morality is at its very best a superior form of natural life." Now natural life is the very thing from which religion points away. (One might add: the better the moral life, the more man is disinclined to listen to religion, which offers something quite different.)

As a consequence, religion and morality have much less in common than is generally supposed. Pradines claims that they do not share positive aims; at the very most they reject the same things, but then it is for different reasons. For example, both religion and morality recommend a struggle against the passions, but morality wants us to resist them "because they are against 'nature,'" while religion demands our struggle because the passions "belong to 'natural' life."

Pradines sums up the radical differences by referring to four contrasts:

(1) "In the moral life everything is the work of man and the fruit of his will, whereas in supernatural life everything is the work of a divine activity, inspired by a pure grace."

(2) "In the moral order we can possess nothing which we have not given to ourselves; in the supernatural order we cannot acquire anything which we have not received."

(3) "The least trace of heteronomy radically vitiates moral life; the least pretension of autonomy radically corrupts supernatural life."

(4) "Moral activity in itself is without any doubt *not* an insult to God. . . . He has granted us our freedom, and we honor him . . . if we make a good use of it . . . but the worship turns into sacrilege if we claim that God's gifts only serve to perfect that which we have given ourselves." [5]

c) Religion offers a good which morality does not understand. "It is absurd to claim that the senseless misery of life, from which man appeals to God (which appeal is the true nature of faith), could be

[4] *Ibid.*, pp. 402, 404, 467. Used by permission.

[5] *Ibid.*, pp. 404-9, 434-36.

deluded by a moral consolation which pulls us down to that same life and which invites us to find our salvation in ourselves."

"Our anxiety as to life and death can be quieted by morality," but it can never be "solaced by it in the way food solaces our hunger." Our moral needs are "contrary" and "alien" to the need to which our faith speaks. "Morality consists always in an activity which sustains the confidence that it can attain all its essential purposes, whereas faith has its principle in the certainty that there exists a Good which is absolutely necessary to us and which we cannot possibly give to ourselves." [6]

d) "The renewal of the Christian faith has always taken the form of a reaction against the moral way of thinking." In the case of crises in which religions renewed themselves, the leaders have always returned to the basic distinction between religion and morals. Pradines gives as examples: Paul, who appeals to this principle in his battle against ritualism and legalism; Augustine, in his struggle against Pelagianism. He remarks that Luther and Calvin protest "not only against the easy moral way of reaching salvation by means of indulgences, but against the difficult moral way of austerity and mortification," i.e., against the moral way as such.[7]

e) Religion and morality have found each other, but this never went further than an uneasy compromise. Pradines dedicates several sections of his book to the demonstration that religion and morality need each other. Something like a real union was never reached because of the basic differences. Pradines discusses several forms of the resulting compromises, one of which is the doctrine of predestination. He claims that neither religion taken in itself, nor morality in itself, needs such a doctrine. Morality does not need it because "it is founded upon the notion of the complete autonomy of the will." Religion does not need the doctrine either, for "it does not require anything of man at all"; God gives him that which he needs more than anything else and this it is which he cannot produce himself. "The problem of predestination arises only when morality and religion interpenetrate." Then it is "unavoidable to bring into accordance with each other the necessary heteronomy of grace and the necessary autonomy of the will. God will order us then to do that which He will yet work in us in another way." "Predestination has nothing whatsoever to do with determinism and fatalism." These two are views which exclude free will. The doctrine of predestination, however, "is the result of a view which reckons with two freedoms which are nearly on equal footing." Man's freedom "must

[6] *Ibid.*, pp. 436, 437.
[7] *Ibid.*, pp. 437, 438.

produce that which, at the same time, it must receive in virtue of God's grace." [8]

f) Pradines gives no stronger expression of the contrast between religious and moral language than by saying that they seem to mean the same God, but that actually they have a different God in mind. "The God who supports religious life, or much more causes it to be born, remains a God who suppresses moral life. The God who sustains moral life, or much more gives it its most lofty meaning, remains a God who suppresses religious life." [9]

B. THE FANATICAL CLAIM

The following analysis is akin to those offered by Marcel and Reinhold Niebuhr.[10] Their interpretations are, however, not wholly satisfactory; hence our own view is presented, with frequent references, especially to Marcel's work.

Marcel rightly warns against the use of the term "fanaticism," because "words in 'ism' often represent an illicit process of thinking." He proposes to speak of "the fanaticized consciousness," following Husserl's phenomenological method, which holds that consciousness is "intentional," or directed toward something.[11] Marcel's objection against the term "fanaticism" is valid, but it seems more appropriate to speak of "the fanatical claim." Such a claim is a language phenomenon analyzable by philosophy. The claim tells us something about the fanatical "consciousness" and the fanatical person, but it is not prudent if we concentrate mainly upon this person or this consciousness in our investigation. These terms suggest too easily that we can divide people into two groups, those who are fanatics and those who are not. An analysis of the fanatic claim does not start from such a preconceived idea. The discussion of the fanatical claim will be followed by an analysis of the fanatical situation. This situation comprises the fanatical person, but also other elements just as crucially important for the fanatical situation.

1. *The fanatical claim*

Webster's New Collegiate Dictionary gives as the most important aspects of the verb "to claim": *authority* by virtue of which something is asked for; the demand that a fact, right, or relation *ought* to be

[8] *Ibid.*, pp. 465, 466.

[9] *Ibid.*, p. 507.

[10] Marcel, *Man Against Mass Society*, Part II, ch. ii. Niebuhr, *The Self and the Dramas of History*, chs. xvii-xix.

[11] *Man Against Mass Society*, pp. 99-100.

acknowledged; the call for *attention.* The examples given in the dictionary are taken from legal language and everyday language. It is clear that the fanatical claim comprises all three elements, but belongs to another type of discourse, that of convictional language. Webster's term "ought" also points in this direction. The fanatical claim requires people's attention for something or somebody which is supposed to possess exceptional, unquestionable value and authority and hence demands their unqualified submission. In other words, the fanatical claim carries a very strong and a very definite conviction; it points to a powerful convictor.

a) The fanatical claim is a form of imperialistic language. It is a convictional encroachment upon all other convictions. If the people addressed by the claim do not answer with the right response, they are *ipso facto* condemned, for instance, as enemies of the working class, as enemies of the Aryan race, as traitors, heretics, Communists. Such disqualifications and insinuations are not to be minimized as forms of extreme intolerance. The fanatical claim implies the conviction that something of ultimate importance is at stake, and testifies to the certainty that everyone who does not worship this convictor trespasses upon a cosmic law.

b) The imperialism of the fanatical claim depends upon the conviction of "knowing" an "absolute" convictor. There is no term which characterizes the fanatical claim better than this word "absolute," provided that it is understood in its unweakened meaning. The English "absolute" points back to the Latin verb *absolvo,* to loosen from, to make loose, to set free, to detach, to untie.[12] Hence we find in the Oxford dictionary, among other meanings, the following pertinent to what we can call the "strong" meaning of the word "absolute": detached, unfettered, disengaged from all accidental or special circumstances, essential, free from all imperfection or deficiency, independent, free from all external restraint or interference, unlimited power, unconditioned, self-sufficing.[13] The fanatical claim points out a convictor which is "absolute" in this strong sense: Hitler, Stalin, God, Reason. Or perhaps we should say that in many cases the claim of absoluteness is made for certain "mediating powers," such as the Church, the Creed, the Prophet, Science, *Das Kapital.*[14] To the absolute convictor or the absolutized mediating element corresponds the absolute certainty claimed for the fanatical utterance.

[12] Harper's *Latin Dictionary, s.v. absolvo.*

[13] *A New English Dictionary on Historical Principles* (Oxford: Clarendon Press, 1888), *s.v.* "absolute."

[14] Marcel, *Man Against Mass Society,* p. 106.

c) The absoluteness of the claim makes understandable the claimer's refusal to have the claim questioned. Nothing is more disconcerting to the person who does not affirm the fanatical claim than this refusal. Still, nothing is more "reasonable" from the claimer's standpoint. Such a questioning is nothing less than an insult to his convictor or the mediating power, a lese majesty, sacrilege, and profanation. The convictor is absolute, that is, out of reach of the arrogant criticism of people who live in the realm of circumstances, of conditions, of what is accidental and imperfect.

This "refusal to question one's basic convictions" is such a crucial issue that it is well-nigh impossible to restrain our convictions in talking about it. Some people will say that the fanatical claim is the perversion of convictional language. This is the tenor of Marcel's and Niebuhr's discussions. Others will claim that all convictional language is basically fanatical, or at least tends to become so. As philosophers we cannot say more than this: some convictional language is saturated with fanatical claims; other convictional languages may not be completely free from such claims, but they are characterized also by demands for self-criticism and criticism by others. We have to notice that there is no convictional world view which can give guarantees that its language is free from fanatical claims. Some Roman Catholic language is full of such claims; other Roman Catholic language is remarkably free from them. The same thing goes for Protestant, for humanistic or for naturalistic language. On the other hand, there are convictional world views, the language of which always seems full of fanatical claims: Communist, Fascist, and nationalistic views.

2. *The fanatical situation*

The foregoing analysis of the fanatical claim calls for a discussion of the fanatical situation: How does the fanatical claimer see his convictional situation?

a) As has been said earlier the fanatical person lives by means of a very specific interpretation of his convictor and himself.[15] He believes that he serves a single convictor and therefore refuses to admit the complexity and ambiguity of his own life. This refusal is the foundation for the refusal to question his basic convictions. A person who bases his whole life upon the denial of part of his own being cannot allow a free discussion, which certainly would bring to light exactly those elements which, unknown to himself, he wants to keep in the dark. An open discussion would endanger the whole existence of the fanatical claimer, that is to say, the existence as he interprets

[15] Chap. I, Sec. B-5-*c*.

it himself. Both refusals are grounded in anxiety. The absoluteness of the claim reveals anxiety, and the anxiety reveals a basic insecurity. This means: they are revealed to the nonfanatical outsider. For the fanatical claimer the whole situation remains hidden.

b) To the fanatical claimer's interpretation of his convictional situation belongs also a specific view of his confessional group. Because of the absoluteness of his convictions he cannot admit that other confessional groups have a right to exist; he cannot see his own group other than as the only real group.

We have to say: the fanatical claimer sees his own group as more than just a group. It is a *fanum.* The word "fanatic" is derived from the Latin *fanaticus,* and this word is related to *fanum,* a temple, a sanctuary. *Fanaticus* meant: first, pertaining to a temple; second, inspired by a divinity, especially with the meaning of a frantic zeal for such a divinity.[16] We can say that for the fanatical claimer his group is such a *fanum,* a sanctuary, a privileged domain which relieves him of his hidden anxieties and insecurity.

Another aspect of the fanatical claimer's interpretation of his convictional situation is the identification of three elements, namely, his own person, his *fanum,* and his god. The fanatical Nazi *is* "the victorious German nation" (his *fanum*); the Orthodox Dutch Calvinist of the war against Spain (1568-1648) *is* the Chosen Nation, and *is* his God of Old Testament wrath. The fanatical claimer cannot permit his basic presuppositions to be questioned because such a questioning would imply a doubting not only of these convictions but of the whole structure (his own person, his *fanum,* his God) cemented together by the process of identification.

This structure has not always the same form. In some cases the god is extremely vague, whereas the *fanum* assumes exceptional clarity and power. For instance, the god of the Communists is the inexorable, irresistible, but vague Force of History; their *fanum* is the Party. In the case of the racial fanatics among the white South Africans and others like them in this country, not the god, but the *fanum* is quite clear: the sacred community of white people. The convictional structure is different when both the god and the *fanum* are represented with equal clearness. We find this structure with those Catholics for whom the church is a *fanum,* and with the Dutch Orthodox Calvinists mentioned above.

Marcel justly points out that there is still another element in the convictional situation of the fanatical claimer, the focus.[17] Marcel

[16] Harper's *Latin Dictionary, s.v. fanaticus.*

[17] *Man Against Mass Society,* p. 102.

suggests that such a focus is an individual; and that is sometimes the case, as with Hitler and Stalin. In our opinion there are other cases where the focus is a creed, as, for instance, the Protestant creeds for the orthodox Calvinists. Whether the focus is an individual or something else, it shares the absolute character of the *fanum,* of which it forms the center of attention.

c) We have not yet discussed the aggression characteristic of the fanatical claimer and his group. It is the counterpart of his refusal to question his basic convictions, that is to say, his whole convictional structure. The very existence of entities outside the group endangers this structure, threatens the fanatic's existence, insults his *fanum.* It is inevitable that the threat is met with aggression. The other, alien entities which evoke resentments are largely of two types. One can be another group with fanatical claims. Niebuhr describes the conflict between two fanatical groups, that of the feudal and Catholic France before the revolution, and that of the revolutionaries who worshiped reason.[18]

The resented entity can also be a nonfanatical group or convictional world view. Nazi Germany destroyed the Jewish congregations and the social democratic formations and intimidated the Christian churches because the convictions of these groups demanded more or less clearly a continuing criticism, a fundamental questioning of their own and of others' basic assumptions. Generally speaking, the "right wings" of churches and political parties are always inclined to resent the questioning which is one of the functions of left wings as "dirty radicalism," as "fouling one's own nest." The Old Testament prophets who questioned the easy identification of the Jewish cause with God's cause were stoned or mistreated.

d) Many of the foregoing remarks have already made clear that fanatical language is a kind of "religious" language. The fanatical claimer serves a god, escapes from the insecurity of life into a *fanum,* a sanctuary, and by identifying himself with these sacred elements elevates himself to a divine status. We can add here that he also knows devils and saviors. The resented alien entities readily assume characteristics of a devil, such as "the Jewish international plutocracy" for the Nazis, "Western imperialistic capitalism" for the Communists, "the Communists" for Western fanatics. Many times the fanatical group lives by the grace of the hope for salvation by a savior, such as the hope of the class of the workers in Karl Marx as their savior. Also Lenin and Stalin (before the denunciation), as they lived in the convictions of the

[18] *Op. cit.,* p. 118.

fanatical Communists, were saviors. Both devils and saviors are foci of anxieties and expectations.

e) There are certain phenomena which can but do not need to play a role in a fanatical situation. They are: creeds, manifestoes, ontologies, and philosophical or theological systems. These phenomena are all of them crystallizations of convictions. They can be interpreted as the expression of a certain convictional world view of a specific group, whereas the conviction is implied that there are other groups with views of their own which are not *ipso facto* evil. It is also possible to interpret a creed or system as the formulation of absolute truth. This is the fanatical interpretation.

Many people are certain that the adherence to a creed is already the first step toward the direction of a fanatical claim. G. J. Sirks reminds us, however, that the term "creed" is derived from the Latin *credo*.[19] This word is not a noun, but a verbal form, namely, "I believe." It is the first word of the "apostolic" confession of faith: "I believe in God, the Father Almighty . . ." Sirks claims that we misunderstand the original meaning of this confession if we treat *credo* as if it were a noun. "The creed" actually means "the I believe." This is neither good grammar nor good convictional language. Sirks asserts that in this way the confession (we should say: the confessing, if the English language would permit us) "is objectified and cut away from the living tissue." We can understand "objectified" as to mean: made into a thing, a tool, which can be used, for instance, in a fanatical situation. The word "crystallization" used earlier points in the same direction. Something which was alive, and therefore not exact, never final, always changing, because individuals and groups change, is deadened into a finished, final product. The problem at hand is that of the function of a "creed" (and of manifestoes and systems) in a confessional group. The nonfanatical interpretation of this function is that such a formulation is the expression of the convictions of a certain group, in a specific country, in a definite century. The fanatical interpretation sees the formulation as the expression of absolute truth.

3. *The nonfanatical attitude*

In the preceding pages the term "nonfanatical person" had to be used a few times. We have to realize that this is a contradiction in terms.

a) A person who is convinced of the dangers of the fanatical attitude will readily admit that some people, and even institutions belong-

[19] *Op. cit.*, p. 15.

ing to his own confessional group, frequently make fanatical claims. The assertion that fanatical claims are to be found only in the language of other groups—of Communists, of Nazis, or of religious people—is itself a fanatical claim.

Niebuhr and Marcel are good examples of "nonfanatical people." Niebuhr tries to show how rationalism and naturalism in modern culture are sources of fanatical claims, but he never distorts the picture by leaving out or condoning or minimizing the devastating role of religious fanatical claims.[20] Marcel is a Roman Catholic. He claims that "genuine religion" is not fanatical, but he admits several times that even such genuine religions can become fanaticized. This admission does not refer only to Christian churches other than his own, but points clearly to the Roman Catholic Church itself.

> But if fanaticism can creep back into such religions [Christianity, Judaism, Islam] . . . that is, it seems to me only due to the growth and intervention between man and God of certain mediating powers, such as the Church or the Prophet, which, instead of remaining mere mediators, are endowed by the fanaticized consciousness with the prerogatives quite incompatible with the weakness proper to the creature *qua* creature.[21]

b) The person of nonfanatical convictions will readily admit the probability that he himself is not completely free from fanatical claims. Such a person will never forget, not only that man is a complex and ambiguous being, but also that he himself is such a man, a being who knows himself only partially. Marcel says: "The first obvious observation to be made is that the fanatic never sees himself *as* a fanatic; it is only the non-fanatic who can recognize him as a fanatic." [22] This holds also for the person who strives to avoid fanatical claims. He may be free from such claims—for instance, in his explicit religious convictions—but it is possible and probable that he entertains fanatical claims in his political convictions, or in his disdain for a certain philosophical position.

We are therefore not allowed to speak of a nonfanatical person. The most we can say is that there exist persons, and convictional groups, who earnestly desire to keep free from fanatical claims as much as possible. We can call them "nonfanatical?" persons and groups, and say that they often assume a nonfanatical attitude.

[20] *Op. cit.*, pp. 149, 153.
[21] *Man Against Mass Society*, pp. 99, 106.
[22] *Ibid.*, p. 101.

C. MAN-WHO-SPEAKS ESTABLISHES HIS EXISTENCE

1. Power is intrinsic in language

In talking about phenomena such as imperialistic and fanatical claims, we should beware of the temptation to suggest that language is sometimes aggressive and at other times not, that it is sometimes decent and peaceful and on other occasions willful and bad. On the contrary, language is always power-full; to speak is always to exercise power.

a) By speaking man intervenes in a situation.[23] Man is a being which does not accept life demurely just as it comes, but he rebels against it and wants to change it. It is man-who-speaks who calls for the change. The leader of an oppressed group "gives the word," and on this sign the rebellion begins and the political situation is basically changed. The word of protest and frustration spoken by the adolescent who defies the paternal authority changes the peaceful family situation. In these examples two factors are present—resentment about an unacceptable situation, and the attempt to change the situation by means of speaking. It seems that these two factors always can be noticed if human beings speak up, however, with this difference, that on most occasions the emotional color is less vehement, so that we do not have to speak of "resentment" but of "disapproval," not of "unacceptable" but of "less desirable." The degree of vehemence, however, has nothing to do with the basic fact that, by speaking, man wants to intervene in a given situation which he would like to see changed. Even in a very quiet and peaceful situation, such as teaching a class of poetry, the underlying motive of the person speaking is that of being dissatisfied with the situation, in this case ignorance about Ben Jonson, and the decision to change the situation.

b) Our language, that is to say, we ourselves, are intervening in situations even when we are not fully aware of our intention to intervene. When we call some action "good," we tacitly invite other people to judge in the same way, and even ask them to act according to the judgment given. Many, however, deny that they are intervening in such a case, or that they want to intervene. They forget that every speaking is a form of propaganda. People speaking moral language on a certain occasion give other people to understand that moral language is the appropriate language for this occasion, because a moral good is at stake.

c) It is not enough to say that man-who-speaks intervenes in a given situation. Speaking is a power which releases power. During World War II Churchill's words redeemed in the British nation the power which

[23] Gusdorf, *op. cit.*, p. 34.

enabled them to keep going even in the darkest hours. In the mid-twenties, in a period of crisis in Communist Russia, Stalin's words that Communism could be achieved "even in one country" released powers in the Russian nation to endure the hardships of the five-year plans.[24]

d) The intrinsicality of power in language is further demonstrated by the fact that we can easily apply to the power of speaking some distinctions made by Bertrand de Jouvenel in view of power as such.[25] De Jouvenel comes to the conclusion that "in the make-up of Power . . . two natures are necessarily found in association. In whatever way and in whatever spirit it has been established, Power is neither angel nor brute, but, like man himself, a composite creature, uniting in itself two contradictory natures." The two natures which De Jouvenel mentions are "the will to dominate" and "the will to serve." His remarks apply surprisingly well to language, or to man-who-speaks. We can notice here both De Jouvenel's "two natures" and perhaps something of his "necessary association." Roget's *Thesaurus* gives *s.v.* "motive" a list of verbs, all of which picture man-who-speaks and clearly show us man-exercising-power-in-speaking. In some verbs the dominating aspect of this exercise of power is prominent; in others the serving element; again others are neutral. To the first group belong verbs such as: incite, tempt, bewitch, wheedle, coax, bribe, overpersuade, lure, inveigle, entice. It is not so clear which words belong in the second and third groups. Perhaps "inspire" and "fascinate" have a serving connotation, whereas "induce," "move," "draw," "prompt," stimulate," "encourage," and "advocate" can be said to be neutral. We may conclude that exercising power is an intrinsic aspect of man-who-speaks.

e) Religions have offered remarkable interpretations of the power of language. The following remarks relate some attempts by people of different religions and of various periods of history to give account of the power of language, something which appears to have impressed them deeply. Their serious concern may count as a support for our thesis about the power aspect of language being intrinsic. The examples are taken from Van der Leeuw's *Religion in Essence and Manifestation.*

Not only the words spoken by gods, such as words of creation, but also human words carry power in the eyes of primitive man. A word is for him not a mere thing, only a name; it is not to be contrasted as something powerless with the deed as the exercise of power. The word is also a deed; it carries power, and it sets power in motion.[26]

[24] Isaac Deutscher, *Stalin, a Political Biography* (New York: Oxford University Press, 1949), pp. 281 ff.

[25] *On Power,* tr. J. F. Huntington (New York: Viking Press, 1949), p. 114.

[26] Pp. 224, 403. Used by permission of George Allen & Unwin.

The power released by the spoken word can be saving and healing power (notice Van der Leeuw's discussion of Empedocles' noteworthy speech); it can also be dangerous. "A word is always a charm." "Whoever asserts anything, 'poses,' and thus exerts some influence, but he also 'exposes' himself." We have therefore to be very careful with what we say: we cannot calculate the consequences. Gods may be insulted; unmanageable situations may be conjured up.[27]

The might of the word "becomes still further enhanced in various ways. Raising the voice, emphasis, connection by rhythm or rhyme, all this endows the word with heightened energy." "Certain unusual words possess intensified power: the term *eilikrineis,* for instance, gives a holy man an 'excellent feeling.' " Van der Leeuw mentions terms such as Hallelujah, Amen, Om. We certainly can add that the key words of a confessional language fill the believer with joy: "the proletariat," "the downfall of Western imperialism" in one case; the *Führer,* "the Aryan race," "the future of the German nation" in another; "eternal, unchangeable moral rules" and "absolute truths" in again another case.[28]

"Words, however, possess the greatest power when they combine into some formula, some phrase definite in the sounds of its terms, their timbre and their rhythm." This holds for creeds, liturgies, recitals of scriptures and of doctrinal statements. We can add: it holds, too, for famous quotations of beloved philosophers.[29]

Van der Leeuw refers not only to words and formulas, but also draws our attention to the man who speaks.

> Whoever speaks . . . not only employs an expressive symbol but goes forth out of himself, and the word that he lets fall decides the matter. . . . It is the word that decides the possibility. For it is an act, an attitude, a taking one's stand and an exercise of power, and in every word there is something creative.[30]

2. *Man-who-speaks establishes his existence*

a) Who is the subject of the imperialism of languages? The term "imperialism of languages" is in a certain sense a misleading one. It suggests that the subjects of the imperialisms are the languages. We have to raise the question as to whether, strictly speaking, languages can be called imperialistic. Perhaps this is a question to which a clear answer is impossible.

One can make a very good case for the position that it is better to say that *human beings* are aggressive and that they are not allowed to

[27] *Ibid.*, pp. 225, 404.
[28] *Ibid.*, p. 405.
[29] *Ibid.*, p. 406.
[30] *Ibid.*, p. 403.

hide behind the skirts of their languages by putting the charge of aggression upon their shoulders. If a pacifist's moral approach to the world encroaches upon the political realm and also intrudes into the religious and vital domains, we should recognize that it is just as appropriate (or even more so) to say that it is the pacifist than that it is moral language which is aggressive. When Wendell Johnson argues that we can build a more peaceful and humane world by freeing ourselves from aggressive language, "symbols of conflict," Leon L. Matthias rightly observes that aggression possibly is as much a basic aspect of human existence as of language.[31]

There are, however, good reasons not to discard the idea that the languages themselves may be called imperialistic. It cannot be denied that languages seem to be powerful structures which take hold of our minds and hearts. It makes very good sense to say that the pacifist, the Communist, and certain scientists cannot escape from the pacifist, the Communist, the rationalist way of viewing the world. Many people will agree that our Western civilization is in the grip of a pragmatic approach to the world from which it cannot extricate itself.

Further, it is impossible to deny the element of truth in Bacon's exposition of the four classes of idols. Let us notice the verbs he uses in order to portray the imperialistic power of these language habits. The strongest expression is "idols which beset men's minds," in Aphorisms xxxviii and xxxix. We should notice that the Latin verb *obsideo,* which is translated here by "beset," is ultimately the origin of our word "obsession." Other expressions used by Bacon to convey the notion of imperialistic power include: "are now in possession of human understanding," "have taken deep root therein," "trouble us" (Aphorism xxxviii); "words plainly force and overrule the understanding, and throw all into confusion" (xliii); "crept into the understanding," "words stand in the way and resist the change" (lix).

We can partly solve the dilemma by saying that there is actually not much of a problem. We cannot separate languages from persons, or, we *are* our language. The subject of the imperialism is therefore quite simply man-who-speaks, *homo loquens.* This solution seems to be too easy a way out. We had better consider the problem raised by the term "imperialism of languages" as a reminder of the fact that language is an ambiguous phenomenon: we ourselves are our languages, but also, they have power over us. Languages possess an individual, a personal aspect,

[31] "Symbols of conflict: Some Language Structure Aspects of Culture Conflicts," by Wendell Johnson, in *Conflicts of Power in Modern Culture* (Seventh Symposium of the Conference on Science, Philosophy and Religion), pp. 463-69; comment by Leon L. Matthias, p. 469.

but also a structural aspect. Languages are also language structures which are available to man, have power over him, present to him the various ways of being human.

b) Why are languages, or man-who-speaks, aggressive? Our answer to this question is that something has to be defended, that values of ultimate importance are at stake. In speaking their languages individuals and groups have in mind concrete goods without which they claim they cannot live, goods which make life so much more worth living that people want to give their lives for these goods' sake. These goods are presented, for instance, in democratic language and defended against a Communist or a Fascist way of viewing life. The convulsions of our time are partly due to conflicts between these and other convictional world views.

Man-who-speaks is aggressive because he is insecure. The complexity and ambiguity of life cause a deep anxiety, and he attempts to escape by presenting to himself the world in a simple pattern by means of his language. Wendell Johnson makes a trenchant remark when he speaks of the "two-valued frame of reference" of our traditional language. "We talk as though a given individual were either a Jew or not a Jew, either a capitalist or not a capitalist." [32]

Man-who-speaks is aggressive because the power of his language invites expansion. The success of a certain language in a specific field prompts him to speak that language also in other fields. When the scientific approach has proved its validity in the investigation of nature, people begin to expand the range of this method and to apply it also in the understanding of history. When philosophers discover absolute, unchangeable, and unquestionable truths in geometry, they claim that "truths" of the same nature must be found in the realm of morals.

c) The answers just given are not sufficient. The reasons mentioned are only partial reasons; the threat to concrete goods, insecurity, and expansion, all point to something which underlies all that, namely, man's existence. Man speaks aggressively because his very life is at stake. If we now, remembering our thesis that power is intrinsic in all speaking, take one step further, we can say: man speaks powerfully because he wants not only to defend but, more fundamentally, to establish his existence. The aggressiveness of the defense is so much more conspicuous than the exercise of power of the establishment that we are in danger of overlooking the latter.

The establishment of one's existence is the background against which imperialistic and fanatical claims have to be understood. Such aggressive

[32] *Ibid.*, p. 468.

claims stand actually in the service of attempts to establish, and this implies: to protect, to reinforce, to widen man's existence. Many times, or to say it better, every moment, such attempts meet and clash with other men's attempts. Hence the necessity of using power, of intervening in a situation. Hence also the frequency of aggressive or overaggressive claims. Man is plagued by the anxiety that he cannot maintain his existence on a level which he deems necessary, or by the anxiety that he will never be able to gain the glorious existence which he feels life ought to grant him.

d) The language in which man establishes his existence is always convictional language. He says: "Here am I, and this is what life means to me." We have to fill in: "Here am I, a mere proletarian, but I belong to that group which will do away with all oppression." Or: "Here am I, a scientist, and I will help to change the life of mankind by means of my research." In establishing his existence, man evaluates himself, his situation, the people and the world around him.

The conflict between imperialistic languages is always a convictional conflict. The languages involved are, for instance, *not* moral against political, religious versus scientific, moral against aesthetic language. The participants in the battle are convictional views, centered around certain goods or interpretations of goods. The cases just mentioned could, for instance, mean conflicts between an interpretation of social institutions and nations which implies a dislike of force, and another interpretation which has a high regard for power; the conviction that for a full life belief in a personal God is necessary, and the conviction that a decent man should not rely upon a god of whom we do not know a thing, but upon responsible, careful science; a preference of thinking in terms of good and bad, and a willingness to use also terms such as "graceful," "full of expression." Hence we had better avoid speaking of the conflict between religion and science, because probably in most cases what is meant is actually a conflict between religionism and scientism.[33]

The various languages seem to be *employed* by human beings, who want to establish, or protect, or improve, their existence. The goods, the way of living, the community, which are at stake, are defended by man-who-speaks by means of impressive languages. In establishing his existence man-who-speaks borrows the authority and the glamour of scientific language or of a specific religious or moral language. Man-who-speaks expects that the (real or supposed) power of such an em-

[33] "In most cases," for there are also tensions between each of the religions and science itself (as distinguished from scientism), conflicts which do not necessarily show forth the confusion characteristic of the above-mentioned imperialistic strifes.

ployed language will shine off upon or even transfer itself to his existence. "Here I am, a faithful orthodox Jew!" "Here am I, a good Reformed Christian, not one with a watered-down liberal faith." "Here am I, a man who keeps up moral values in an amoral and immoral age." "Here I am, and O Lord, help me to make a decent thing out of my life." "Here I am, and I want to live as honestly and justly as possible."

3. In what ways is man's establishment of his existence achieved?

We have to explain some of the terms of the sentence "Man-who-speaks establishes his existence." "Man-who-speaks" is better than "man, by means of his language," for the last expression might suggest language *used* as a tool, such as in scientific language. In establishing his existence man *is* his language and he *employs* some language. Man-who-speaks is *homo convictus*.

The other term in need of an elucidation is "establishes." The term "create" used by Gusdorf is clearly too strong.[34] We do not create our existence, strictly speaking, but we do something to what has been given to us (or to our "being thrown into the world," Heidegger). On the other hand, a term such as "affirm" seems to be too weak. That would suggest that our existence was already established for us and that it was only up to us to affirm it.

The question now to be considered is: What are the different forms in which the establishment of existence is achieved?

a) Gusdorf points to an interesting expression which illuminates the act of establishing our existence. The French expression is *prendre la parole,* of which no exact English equivalent exists.[35] It means: to begin to speak, to speak up, to rise and speak.

To speak up is one of the major tasks of man. . . . Language does not exist before the personal initiative which sets it in motion. The given language merely offers a frame to be used by man's verbal activity. The words and their meanings formulate all kind of possibilities . . . and these are presented to the man who speaks.

Gusdorf follows up these remarks by a discussion of what he calls "the creative nature" of language:

The name creates the thing. . . . But the name also creates the personal existence. . . . If one says to himself "I am sick," or "I am in love," "I am

[34] *Op. cit.*, p. 35. Also Jean Paul Sartre uses a terminology which is too strong, namely, in the passage where he discusses the meaning of the saying that existence precedes essence, *op. cit.*, p. 28: "We mean that man first of all exists . . . and defines himself afterwards. . . . To begin with he is nothing. He will not be anything until later, and then he will be what he makes of himself."

[35] *Op. cit.*, pp. 8, 33, 56.

bashful," or "I am stingy" then that means that . . . one gives a name to the enigma of personal incertitudes and hereby passes beyond these incertainties. The operation of language creates for us a persistent nature, beyond the present, fitting to explain the past and to engage the future.[36]

As intimated earlier, Gusdorf does not seem to give here an accurate analysis of the human situation. Indeed, man speaks up, gives names to things, and addresses himself, but in this picture some elements are left out. In all these ways of speaking a *response* is implied. Man considers himself *addressed* by his fellow men or his convictor, and he is *challenged* by events, by goods which he desires, by persons or events which threaten goods which are highly appreciated. When man-who-speaks establishes his existence, his speaking always implies answers to such addresses and challenges. In other words, in establishing his existence man-who-speaks relates himself not only to himself, but also to other people, to what is "real" for him, that is to say to concrete goods, and to what is for him his convictor. Gusdorf's examples just quoted are therefore not quite right. Man's "I am in love" is unthinkable without an "I love you!" We may suppose that somebody decides to be a Communist not by saying, "I am a Communist," but by committing himself in this way, "I will help in driving out the imperialist scoundrels," just as people in 1948 established themselves as Republicans by saying, "Let us clean up the mess in Washington." We have to add that we should supplement Gusdorf's little list of sentences by the following examples: "Thou art my God," "Heil Hitler," "Stevenson is the incarnation of the liberal spirit," and "Down with Truman; MacArthur is our national hero." Gusdorf would not have omitted this kind of sentence if he had realized that man-who-speaks, when establishing his existence, speaks convictional language and therefore either explicitly or implicitly relates himself to his convictor. Some of the most typical pronouncements in which man establishes his existence are couched not in terms of the "I" but in terms of the convictor. Many times man-who-establishes-himself forgets about his own existence in a concentrated attention upon a god, a cause, a "good," upon that which has overpowered him and which makes life possible for him.

The importance of concrete goods in this connection is clearly demonstrated by Marcel's discussion of what work, or better, what "being at work" means. The unemployed

has no further part in reality. To be at work, on the other hand, is to be possessed by the real in such a way that we no longer know exactly whether it is we who are fashioning it, or it which fashions us. . . . We can say that [this

[36] *Ibid.*, p. 35.

operation] involves the reciprocal movement by which man and reality embrace each other, which is none the less effective in the artist and the scholar than in the artisan, for instance, or the laborer.[37]

Man-working is very intimately related to man-speaking. Human work and human speaking is unthinkable without a commitment, and this is a response to a challenge by goods which are concrete (by what is "real" in Marcel's sense).

b) Marcel gives a profound discussion of two different ways in which human beings can establish their existence. He discriminates between establishing oneself as an ego or as a person.[38] Marcel does not refer to man-speaking in his essay, but if we read it carefully we will notice how according to Marcel's interpretation these establishments are actually performed by man-speaking. The *ego* is established in exclamations of a child, such as, "Look, . . . I picked these (flowers)!" A parallel utterance for an adult would be, for instance, the words of a man who in each conversation is waiting for the moment that he can say, "Now listen to what happened to *me!*" Man who has established himself as an ego is, according to Marcel, the typical *poseur*. A *poseur* is an actor; he "plays to the gallery," be it that the gallery is not only other people but also, and even in the first place, the self. We should not forget that this play-acting, which Marcel stresses so much, is a form of speaking. The *poseur* is man-speaking, who addresses himself as well as others. Also the etablishment of the *person* is, according to the account which Marcel offers, a typical language act. Some of the elements of this act are: committing oneself, i.e., responding to a call; binding oneself, with a vow; and believing in the existence of others.

In connection with Marcel's discussion we can say that the fanatical claim (mentioned elsewhere in this chapter) is an extreme example of man-speaking establishing himself as an ego.

c) An important characteristic of the establishment of our existence is the fact that one of the ways in which it is achieved, the speaking of a vow or a commitment, is often repeated. Our wife wants us to say again and again, "I love you," and a Christian repeats each week, "Thou art my God." On the one hand, the act of establishing our existence is the decision of a moment; on the other hand, we have to establish ourselves each time anew, in each new situation.

The necessity of testifying repeatedly to our act of establishment is related to our being complex and ambiguous beings, with many convictors, and many often conflicting loyalties. It has also to do with the

[37] *Homo Viator,* p. 145. Used by permission of Editions Montaigne and Henry Regnery Co.
[38] *Ibid.,* pp. 13-28. A fuller discussion of this essay is offered in Chap. VII of this book.

counterpart of this fact, namely, life being full of possibilities. Gusdorf rightly points out that it is language which enables us to identify and formulate the range of possibilities.[39] In view of this range of ever new possibilities, man-who-speaks feels the need of fortifying his establishment by repetition of the commitment. It will also happen that out of consideration for the new possibilities a new decision arises; that is to say, man establishes himself in a way more or less different than before. Many people who took a strong stand against McCarthyist slander had never before committed themselves so seriously.

d) Another way in which man-who-speaks establishes his existence is to be found in his mastering of the world of nature. Western man has realized the possibility of approaching nature in a detached way. That is to say, he knows that, to a certain extent, he can detach himself from his convictions, his commitments, his convictor, and in this way ask nonconvictional questions about what surrounds him and even about himself. Modern man has started to speak artificial, depersonalized languages, those of the sciences. This means that modern man has established himself as *homo sapiens,* as man-who-knows. If one asks such a question as "Why did the modern Western civilization arise?" part of the answer should be, "Because Western man has decided to establish himself as *homo sapiens.*"

It should be noticed that "the world of nature" to which man-who-knows relates himself differs from "the concrete goods" in relation to which man can also establish himself. This last relationship is more intimate, so that Marcel when describing it can speak of "man embracing what is real" (see Chap. VII). We can also borrow a set of terms of K. A. H. Hidding, a historian of religion who developed an anthropology in connection with the philosophy of Merleau-Ponty. Hidding's method will be discussed in Chap. V. Here we point only to his pair of concepts, "participation" and "objectification." We can say that man-who-speaks as *homo convictus* participates in the concrete goods in relationship to which he establishes his existence, whereas man-who-speaks as *homo sapiens* objectifies the world of nature. In speaking the language of scientific cognition, he makes this world of nature into an object which to a certain extent he can control and dominate, by setting himself apart from it. The term "world of nature" has to be taken in a wide sense. It comprehends not only what one usually calls nature but also man's culture, his history, his language. Also these can be objectified, that is, can be known in the way of scientific cognition.

In objectifying his culture, his history, his language, man objectifies

[39] *Op. cit.*, p. 33.

himself, for he *is* this language and this history. We can therefore say that man-who-speaks relates himself to himself at least in two different ways. As *homo convictus* he is himself in the way of being his convictions, of living in relationship to what he is convinced are his goods, his convictor. As *homo sapiens* he is himself in the manner of setting aside, for a moment, his deepest self, i.e., his convictions, and thus looking at himself and at what is not himself in a detached way.

e) If we consider again the diagram on *homo loquens* as shown in Chap. I, we will read it in a different way. Now the diagram represents the power of man-who-speaks. *Homo loquens* exercises his power and therewith establishes his existence in a variety of ways. The arrows present not only relationships, but also man's going forth out of himself to meet his convictor, his goods, his fellow men, the world of nature.

f) The most appropriate answer to the question, In what manner does man establish his existence? has not yet been given. This answer will be developed in the following chapter: man-who-speaks establishes his existence by means of the language-structure which we will call "world view."

CHAPTER THREE

WORLD VIEWS

Man-Who-Speaks Establishes His Existence in Drafting World Views

A. THE PROBLEM

1. *Terminological vagueness*

The body of convictions held by an individual or a group possesses a certain structure. People have used various terms to indicate this structure.

a) We noticed in Chap. I that James, in "The Sentiment of Rationality,"[1] used the following expressions: a conception of the frame of things (page 3), modes of conceiving the cosmos (page 4). We now add: conception of the universe (page 12), a philosophic conception (page 13), ultimate explanations of the universe (page 15), a philosophy (page 16). In Whitehead's *Science and the Modern World,* we find a great variety of expressions already in the first two paragraphs of the preface: view of the world, scheme, cosmologies, effective outlook, intuitions as to the nature of things, ultimate ideas, cosmological scheme.[2] Neither of these authors seems to have taken the trouble to define any of these concepts, each taking it for granted that his meaning was well understood.[3]

b) The German language seems to be privileged in regard to our problem because it possesses a specific term for what we have in mind (the nature and the structure of the body of convictions of a group or an individual), namely, the word *Weltanschauung.* German dictionaries, however, even philosophical dictionaries, do not suffice for a clear notion of what is involved in this concept. Eisler offers no separate discussion of the term; Felix Fluegel gives *s.v. Weltanschauung,* contemplation of the world, view of life. Runes, under the same head, world-view, perspective of life, conception of things. Baldwin, *s.v.* "world-view" (suggested rendering of the German term), the general way of regarding the world, more or less philosophically, personal to this or that individual. Webster, *s.v. Weltanschauung,* a conception of the course

[1] In *Essays in Pragmatism,* ed. Alburey Castell (New York: Hafner Publishing Co., 1952).

[2] New York: The Macmillan Co., 1925.

[3] James goes on to analyze the elements of a satisfying world view, but he omits a discussion on the term "world view" itself.

of events in, and of the purpose of, the world as a whole, forming a philosophical view or apprehension of the universe: the idea embodied in a cosmology.[4] None of these descriptions escapes the vagueness which we noticed in James and Whitehead. It is, however, possible to distinguish some of the major elements which are vaguely indicated in the definitions of these philosophers and dictionaries as follows:

(1) *Totality* is suggested by the terms "frame," "cosmos," "universe," "cosmology," "ultimate," "world as a whole," "life."

(2) The *essence* of the totality is suggested by "the nature of things."

(3) *Seeing* the totality is indicated in the terms "view," "outlook," "intuition," "idea."

(4) The *intellectual* aspect of this seeing appears in "explanation," "conception."

(5) *Other than purely intellectual* aspects are shown by "intuition," "personal," "purpose," and perhaps also "contemplation," "apprehension."

2. *Existentialist objections*

A protest against the term *Weltanschauung* has arisen largely under influence of existentialist philosophy. We find a typical example of this reaction in an official document of the Reformed Church of The Netherlands called *Being a Christian in Netherlands' Society*. The passage runs, "Being a Christian is in the first place a way of being, a way of existence. It is not having a philosophy about the significance of life and the world. It means to have a Lord and to be under the authority of that Lord." [5] This "philosophy about the significance of life and the world" is a way of rendering *Weltanschauung*. The protest seems to be directed against the mere spectator or "onlooker" attitude.

a) The term *Weltanschauung* suggests an attitude which does not go further than contemplation, or seeing (notice the preponderance of this element in the series of five elements listed in sec. 1-*b*). This contemplation is so detached that no reference is made to any action.

b) The term betrays the tacit assumption that one can construct his own *Weltanschauung* by a detached checking off of various considera-

[4] R. Eisler, *Wörterbuch der Philosophischen Begriffe* (2nd ed., Berlin: Mittler, 1904). F. Fluegel, *Allgemeines E.-D. und D.-E. Wörterbuch. The Dictionary of Philosophy*, ed. Dagobert D. Runes (New York: Philosophical Library, 1942). *Dictionary of Philosophy and Psychology*, ed. J. M. Baldwin (New York: The Macmillan Co., 1902). Webster's *New International Dictionary*, 2nd ed.

[5] In *Background Information* (published by the World Council of Churches, Department on Church and Society, Geneva, Switzerland), No. 12 (November 1955), p. 24.

tions against each other. That is to say, one can choose his *Weltanschauung* at will.

c) Such a *Weltanschauung* would be virtually a valueless thing, an armchair philosophy, a pretentious speculation, not determined by deeply rooted elements of the personality, but by trivial, playful, not serious constructions; the whole person would not be involved.

It is clear from what has been said in Chap. I that I do not have in mind such a *Weltanschauung*. Still, I think that a term such as "world view" is indispensable. Not only do we entertain a variety of convictions, but these form a more or less coherent whole. Further, such convictions are not merely the subjective expressions of one person, they represent an account, a *view* of the world, of life, of other human beings, of the All, of what for somebody may be his God. On the other hand, the terms "world," "view," and "world view" may be of doubtful value. There are indeed serious problems involved in all of them. We will approach them by entering more carefully into the principal existentialist objections. This can be done most suitably by analyzing the conception of "world" and our relationship to it as it plays a role in the works of some twentieth-century existentialist thinkers. As representatives of this phenomenological existentialism, we have chosen a philosopher, Martin Heidegger; a psychologist, Ludwig Binswanger; and a historian of religion, Gerardus van der Leeuw.

B. EXISTENTIALIST CONCEPTS OF THE "WORLD"

1. Heidegger's concepts of "world" and space

We have in mind Heidegger's philosophy of his first period, that of the volume *Sein und Zeit*. It would not be too much of an exaggeration to say that the actual preoccupation of this book is more accurately expressed as *Dasein und Raum* (man and space), or better *Dasein und Welt* (man and world), than in the actual title *Sein und Zeit* (being and time). Heidegger says that he is interested essentially in *Sein*, being, but his actual discussion centers around *Dasein*, human reality. The second half of the book deals with time, but the foundation of this discussion is given in the first half, in which the concept of "world" and the understanding of man as being-in-the-world are the central issues.

a) The main thesis of Heidegger in regard to our subject is that we have to distinguish sharply between the world which is described as the space of geometry and the world which is lived in by human beings. The first world does not found the second, but the second founds the first. Hence we have to begin our attempt to understand Heidegger's standpoint with an analysis of his concept of this human world. The term "world" will be used in the pages that follow, to indicate this human world, as distinguished from geometrical space.

b) Heidegger begins his discussion with the distinction between *Sein in* . . . (being inside . . .) and *In-Sein* (inhabiting). The first term points to the way of being a *thing,* the last to the constitution of being of *human reality.* A thing is inside another thing; for instance, there is water "in" a glass, that is to say, inside it. The glass is inside a room, the room inside the building, and so everything is inside world-space. But very different is the word "in" as it is used in "inhabit," "dwelling in," "living in," which has quite a different philosophical meaning from the "in" of "inside." Inhabit is related to abide, sojourn, and even to "being familiar with." *In-Sein* therefore means: staying in a "world" in which one is at home. Heidegger lists several modes of *In-Sein,* such as "produce, . . . use, . . . investigate, . . . contemplate, determine, discuss," and also "neglect, rest, omit." [6]

c) The meaning of the term "world" becomes more clear if we investigate the nature of knowledge. According to Heidegger, traditional epistemology is on the wrong track if it presents the "problem" of knowledge in terms of an "internal" and an "external" realm. This approach suggests that knowledge is first internal, and then the problem remains of how it "can get outside this internal realm into 'another and external' world." Heidegger claims that knowledge is not of a primary nature. There is something prior to it, namely, being-in-the-world, and this implies a dealing with the realities which one meets in the "world." Thus, the entire notion of the contrast between internal and external is completely false. To say "man" means to refer to a being which in its very nature is not an isolated internal realm, separated from an external domain, but a being which is always already part of a "world." Man is always "concerned about something," he is "out there" from the very beginning. The problem of how to get from the internal to the external, therefore, is no real problem at all; it is a pseudoproblem fabricated by a faulty epistemology. Furthermore, Heidegger points out that knowledge (or better, knowing) is a specific mode of "dealing with," namely, one which "abstains from all . . . handling" and which confines itself expressly to "merely-looking-at things." [7]

d) The "world" is therefore a basic characteristic of human existence. Although this thesis of Heidegger's may sound paradoxical, it is of the very essence of his philosophy. The "world" is not something "objec-

[6] *Op. cit.,* pp. 53-57.
[7] *Ibid.,* pp. 59-61.

tive," something which exists prior to and independent of man. Man and "world" belong together. "World" is "that wherein . . . man . . . lives." For one who accepts this point of view, it is clear that all attempts to find something prior to the "world" are in vain. "Nature," for instance, does not enjoy this a priori position. Man can discover nature only because he already lives in the "world," and this being-in-the-world enables him to meet nature.[8]

e) The first thing which man encounters in the "world," however, is not nature. Man is first and foremost concerned with some specific realities which he meets in the "world," such as other men, and tools. Heidegger's treatment of the concept "tool" (*Zeug*) is most characteristic for his philosophy. For tools he means not only hammers and pliers but also trains, cars, houses, clothes, i.e., everything which human beings use in living.

Strictly speaking, a tool *is* not, but it is *something in order to* . . . A pen is in order to write. Each tool points to the totality of tools, for the structure "in order to" implies references to the job which is undertaken, to the material of which the tool is made, to the people who use the tool, to the other people who manufactured it, to the people who will use the "job" when it is finished. The "world" is therefore "a system of references," a "totality of tools," a workshop.

Though the handling of tools is quite different from the merely-looking-at-things, that is to say, from knowing, it is not "blind." " 'Handling' possesses a way of looking of its own," namely, "a reckoning with the structure of the in-order-to." This way of looking is that of the *Umsicht,* practical wisdom, or know-how. The literal meaning of *Umsicht* is caution, prudence, care. Heidegger stresses, however, the aspect of looking implied in this term: *-sicht* coming from the same root as the English "sight." This view of practical wisdom is implied in the using and handling of the tools and is opposed to the theoretical attitude toward things which consists in merely looking at them without practical interest (*unumsichtig*).[9]

f) Heidegger discusses extensively the spatial status of tools. Tools belong in a place, or better, in their own place. This spatial relationship is fundamentally different from *mere occurrence* at a point in geometrical space (this holds for things) as well from *occupying a place* (this holds for human reality). Tools are "at hand" (*zuhanden*) in their place.[10] A dishtowel belongs, is "at hand" on its own hook near the sink in the kitchen. Tools belong in their own area, and areas are chosen sometimes

[8] *Ibid.,* p. 65.
[9] *Ibid.,* p. 69.
[10] *Ibid.,* pp. 102, 104, 107.

in view of the sun, e.g., the living area at the sunny side of the house. The sun, with its light and warmth, also belongs to the world of "at-handness." [11]

The spatiality of human beings can be characterized in its difference from the spatiality of tools as "giving a place to," or "making room for" tools.[12] The "world" is thus a workshop.[13] Furthermore, it is a system of reference, because each tool refers to other tools (a hammer to a chair which will be produced), and tools refer to human beings (those who cut the tree and those who will sit in the chair). A main characteristic of human existence and its "world" is "putting a thing in its right place" (*Ent-fernung,* lit., taking the distance away), whereas the spatiality of tools is characterized by "being somewhere at a place" (*Entferntheit,* lit., distance).[14] A chair, e.g., can be at the door, but a human being can put it at its right place, where it belongs.

g) Geometrical space, according to Heidegger, can be understood only within the frame of the "world." [15] One can consider it only if one gives up the practical approach. The discovery of geometrical space, in pure contemplation, free from practical considerations, "neutralizes the areas of the 'world' to pure dimensions." Instead of places where tools belong, we now get points in mathematical space. Instead of the "world" as "a totality of tool relationships," we get space as a container for bodies; instead of practical know-how, theoretical contemplation.

h) Heidegger claims that he discusses the "world" in two different ways. The above analysis belongs to the "ontological" approach. Heidegger adds to it an "ontic" approach, i.e., one which asks what actually is the case. The ontological answer to the question who it is who lives in the "world," is "human reality" (*Dasein*). The ontic answer says that we have to distinguish between two selves, the authentic self and "one," "people" (*Das Man*).[16] It is the "one" of "one does not do such things," and "people say that . . ." The *who* who lives in the "world" is first and foremost designated by "one" and "people." "One" has "surrendered to the 'world,' " has been taken in by it; "one" is "wrapped up in the 'world,' " say in public life (*Oeffentlichkeit*).[17] The relationship between these two ways of being ourselves is indicated as follows: the authentic self is "an existential modification of the 'one.' " [18] "One" itself has its

[11] *Ibid.,* p. 103.
[12] *Ibid.,* p. 111.
[13] *Ibid.,* p. 75.
[14] *Ibid.,* pp. 103, 105.
[15] *Ibid.,* pp. 111-13.
[16] *Ibid.,* pp. 114 ff.
[17] *Ibid.,* p. 127.
[18] *Ibid.,* p. 130.

own ways of being (*Seinsweisen*), e.g., averageness, leveling down, dependence, and inauthenticity." [19]

2. *Binswanger's "home-world"*

Though Binswanger's main work is largely based on Heidegger's method and achievements, it offers a fundamental criticism.

a) Binswanger adds to Heidegger's two ways of being ourselves a third one, the "dual we-ourselves" (*das duale Wirselbst*).[20] It is "the being together of I and Thou, of the We of love." "This loving-being-together can not be described as a feeling or an affect, but only as a unique way of being (*eine eigene Weise zu sein*), as distinct from the 'one' and the authentic self." [21] "I and Thou gain their 'selfness' only through each other, emerging out of the undifferentiated fullness of togetherness." "The question 'who man is' receives its real directives" and motivations exactly from "the loving togetherness." [22]

b) Binswanger adds to Heidegger's two spatialities (space and "world") a third one, the spatiality of love. Whereas not only the "one," but even Heidegger's authentic self, lives in the "world," the "we" of love lives in a "home" (*Heimat*,[23] *Wir-Raum*[24]). The "who" is no longer a single individual, but we-both, "the two of us" (*Wir-beide*).[25] Binswanger considers it a revealing trait that Heidegger calls his "world" a workshop (*Sein und Zeit*, page 75); this term shows that Heidegger overlooks the fact that the "we" of love lives in a "home." In this "home" an "encounter of loving beings . . . takes place, and in this encounter I and Thou are born as We-both." [26] Bingswanger's "home" does not mean a specific house which has been furnished and lived in and is now a real home, just as Heidegger's "workshop" is not a hobby-shack in the back of your garden. "Home" suggests a view of the All, an arrangement of everything, of the human world, nature and history; it is a specific way of seeing the structure of the universe. This universe possesses "an unbounded expansion and at the same time a groundless depth." It is "like the ocean," revealing "an inexhaustible fullness." We are safe, out of danger in this "home"-universe, embedded in its security.[27] Man's approach to this "home" is "not the careful handling of

[19] *Ibid.*, pp. 127-28.

[20] *Grundformen und Erkenntnis Menschlichen Daseins* (2nd ed., Zurich: Max Niehans, 1953), p. 69.

[21] *Ibid.*, p. 54.

[22] *Ibid.*, p. 21.

[23] *Ibid.*, pp. 72 ff.

[24] *Ibid.*, p. 82.

[25] *Ibid.*, p. 71.

[26] *Ibid.*, p. 83.

[27] *Ibid.*, p. 74.

tools which are at hand," but "the deep longing for union and totality."[28]

3. *The "world" of primitive man, according to Van der Leeuw*

Binswanger's discussion of *Sein und Zeit* raises a crucial question. Since Binswanger makes clear that it is arbitrary to assume that man knows only two worlds (geometrical space and the workshop), and makes a case for our living in a "home"-world, we have to ask ourselves whether also Binswanger is not arbitrary in assuming that we know only three "worlds." The publications in the field of history of religions seem to indicate that primitive man lives in a "world" which possesses a unique structure, which differs as much from Binswanger's *Wir-raum* as this from Heidegger's workshop.

a) According to Van der Leeuw[29] the people of primitive culture do not entertain explicit conceptions of the universe, although this does not mean that they do not live by an implicit view of the world. We will follow Van der Leeuw's description of (what *we* call) tools, things, animals, celestial bodies, and places in order to see in what kind of "world" primitive man lives.

b) Since the concept of "tool" plays such a crucial role in Heidegger's analysis, we begin by asking what is the primitive's understanding of it. The answer is that he does not know tools, strictly speaking. Life, which for primitive people is always sacred life, is never taken for granted. It is a possibility. "Man must succor feeble life with his own magic rites, or implore the powers to do so." Man makes tools for himself "in order to correct life." This means that he creates a culture. Man produces clothing, builds homes, and cultivates the fields.[30] For this reason *work* for primitive people does not mean the same thing as for us. It is "the very antithesis of technical occupation—it is creative. The primitive craftsman experiences the power, in virtue of which he completes his task, not as his own." This power (or better: Power, for it comprises the notions of "Majesty, Authority, Deity, Capability," *tremendum*, tabu[31] resides "within the implements themselves." This explains why primitive man handles the "tools" with a religious respect. For example, "The Toba-Batak of Sumatra sacrifices to his forge, hammer and anvil, to his canoe, rifle and furniture."[32]

Primitive man, further, does not know "things" in our sense of the

[28] *Ibid.*, p. 33.
[29] *Phaenomenologie der Religion* (Tubingen: Mohr, 1933); English trans., *Religion in Essence and Manifestation.* The quotations are from the English translation.
[30] *Ibid.*, p. 209.
[31] *Ibid.*, p. 24.
[32] *Ibid.*, p. 40.

word. What we call a thing is for him "the bearer of a power; it can effect something, it has its own life which reveals itself, and once again wholly practically. During an important expedition, for example, an African negro steps on a stone and cries out: 'Ha, are you there?' and takes it with him to bring luck. The stone, as it were, gives a hint that it is powerful." [33] According to Van der Leeuw, several factors, such as "the prevailing emphasis on the spiritual" and the influence of modern machinery, "have transformed the living, 'self-activated' things" of primitive man "into the merely dead material" which we reckon with in the modern "world."

c) The difference between the mentality of primitive peoples and that of twentieth-century Western man shows again clearly if we compare their understanding of *celestial events* with ours. What happens in the skies is not a process, "but rather a revelation of Power. Life in the heavens deploys itself spontaneously just as it does on earth." The stress is here on the word "spontaneously." The planets, sun, and moon do not "obey" certain "laws." Primitive man "is by no means certain about the daily return of the heavenly light, and the fear that the sun may some day fail in its course is to him in no way a mere phantom of the brain." [34]

d) The spontaneous, awful, majestic Power of Life manifests itself very vividly in the *animals*. It is especially the nonhuman nature of animals "that impels man to regard them as being bearers of power." The animal appears to be far superior, for "it controls powers in which man himself is deficient: muscular strength, keenness of sight and smell . . . flying, running with terrific speed." "Thus the animal is on the one hand the non-human, the wholly different, the sinister or the sublime; on the other it is intimately attached and familiar; and this union of both aspects renders the worship of the animal as a numinous object comprehensible." [35]

e) A crucial issue for our discussion is the understanding of *space*.

> Parts of space . . . like instants of time, have their specific and independent value. They are "positions" but they become "positions" by being "selected" from the vast extensity of the world. A part of space, then, is not a "part" at all but a place, and the place becomes a "position" when man occupies it and stands on it. He has recognized the power of the locality. . . . Sacred space may also be defined as that locality that becomes a position by the effects of power repeating themselves there, or being repeated by man. It is the place of

[33] *Ibid.*, p. 37.
[34] *Ibid.*, p. 65.
[35] *Ibid.*, pp. 75, 76.

worship, independently of whether the position is only a house, or a temple, since domestic life too is a celebration constantly repeated in the regulated cycle of work, meals, washing, etc.[36]

House and temple, still further, are essentially one: both can stand firmly only in virtue of the power residing in them. The house is an organic unity, whose essence is some definite power, just as much as is the temple or the church. . . . For the house with its own fire, which must produce its own means of life, manufacture its own clothing . . . is a world in itself. And we who purchase the objects we require when we want them, and buy furniture in this or that style, perhaps know only very little about the community of essence between all parts of the house and its inhabitants, of that participation which fits each member of the domestic group into the same structure, whether it is a so-called "thing," an animal or a human being.[37]

f) One of the leading concepts, not only of Van der Leeuw's work, but of all history of religion of the last decades, is that of "participation." It has been formed by Lucien Lévy-Bruhl. Van der Leeuw writes:

Things do not encounter each other "solidly in space" but have some share in one another and may mingle with, and appear in place of, each other. Accordingly, man does not conduct himself "objectively" towards the "world": he participates in it, just as it does in him. His path to the world, therefore, is neither that of contemplation nor reflection . . . but of existing as oriented *towards* the world.

Participation is thus the mental attitude "which neither dissects nor abstracts, neither infers nor analyzes, but deals with the whole, grasps it concretely, connects together its essentials."

Lévy-Bruhl and Van der Leeuw both warn us not to oversimplify matters. Participation is not only a characteristic of primitive man, but also of modern man; for it is "an attitude deeply rooted in human nature." On the other hand, the "so-called primitives are obviously 'modern' also, and are quite familiar with analytical and logical thought." [38]

g) We notice in Van der Leeuw a suspicion of the notion of *Weltanschauung* which is not so blunt as the statement of the Netherlands Reformed Church (Sec. A-2), but which is certainly one of its roots: "A 'religious Weltanschauung' is never merely a 'point of view' but is always a sharing, a participation." [39] Also at another place Van der Leeuw contrasts *Weltanschauung* and participation. He condemns vehemently

[36] *Ibid.*, p. 393.
[37] *Ibid.*, p. 396.
[38] *Ibid.*, pp. 543, 544.
[39] *Ibid.*, p. 543.

the attitude of those scholars who claim that they can discuss matters of religion in a manner which is free from prejudice. He says:

> This attitude . . . was associated with the grave error of supposing that, in the spiritual realm, one may adopt any desired position or abandon it at will, as if it were possible to choose any Weltanschauung whatever, or to abstain provisionally from all partisanship. But gradually it is being perceived that man *exists* in the world in some quite definite way and that—with all due respect to his own Weltanschauung—any "unprejudiced" treatment is not merely impossible but positively fatal.[40]

C. A VARIETY OF "WORLDS" AND "VIEWS"

1. *"World" or "worlds"?*

a) On the basis of Van der Leeuw's discussion we may say that Heidegger's "world" does not possess the rank which he demands of it. Whereas Heidegger seems to offer the philosophical analysis of *the* "world" of human reality, i.e., of man *in general,* he appears to have given an analysis of one specific "world" of one specific man, twentieth-century modern man. We have to sharpen the term "modern man" to "modern secularized man." The word "secularized" does not refer to the contrast between the churched and the unchurched, but to that between "primitives" and "moderns," the latter including the Christians, Jews, Buddhists, and other believers of our modern Western civilization. Primitives see animals, tools, things, sun, and moon in a religious light, immediately related to the religious Power and ground of all that is, the awesome, majestic Power of Life. Just as self-evident as this way of looking at the world is for them, so self-evident it is for modern men to look at the world in terms of tools, "mere things," "mere animals," i.e., in terms of utility. Actually, neither of these "worlds" is self-evident. Both of them are related to specific periods of history and specific civilizations.

Binswanger's protest means that he claims it is not true that the workshop-"world" is actually the world in which modern man lives. One could say that he accuses Heidegger, who looks so extremely "European" to Americans, of what part of the European intelligentsia calls "Americanism."[41] This word is a term of abuse, used to indicate and condemn the technological aspect of modern civilization in which "real" values are crowded out by mass production. We do not deny, on the basis of Binswanger's and Van der Leeuw's analyses, that Heidegger's "world"

[40] *Ibid.*, p. 645.
[41] See, e.g., Van der Leeuw, *op. cit.*, p. 396, "semi-Americanized as we already are. . . ."

"exists." We merely assert that it is arbitrary to place over against geometrical space only one "lived-in world." There are several of these "worlds."

b) The question has to be raised as to the *historical* relationships between the modern mentality and its "worlds," and the primitive mentality and its "world." This is a problem which lies outside the range of this book and the competence of its author. The members of the Dutch school of history of religions (W. B. Kristensen, its founder; Van der Leeuw; K. A. H. Hidding, *et al.*) have given much attention to this problem. Whereas Kristensen does not want to give more than extremely cautious suggestions, Van der Leeuw and Hidding describe a development (not evolution) in several stages. Perhaps one may say that our modern "world" is the result of a process of gradual demythologizing or deconvictionalizing of primitive man's "world." It could, e.g., be asserted that the conformism of the public world of the "one" is a pale replica of the conformism of primitive society with its powerful taboos. Such a view, however, is too simple, because we are dealing not with "the" primitive world and "the" modern world, but with primitive tribes of an older Europe and Asia, with the ancient cultures around the Mediterranean, with the Hebrew culture, with medieval Europe, etc.

c) Another question to be asked is that of the *ontological* relationships between the various spatialities which we have met so far: geometrical space, Heidegger's "world," Binswanger's *Wir-Raum,* the "world" of primitive cultures. It seems to me that Heidegger has demonstrated that his "world" is prior to geometrical space, not, however, ontologically[42] prior but psychologically. Furthermore, we have the right to say that several religious, more or less primitive "worlds," are historically prior to Heidegger's world. The question as to the ontological priority cannot be answered. One should not say more than the following: it is clear that primitive people live in one "world," and that modern Western man knows several "worlds," in which he lives by turns. As philosophers we cannot go further than that. As soon as we begin to claim that one of these worlds is the real one, or the authentic one, we speak convictional language. We cannot replace Heidegger's workshop-"world" by another "world" as the foundation of all other "spatialities." Which of the many primitive, and religious, or lived-in "worlds" would have the right to claim to be that basic one?

d) This is not to say that the concept of "lived-in worlds" is not exceedingly important. The task of describing and analyzing them

[42] In any meaning of the word "ontological."

belongs to psychologists, philosophers, and theologians. Among psychologists, besides Binswanger, J. F. Buytendijk and E. Minkowski are doing pioneer work. Part of the work of theologians (in the wider sense, Chap. I, Sec. B-2) is to describe the "world" in which the members of their confessional group live, or are supposed to live.

2. *Can any "view" of or approach to the "world" be said to possess ontological priority?*

a) The existentialist thinkers may differ considerably in regard to the nature of the "world"; they are united in their interpretation of man's relation to it: this is one of participation—man has specific ways of "being-in-the-world." This relationship is contrasted with one of mere thinking, mere reflection, contemplation. We misunderstand man, it is said, if we assume that such a reflective view, such a *Weltanschauung* is connected with the center of his existence. Heidegger's terms are, e.g., *In-Sein, In-der-Welt-Sein, das Sein zum Tode, Seinsweisen* (being-in, being-in-the-world, living in relationship to death, ways of being). Binswanger uses, e.g., *eine eigene Weise zu sein* (a unique way of being). Van der Leeuw speaks of *ein Sein zu der Welt* (existing as oriented *toward* the world). It is Van der Leeuw who formulates the contrast most sharply: "*. . . nicht eine Betrachtung, ein Denken über . . . sondern ein Sein zu der Welt.*"[43] The English translation (*Religion in Essence and Manifestation,* page 543) renders *Betrachtung* with "contemplation." It should be well understood that the contemplation meant here is the mere contemplation of the onlooker, who is not existentially involved. Hence it is a contemplation with the connotation of speculation, or (Roget's *Pocket Thesaurus,* No. 451, *s.v.* "thought") meditating, pondering, musing, dreaming, ruminating. We meet here one of the main theses of phenomenological existentialist thinking. Reflection is not a "first" thing. It comes "later than" and is founded by another approach to the world. Very revealing for this thesis are some of the key terms of Sartre's chef-d'œuvre, namely, "the prereflexive cogito," "a pre-interrogative familiarity with being," and "a pre-judicative attitude."[44] The shortest formulation is "existence precedes essence."

b) I fully agree with the existentialist position in its negative aspect, i.e., in its rejection of idealist claims of the apriority of reason, *Vernunft, cogito.* I question, however, the existentialists' attempts to establish an a priori of the "familiar know-how" or of "participation." Can we

[43] *Phaenomenologie der Religion,* p. 516.

[44] Jean Paul Sartre, *L'Etre et le néant* (Paris: Gallimard, 1950), pp. 16, 39, 42. English translation by Hazel E. Barnes: *Being and Nothingness* (New York: Philosophical Library, 1956), pp. lii, 5, 7.

speak at all of an a priori? Should we search for one at all? Whereas "familiarity with" is psychologically and historically "earlier than" theoretical knowledge, and also earlier than any other conscious considerations, it is doubtful as to whether these facts warrant far-reaching philosophical conclusions. The existentialists overdo the contrast between "being-in-the-world" and mental activities which are more or less conscious. We think especially of the element of "giving account of," an accounting, that is to say, which is not purely rational but guided by specific convictions. The way in which a human being is-in-the-world is partly the result of an ongoing process of checking and changing his existential stand by means of "giving account of" his life and all events in which he takes part. A never-ending *interaction* takes place between the deepest motivating center of the person and the element of "giving account of." This element is, exactly because it is guided by convictions, just as much related to the center of man's existence as any prereflexive familiarity with the world.

(1) The accounting element is related to *language*. Accounting is not possible without concepts, i.e., without language. Language is one of the approaches to the world, one of the most important ways of communicating with other human beings and with one's convictor. One cannot handle a Heideggerean tool, nor build a primitive home in which meals are celebrated as rites, without the help of language. Tools, homes, and meals presuppose other human beings, i.e., community, and community is unthinkable without language. In other words, being-in-the-world is always expressed in language. "Expressed" does not mean here "only an expression"; the expression is an integral part of one's *Seinsweise* (way of being in the world).

(2) The accounting element is also related to a *view*. The convictional accounts which we form of tools, other human beings, animals, goods, a convictor, witnesses, etc., arrange themselves in a structure, and a structure is something which has to be seen. The metaphor of seeing is indispensable in the "giving account of" life. We "look at" certain problems or goods "in the light of" our highest good. We act "in view of" some value which is at stake. The undeniability of the importance of the "view" element forces us to ask again for the reason of the vehement protest against *Weltanschauung*.

c) Before we enter upon this issue we have to elaborate a point just made. If the element of "giving account of" is guided by our convictions and hence is related to the deepest motivating center of the person, what then is the place of *reason*?

One of the major themes of Reinhold Niebuhr's work is the warning that "reason is always a servant." I agree but not without some hesitation. This reluctance is rooted in a certain uneasiness about the terminology. Should we speak of "reason" at all? Such a usage suggests that there is something like an isolated entity, a faculty, a power "reason."

Perhaps we should drop the term and refer only to man-who-speaks. In the act of speaking, what people mean by the word "reason" is always implied, whether the people who speak are aware of this fact or not. In other words, we may doubt whether something like "reason" really exists. What exist are: people who speak, human beings, language structures. If this holds true, "reason" is an abstraction, and to speak of "reason" is falling into a language trap.

Just as people many times use the term "reason" as if they were dealing with an independent faculty, in the same way they refer to "our critical faculties." Here similar objections have to be raised. It is misleading to say, for instance, that some people (modern Westerners) use these critical faculties, whereas others (so-called primitives) do not. It is better to say that modern people speak other languages than primitives do, and that several of these modern languages (such as science, philosophy, and theology) imply standards which make them critical of each other and of themselves.

To drop the term "reason" and to follow the terminology here proposed is perhaps one way to disengage ourselves from the morass of the old quarrel between "rationalism" and "irrationalism." This is not to deny that there *are* people who overdo, and others who underestimate, the importance of the thinking aspect of our speaking and living. However, both schools of thought contribute to the confusion by isolating this thinking aspect ("reason!"), and then either glorifying or belittling it.

3. *Three different kinds of "views"*

We have to distinguish between three kinds of views, and will claim that the existentialist protest is legitimate in connection with one of them, but not in regard to the other two kinds of views.

a) There is something like a *scientific picture of the world*. It gives account of reality in strictly indicative terms, such as atoms, light years, H_2O, market, Middle Ages, organism, trilobites, paleozoicum. Such a picture possesses the hypothetical, relative, and provisional character of the theories of which it is a composition. It is presented in the indicative language of empirical science. In German it is sometimes called *Weltbild*. The existentialists cannot have any quarrel with this kind of view because it does not pretend to speak about the significance of life or about the meanings and values of the phenomena it describes.

b) There exists a being-related-to the world which involves a person's existential center. This relation is expressed in several ways, e.g., in discursive behavior, in this case, convictional language; and in non-discursive behavior, in gestures, actions, and attitudes. The discursive expression of this relation implies a view of the world, an arrangement of a person's convictions which mirrors the order in which the world appears to him.

This *implied,* existential, *convictional view* differs from the convictional account which the person himself gives of his attitude toward life. This last, *explicit view* is largely what is meant by the term *Weltanschauung,* and it is this view which is attacked by the argument of the existentialists. It seems that their criticism is sometimes justified but other times scarcely deserved. This depends upon several factors, some of which will be mentioned here.

It has to be stressed that both the explicit and the implicit world view are convictional in character. The explicit view represents the face which a person wants to present to the world and to himself. It expresses the approach to the world which we *want* to assume, which we *claim* we assume. The implicit view represents our actual relation. It is connected with the deepest layers of our personality, i.e., to what we really are. This view appears in our language unintentionally, without our foreknowledge, many times without our even realizing and recognizing it in its true meaning, sometimes even against our explicit wishes and claims. This implicit, existential view can never be fully known to our conscious considerations. One of the reasons for this is that nobody can be sincere enough for a complete self-understanding. All of us are inclined to present ourselves (both to others and to ourselves) as more glorious than we actually are. We dearly love to identify ourselves with impressive and brilliant accounts of life and the world. We offer to ourselves and to the world a glamorous façade of lofty and lordly ideas.

At this moment of our discussion the names of several great philosophers, psychologists, and novelists come to mind: Freud, Marx, Nietzsche, Dostoevsky. Terms offer themselves, such as "mask," "rationalization." We will have to leave it undecided as to what extent we have the right to call the explicit convictional world view a rationalization of the implicit one. And is it not true that all of us wear a mask, without being able at all to determine where the mask ends and where the authentic person begins?

c) It is time to give an illustration. Marx's *Weltbild* consists largely of the historical, sociological, and economic data at his disposal. His implicit convictional world view consists (so far as an outsider can judge) of the moral and cryptoreligious convictions which we analyzed in Chap. I. Marx's explicit world view consists of what he himself presents as an unbiased, scientific, matter-of-fact picture of what "is going on before our very eyes." A typical term of Marx's *Weltbild* is "price"; a term of his implicit world view, "the icy waters of egotistical calculation," revealing his moral indignation; again of his explicit world view, dialectical materialism.

Marx is but an extreme case. It happens many times that an individual or a group claims to possess a certain view of life, and that a careful analysis of their language and behavior shows that they are moved by quite a different view. Many liberal Protestants of the nineteenth century did not realize at all how much their being-in-the-world and their convictional world view were determined by Enlightenment convictions. Sometimes it happens that people who claim to possess an explicit world view which is "materialistic" or "naturalistic," in their own eyes, and "superficial" or "shallow" in the eyes of others (who are naturally really "spiritual" people), appear to be motivated by implicit convictions which are of a more "spiritual" character than meets the eye. Classical examples are Marx, Freud,[45] and logical positivism.

d) The relationship between an individual's or a group's explicit world view and his implicit view discloses to us something about him. The depth or the lack of clarity of his self-understanding, his sincerity, and his pretensions are revealed. The prevalence of misunderstanding ourselves and the nonexistence of complete self-understanding, these facts in themselves would be sufficient reasons to suspect all-embracing, pretentious views of the world, and closed systems of philosophy. Nobody, no wise man, neither a church, nor a philosophical school, nor any other institution is wise enough to command a completely satisfying, exhaustive interpretation of life. It seems that in the existentialist protest against *Weltanschauung*, in the logical positivist aversion to metaphysical systems, and in the liberal Protestant rebellion against authoritative church creeds, the suspicion of arrogant constructions is a leading element.

e) The distance between our implicit convictional world view and our explicit view can be noticed not only by others but in rare cases also by ourselves. This may be a reason for reconsidering ourselves. Is it not,

[45] See, e.g., Edgar Michaelis, *Die Menschheitsproblematik der Freudschen Psycho-analyse* (2nd ed.; Leipzig: Ambrosius Barth, 1931).

more or less, when brought to the full light of consciousness, one of the driving powers behind the theological activity analyzed in Chap. I? One of the motivations is an urge for greater clarity about the most real and deep convictions of the group.

The term "convictional world view" dissolves a difficulty implied in the harangue of the Netherlands Reformed Church (Sec. A-2). It is said there, first, that being a Christian is a way of being; second, that it is not to have a philosophy of life; third, that it means to be under authority of a Lord. The third part of the statement shows that the first part is insufficient in itself; it needs to be supplemented with a reference to a Lord. This insufficiency of the term "way of being" holds also for other than Christian world views. Man's attitude toward life is not sufficiently characterized by his attitude toward the world in general; it needs specification by disclosing who is his convictor. Whereas the Dutch statement needs *two* sentences, which are furthermore not clearly related, we have expressed the same thing in one term, "convictional world view," in which the prominent place of the word "convictional" suggests the prominence of the convictor.

The weakness of the Dutch statement becomes the more conspicuous if we consider the following problem. In some convictional world views, the convictor is believed to exist *beyond* the cosmos, such as in the Hebrew, the Christian, the Moslem religions. In these cases a philosophical term such as "being-in-the-world" offers not merely an insufficient account of man-who-speaks, but frankly a misleading one. If one wants to begin with being-in-the-world, one should use being-in-the-world-and-in-relationship-to-the-creator-of-this-world. The term "convictional world view" is not only more elegant, but it is also wide enough to comprise the conception of convictor which is characteristic for these religions. It is strange that the Christian theologians who hail the existentialist terminology as such an improvement upon the traditional one, have not realized the weakness of this new terminology.

4. Convictional world views replace convictors

a) One of the characteristics of the modern Western world is that many people no longer believe, strictly speaking, in a God but in a *Weltanschauung*. The kind churchgoer is not a man who is fervently dedicated to Christ; his life is guided by a benevolent belief in Christianity, in religion, in the "Christian way of life," or in religious experience. The "church"-goer believes in the American way of life, in democracy, or even in the search for the Absolute. The last decades of the modern era show, however, people who are much less pleasant, less tolerant, because they believe in a powerful convictor: Nazis believing in the Aryan race, Communists believing in the coming of their millennium, a handful of Christians believing in Christ. The convictional situation possesses a different structure in these two cases. First, a powerful convictor occupies the central place; second, the convictional world view as such occupies this place.

It seems permissible to place these facts in a historical perspective. For Christians it seems that some centuries ago the structure with a convictor in the center was predominant, as, for instance, in the era of the Reformation. Gradually the convictor's power slipped away, and Christians came to believe in religious experience instead of in God. After the end of the First World War large groups of people were dissatisfied with this development and surrendered to the more powerful convictors of Nazis and Communists. It is not only the convictional world view which takes the place of the convictor. Sometimes people believe in the group, in the church, or in the party. There are therefore three possible structures of the convictional situation, according as the center is occupied by the convictor, by the convictional world view, or by the group.

b) On the basis of the preceding considerations we seem to have the right to distinguish between "genuine," "real" convictors and pale, shadowy convictors. Convictors, like generals, sometimes fade away. The terms "real" and "genuine" do not imply any evaluation or any assertion as to the reality of this first group of convictors. They are meant to be descriptive, to point to the convictor's sway over the believers. A faded convictor is like an ideal Republican president: he does not interfere, but leaves his fellow citizens alone. The nice, friendly "church"-goer feels safe in his Christian or American way of life, as in a snug home. A genuine convictor is so powerful that he disturbs his adherents, shocks them out of their "home," and breaks up ways of life and religions. A real convictor makes people "quake," turns them passionate, ascetic, so that they disregard the values of ordinary life and of safe moralism.

Here are some examples of genuine convictors breaking up convictional world views and confessional groups. The "Aryan" race destroyed the convictional world views of both Christianity and humanism, as well as the confessional groups of the churches and of the socialist and conservative parties. The God of the Reformers broke up settled medieval views and even damaged the powerful church. The Communist cause demolished Christian and aristocratic world views and wiped out several social groups, pushing back the church.

c) Heidegger refers to the problems at hand in a passage in his essay "Die Zeit des Weltbildes," which is included in his volume *Holzwege*.[46] He lists several phenomena which he considers characteristic for the modern era:

> A fifth phenomenon of the modern world is the *Entgötterung* [literally: letting the gods go]. This expression does not mean the mere discarding of the gods, or crude atheism. *Entgötterung* is a process with two aspects. First, the view of the world is Christianized, in so far as the ground of the world is taken to be the Infinite, the Unconditional, the Absolute. Second, Christendom reinterprets its Christianity and changes it into a world view (the Christian world view) and in this way it gives itself a modern form. *Entgötterung* is here the condition of indecision about God or the gods. Christendom itself has offered the greatest contribution to the bringing about of this condition. The *Entgötterung* does not exclude religiosity at all. Actually the relation to the gods changes into religious experience only by means of the *Entgötterung*. If things have come this far, the gods have fled. The resulting vacuum is filled by the historical and psychological research of myth.

Heidegger's picture is inimitable in its vigor and conciseness. It is, however, dated. Heidegger interprets the situation of the nineteenth and early twentieth centuries, but he does not take into account the new and powerful gods of several decades just past.[47]

5. *In drafting convictional world views man-speaking establishes himself*

It is not quite accurate to say that man establishes his existence "with the help of" his convictional world views, for the establishment and the drafting of his views go hand in hand. Man establishes himself by "seeing" the "world" and his own place therein. The seeing of the place and the occupying of the place are the same act and are accomplished by one and the same act.

We have to realize the complexity of this establishment, and perhaps it is necessary to speak of two establishments. One is accomplished in the drafting of one's implicit convictional world view, the other in the drafting of one's explicit convictional view. For instance, a man can explicitly establish himself as a "Christian," and think about himself as a "Christian gentleman," while implicitly he sees the world centered around his important person, to be served, recognized, and respected by his wife, children, and friends.

[46] Martin Heidegger, *Holzwege* (Frankfort am Main: Klostermann, 1952), p. 70.

[47] It is true that there are passages in Heidegger's later work which reveal his expectations of new gods to arise. These passages, however, are open to various interpretations, and since their meaning is not clear, they are not taken into account in our remarks just made.

In order to understand these establishments better, we have to ask for the structures of both the implicit and the explicit convictional world views.

a) The discussion of the structure of the *implicit* convictional world view cannot be more than a mere sketch, since a satisfying treatment would require a whole book. It is probable that a more thorough investigation will point out the following elements as among the crucial ones.

(1) A center. In the case that the individual establishes himself as an *ego,* he himself is the center. The individual who sees himself (herself) as the original scholar, the ideal wife, the successful businessman, the dedicated missionary, the leading statesman, that is to say, who takes himself quite seriously in this status, is the center and *raison d'être* of his world. The individual who establishes himself as a *person* has as his center a convictor, a cause. He becomes a person by the very act of allowing himself to be grasped by a god. For a person this convictor, this cause, is the center and *raison d'être* of the world.

(2) Other "realities." For the self who establishes himself as a person the world is full of entities which are "real" in their own right, such as other human beings, concrete goods like towns, schools, hospitals.[48] These entities truly exist and have meanings independent of our own existence and desires. For the self who establishes himself as an ego, these "realities" as such simply do not exist. His world is filled with shadowy entities which only echo the preoccupations of the ego.

(3) Relationships. Man relates himself to the fundamental events of life: birth, marriage, death. In his convictional view of the world is implied a certain way in which man interprets, sees, and lives in relationship to those events. Then, man establishes himself in setting up relationships to the just-mentioned "realities," approving or disapproving of them. Finally, a special relationship to events and "realities" is found in man's task, his work, his vocation. A person establishes himself in selecting certain "realities" or a certain event with which he enters into a more intimate relationship, with which as it were he mingles himself. A farmer merges with the soil, a teacher with her school and "her" children, a doctor with his patients, a woman with her family. For the individual who establishes himself as an ego, all these relationships are different. He cannot merge in

[48] This concept of "reality," just as the contrast between "ego" and "person," is borrowed from Marcel, *Homo Viator*.

anything or anybody other than himself. His relationships are those of a worker using a tool. He is not a farmer but uses his farm to raise corn and sell it. He is not a doctor but a businessman who sells special services.

(4) Dimensions. Man establishes himself in view of the past, *his* past, his future, his present. Man sees and establishes himself as the son of his father, whether that is a thing of glory and gratitude, a matter of rebellion, of disgust, or of indifference. Man establishes himself also in regard to past generations, proud that his forefathers have lived in this country for several generations, or respecting himself as a new immigrant bringing with him some of the achievements of an old civilization.

Man establishes himself also in view of the future. It makes very much sense to say that we *are* what we hope for, what we hope in, the one in whom we hope. We see opportunities and possibilities and choose between them. Our convictional view of the world consists to a very large extent of these possibilities, their values and meanings. Again, for the self establishing himself as an ego, these dimensions are "unreal." He is so taken up with himself that he has no "real" hope.

(5) The source of certainty. Man establishes himself in view of a fundamental factor which guarantees the basic meaningfulness of his "world." He needs this guarantee because he is moved by anxiety. His world changes, is full of conflicts and crises. He himself suffers defeats. He is disturbed by the complexity and ambiguity of his own existence.

For the man who has established himself as a person the source of certainty is his convictor or his cause. For the ego the source can be found in the individual's own self, but more often in the group or the convictional view which take the place of the convictor in the absence of a "real" convictor. Perhaps we are allowed to say that in these cases the group and the world view are part of the self, serve the self by producing the consolation which silences the anxiety.

b) The structure of the *explicit* convictional world view is basically the same as that of the implicit view. One of the differences lies in the frame. Whereas the implicit convictions do not form a well-ordered whole, the explicit view is always a systematization. Here two extremes are possible. Some explicit views take into account the inconsistencies, the gaps, the tentative character of the implicit convictions. Their authors do not want to systematize away these order-resisting aspects. Other explicit views attempt to offer an individual's or a group's convictions in a rational order. This is done, for instance, in theological, metaphysical, and ontological *systems*. We will meet these last two in the next chapter.

Here follows a short survey of the various elements of explicit convictional views, the counterparts of the elements of the implicit views.

(1) The center. Explicit views are not apt to admit that the self is the center of the world. Some individualistic "philosophies" (read: theologies) form an exception. On the other hand, countless are the theologies which give ample account of the convictor, for instance, in the chapters "On God" in textbooks in Christian, Moslem, or Jewish theology.

(2) The "other realities" receive an equal amount of attention. They are dealt with in books on ethics, and social ethics.

(3) The relationships to the events are very widely and intensively discussed. The primitive religions possess highly elaborate cosmologies in which the nature and meaning of these events are accounted for and man's attitude in relation to them is prescribed. The other relationships are dealt with in ethics and theologies.

(4) The dimensions form the material for theologies and "philosophies" of history, for eschatological treatments. For instance, Tillich's concept of *kairos*, and various theologies of revolution and of progress, belong here, as well as existentialist "philosophies," which struggle with the individual aspects of these dimensions.

(5) The source of certainty is searched for more fervently than the Holy Grail. This source has been found in an amazing variety of ways. One could distinguish as follows:

Substance "philosophies"—*res cogitans*, Whitehead's underlying energy, the *Blut und Boden* of the Nazi "philosophy"

Person theologies—several religious theologies

Group theologies—Communist, Fascist, Nazi, nationalist "philosophies," certain aspects of Roman Catholic theology

Cosmic order theologies—primitive and ancient religious theologies, classical "philosophies," Roman Catholic and orthodox Protestant ontological theologies

A priori "philosophies"—in which the certainty is founded upon aprioristic truths or aprioristic moral laws

It will seldom occur, except in elaborate theological systems, that an explicit convictional world view offers an extensive account of all five of these categories of its structure. Nearly always the fifth category, the source of certainty, will receive the main emphasis. This is only natural, since it most impressively banishes the anxiety which is prominent among the motivating powers in the construction of explicit convictional world views. Man feels that his establishment is uncertain, too provisional, too questionable, if he cannot justify it by means of a view which puts everything, or at least nearly everything, in its right place.

c) We meet here again the structural aspect of language, as distinguished from the individual, personal aspect. A human being *is* his language—this holds for the implicit convictional view. Language is a structure available to the individual—this holds for the explicit convictional view. Such a language structure is ready for the individual in the sense that he can walk into it, make his home in it. This structure becomes his habitation, his *Gehäuse,* in which he establishes his existence, where he feels "at home."

The metaphor of "walking into" should be balanced by another. These language structures are not only available to man, ready for him, offered to him, but they are also pressed upon him. Churches, political parties—that is to say, confessional groups—urge and force him to enter a specific language structure. All kinds of pressure are used, as for instance the threat of heresy or eternal damnation. Groups which are scarcely organized or not at all, such as that of the enlightened humanists, exercise pressure by means of the powerful "common opinion" that declares which language structures are "natural" and "self-evident" for a civilized person.

The promptings and proddings of the confessional groups, especially those of the highly organized ones, correspond to the uncertainties and anxieties of many people. Young people and insecure men crave for the protective shelter of powerful and reassuring "homes." They are very happy if men of authority assure them that they have entered "the only true" abode.

CHAPTER FOUR

METAPHYSICS

Man-Who-Speaks Is Inclined to Draft Closed Systems

A. INTRODUCTION

1. *Meaningless language*

One of the outstanding characteristics of logical positivism is the disqualification of "metaphysics" as meaningless language. We cannot say that the positivists take it for granted that religious language as such is included in this censure.[1] Still, it is an important task for a philosophy of religion on an analytical basis to set forth to what extent this attack upon metaphysics is "meaningful," and what sense needs to be ascribed to the word "metaphysics." For up to this very day there has been, in the fields of philosophy and theology taken together, a sharp distinction between those who defend metaphysics (theologians and most philosophers, whether idealists or not) and those who condemn it (skeptics, Hume, positivists, and empiricists). How can philosophy of religion be "analytic" if that term implies an alignment with antimetaphysicians? Indeed, the present book defends a *renversement des alliances;* it sides on several issues with the positivists and rates the conception of "metaphysics" as inappropriate language, a gain for philosophy of religion.

2. *The background of the attack on metaphysics*

A very sketchy survey of some intellectual forefathers of the logical positivists should help to remind us that a certain suspicion of the metaphysical enterprise is nearly as old as philosophy itself and has accompanied it throughout its whole course.

a) Skepticism, with its *epoche,* its suspension of judgment.

b) William of Occam, with his razor.

c) Francis Bacon, *Novum Organon,* Aphorism xiv, "The human understanding is of its own nature prone to suppose the existence of more order and regularity in the world than it finds."

[1] Notice the reservations made, e.g., by Von Mises, *Positivism,* pp. 58-59; A. J. Ayer, *Language, Truth and Logic,* pp. 118-19.

d) David Hume, with his claim that no reality answers to terms such as "I," "cause," and "substance."

e) Auguste Comte, with his thesis of three stages in the development of man's thinking—the theological, the metaphysical, and the positive. In the second stage natural phenomena are explained with the help of hidden powers, such as Nature, Vitality, or the Final Purpose.

f) Jeremy Bentham, with his tenet that error lurks in generalities. High-sounding generalities which excite Bentham's indignation are: common sense, moral sense, the Rule of Right, the Law of Nature, Right Reason, Natural Justice.[2]

B. HUME

1. *Introduction*

Hume has inaugurated a revolution in philosophy, the full scope of which has been realized only in our time. This revolution has its central force in Hume's conception of reason. One of the main results of Hume's new manner of philosophizing was the undermining of the metaphysical enterprise.

The majority of the philosophers before Hume had philosophized under the guidance of the conviction that reason is both the essence of man and of the cosmos. For Hume reason is a faculty of man's mind, or to say it more accurately, one out of several faculties of man's mind. Further, it is a faculty which labors under considerable limitations. Finally, man is inclined to disregard the importance of these limitations. Thus, in regard to man, reason is for Hume not his essence but only a faculty and one which presents us with peculiar problems. As regards the universe, Hume is on this point even more doubtful as to the possibility of identifying reason with its essence. He claims that we are not in the position of being able to make definite statements about the nature of the universe. On the basis of such an approach, metaphysics becomes a very questionable effort.

a) The reduced significance of reason becomes nowhere so clear as in the relationship between reason and idea. Hume says that "reason alone can never give rise to any original idea." [3] It is impossible to overestimate the revolutionary impact of such a statement. With the exception of some "pedestrian" empiricists, every respectable philosopher before Hume had thought of reason as possessing creative power. According to the classical view, reason was capable of producing order,

[2] See John Stuart Mill's essay on Bentham.

[3] *The Treatise of Human Nature*, Bk. I, Pt. III, sec. 14, from *Selections*, ed. Charles W. Hendel, p. 46.

harmony, and goodness; and this conviction meant not only the world-reason but also man's reason, which was a spark of the reason which sustained the cosmos. Hume, shockingly, robs reason of its creative power and ascribes to it a moderate place among a whole group of factors which decide a man's mental life. Ideas cannot be produced by reason alone; they are linked by Hume to impressions. Hume aims another blow at the alleged prominence of reason when he discusses complex perceptions and ideas. He says that simple ideas can be separated and may be united again, and it is not reason which performs this important operation, but the faculty of imagination. Further, when Hume discusses the principles which guide the imagination at this point, he rejects a rational principle such as that of "inseparable connection," and introduces the principle of association.[4] All through the first book of Hume's *Treatise* the key terms are "custom," "habit," "experience," "imagination," and not "reason."

b) The reduction of the significance of reason is the basis for two of the main tenets of Hume's thought, both tending to disqualify metaphysical thinking: first, the rejection of the traditional meanings of some of the major concepts of philosophy, which meanings formed the foundation of *metaphysical philosophy;* second, the rejection of some ways of establishing the nature of God by means of reasoning, which methods formed the foundation of *metaphysical theology*.

Hume's elaboration of the first tenet forms one of the best-known chapters in the history of philosophy. He discusses the ideas of extension and of time, the ideas of cause, power, and necessity, and shows in each case how these ideas are not derived "from knowledge or any scientific reasoning," but "arise from observation and experience." [5] A straight line runs from Hume's discussion of these terms to the present-day logical empiricist attack upon metaphysics.

In view of the discussion of this attack in the next section of this chapter, it would have been very proper to deal in this section with the first of Hume's tenets. I have, however, decided to omit a treatment of this subject. It seems that enough has been said about it. Hume's second tenet, however, has not received due attention, and moreover, its subject matter is very appropriate for a text on the philosophy of religion. The section on Hume will therefore offer a discussion of the way in which Hume applied his notion of the limited significance of reason to the problem of metaphysical reasonings regarding God's nature.

[4] *Ibid.*, Bk. I, Pt. I, secs. 1 and 4, pp. 9-13.
[5] *Ibid.*, Bk. I, Pt. III, sec. 3, p. 32.

2. Hume's problem in the Dialogues

Hume is concerned with the role of reason in religion. His main question in the Dialogues is: "To what extent can reason help us to establish the nature of God?" His answer runs that it is difficult to see how reason, as it functions in science or in logic, can assist us in any satisfactory way.

a) The necessity of giving full attention to the cautious form of Hume's formulations cannot be underlined too heavily. He does not like to make clear statements such as, "Reason does not play a role in religion." Hume seems to feel that the matter under discussion is too involved for such apodictic statements, and that he himself has not thought his way through to a clear-cut position. These reservations have to be borne in mind in considering the following attempts to render Hume's considerations in the form of a short thesis. The difficulty in doing this is enhanced by the fact that we are not in a position to identify Hume with one of the participants in the dialogue.

(1) Perhaps we may say that Philo expresses Hume's own ideas in Part I when he describes reason as weak, blind, frail, uncertain, in contrast to those half-taught people who "think nothing too difficult for human reason." Because of these weaknesses Philo speaks of the "narrow limits" of human reason.[6]

(2) In this context Philo indicates the range and limits of philosophy. He says it is a continuation of what everyone does in common life—that is, giving account of life and its phenomena—only that in philosophy this account is more methodical. Such philosophizing may be trusted if it concerns itself with human affairs and with the physical world, with "natural or moral subjects," but not when it launches out into "the two eternities, before and after the present state of things." Speculating about creation, spirits and one universal spirit, is "beyond the reach of our faculties." [7]

(3) It seems plausible that in Part II it is again Philo who comes closest to representing Hume's position. Here the question is as to whether arguments a priori and a posteriori possess any validity in establishing God's nature. Philo does not assert that reasoning from experience (a posteriori) is completely without value, but he regards its results as at the utmost very uncertain. First, we may not suppose that there is any analogy between God's perfections and man's. Therefore the comparison of the universe with a machine is faulty, and we may not infer that God is a supernal artisan, an immense

[6] Hume, *Selections*, p. 288.
[7] *Ibid.*, pp. 292, 293.

mind. Second, making inferences on the basis of similarity requires great caution, even if one deals with observables; in this case doubts and new experiments play a role. Thus the most extreme prudence is required where a similarity is assumed between something observable and the universe; in this case experiments cannot be set up at all. Third, it is an unpardonable and arbitrary preference to conclude, from elements of thought and design in the observable world, to a universal mind as its cause, because design "is no more than one of the springs and principles of the universe." Fourth, we may not conclude, from the nature of a part, to the nature of the whole, in this case, from our brain to the universe. Fifth, while in regard to observables we make inferences by custom, how is such inference, even though validated in a certain sense by experience, possible when we discuss God who is "single, individual, without parallel or specific resemblance"? [8]

Whereas Philo ascribes little value to the arguments a posteriori, but does not discard them completely, he has no use at all for the reasoning a priori, where one "abstracts from everything which he knows or has seen." To determine the nature of God or the universe in this way merely opens the gates to rambling fancies and chimeras.[9]

(4) The issue of Part III is whether there is any correspondence between men's ideas and God's attributes. If we may assume that in this part Demea represents Hume pretty closely, we are allowed to conclude that Hume rejects the notion of correspondence for this problem. He seems to hold that we do not entertain any adequate ideas as to God's nature and his attributes.[10]

3. *Agnosticism?*

Hume's delicate handling of the problems involved should prevent us from drawing too far-reaching conclusions in regard to his own position. He certainly does not say, "There is no God," but we should even beware of calling him an agnostic. He does not state, "We cannot know God," either. We should not say more than this: according to Hume neither the a priori nor the a posteriori method of reasoning seems to be an appropriate way of referring to God or to the nature of the universe. It has to be added that Hume does *not* supplement his analysis either with an indication of what is the appropriate way in which to discuss the nature of God and the meaning of the universe,

[8] *Ibid.*, pp. 301-11.
[9] *Ibid.*, p. 305.
[10] *Ibid.*, pp. 318-20.

or with a discussion of what might be the role of reason in such an appropriate way.

4. Which God?

There is one problem in the Dialogues about which I cannot be sure as to whether Hume raised it intentionally. One cannot be certain that the three participants in the dialogue are talking about the same thing. When Cleanthes refers to "God," does he mean a personal God? It seems to me that he refers to something like an Ideal World which causes this world, something like Mind, a Universal Mind, or a God, one of whose major attributes is mind. Philo and Demea seem to mean something different when they speak of "the adorable mysteriousness of the Divine Nature." Philo asserts that to suppose a resemblance between God and man degrades the Supreme Being.[11] Demea condemns attempts to "penetrate through these sacred obscurities" as profaneness." [12] In other words, do Philo and Demea stress merely God's otherness from man (in opposition to Cleanthes' emphasis upon his likeness to man), or do the first two have a different God in mind from the latter?

Certainly in the latter case, but even in the former, we have to ask ourselves whether the problem of the appropriateness of the two ways of reasoning in references to God is not more complicated than Hume seems to have realized. It is no wonder, if they do not agree as to what the reasonings should refer to, that Philo and Demea on the one hand, and Cleanthes on the other, differ as to the problem of the appropriateness of ways of reasoning.

In this light it becomes clear why Philo and Demea, who agree in their rejection of Cleanthes' favoring of a posteriori language, differ in view of the a priori language. Philo speaks merely of God's mysteriousness, but Demea also refers to his immutability and simplicity.[13] It is highly probable that there is a connection between these supposed attributes of God and Demea's openness to an a priori approach to such a God.

If these considerations are true, we have to add to Hume's disqualifications of the a priori and the a posteriori methods as inappropriate means of reference to God, the supposition that a preference for such unsuitable approaches may be connected with specific beliefs in specific convictors.

[11] *Ibid.*, p. 307.
[12] *Ibid.*, p. 300.
[13] *Ibid.*, p. 731.

C. THE POSITION OF LOGICAL POSITIVISM

1. *The attack upon metaphysics changes its form*

We will follow Ayer's example and take as a starting point for our discussions not metaphysics "in general" but a specific metaphysical thesis, namely, the assertion that "philosophy affords us knowledge of a reality transcending the world of science and common sense." [14] Ayer does not want to denounce this thesis "by criticising the way in which it comes into being," e.g., by pointing out that one cannot "legitimately . . . infer . . . the existence of anything super-empirical . . . from empirical premises." "For the fact that a conclusion does not follow from its putative premise is not sufficient to show that it is false." Ayer wants to use another kind of critique, "a criticism of the nature of the actual statements which comprise [the metaphysical thesis]." Hence he claims that "our charge against the metaphysician is not that he attempts to employ the understanding in a field where it can not profitably venture, but that he produces sentences which fail to conform to the conditions under which alone a sentence can be literally significant." [15]

What has to be noticed here is the difference between this standpoint and that of Hume and the replacement of his method of discussing the limits of the faculty of reason by that of the linguistic approach. A metaphysical utterance is rejected because of its linguistic characteristics. Logical positivism began as *Sprachkritik* (criticism of language), as appears clearly from one of the first publications, *Wissenschaftliche Weltauffassung, Der Wiener Kreis.*

Metaphysical theories suffer from several errors, one of which is a naïve dependence upon a conversational language and its vague, uncritical use of words. "Ordinary language, e.g., uses the same form of speech, namely, the substantive, for things (apple), for characteristics (hardness), for relations (friendship) and for processes (sleep). Therefore it tempts people to a thing-like conception of functional concepts (hypostatizing, substantiation)." [16]

Linguistic method means also logical approach. Feigl, referring to Ayer's treatment of the subject, says: "This is simply empiricism brought up to date. The psychologistic formulations, an example of which may be found in Hume (ideas must have their origin in impressions), are replaced by logical ones." [17]

[14] A. J. Ayer, *Language, Truth and Logic* (2nd rev. ed.; London: Victor Gollancz, 1946).
[15] *Ibid.*, pp. 33, 34, 35.
[16] (Wien: Artur Wolf Verlag, 1929), herausgegeben vom Verein Ernst Mach, p. 17.
[17] *Op. cit.*, p. 10.

2. *An example of the argument in its present-day form*

Feigl treats the problem of metaphysics in the context of a discussion of "meaning," that is to say, of a variety of meanings. Sentences which are *factually meaningful*, e.g., those which are factually true and those which are factually false, have a different type of meaning than logically true sentences, or emotive expressions. Metaphysics is seen as a problem of confusion of meanings. "The positivistic critique of metaphysics is primarily an attack upon confusion of meanings and is not intended as a wholesale repudiation of what has been presented under that label."

In order to unmask these confusions it is necessary to see that general definitions of metaphysics are unsatisfactory ("the discipline concerned with 'first principles' or with reality as a whole"). Feigl discerns, therefore, five types of metaphysics: intuitive, deductive, dialectical, transcendental, and inductive. Feigl claims that *inductive* metaphysics, "a speculative cosmology derived by extrapolation from scientific evidence . . . need not contain factually-meaningless elements at all. . . . Conjectures regarding . . . the future of evolution may be perfectly meaningful. But anyone . . . will realize how uncertain and vague these guesses must be. . . . They are apt to remain barren, if not actually misleading." Feigl states that the other four types of metaphysics are wide open to linguistic criticism:

(1) *Deductive* metaphysics indulges in the rationalistic practice of producing factual conclusions of a relatively specific character from a few sweepingly general (and often completely vague) premises. It thus misconstrues the nature of logical derivation and is guilty of a confusion of logical with factual meaning.

(2) Similarly *dialectical* metaphysics, especially the Hegelian, confuses what—most charitably interpreted—may appear as a psychological thought-movement or as a form of historical processes with the logical forms of inference.

(3) *Intuitive* metaphysics, convinced of the existence of a privileged shortcut to "Truth," mistakes having an experience for knowing something about it. Then too, it is habitually insensitive to the distinction between pictorial and emotional appeals and factual meaning.

(4) Finally, *transcendental* metaphysics in its attempt to uncover the basic categories of both thought and reality may turn out to be nothing else than an unclear combination of epistemology and cos-

mology, which is then dignified with the name "ontology." It could thus be salvaged and restated in purified form. But it is precisely in ontology that we find the greatest accumulation of factually-meaningless verbalisms.[18]

3. *Psychological interpretations*

Sometimes logical positivists add psychological interpretations to their logical criticism of metaphysics. Von Mises argues the necessity of a psychological analysis of the personalities of metaphysical philosophers in order to attain a better understanding of the cause and effects of metaphysical structures. Anticipating this research, he enumerates some elements which he assumes will be revealed by further study.[19]

(1) The existence of apodictically valid propositions in science and in logic which, however, are not recognized in their character as tautologies, and which evoke the desire to find similar, absolutely valid principles also in the domain of other sciences and in philosophy.

(2) The presence in the human sciences of well-known propositions which admit of no doubt.

(3) The experience that our sense organs sometimes deceive us, and the idea which results from this, that there should be a true reality which supplies us with knowledge which does not deceive us.

(4) The universal desire for security, rest, the absolute, which is not satisfied with knowledge that is not entirely secure, that might change, or that only holds good conditionally.

(5) The general tendency of man to hypostatize ideas which he himself has created.

(6) The special tendency to give an absolutely firm foundation to certain traditional conceptions essential for life.

Von Mises is of the opinion that an exact insight into the nature of our knowledge should make it clear to us that all our knowledge is provisional, subject to revision, only signifying a stage in the process of the scientific forming of knowledge, a process that never ceases.

The more self-assuredly, the more arrogantly a certain view functions, the more clearly it shows that it is still in the uncritical stage of knowledge. Von Mises chooses, in contradiction to this, Mach's attitude. For Mach it is the highest philosophy to endure an imperfect outlook on the world and to prefer it to one which only *seems* to be complete but is in reality insufficient.

[18] *Ibid.*, pp. 11, 12.

[19] Richard von Mises, as discussed in my *Research for the Consequences*, etc., pp. 85, 86.

D. AN ATTEMPT TO REFORMULATE THE PROBLEM

1. *The necessity of a reformulation*

I agree largely with the intentions of Hume and the logical positivists, but consider the ways in which they formulate the problem not altogether satisfactory. The main issue is that there are more factors involved in the problem of metaphysics than the approach of either school admits.

a) Especially the logical positivists' position is very plausible. They are right in rejecting Hume's conception of reason as a faculty of the mind. The transfer they have made from a psychologistic to a logical treatment has many advantages. Metaphysics often involves a confusion of meanings and of languages. Feigl fully realizes the complexity of the problem and therefore carefully avoids giving a definition of metaphysics. Instead he offers a description of certain types of metaphysics.

The fundamental intention, not only of the logical positivists but also of Hume, exhibits a profound insight. Hume duly stresses the phenomenon of "overreaching" the range and possibilities of certain types of thinking.

b) Some of the factors not satisfactorily accounted for are as follows:

(1) There are more languages involved in the problem of metaphysics than Hume's a priori and a posteriori approaches and than Feigl's cognitive languages. There is, for instance, a typical metaphysical problem in connection with an "overreaching" of the range of moral language.

(2) We have to ask ourselves, What kind of thing is a linguistic "error"? Do these errors—the confusion of which Feigl speaks, the overestimation of the powers of reason against which Hume warns—lie on the intellectual level (and this is suggested by the word "error"), or are these errors expressions of an attitude in which the whole person is involved? Freud's analysis of some linguistic "errors" such as *Versprechung* and *Verhörung* strongly suggests the latter. Our respect for Freud's insight should make us want to lift the masks, the presence of which is shown up by the metaphysical "errors."

2. *The reformulation*

The mentioning of Freud brings us back to the realm of psychology, and therewith to the very thing which logical positivism wants to avoid: the confusion of philosophy and psychology—or does it? It is better to say that metaphysics is neither a problem of the science of psychology nor of philosophy understood as logical analysis, but that it is a concern of that branch of analytical philosophy which intends to analyze language situations. Metaphysics is a language act committed by man-who-speaks. That means that those who disqualify metaphysics actually claim that man-speaking-metaphysical-language speaks in a way against which objections can be made.

There are signs that at least some positivists have realized that metaphysics is not just a problem of linguistic errors, but a problem of man. When Von Mises asserts that the logical analysis of metaphysical language has to be supplemented with a psychological analysis of the metaphysicians, he inadvertently warns us that logical analysis is insufficient because it does not really attack the problem in its entirety.

The problem of metaphysics needs therefore to be reformulated in the following manner:

(1) Whereas Hume saw metaphysics as *an imprudent use of the faculty of reason,* to be distinguished from a modest use which reckons with the weaknesses of this much overrated faculty; and

(2) Whereas the logical positivists see metaphysics as *a confused use of language,* to be opposed to a clearheaded use which takes into account the characteristics and possibilities of each language;

(3) The present approach interprets metaphysics as *a certain objectionable way in which man can speak,* to be distinguished from other, more appropriate ways of speaking.

This reformulation requires clarification on several points. First, we need to develop exactly what the objections are which an analysis of the language situation will bring against the metaphysical way of speaking. Second, if metaphysics is not a problem of *use*-language (both Hume and the logical positivists seem to think in terms of *use*), to what kind of language does metaphysics actually belong: *is*-language or *employ*-language?

3. *Man-speaking-metaphysically makes a metaphysical jump* (first objection)

The first of our objections is very close to Hume's basic argument. Hume protests against the use of scientific and logical reason in a domain where it cannot be used fruitfully, namely, in man's thinking about the nature of God or of the universe. We claim that metaphysical speaking means that man-who-speaks, in his longing for an intelligible account of the All, *employs* language which is properly *use*-language.[20] In other words, if one speaks metaphysically he makes a jump from one realm of discourse to another, he commits a *metabasis eis allo genos.* The jump means that concepts which are legitimately used in the first realm are

[20] Sometimes also a certain kind of *is*-language, namely, moral language, is employed. This problem will be raised later in this chapter.

suddenly employed in the second realm, whereas no account is given of this change. Characteristics which belong to the first meaning of the concept (the *use*-meaning), such as its authority or its type of truth, are transmitted to the second realm of meaning (the *employ*-meaning).

For example, the term "evolution" has a legitimate position in indicative language. It is a part of a certain hypothesis, especially in the biological sciences. As the key term of a theory which is supported by a very large group of leading scientists in the twentieth century, it possesses a certain authority. In the same capacity, the term is connected with a particular type of truth; the validity of the hypothesis, though provisional and relative, is "highly probable."

However, the same term "evolution" is also employed to proclaim a certain interpretation of the meaning of history. Actually, we should speak of "Evolution" and not of "evolution" in this case. *E*volution indicates the employ-meaning, *e*volution the use-meaning of the term. The term "Evolution" then discloses a particular theology, characterized by the doctrine that the qualification "good" must be given to everything which supports the Evolution of the human race to ever greater perfection. The employment of this term in convictional language borrows the authority of science for this specific convictional world view. The conviction is implied that whereas other views are biased, based upon "subjective" emotions, the Evolution world view possesses a general validity, because it is based upon the public, unbiased language of science. The naïve nineteenth-century Evolution world view herewith misinterpreted the type of truth of scientific, hypothetical language, overlooked the "highly probable" character of its validity, and in this way transferred to convictional language an unquestionable kind of certainty which scientific language actually does not possess. We disqualify the world view fabricated with the help of this jump procedure as being couched in metaphysical language.

4. *Man-speaking-metaphysically prefers to work with key terms*

The metaphysical procedure many times, perhaps always, is concentrated upon one or more key terms which are transmitted to another realm. We find that the key terms are derived from various fields, but that they are transferred always to one field, the convictional realm of discourse. In the diagram on page 132 some examples are given, two or three for each of the starting languages.

5. *Man-speaking-metaphysically fabricates convictional world views which possess the character of closed systems* (second objection)

In regard to the problem of metaphysics one can discriminate between two kinds of convictional world views, to wit, open views and

KEY TERM	FIELD	REAL OR SURMISED AUTHORITY	REAL OR SURMISED TYPE OF TRUTH	OTHER ATTRACTIONS
A. *Indicative*				
sex class struggle matter organism	biology sociology physics biology	public, unbiased, objective language	empirical; practically unquestionable	
B. *Tautological*				
absolute universal necessary dialectic	logic logic logic logic	public, unbiased, objective language	necessary, apodictic, unchangeable	
C. *Analytical*				
noumenal idea goodness	philosophy philosophy ethics	"more - than - scientific" access to truth	of "higher" spiritual quality, or correspondence between mind and Mind	
D-1. *Convictional*				
good just	morals morals	language referring to the "really" important	of "deeper," personal validity	
D-2. *Convictional*				
savior eschaton	religion religion	language referring to the "really" important	of "deeper," personal validity	suggesting power which will ultimately solve all problems
E. *Aesthetic*				
beautiful harmonious	art art	"more - than - intellectual" access to reality	intuitional	seeing the totality, the wholeness of life

closed views. Our second objection against metaphysical language is that the views which it produces are closed systems. These systems have to be disqualified for two reasons: first, because they offer a pretentious picture of the All, one which cannot be legitimately attained in any human language; second, because they imply the claim that their validity can be proved, or at least made plausible, by intellectual means.

a) We want to illustrate what we mean by such closed systems, first of all by mentioning two of them which in a popularized form are widely adhered to in the present Western world. More sophisticated closed systems will be discussed later in the chapter.

A large majority of Americans and even yet some Europeans, Christians as well as non-Christians, believe in a "Higher World." The All is divided into two sections, characterized by contrasting pairs of concepts, such as real-unreal, spiritual-material, unchangeable-changeable, infinite-finite, essential-accidental. All these key terms are employed in the procedure of the metaphysical jump. The terms are borrowed from nonconvictional languages and are supposed to express the nature of a "lower" world (finite, accidental, etc.), and a "higher" realm (infinite, essential). According to this convictional view man participates in this dichotomy. His instincts, his desires, and his body are bad, or at least much less valuable than his knowledge, his mind, his spirit, and his soul.

This convictional world view is one of the most powerful which ever existed. The power of its present popularized form lies largely in the fact that most people who entertain it are unaware that they do. These convictions seem to them "natural," "self-evident," "common sense." Another reason is probably that *everything receives its place* in the all-embracing frame, the closed system, which this view offers. Good and bad, the meaning of life, the significance of the future, death (shake off the worthless body and enter the spiritual world!), God (summit of all that is good and beautiful, and at the same time the guarantor of this whole cosmic structure and of the final prevalence of the good), moral rules (essentially the same, everywhere and for everyone)—all this and more forms the well-ordered harmony which is fundamentally unquestionable.

It will be shown in Chap. VI that this popular view originates in sophisticated systems of classical and medieval "philosophy." These original systems showed both characteristics of closed systems. Not only did they exhibit the "universality" of the picture of the All in which everything was accounted for, but they also presupposed the validation of the system by "philosophical" means (e.g., metaphysical systems of Aristotle, of rationalists, mystics, and Platonists; proofs for the existence of God). It is natural that in the present-day popular form we can uncover only the first of these characteristics. Nine out of ten people who are quite certain that America is spiritual and therefore good, and that socialists and Communists are materialists and therefore bad, have never heard of such a thing as philosophy.

There is another closed system which is a parallel case to the one just mentioned. The major difference is that whereas the first view stressed the contrast between the good and the bad, this second view is inspired by a strong belief in the Unity of all that is. The All is a Whole, an Organism, a Totality. Man in this view shares the monistic character of the All. The conflict between good and bad is de-emphasized so that man mirrors the beautiful and rational harmony of the Whole. Many times the dualism of the convictions about "higher" and "lower" worlds is combined with the belief in the cosmic Whole, the dichotomy being easily *aufgehoben* in the final Unity.

If one wanted to list all cults, groups, movements, churches, and synagogues where the message of salvation is based upon one of these convictional systems, one could easily fill several pages of this book. The reason for stressing here the preponderance of these popular forms of metaphysical systems lies in my intention to demonstrate that metaphysics is completely misunderstood if it is seen as a problem of importance solely for professional philosophers.

Metaphysics is a universal human problem, in the sense that it is not to be located exclusively in a specific intellectual discipline, but that it must be recognized in its "existential" nature. Something of ultimate importance is at stake for those who believe in such systems. It seems that many people (or most?) cannot find a comfortable place in life, cannot establish their existence, without the support and solace which the all-embracing systems generously provide. Interpreters of metaphysics who concentrate upon an immodest use of reason or upon linguistic errors, instead of thinking in terms of the various ways in which man can establish his existence and in that way can encounter or escape the difficulties of life, are likely to offer learned but superficial interpretations.

b) A term must now be introduced which many readers will have expected for a long time. What is the relationship between metaphysics and ontology? In this book we will use the term "ontology" in the traditional sense, so that "ontology" as it is used in the newest Anglo-American epistemological research, and also as it is used by Heidegger, is excluded. In the traditional sense ontology meant: the *logos* of *to on*, or *ta onta*. The translation "the science of being" is misleading because of the ambiguous character of its main terms. It seems that a translation of ontology by "an intelligible account of all that is," or "of the All," is open to less misunderstanding.

If this interpretation is right, ontology and metaphysics are inseparable. Perhaps the best way to say it is by asserting that a closed system has two aspects, a metaphysical and an ontological. The metaphysical aspect refers to the metaphysical jump, the ontological aspect to the "universality" of the all-embracing system. The demand for "philosophical" validation of the system is characteristic for both aspects.

Philosophers who are critical of ontology are often attacked by the argument: everyone uses ontological elements in his thinking, whether he realizes it or not, and whether he intends to or not. This objection rests upon a very simple misunderstanding. Everyone lives by convictions and is therefore influenced by them in his philosophizing, but not all convictions are ontological in nature. As we stated above, some convictional world views are open, others are closed, and only the latter are ontologies.

Examples of nonontological world views can be found in those religions which take the starting point for their theologizing in a revelation, such as Judaism, Christianity, and Islam. Here the theologians are fully aware of the fact that their theologizing starts with specific convictions, presented to them in a holy Law, the life and teachings of a holy Person, or in a holy Book.[21] Theology in these cases starts with the admission of a mystery; that is to say, the origin of the convictions is acknowledged as lying in a domain which is inaccessible to rational understanding (God's will, as revealed in Law, Person, or Book), and thus the desire for an intelligible account of the All does not arise at all. It has to be admitted that there are numerous Jewish, Christian, and Moslem theologians who still have offered closed systems, but in these cases their thinking was fundamentally influenced by metaphysical and ontological "philosophy."

It is not so easy to point out open convictional world views (and therefore open theologies) outside the province of these three religions. In principle, open convictional views are those wherein the author admits both to his reader and himself that his convictions possess a unique character, are *sui generis,* are not the logical implications of some rational principle or a universally accepted fact.

6. ***Man-speaking-metaphysically regards philosophy as a savior* (third objection)**

A third objection against metaphysics is that it demands a very special interpretation of the function of philosophy. Philosophy is not considered to be a mere discipline; it possesses a much loftier rank, that of a savior. The elements entering into this picture are as follows:

(1) Philosophy is contrasted with science. The latter is, for metaphysical thinking, the "ordinary" approach to the "ordinary" world, whereas philosophy offers a special way of access to the Higher World.

[21] K. A. H. Hidding, *Mens en Godsdienst* (Delft: Gaade, 1954), pp. 96 ff.

(2) Philosophy is seen as the critic of all disciplines, sorting out their valid contributions to the final vision of the All.

(3) Closely related to the foregoing is the conviction that philosophy "harmonizes all human experiences," not only the scientific, but also the aesthetic, the moral, and the religious. Some "Christian" philosophies make a bid for the prize of broad-mindedness by proclaiming that even non-Christian experiences should be included.

(4) By means of this critical and harmonizing activity, philosophy can reach the one Truth, and present the image of the All-unity in one system of thought. (In our terminology, philosophy is the agent who performs the metaphysical jump. The jump is not recognized, at least not in its questionable character. Instead of being criticized the jump is praised.)

(5) It is an insult to think of philosophy as just one discipline among others: it is a high calling. Its adepts are special people who have committed themselves to defend the belief in the All against all doubters; to proclaim a way of life, flowing from this belief; even to defend the All itself against its enemies: skeptics, agnostics, materialists, and positivists. The marked hostility toward logical empiricism has its origin in this belief. The positivist or empiricist is not merely an adherent of a rival philosophical school; he is a traitor who uses his philosophical erudition, not for the exercise of his high calling, but even to denigrate and blacken what he ought to defend. Hence, he is "not a philosopher at all." The "real philosopher" has a calling to use all available intellectual and intuitional means to establish the reality, the truth, and the glory of the All.

(6) In other words, philosophy is both a savior and a guide. It is a savior to the extent that it will *rescue* man *from* life as it appears to his unpurified experience, ridden by the powers of disorder, ignorance, and materialism. Philosophy is a guide to the extent that it *leads* man *toward* life as it should be and "really" is; that is to say, philosophy teaches man how to establish his existence in harmony with the "really Real." In the ideal state it is the philosopher who is king, and who in this function establishes the existence of the community. In later, more individualistic ages it is the philosopher who shows the way to the establishment of a personal existence "in harmony with the Infinite."

Each of these six elements is not openly admitted, or even clearly recognizable, in all metaphysical systems, because the metaphysician is seldom fully aware of them. We should realize, however, that these elements do not occur in metaphysical language by accident. A closed system *demands* a philosophy-savior. The harmonious, intelligible picture of an ultimately harmonious, intelligible All, which the "ordinary" man cannot recognize, *demands* a factor which can guide and illuminate the blind. Without the illuminating activity ("enlightenment") of this factor, the All would suffer from a gruesome dark stain, unharmonious, antirational, defying and spurning all fullness of meaning: the ignorance of an important portion of the All about its "real" grandeur. Hence, this enlightening factor cannot be anything else than harmony and intelligence itself—in other words, philosophy!

7. *Metaphysical speaking is rooted in anxiety* (fourth objection)

Another objection against metaphysics is that this language does not tell us anything about "Being" or the "All," but gives us some interesting information about the man who speaks it. If our first three objections are valid, metaphysics only *seems* to disclose the "real" structure of the universe, and actually exposes deeply hidden strivings which lead men to speak metaphysically. For instance, the craving for a closed system unveils the remarkable compulsion to claim that there *must* be a well-ordered, recognizable pattern behind the distressing manifoldness of things. A metaphysician just cannot stand the idea of a universe which cannot be grasped, either by reason, by meditation, or by intuition, for it would fill him with horror. How could he establish his existence if there were no intelligible frame wherein he could find his place?

In other words, man-speaking-metaphysically is in the grasp of a strong anxiety, which allows him no rest. The anxiety must be exorcized by means of a system which assures him that life is not as it seems, but that "Order" is hidden behind its alarming opaqueness and disorder. How deeply satisfying and reassuring is the message that a time-honored activity exists—philosophy—which guarantees to introduce him into the final secrets and mysteries of this beneficial "Order."

We meet here the very same problem which has been discussed earlier in other terms. Man is deeply disturbed by the ambiguity and complexity of life, and of himself. He wants to silence these distressing elements, to ignore them, to give them the lie, all at the same time. Man wants to be solaced, by religions, by *Weltanschauungen*, by august philosophical systems—or does he want to console himself?

Metaphysics must therefore be considered as a typical example of experience theology, that is, experiential cryptotheology, to be sure. Not only is its starting point a very personal experience, anxiety, but it can never disentangle itself from this experience. The metaphysician begins and ends as the prisoner of his experiences, that is to say, of himself.

8. Logical empiricism is "soft" on metaphysics

The four aspects of metaphysics pointed out in our four objections belong together. They form a whole, each element conditioning the others. This assertion does not need any validation after what has been said in the last paragraphs. This fundamental unity of the four aspects places the position taken by the logical empiricists in a peculiar light.

It is highly probable that the logical empiricists would in principle agree with all four objections. They have, however, place for only one or two of them in their kind of philosophy, which is logical analysis. And even one of these objections, the protest against the metaphysical jump, is formulated in such a careful way (confusion of language characteristics, linguistic errors) that it loses much of its force. If one accuses a metaphysician of making linguistic errors, he shrugs his shoulders, for this attack does not have much impact. It hits only the intellectual side of the metaphysician's existence, and if our analysis of the problem of metaphysics is correct, the roots of metaphysical "thinking" do not lie on the level of thought but reach back to a much deeper realm; they are related to the very center of man's life.

In other words, the logical empiricists "pull their punches," and perhaps one is allowed to say that they are largely aware of doing so. The "psychological" remarks which Von Mises wants to add to the positivists' logical analysis of metaphysics, and the famous remark of Ernst Mach about the highest philosophy existing in a courage to give up the alluring notion of a *Weltanschauung* which can explain everything, show that the logical empiricists are aware of the existence of arguments against metaphysics other than those of logical analysis. The fact that these remarks are not elaborated and have not been brought into a closer connection with that analysis shows that the logical empiricists actually cannot give them a significant place in their philosophical approach.

Our criticism leads up to the thesis that logical empiricism offers in its logical analysis a very insufficient tool for raising the question of metaphysics. The empiricists either should say more, but that would require a broadening of their concept of philosophy into the direction of situational analysis, or they should not say anything at all against metaphysics, and that would take much of the vigor out of the movement, for the battle against metaphysics has been one of the major sources of its inspiration.

Perhaps Karl Menger, one of the members of the Vienna Circle, was the only logical positivist who realized the seriousness of the dilemma into which the positivists brought themselves by attacking metaphysics with the instrument of logical analysis. In my *Research for the Consequences of the Vienna Circle Philosophy for Ethics,* Menger's standpoint is characterized as follows:

> In his *Moral, Wille und Weltgestaltung, Grundlegung zur Logik der Sitten,* 1934, he appears to share entirely the other Vienna Circle aversion to terms such as Wesensschau, evidence, intuition, das Reich der Werte, and such metaphysical expressions. But he considers it a great danger to call such propositions and questions which contain these terms, meaningless. Menger simply does not wish to enter into discussion with people that use these metaphysical terms.
>
> As soon as we put the question whether such terms are meaningless, Menger avoids giving an answer. Woe to him who declares certain propositions to be meaningless! "He resembles the man who, having thrown his enemy into a swamp, jumps into the swamp himself with a dagger in his hand." Assertions such as: these terms or methods are meaningful and those are meaningless, are an infringement of psychological and appreciating propositions in science. Such propositions belong to the biography of those who give the utterance. In other words, Menger sees in the proposition "this or that is meaningless" a metaphysical proposition (pages 28-29).[22]

In view of the insufficiency of the logical empiricists' treatment of the problem of metaphysics, and the more thorough discussion offered by the method of situational analysis, we can claim that this last method is not a dilution of logical analysis but, if anything, its completion. We must distinguish between the vehemence of the logical empiricists' feelings against metaphysics and the effectiveness of their philosophical attack. Whereas no one can outdo them on the first point, in the second matter they are weak. On the other hand, it would seem that situational analysis comprises all that is valid in the logical-analytical disqualification of metaphysics, gives a full account of the nonlogical objections which could find no place in the logical analysis, and combines all these elements in an approach which is more appropriate to the topic under discussion.

9. *The relationships between metaphysical, religious, and moral language*

In order to prevent misunderstandings we have to make clear what are the agreements and the differences between metaphysical, religious, and moral language. All that these three languages have in common is that they are all convictional languages. The differences are the follow-

[22] (Utrecht: Kemink en Zoon, 1946), pp. 65-66.

ing: First, we usually understand by religious and moral language a kind of *is*-language. As soon as the element of intentionally giving account of one's convictions enters in, we speak of theological language, and this is an *employ*-language. Metaphysics is also an employ-language. Second, the difference between religious, moral, and theological language on the one hand, and metaphysical language on the other, lies in the fact that the first three languages do not deny that they are convictional languages, whereas metaphysical language presupposes the claim that it possesses a purely rational basis.

Third, there is a difference between moral language on the one hand, and religious and metaphysical language on the other. Convictional language which carries evaluations of human behavior is called moral language. Religious and metaphysical languages also have human problems in mind but refer in the first place to the meaning of the All. This third difference is of great importance, because it makes clear how a metaphysical jump can be made with a convictional language (namely, that of morals) as the springboard. For instance, some people infer from the importance of the term "good" in the judging of human behavior that the nature of the All "must" also be "good." Other people, impressed by the absurdity of life, and morally rebelling against it, cry out that the All is fundamentally an absurd, meaningless joke.

On the basis of the discussions so far offered in this chapter we can expand (see page 141) the diagram on *homo loquens* which was given in Chap. I.

10. *The third aspect of the term "analytical"*

a) We must now enlarge upon the third meaning of the term "analytical" mentioned briefly in the Introduction. Analysis in this essay means not only the *logical analysis* of the logical empiricists, and the broader *analysis of the language situation,* oriented toward existentialism and Dewey, but also *distrust of lofty words.* Misgivings about grandiose ways of speaking are certainly not absent from logical empiricism, existentialism, and pragmatism, but this suspicion is an element in its own right. It is of a much wider range of influence than these particular philosophical schools.

This suspicion is fed by various sources, one of the most important being that of Freud's psycho-*analysis.* We must recognize, however, that most of the leaders of nineteenth-century thinking contributed to the understanding of man implied in this distrust: Marx, Feuerbach, Kierkegaard, and Nietzsche.

Perhaps we can discriminate between three stages in the development of this "analytical" distrust of man's impressive speaking. First, this dis-

HOMO LOQUENS II

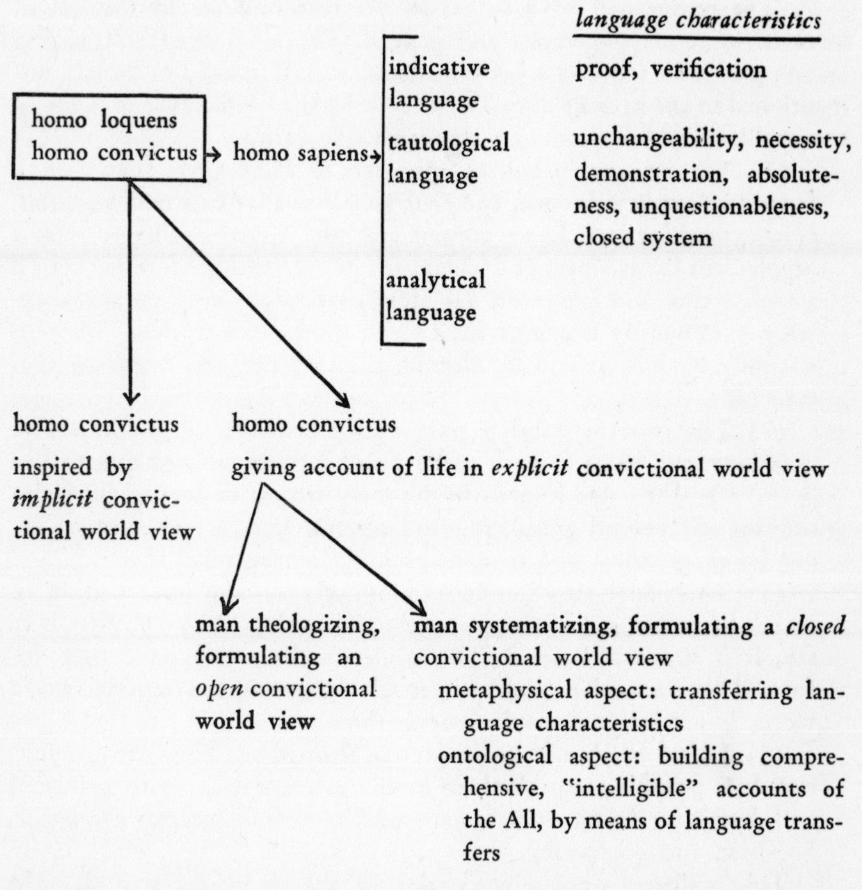

trust has never been completely absent in Western civilization. It was one of the major motivations of the minority philosophy of empiricism; notice the sophists, the skeptics, the nominalists, Francis Bacon, and David Hume. It was a definite element in the way in which the Hebrew prophets and Jesus of Nazareth looked at man. Second, this distrust did not play an important role in the idealistic, rationalistic, church-religious, metaphysical eras of Western civilization, but was brought into focus by certain thinkers of the nineteenth century. (See page 140.)

Third, whereas the "analytical" distrust of loftiness was a matter of some individuals in the nineteenth century, it is an attitude shared by large groups in the twentieth century. It is therefore not surprising at all that in this century two new revolutionary schools of philosophy arise—logical empiricism and existentialism—each of which has this "analytical" understanding of man as one of its main motivating powers.

b) The reader will have to excuse my referring to the distrust of loftiness in terms too vague and general. The analysis of this understanding of man requires a book in itself. Still, it could not be left unmentioned in the present essay. What follows is an indication of some of the problems which demand a thorough elaboration.

(1) We can say, using an approach of Heidegger, that man is *homo loquens* in principle, and that he is actually, first and foremost, *homo grandiloquens*. If we are not too bold in attempting to offer a supplement to an aspect of Heidegger's interpretation of man (man is actually, first and foremost, *das Man*), we might say that speaking-lofty-words-easily is one of the characteristics of *das Man*. "Man" is not only *homo loquax* (*das Gerede,* chatter) but also *homo pomposus*.

(2) The issue at hand is part of the problem of mask. *Homo grandiloquens* wears a mask made up of language; he wants to impress both others and himself by his lofty words, to conceal his insignificant self behind grandiose word screens. If it is true that we *are* our language, then who *is* man-speaking-impressively?

(3) This "analytical" understanding of man is in itself neither an attack upon nor a defense of any convictional world view; that is to say, it is not convictional. This understanding may have been informed by particular (but very much different) convictional world views, but it is not dependent upon them.

(4) Lofty words are not suspect in themselves. They are ambiguous. It is possible to speak them in an authentic way, with prudence and humility, being fully aware of the possibilities of arrogance, bombast, and pomposity.

This position is not a weakening of the suspicious attitude. The radical disavowal of lofty terms *as such* oversimplifies and hence distorts the problem. In this manner the ambiguity and complexity of man's speaking is denied.

(5) It is understandable that the "analytical" understanding of man does not have much chance in large groups which are kept together by the proclamation of lofty words, such as churches and political parties. People are inclined to take these words at their face value, to admire lofty language for its own sake. It is, however, characteristic for the leadership of modern churches to encourage the suspicious, "analytical" attitude among their members. On the other hand, the way in which so many theologians are irritated by logical

positivism demonstrates that this "analytical" attitude is not so strong in theological circles as one might believe.

c) It is in accordance with this understanding of man not to join Marcel in his attack upon Sartre for his denial of Grace, but to respect the latter (in spite of obvious shortcomings) for his refusal to sweeten the vehemence of his bitter analysis of the human situation with the syrup of comforting, lofty words. In the same way, this understanding implies the refusal of a wholesale condemnation of logical empiricism for its atheism and "lack of spirituality."

E. SOME EXAMPLES OF METAPHYSICS

1. *Whitehead*

a) We begin with an exposition of Whitehead's method.

(1) In his *Science and the Modern World* Whitehead's main purpose is not so much to deal with science itself as with the "general climate of opinion," the "outlook," the "mentality," which lies deeper than science and which colors our whole way of thought. "The new mentality is more important even than the new science and the new technology. It has altered the metaphysical pre-suppositions and the imaginative contents of our minds." Whitehead calls it "scientific materialism," and describes it as "the fixed scientific cosmology which presupposes the ultimate fact of an irreducible matter, or material, spread throughout space in a flux of configurations." Whitehead repeatedly qualifies this "cosmology" with the term "simple location." It is determined by the assumption that matter "has the property of simple location in space and time." [23]

(2) Whitehead offers several objections against scientific materialism, the most important of which are: that it encumbers the development of science in our century; that it distorts the concrete facts of our apprehension; that there is a "discrepancy between the materialistic mechanism of science and the moral intuitions, which are presupposed in the concrete affairs of life"; that it leads to the doctrines of the "Struggle for Existence" and "Natural Selection," because it neglects creativeness, co-operation, friendly help, i.e., "the whole ethical aspect of evolution." [24]

(3) Whitehead deems it necessary to replace scientific materialism by the theory of Organic Mechanism. Perhaps the most decisive term for this view of nature is *mirror*.

[23] Pp. 3, 25, 71, 72. Copyright 1925 by The Macmillan Co. and used by their permission.
[24] *Ibid.*, pp. 22, 116, 163, 164.

The body is the organism whose states regulate our cognizance of the world. The unity of the perceptual field therefore must be a unity of bodily experience. In being aware of the bodily experience, we must thereby be aware of aspects of the whole spatio-temporal world as mirrored within the bodily life. . . .

My theory involves the entire abandonment of the notion that simple location is the primary way in which things are involved in space-time. In a certain sense, everything is everywhere at all times. For every location involves an aspect of itself in every other location. Thus every spatio-temporal standpoint mirrors the world. . . .

That which endures is limited, obstructive, intolerant, infecting its environment with its own aspects. But it is not self-sufficient. The aspects of all things enter into its very nature. It is only itself as drawing together into its own limitation the larger whole in which it finds itself.[25]

The quotations cited above also contain the second important key term, *organism*. This term is not to be understood exclusively in a biological sense. The atom is an organism; electrons are the ultimate smallest organisms. We should not be surprised about this terminology, for Whitehead claims that whereas "materialism only applies to very abstract entities," he considers that the "concrete enduring entities are organisms." There is a difference between the organism of an atom and that of an animal, but it is not very important. "In the case of an animal, the mental states enter into the plan of the total organism." Hence, "Science . . . is becoming the study of organisms. Biology is the study of the larger organisms, whereas physics is the study of the smaller organisms."

Other crucial notions are closely related to "organism." Whitehead asks, e.g., for the "primary entities," the "primary organisms which are incapable of further analysis." He calls this primary entity "the *event* as the ultimate unit of natural occurrence." [26]

(4) Whitehead gives full account of the way in which he receives his outlook of organic mechanism. It is certainly suggested by modern science, or at least compatible with it. But other factors are not less important. First, there is the appeal to empirical observation. This shows which property makes for self-identity, namely, "retention, endurance, or reiteration." Second, there is "the process of analyzing the character of nature in itself," which discloses "a selective activity which is akin to purpose." Related to this sentence is the statement—"Nature exhibits itself as exemplifying a philosophy

[25] *Ibid.*, pp. 116, 133, 137.
[26] *Ibid.*, pp. 115, 149-51.

of the evolution of organisms subject to determinate conditions." [27]

A factor of a somewhat different kind is, third, "that fundamental intuition of mankind which finds its expression in poetry." "I hold that the ultimate appeal is to naïve experience and that is why I lay such stress on the evidence of poetry." What poets such as Wordsworth and Shelley teach is "that a philosophy of nature must concern itself at least with these six notions: change, value, eternal objects, endurance, organism, interfusion." [28]

(5) The second of these factors points to the most fundamental problem of all: "What is the status of the enduring stability of the order of nature?" Whitehead says that two classes of answers are possible. First, those which "refer nature to some *greater* reality standing *behind* it." These realities carry various names, such as "The Absolute, Brahma, The Order of Heaven, God." Second, the assumption that nature is *self-explanatory*. Whitehead espouses the second position. He claims that the first kind of answer implies an unwarranted jump from "our conviction of the existence of such an order of nature to the easy assumption that there is an ultimate reality which . . . is to be appealed to for the removal of perplexity" and censors such procedure as "the great refusal of rationality." Whitehead elaborates thus:

> The sheer statement of *what* things are, may contain elements explanatory of *why* things are. Such elements may be expected to refer to depths beyond anything which we can grasp with a clear apprehension. In a sense, all *explanations* must end in an ultimate arbitrariness. My demand is, that the ultimate arbitrariness of matter of fact from which our formulation starts should disclose the same general principles of reality which we dimly discern as stretching away into regions beyond our explicit powers of discernment.[29]

(6) Whitehead's analysis of nature's self-explanation ultimately leads to the vision of "the metaphysical situation." If I interpret Whitehead well, the foundation of the metaphysical situation is the underlying, substantial activity. This activity possesses three attributes, to wit:

eternal possibility
modal differentiation into individual multiplicity
the principle of limitation

[27] *Ibid.*, pp. 135, 152, 157, 158.
[28] *Ibid.*, pp. 125, 127, 129-30, 139. Eternal objects are, e.g., colors and shapes.
[29] *Ibid.*, pp. 134, 135. Italics mine.

Further, this principle of limitation is called "God." "God" is the ultimate limitation, and his existence is the ultimate irrationality. "No reason can be given for just that limitation which it stands in His nature to impose. God is not concrete, but He is the ground for concrete actuality." God's metaphysical position is finally clarified with these words:

> Among medieval and modern philosophers . . . an unfortunate habit has prevailed of paying to Him metaphysical compliments. He has been conceived as the foundation of the metaphysical situation with its ultimate activity. If this conception be adhered to there can be no alternative except to discern in Him the origin of all evil as well as of all good. . . . If He be conceived as the supreme ground for limitation, it stands in His very nature to divide the Good from the Evil, and to establish Reason "within her dominions supreme." [30]

(7) An account of Whitehead's method is incomplete without a reminder of the crucial role of philosophy in his system. "Philosophy . . . is the critic of cosmologies. It is its function to harmonise, refashion, and justify divergent intuitions as to the nature of things. . . . Its business is to render explicit, and . . . efficient, a process which otherwise is unconsciously performed without rational tests." "It brings to this task, not only the evidence of the separate sciences, but also its own appeal to concrete experience . . . and the aesthetic intuitions of mankind." Hence, it is the task of philosophy in our time "to bring together the two streams[31] into an expression of the world-picture derived from science, and thereby end the divorce of science from the affirmations of our aesthetic and ethical experiences." [32]

b) A discussion of Whitehead's method has to raise the following points.

(1) Scientific materialism is not a unity. What Whitehead indicates with this term are actually three different items:

(*a*) Scientific materialism as an aspect of the *Weltbild* of the sixteenth and following centuries, an account of the physical universe in scientific terms, such as time, space, and matter.

(*b*) Scientific materialism as an aspect of an *explicit convictional world view* of the same centuries, an explicit account of the meaning of life and the nature of the universe; the world *is* a large space with matter spread throughout it.

[30] *Ibid.*, pp. 255-58.
[31] The two streams are: mechanism, e.g., Descartes, and organism, e.g., Leibnitz.
[32] *Op. cit.*, pp. ix, x, 126, 127, 225.

(*c*) Scientific materialism as an aspect of an *implicit convictional* world view of the same centuries, that which Whitehead himself calls the "mentality" which lies deeper than science.

(2) Whitehead is right in criticizing scientific materialism as a *Weltbild*, but he is confused as to the legitimate grounds for such critique. A *Weltbild* with its scientific theories and hypotheses can be judged only on the basis of other hypotheses. Whitehead joins in this legitimate discussion, but the vital power of his arguments lies elsewhere, in his references to aesthetic and moral considerations. A typical case of metaphysics! It is disastrous for scientific integrity either to reject or to accept scientific theories in view of convictional requirements. It belongs to the honor of the "modern" world to consider scientific and philosophical proposals apart from their implications for convictional beliefs.

The situation is, however, more complicated than suggested by these remarks. Whitehead is right in accusing scientific materialism of encumbering the recognition of new scientific theories. The scientific materialism which is guilty here is, however, this materialism as an implicit convictional world view.

(3) In the same manner as "scientific materialism," the term "Organic View of nature" is used by Whitehead in a confusing way. We should discriminate between:

(*a*) The Organic View as an aspect of the *Weltbild* of the eighteenth, the nineteenth, and especially the twentieth centuries, a scientific account of the world in terms such as energy, event, and organism.

(*b*) The Organic View as an aspect of the many *explicit convictional world views* of the same period, an explicit account, convictional in character, though this character is not recognized; its key terms are, e.g., mirror, substance, organism (nonbiological meaning), underlying activity, and God as the principle of limitation.

(*c*) The Organic View as an aspect of the *implicit convictional world view* hidden behind that explicit convictional view.

(4) The following attempt to analyze the Organic View as an implicit convictional view is offered with hesitation, because of the danger of misinterpreting the person who did not avowedly adhere to the convictions presented in the following.

(*a*) Whitehead's real god seems to be the underlying activity. It is this activity and not "God," the principle of limitation, which receives the highest place in the metaphysical hierarchy. Our surmise is strengthened by the central role of concepts related to activity, such as energy, or process, and by the entire stress upon change and growth. Therefore the name "Process Philosophy" for the Organic View as an implicit convictional view is very appropriate.

(*b*) We could also make a case for Nature as Whitehead's *summum bonum*. The rejection of the traditional gods, all of which transcend nature, and the claim that nature is self-explanatory, point decidedly in this direction. Therefore, the name Naturalism for the Organic View as an implicit convictional view is also very appropriate.

(*c*) Philosophy plays, as in so many traditional metaphysical systems, the role of a savior. It has to save civilization from falling victim to partial interests (science, isolated from philosophy and poetry) by harmonizing the various interests of man, testing them as to their validity.

(*d*) The harmonious life to which philosophy would guide us is a mirror of the harmonious cosmos, a true microcosmos. Whitehead appeals from a submission to dull matter to a vision of a real "kosmos," a well-ordered whole which is reasonable, good, and above all beautiful. Perhaps we may divine this strong preoccupation with the "Whole" in Whitehead's attempt to minimize the difference between physical and animal organisms, not to mention human organisms.

(*e*) Whitehead's doctrine of man is not very well elaborated. He stresses goodness (friendly help, co-operation) but especially wisdom (philosophy) and poetry.

(5) The *vitium originis* of metaphysics is to claim or tacitly assume that a specific *Weltbild* and a specific explicit convictional world view necessarily presuppose each other. The present book defends the position that these two views and also the implicit convictional world view are related but not in a cogent way. Neither do scientific materialism as a *Weltbild*, scientific materialism as an explicit convictional view, and this materialism as an implicit convictional view mutually presuppose each other, nor is that the case with the Organic View as a *Weltbild*, the Organic View as an explicit convictional view, and this view as an implicit convictional view. It is preposterous to suggest that scientific materialism as a *Weltbild* (and the Organic View as a *Weltbild*) cannot go together with explicit convictional views which are completely different from scientific materialism (and the Organic View) as an explicit convictional view. Actually, many scientists who call themselves Jews, Christians, Buddhists, and Mos-

lems, adhere to a *Weltbild* which possesses many traits both of the scientific materialistic and the organic *Weltbild*.

2. *Logical empiricism*

We have to consider the problem whether the logical positivists themselves are free from metaphysics. In order to answer this question we do not want to attempt giving a definition of this movement, but to work with an attempt to describe its structure.

a) We should ask this question: What do people mean when they use terms such as positivism, empiricism, logical positivism, logical empiricism, neopositivism, and Vienna Circle philosophy? We have in mind the opinions, not only of the positivists themselves, but also those of outsiders, even of opponents.[33]

It then appears that people mean a variety of things with these names, that is:

(1) A certain stand in regard to the problem of the legitimate *scientific* method.

(2) A certain stand in regard to the *epistemological* problem.

(3) A certain conception of the *function of philosophy.*

(4) A certain group of *convictions* about the meaning of history, the nature of man, the value of religion, convictions which are partly *explicit*, partly *implicit*. The terms of the series positivism, empiricism, etc., are all in turn used for the various standpoints in the four mentioned fields. This situation is accounted for in the diagram on page 150.

b) A positivist can be called a metaphysician if he claims that the five standpoints—A, B-I, B-II, C-I, C-II—are necessarily related; in other words, that the validity of one standpoint guarantees the validity of the others. In that case he will, for instance, employ B-I to "prove" the validity of C-I.

c) An antipositivist can be called a metaphysician if he claims that the five standpoints are necessarily related, so that the nonvalidity of one standpoint guarantees the nonvalidity of the others. He will, for instance, employ "the low spiritual value" of C-I and C-II to stigmatize A, B-I, and B-II. Actually, the validity of these last three standpoints is independent of any explicit or implicit convictional world view.

[33] We do not enter at all into a discussion of the question on which issues logical empiricism differs from logical positivism. This problem is complicated by the fact that the usage of these two terms is uncertain, different in Britain from that in the States, even different from one to another author.

LOGICAL EMPIRICISM

LOGICAL POSITIVISM
NEO-POSITIVISM
THE VIENNA CIRCLE
RELATED: THE ANALYTICAL MOVEMENT

ELEMENTS	MAIN THESES	BACKGROUND		REJECTED
		IMMEDIATE	FARTHER BACK	VIEWPOINTS
A. Scientific method	observation experiment verification prediction	Mach Heisenberg	Bacon	normative science *Einfühlung* *Verstehen* *Wesensschau*
B-I. Epistemology	meaningful languages: mathematics, logic, empirical science; meaningless language: metaphysics	Mach Wittgenstein	skeptics nominalists older empiricists	proofs of existence of an Intelligible World; access to this world by means of reason, intuition, faith
B-II. Function of philosophy	*wertfreie* analysis of languages	Lichtenberg Wittgenstein	Bacon Bentham	guide to happiness, establish hierarchy of values, validate eternal truths and absolute norms
C-I. Explicit convictional world view	(1) neutrality *re* languages (2) admission of own convictions playing a role (3) neutrality *re* religion (4) religion a cultural lag	positivism pragmatism naturalism behaviorism agnosticism	skeptics Hume Comte	metaphysics
C-II. Implicit convictional world view	(1) strong preference for cognitive languages (2) religion an enemy of philosophy and progress	modern atheism and secularism		religion

F. THE PROBLEM OF ONTOLOGY

1. *Introduction*

The philosophy which we have chosen as an example of an ontological system is that of Paul Tillich. I wish to explain why my objections to

Tillich's method of philosophizing are so strong that I feel obliged to disqualify it as ontology. Especially the theologians among the readers, and those philosophers who are sympathetic toward theology, may feel that this disqualification goes too far, the more so since on some very essential points Tillich and I seem to say the same or at least similar things. Here follow some of the major issues raised by Tillich. I shall not try to give a discussion of Tillich's stand on these problems, but merely attempt to indicate how closely akin the position of this book is to these basic ideas of Tillich.[34]

a) The term "ultimate concern" points to the same problems as our "convictional language." One of the insights Tillich wishes to convey with this term is the notion that religion, philosophy, art, and politics are not so much different and isolated fields of interest as various ways in which man expresses his concern about what is of ultimate importance for him. One of the implications of this approach is that Tillich in all his publications shows the intimate relationship between the deepest motivations of artists, theologians, philosophers, and scholars, and in this way redeems theology from the isolation into which it has brought itself.

b) We may perhaps say that the term "the demonic" reveals according to Tillich the unwarranted, arrogant claim of a *finite* power to be *ultimate*. For me, this is too convictional a notion for use in philosophical language. Yet Tillich's view shows kinship with the analytical position that every man is overcome by a convictor, and that many people's convictors are the result of a metaphysical jump (in the case of the demonic, a jump from the finite to the ultimate).

c) In the book which we here discuss in detail,[35] Tillich defines religion as "the state of being grasped by the power of being-itself." The words "being grasped" express very beautifully the element of "being overcome thoroughly."

d) Tillich has made a significant contribution to the understanding of modern man, and therewith to analytical philosophy, by selecting courage as a topic for a philosophical treatise, and especially by the way he handles the subject. Before World War II scarcely anybody realized the importance of courage in man's life. Scholars wrote about knowledge, love, faith, duty, and justice, but not about courage. The last war, with its underground resistance groups, with its necessity for every citizen

[34] We suppose that the reader possesses some knowledge of the ideas involved. If necessary he can look them up in the index of Tillich's *Systematic Theology*, Vol. I (Chicago: University of Chicago Press, 1951).

[35] Paul Tillich, *The Courage to Be* (New Haven: Yale University Press, 1952), p. 156.

to determine his attitude toward Fascism, and to remain loyal to that stand, suddenly made clear how immensely significant and noble a virtue courage is. Tillich, however, does not treat courage as a "virtue." He realizes that we encounter here an issue which is more comprehensive and deeper than moral life. He considers courage as "the universal and essential self-affirmation of one's being." [36] Tillich's approach in regard to this ontological courage displays affinity with the notion of man's establishment of his existence, as developed in this book. We can say that Tillich describes three modes of this establishment—an individualistic, a collectivistic, and a transcendental mode ("the courage to be as oneself," "the courage to be as a part," and "the courage to accept acceptance").

On the surface it would seem that no philosophy is closer to our own than this. However, we cannot follow Tillich's way of philosophizing because of the ontological framework within which his questions are raised, or should we say "imprisoned"? Tillich's questions are therefore less similar to ours than one might think at first view. We can go along with terms such as "concern" and "being grasped by," but not with "ultimate," "finite," "*the* demonic," and "being-itself," because these last terms reveal the ontological framework.

In our eyes Tillich's philosophy is inacceptable because of this fundamental self-contradiction. There is a modern element in the problems which he discusses, but the way in which these problems are treated appears to be far from modern. The suspicion of ontology and metaphysics which characterizes modern philosophy is alien to Tillich's thinking.

We will continue this section by first describing and then discussing Tillich's ontology; further we will offer our analysis of the problem of ontology; in an appendix we will briefly indicate the attitude of some modern Christian theologians toward ontology.

2. *Tillich's ontology*

We will describe this ontology only insofar as it is set forth in *The Courage to Be*. A fuller exposition of Tillich's standpoint can be found in his *Systematic Theology*.[37]

a) If one wishes to understand Tillich's ontology, one has to start with the concepts of being, being-itself, and non-being. Tillich sees the relationships between these elements as follows: "Being embraces itself and non-being." "Being has non-being within itself as that which is eternally present and eternally overcome in the process of the divine life." "Non-being (that in God which makes his self-affirmation dy-

[36] *Ibid.*, p. 3.
[37] I, Pt. II, "Being and God," 163 ff.

namic) opens up the divine self-seclusion and reveals him as power and love." Being is ontologically prior to non-being. Therefore "non-being is dependent on the being it negates," in the sense that it "is dependent on the special qualities of being." [38]

b) Now we turn from being to man, a finite being. He is characterized by anxiety, among other things. "Anxiety is the state in which a being is aware of its possible non-being," or: "Anxiety is the existential awareness of non-being." It is "finitude, experienced as one's own finitude." Anxiety is produced by the "naked absolute," for "facing the God who is really God means facing also the absolute threat of non-being." [39]

c) The next question is as to the relationship between finite beings, anxiety, and non-being. Beings affirm their own existence. This self-affirmation can assume three forms—ontic, spiritual, and moral self-affirmation. Non-being threatens being in three different directions, which correspond to the forms of self-affirmation. It follows that there are three different forms of anxiety in which finite being reacts to the threat of non-being. This leads to the following set of correspondencies:

Self-Affirmation of Beings	Threats by Non-Being	Anxiety in Beings
i. ontic self-affirmation	fate, death	anxiety of death
ii. spiritual self-affirmation	emptiness, meaninglessness	anxiety of meaninglessness
iii. moral self-affirmation	guilt, condemnation	anxiety of condemnation[40]

d) Finite beings do not just succumb to these anxieties; they try to meet them in courage. Courage is not only a *moral* concept, indicating a human act of which we morally approve; it is also, and in the first place, an *ontological* concept. It is "the universal and essential self-affirmation of one's being," that is to say, self-affirmation "in spite of." The main part of the book is taken up by a discussion of the various forms of this "courage to be": "the courage to be as a part," "the courage to be as oneself," and "the courage to accept acceptance." The first two forms of courage are one-sided. They stress too much either

[38] *The Courage to Be,* pp. 34, 40, 179, 180.
[39] *Ibid.,* pp. 35, 39.
[40] *Ibid.,* p. 41.

the community or the individual. The third form unites the valid elements of the other two on a higher level.[41]

e) The circle is now nearly closed. We started out with being and non-being, and our discussion of Tillich's ontology has brought us via finite beings and anxiety to courage. This last element *leads us back again* to being, or being-itself. For Tillich calls courage "the key to being-itself." This notion is the "key" to Tillich's ontology. It is made clear to us in the following statements: "Courage is the key to the interpretation of being-itself." "Courage to be is key to the ground of being." "Courage to be in its radical form is a key to an idea of God which transcends both mysticism and the person-to-person encounter." Tillich even uses a much stronger term than "key," namely, revelation. "Courage to be in all its forms has, by itself, revelatory character," and "courage has revealing power, the courage to be is the key to being-itself." [42]

We can visualize the structure of Tillich's ontology by means of a diagram:[43]

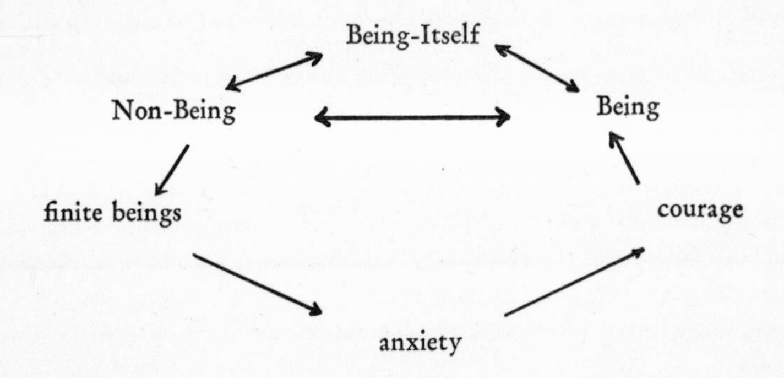

f) The character of anxiety and courage has to be determined further as experience, or awareness. About anxiety, we have already seen that it is considered as "experience" of finitude, and "awareness" of non-being. Also, courage belongs to "experience": "The courage to be (in a certain respect is) . . . the fundamental experience in the encounter with God." The use of the term "experience" is not an accident; in the last chapter it occurs on nearly every page; seven times on page 177.[44]

[41] *Ibid.*, pp. 3, 32, *passim.*

[42] *Ibid.*, pp. 32, 156, 178, 181.

[43] The figure suggests a cosmic process. In neoplatonic philosophies the cosmic process plays a crucial role, e.g., in those of Meister Eckhart and Jakob Boehme.

[44] *The Courage to Be*, pp. 35, 165.

g) Tillich's ontology is much more complicated than the simple structure which we have discussed up to now. We do not aim at completeness but one more element has to be mentioned. It is the "basic polar structure of being." From it are derived ontological principles. This polar structure can be found on several levels of being. On the level of the universe, it is the polarity of "self and world"; on the level of finite beings, it is the contrast between "individualization and participation"; in regard to man's courage, we distinguish the courage to be oneself, polar to the courage to be as a part.[45]

h) Closely related to this ontological element is that of transcendence. This term is used to indicate both a characteristic of the domain of being and God, and of the right attitude of finite beings. About the divine realm, Tillich asserts, "The power of being transcends nonbeing." "Encountering God means encountering transcendent security and transcendent eternity." "Being-itself transcends every being infinitely; God in the divine-human encounter transcends man unconditionally."

In regard to finite being, Tillich says that the right courage to be "transcends both the courage to be as a part and the courage to be as oneself." This right courage also "transcends both self and the world." Further, "Only if the God of theism is transcended can anxiety be taken into the courage to be." [46]

These last paragraphs can be visualized in the diagram on page 156.

i) Another concept which belongs to this same section of Tillich's ontology is "absolute faith." It is closely connected with transcendence, namely, the transcendence of finite beings. "It is simply faith, undirected, absolute. It is undefinable, since everything defined is dissolved by doubt and meaninglessness." It is "a faith which has been deprived by doubt of any concrete content." Further, it is "the state of being grasped by the God beyond God . . . a movement in, with, and under other states of the mind." [47]

j) Tillich gives the following account of his ontological method. Ontology is the philosophical analysis of the nature of being. As such it precedes all other mental activities: theology and medicine, metaphysics, ethics, and religion. The ontological method consists of the following five steps:

(1) It uses "some realm of experience."

(2) It points "to characteristics of being-itself."

[45] *Ibid.*, p. 86.
[46] *Ibid.*, pp. 123, 131, 155, 170, 172, 186.
[47] *Ibid.*, pp. 176, 177, 188.

(3) It "speaks analogously."

(4) It offers cognition.

(5) It chooses its concepts on the basis of "experience and thought." [48]

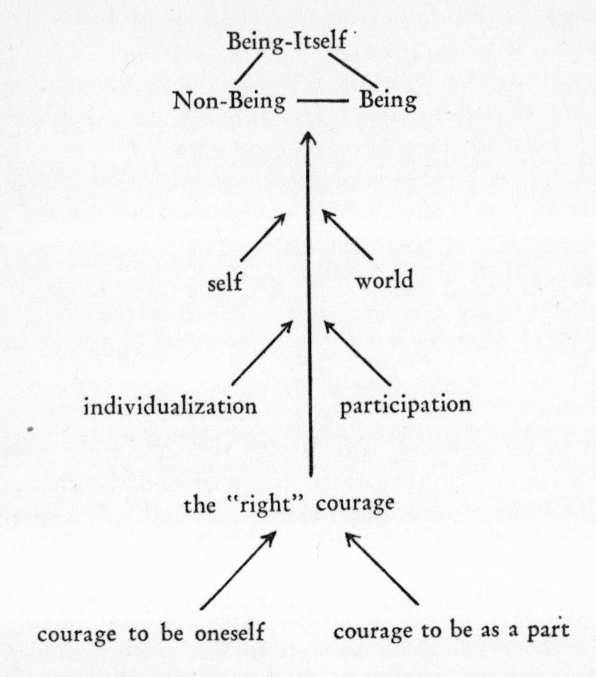

3. *Discussion of Tillich's ontology*

We will try to show that Tillich's so-called ontology actually is a cryptotheology. This means, first, that what is offered here is not a philosophy but a theology, the defense by intellectual means of a specific set of convictions; second, that the specific character of this group of convictions is not admitted, but hidden behind the façade of the authority of a seemingly pretheological, ontological system.

a) The basic term of Tillich's ontology is "experience." [49] He adheres

[48] *Ibid.*, pp. 42, 72, 87, 25.

[49] It seems that our procedure of classifying Tillich as an experience theologian is mistaken. Tillich raises objections against a too naïve use of the term "experience" in his *Systematic Theology*, I, 42 ff. One might even say that he explicitly rejects the theology of religious experience. This same standpoint was already taken in Tillich's article on "The Problem of Theological Method" (*Journal of Religion*, Vol. XXVII, 1947), from which the following quotations are taken: "The religious experience of the theologian is not a positive source and not a norm of systematic theology. Everybody's religious experience is shaped by the denominational group to which he belongs." "It contradicts the basic principle of the Reformation to look at one's self instead of looking beyond one's self at the new reality which liberates man from himself."

to the doctrine that man can "understand" the universe on the basis of his experiences, namely, anxiety and courage. (The term "understand" is not used by Tillich; what we mean by it will be explained in sec. 4.)

The term "experience" is ambiguous. Experience is determined by what we are, that is to say, by our particular convictions. The events of World War II were experienced in very different ways, depending upon whether people were courageous or cowardly, convinced Christians or Christians in name, committed humanists or would-be humanists, democrats or Fascists. Experience therefore does not offer at all the kind of insight which would enable us to know, or "understand," the universe, being, being-itself, or God. People's experiences do not reveal the nature of Being, but they disclose the specific character of the convictions of the persons who voice their experiences, or the ways these persons have established their existence in view of certain events. Starting from ex-

---

Tillich, however, does not live up to his own theology. The rejection of a theology of experience was stated explicitly in 1947 (the article in the *Journal*), and in 1951 (the section in *Systematic Theology*), but the book on *Courage*, which is built on a theology of experience, was published in 1952! In other words, Tillich's explicit theology and his implicit theology are in conflict with each other.

We have to realize that the decisive role attributed to experience and awareness was not introduced into Tillich's theologizing by accident. The emphasis upon experience and awareness is a major characteristic of Tillich's thinking from his earliest to his latest writings. We find an *explicit* formulation of an experience theology as late as 1946, in an article on "The two types of Philosophy of Religion" (*Union Seminary Quarterly Review*). Tillich develops here the conception of the "ontological awareness of the unconditional." It is true that Tillich explains why he prefers the term awareness to other terms such as intuition, experience, knowledge, but even his argument shows that awareness is in reality a kind of experience. The awareness of the unconditional is itself unconditional. It is "immediate awareness," and is more fundamental than any psychological function. It is "the prius of the separation of subject and object." Very enlightening is the explanation of this awareness: "The immediate awareness of the unconditional has not the character of faith but of self-evidence. Faith contains a contingent element and demands a risk. It combines the ontological certainty of the unconditioned with the uncertainty of everything conditioned and concrete."

It is our impression that immediate awareness of the unconditioned is a basic experience, which is prior to all concepts, symbols, and words, and further constitutes them as religious concepts and at the same time transcends them as being too concrete. This reasoning is closely akin to that in *The Courage to Be*. We are allowed to say that the book on *Courage* of 1952 sides with the article of 1946, over against the article of 1947 and the *Systematic Theology* of 1951.

A quotation of one of Tillich's earliest writings will show how deeply rooted experience theology is in Tillich's thought. In his work *Ueber die Idee einer Theologie der Kultur*, 1919, p. 35 (quoted and translated by J. L. Adams, Ph.D. thesis, Divinity School, University of Chicago, 1945, p. 42), Tillich delivers a quite revealing statement. He defines religion as "an experience of the unconditioned and that means an experience of absolute reality on the ground of absolute nothingness; it will experience the nothingness of all existing things, the nothingness of values, the nothingness of personal life."

It seems to be beyond doubt that experience theology is one of the major powers in Tillich's thought, and that his later rejection of this element has influenced only Tillich's explicit and not his implicit theology.

perience, therefore, means to assume that a starting point, very arbitrary in itself, possesses a kind of objective authority.

For this reason many people who belong to the churches which participate in the World Council of Churches feel that the only right starting point for a theology is in the convictions of a specific group. According to this point of view, it is misleading to claim that one can start his theologizing with any factor which is not touched by our convictions, be it experience, or the Bible, God, or revelation. People's "Christian experience," as well as their thinking about God or scripture, depends upon the convictions held by the specific confessional group to which they belong.

b) The arbitrariness to which an experience theology leads is more than clear in Tillich's case. He claims that the basic structure of being is polar; it is the polarity of self and world. If man could know the structure of being at all, who could tell us whether it consists of two basic elements, or of three, or five? One could make a case for three elements: self, community, world; a case for four elements: self, community, nature, history; a case for five, by adding the convictor. Tillich, however, is *not free to choose* three or more elements, for he has tacitly committed himself to a semi-Hegelian system.[50] The two basic elements are supposed to be partly valid, partly nonvalid, like a Hegelian thesis and antithesis. The valid aspects have to be *aufgehoben* in a synthesis. In this way, the polar contrast between the two one-sided kinds of courage—the courage to be as oneself and the courage to be as a part—is *aufgehoben* in the courage to accept acceptance. In this manner the transcending movement is started which leads beyond all polar contrasts to being-itself.

Another trait which shows the arbitrariness of Tillich's approach is the use of the term "participation" in the polar contrast between individualization and participation. The last term goes back to Lévy Bruhl, who uses it, not in an ontology, but in an attempt to describe human attitudes; he places participation over against objectification. Several historians of religion, sociologists, and philosophers have been using these two terms and have shown their usefulness. Tillich could have used them too and could very well have added individualization as a third human attitude. He found it difficult to follow this course because of Hegel's influence upon his thinking. One of the three terms had to be left out in order to maintain the bipolar structure required by his system.

[50] Tillich's point of view is only semi-Hegelian because, though he uses the triad of thesis, antithesis, synthesis, he does not go on to use the synthesis as the starting point of a new triad.

c) It is difficult to state definitely what is actually, implicitly, God for Tillich.

(1) Tillich's explicit statements refer to the "God above God," the God whom we reach when we transcend theism.

(2) We have to say that being, being-itself, and non-being together form a divine realm. The interaction between these elements makes for a dynamic movement, a life-sustaining process within the godhead. For Tillich, God is the power of being itself. This interpretation is strengthened by the important role of the arrows in the two diagrams presented on pages 154 and 156. The arrows suggest two powerful circular movements (first diagram) which prevent the death of the All in a stagnant, arrested being. In the second diagram, the rising arrow suggests a powerful saving movement, a climbing up to the fullness of being.

(3) In another sense the universe, the All, being-itself, is God: for there is nothing which is really outside the realm of being for Tillich. "For everything that is participates in being-itself." [51]

(4) Furthermore, we can distinguish within the realm of being specific titanic entities to which superhuman powers are ascribed; these entities are personified, they become "goddesses." Non-being threatens.[52] Non-being is omnipresent, it stands behind insecurity, it actualizes itself (all these on one page!).[53] Other goddesses are Contingency, Ultimate Reality, and the Unconditional.[54]

d) The specific faith for the sake of which Tillich writes an apologetic is related to mysticism.

(1) This faith differs considerably from what modern Protestantism takes to be typically Christian. First, Tillich rejects the Christian conception of God in favor of the "God above God." Second, Tillich condemns definiteness, but the Christian faith tells of several definite acts committed by its God. Third, the God of the Christian faith is one about whom narratives are told. However, it would be difficult to say that being-itself led the chosen nation out of Egypt. Fourth, salvation is, according to the Christian faith, by Christ, and not by "understanding" (experience, courage). Finally, man, in the eyes of a

[51] *The Courage to Be*, p. 156.

[52] *Ibid.*, pp. 41, 51, 155, *passim*.

[53] *Ibid.*, p. 45.

[54] In *The Courage to Be* Tillich shows more restraint than in earlier works, wherein the number of deities created *ex nihilo* was much larger. At one place Tillich suggests an eschatological battle between the Titans Autonomy and Heteronomy (*R.G.G.*, 2nd ed., *s.v. Theonomie*).

Christian, is not a finite being but a creature, a sinner, a forgiven sinner.

(2) Tillich's faith is connected with the convictions of old Greek philosophy; these will be discussed in Chap. VI. We assume, however, that it can already be agreed upon that an important part of these Greek convictions is formed by the notion that man is a microcosmos. This conviction lies behind the fact that Tillich discusses both individual man and the world as a whole with the help of the pair of terms "potentiality-actualization." Again the term "unconditional" is used to characterize both God and a required attitude of man. We have noticed already that the term "transcendence" likewise indicates both the nature of the power of being and the right courage.

The microcosmos conviction is the basis of Tillich's doctrine of experience. This doctrine implies a very particular conviction about the nature of man and the nature of the universe, namely, the conviction that they are fundamentally akin, and that to such an extent that man (finite being) can "understand" the universe (infinite being, being-itself). These teachings imply a tacit doctrine of salvation. Salvation is by way of transcending experience, which leaves behind all particulars and definites, and climbs beyond all contrasts and gods to being-itself, or to God above God.

(3) It is not clear what Tillich means by his rejection of "the theistic objectivization of a God who is a being." [55] If he intends to point out here a weakness of the Hebrew-Christian faith, he could be proved wrong. A much more plausible discussion of this issue is offered by a modern historian of religion, K. A. H. Hidding, whose position will be discussed more fully in Chap. V. Hidding tells us that in the primitive and ancient religions God or the gods were thought to be identical with the cosmos or its very being. In other religions—namely, Judaism, Christianity, and Islam—God is considered to be wholly other than the cosmos. He is its creator, and not a part of it. This view of the relationship between God or gods and the cosmos has its implications for the problem as to whether man can *know* the gods, can understand the nature of the All. Hidding says that in the primitive and ancient religions the gods and the universe can be known by man, because the universe, the gods, and man participate in each other. In Judaism, Christianity, and Islam, man can *not know* God; a revelation in a law, a person, or a book tells man, not about God's nature, but about God's will.

If this account is right, Tillich's ontology is a rebirth of primitive

[55] *The Courage to Be,* p. 186.

religion; a man, a finite being, participates in being, even in being-itself, in the cosmos. There is nothing strange in the grouping of Tillich with primitive religion. He is not the only one who belongs in this milieu. According to Hidding there is no clearer account of the primitive High God than Karl Jaspers' *das Umgreifende* (the All-embracing). Furthermore, there is an example on quite another level; we have witnessed in the *Führer* the resurrection of the primitive tribal king, the representative of the High God on earth.[56]

4. *Some philosophical remarks about ontology*

a) We have to distinguish between various types of ontology. The first distinction is that between hard and soft ontology. By *soft* ontology we mean a cryptotheology which confines itself to the claim to furnish "understanding" of the universe, or of God, or of the nature of being. We call a cryptotheology a *hard* ontology if it moreover goes on to supply predictions about the future, on the basis of its "understanding." An example of soft ontology is Tillich's system. The clearest examples of hard ontologies are those systems which enabled people during the last war to "know for certain" that the war would end in a victory for the Allies. These systems guaranteed that "evil and injustice will not prevail in the end."

b) Another distinction to be made is that between various types of "understanding." "Understanding" can be furnished either by reasoning, or by experience, or by religious belief. We encounter *reasoning ontology* in idealist philosophies with an emphasis upon reason, for instance in Aristotle and Thomas. We find *experience ontology* in a variety of philosophies, which offer "understanding" by intuition, moral sense, feeling, and *Ahnung*. Tillich belongs here with his experience of courage. Another example is early liberalism, which based its theology upon "religious experience." It is not impossible that Tillich has never completely shaken off old-liberal influences. We meet *religious ontology* in those sections of Christianity which have been deeply influenced by Greek ontology, e.g., Thomas, Protestant orthodoxy, and a certain type of early liberals. It is probable that each of the three types—reasoning ontology, experience ontology, and religious ontology—can be found in both the hard and the soft variety.

c) We have to add one more member to the small series of the soft and hard types, namely, *double hard* ontology. To the characteristics of understanding the cosmos, and of predicting cosmic events, is added

[56] A. C. Garnett offers a philosophical criticism of Tillich akin to ours. Cf. his discussion of Tillich's *Biblical Religion and the Search for Ultimate Reality*, in *Encounter*, Vol. XVII No. 2 (Spring, 1956).

here that of influencing these events. Especially primitive religion is full of hard-ontological elements. The cosmic powers are not only "known" by meditation and speculation, but their workings can be understood also by augury, astrology, and the interpretation of oracles. We find that, moreover, the shaman and the priest, on the basis of their understanding, can *force* the cosmic powers to act in a certain way, by performing a rite, by praying, by ascetic acts.

d) It is scarcely necessary to add any reasons to those mentioned in the discussion of Tillich's system, as to why ontologies are unacceptable for an analytical philosopher. There is no guarantee that any knowledge or "understanding" of transempirical realities is possible. The combination of two facts—first, the nonvalidity of the ontological enterprise, and second, the high frequency of ontologies—asks however for an interpretation.

5. *Ontology and anxiety*

a) Ontology is an attempt to silence the anxiety evoked by the impression of unfathomable mystery which life makes upon man. The voice of anxiety is drowned out by persuasive and seemingly authoritative pronouncements about the structure of the universe. The impression of chaos, meaninglessness, and denial of value is overcome by projecting more order into the world than a nonontological person detects.[57] For this reason in periods of crisis ontologies sprout up like mushrooms. Hard ontologists are much more in demand in such eras than at other times. During World War II, people calculated the downfall of Hitler on the basis of the most divergent ontological systems. Some people applied biblical arithmetic, founded upon verses from the Apocalypse. Others sought solace in a book which interpreted texts taken from the pyramids, which were thousands of years old; they juggled the texts around until these documents "proved" that Hitler would die within a year.

It is not true to say that the crisis of the war only evoked new ontologies. The shock of defeat and occupation also revealed the presence and power of age-old ontologies. Some people saw their systems smashed to pieces; they either sought for new ones or gave up the attempt in defeat and bitterness. Other people felt their ontological constructions totter crazily like a building in an earthquake; they patched it up and even strengthened its foundations.

In a country like Holland it did not make much difference whether ontologists were churchgoers or not. The universe was seen as con-

[57] Compare Francis Bacon's aphorism xlv, "The human understanding is of its own nature prone to suppose the existence of more order and regularity in the world than it finds."

sisting mainly of two elements: a solid earth beneath, and the vault of heaven arching above it, protecting the earth and its inhabitants, guaranteeing their earthly and sometimes also their eternal destiny. The accompanying diagrams offer two examples of the way in which this basic pattern was elaborated.[58]

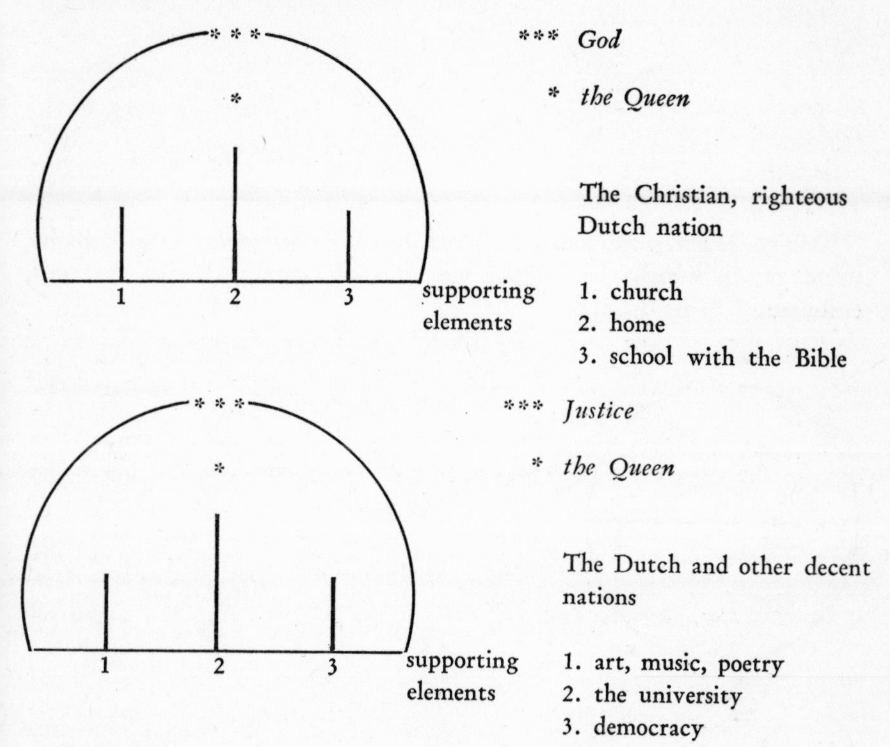

It is probable that there is no nation in which large numbers of people do not live by such ontologies. George F. Kennan pictures the national ontology of contemporary Americans in his *Realities of American Foreign Policy*.[59] Kennan refers to "two planes of international reality." "We found ourselves [in the postwar era] living in two different worlds: one world a sane and rational one . . . and the other world a nightmarish one, where we were like a hunted beast." In our terminology,

[58] After the Dutch army surrendered to the Nazis in May, 1940, a friend of our family was so deeply disturbed that he walked up and down the room, on and on. He cried out, "Where is Justice? I always have believed that Justice ruled the world! Justice has forsaken us!" This man, and others like him, had been sure that Justice (or God) would not have allowed the powers of evil, that is, the Nazis, to overcome the powers of goodness, that is, the tolerant, democratic (or truly Calvinist) Dutch nation. Their universe, their ontological system, collapsed.

[59] (Princeton, N.J.: Princeton University Press, 1954), p. 29.

this sane world is the national American ontological system; the nightmare world is the power which threatens to break up this familiar universe, and which therefore evokes anxiety.

Tillich's ontology is not so naïve as that represented by the preceding diagrams. Still, it is an ontology. Perhaps the following diagram would picture it satisfactorily.

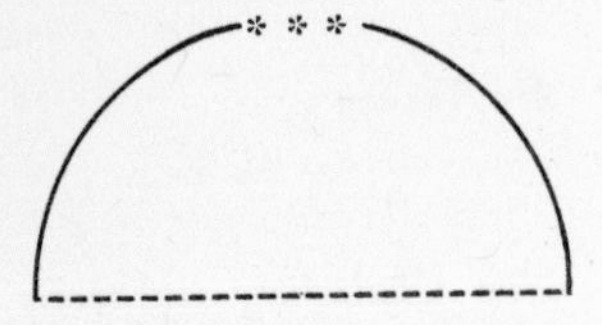

One could also make a case for the following representation of Tillich's ontology, in which the broken world is ultimately safe in the total embrace of Being-Itself.

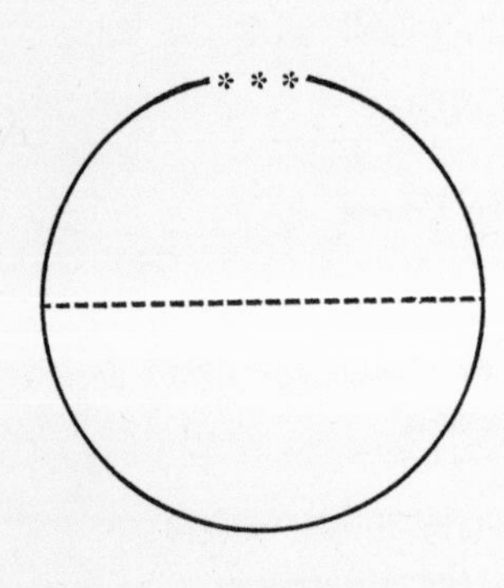

b) Ontology is not merely a matter of making philosophical mistakes; it is in the first place a symptom of a specific "way of being in the world," or more accurately, a specific way of being convinced, a particular way of being related to one's convictor, to one's fellow human beings, to one's world, to oneself. These relationships are seen in such a way that their totality offers a safe home to live in, a possibility to establish one's existence in a manner which keeps death and disaster at a safe distance.

c) Anxiety does not per se disqualify any of its products. Some ontologies represent the outcome of a person's serious struggle for meaning and value; he has been moved existentially, his whole being was involved. Such a system is not mainly a product of the playfully constructing intelligence, but expresses insights gained by painstaking convictional struggling with what are for such a man the deepest and highest realities. It would be boorish to deny that Plato's, Hegel's, or even Tillich's efforts are of this kind. This is undoubtedly true of the ontological convictions of primitive and ancient religions. Such ontologies demand our respect, even if we regard their method as invalid.

It becomes quite another matter, however, if we consider the ontologism of the people who *read* the works of Plato, Hegel, or Tillich, and in their anxiety cling to such systems, without anything comparable to the efforts of these thinkers. For such people an ontology is a temptation to stop thinking, an invitation not to work out their own convictions, meager and vague though they may be, but to accept too easily impressive structures of thought. It is to be feared that the attraction of many institutions, such as theological seminaries, political parties, and churches, consists at least partly in the fascination of the ontologies which they offer. Persuasive institutions and their impressive leaders, professors, statesmen, ministers, and priests, prevent people from forming their own convictions; that is to say, they keep them from becoming what they really are. A person who escapes into an ontological system is afraid to have his own convictions, to be himself, and he tries to become a more glorious person than he fears he is, by selling out to lofty convictional structures.

d) It is not to be overlooked, however, that anxiety also mars the lives of those who *create* ontologies. For the Aristotles, Schellings, and Tillichs, philosophy is a kind of savior, a guide to salvation by "understanding." Philosophy guides reasoning (Thomas), experience (Tillich), and religion (Hegel).

The divine, savior-status of philosophy is seldom fully admitted by these ontologists. If, however, this savior-like role is ignored or denied, the veneration and anxiety underlying it are revealed. Philosophers who think of their discipline as having a more mundane task, such as analysis, are treated with disdain. Empiricists, logical positivists, and others who deny that their task has such a divine character, are suspected of fouling their nest. That is the way in which philosophers such as Berdyaev and Tillich, and theologians like Emil Brunner, look at materialists, positivists, and naturalists. In their writings they never allow philosophers of these schools an honest chance. They either ignore them or disqualify them in short paragraphs.

Even a school like existentialism receives a remarkable treatment from Tillich. In his *Courage to Be* Tillich gives much attention to existentialism but leaves out those aspects of this philosophy which do not fit into his system. He mentions Kierkegaard but neglects to mention that Kierkegaard denounces ontology. He claims that for him Heidegger and Sartre represent existentialism but does not focus the reader's attention upon the strong antiontological tendencies in both men. He shoves aside Marcel as not really being an existentialist, and in this way gets rid of an opponent whose devastating critique of any "system" would have punctured his ontological balloon. In this manner Tillich can fit existentialism into his scheme by ignoring, to all appearances, the devastating criticisms implied in the works of these gentlemen.[60]

[60] *The Courage to Be*, p. 150.

APPENDIX

Antiontological tendencies in the Christian church

It is clear that religions, with their messages about the meaning of this life and the life hereafter, are wide open to ontological interpretations. Therefore, not the frequency of ontology in religion is remarkable, but the occurrence of antiontological tendencies. We will discuss here such tendencies within the churches participating in the World Council of Churches.

a) One of the most explicit examples is Reinhold Niebuhr's debate with Tillich, as it appears in one of Niebuhr's latest works.[61] He does not attack Tillich directly, but denounces the "efforts to comprehend history ontologically."

> Every philosophical effort to understand history is based on the assumption that in some depth of reality a pattern may be found in which that which seems "contingent and unforeseen" takes its place as a "necessary" development, as a servant of the hidden logic which underlies and informs all things.[62]

For instance, Niebuhr makes it clear that the "idea of progress" is based upon an ontology. If we may translate his arguments into our terminology, the conviction that life progresses to ever greater perfection is an implication of the conviction that the fate of reality is dependent upon a deeply hidden core, which is good, rational, and harmonious, and, furthermore, so powerful that it guarantees and establishes its own final victory. The crust of reality will peel off of itself (Western democracies) or it has to be peeled off by human beings (Russian Communism), so that the essential structure of reality will be gloriously manifested.

b) The implicit antiontological tendencies in the church bodies mentioned earlier seem to be more important than Niebuhr's more or less isolated discussion suggests. As far as I know, these tendencies can be noticed in the United States, Germany, and Holland. It is highly probable that they can be found in other countries too, especially in Britain and Sweden. We can speak of a *radical Protestantism* and say that it stresses the atheistic and agnostic aspects of the Hebrew-Christian faith.

(1) The interpretation of Christianity as an *atheism*. According to this radical movement, being a Christian in our time means, in the first place, to refuse to believe in the gods. If one listens to the discussions in some seminaries, the representative church press, and

[61] *The Self and the Dramas of History* (New York: Charles Scribner's Sons, 1955), pp. 49 ff.
[62] *Ibid.*, p. 50.

the publications of the World Council, one receives the impression that the vanguard of the churches involved constantly warns against the worship of the gods of the nations. These gods are: the sacred white race, the sacred middle class, the sacred proletariat, the sacred Western civilization, the holy Russian nation, the divine American way of life, the sacred labor unions, divine and untouchable capitalism, the goodness of man, the goddesses of education and progress, incarnations and bodhisattvas, such as Hitler, Lenin, and General MacArthur. Tillich would be the first one to agree with this warning, but it seems that Niebuhr's protest against ontology is much more in the spirit of this critical theology than is Tillich's creation of the goddesses Being, Non-being, and the Unconditional. The more sophisticated of the radical theologians add to the list of gods in which they refuse to believe Tillich's ontological entities and Berdyaev's noumenal world.

(2) The roots of the atheism of the modern Protestants lie partly in the immediate past. The radicals have been influenced very little, if at all, by any form of empiricist critique of metaphysics and ontology, but Freud and Marx have impressed them deeply. The unmasking of the hypocrisy of the complacent Christian and the worthy bourgeois, the demonstration of man's ineradicable inclination to project lofty structures of ideas behind which he hides his not-so-lofty desires, have made the radical theologian extremely wary of everything which looks like wishful thinking, or the facile surrender to illusions. We are, however, not allowed to overlook the fact that the most important source of the atheism of the radical Protestant is the prophetic trend in the Hebrew-Christian tradition. The very first of the Ten Commandments is the requirement not to believe in the many gods. The prophets sound their warning against the worship on the green hills; Jesus warns against the worship of Mammon. The early Christians were accused of *asebeia*, or godlessness, because they refused to worship the many gods of the Roman Empire, against which worship none of the various Hellenistic religions protested.

(3) The opponent of this atheistic trend in Christianity is *polytheism*. Polytheists are people who believe, not only in many gods, but in as many gods as possible.[63] The Christian world is full of such polytheism. The old liberals believed in God plus civilization plus

[63] We use the term "polytheism" in a typological, not in a historical, meaning. It is highly questionable whether this term is a useful tool in characterizing the primitive and ancient religions.

democracy plus science. The present-day churches are nearly completely polytheistic; people believe in God plus democracy plus the American way of life. Tillich's ontology shows this same character of "plus plus plus" thinking. He seems to believe in the God of the Bible (if He is transcended in the direction of the God above God), plus Being, Non-Being, the Unconditional, and several titans. To express it otherwise, he appears to believe in the gods of several of the theologies and philosophies which he has studied: neo-platonism of the Boehme-Schelling type, mysticism, the biblical tradition, Hegel, etc.

(4) Closely related to the atheistic trend in Hebrew-Christian thinking is the *agnostic* tradition. One of the cornerstones of the radical theology is the distinction between Calvin and Calvin*ism*, between Luther and Lutheran*ism*. Calvin and Luther intentionally avoided constructing theological systems which would *explain* sin and salvation, and would give a reasonable account of God and man, of Christ and the devil. Later Calvinist theologians, however, offered a rationale, in which everything was neatly explained. God's grace, which Calvin left a mystery, was by them subsumed under the "Law," which formed the framework for the rationale. Very soon, revelation was considered to consist of the communication of a set of divine truths, on the basis of which man could *know* history, know his own status, know the exact working of the divine mind. Present-day radical theology wants to go back to Calvin himself, and to stay free from Calvinism and orthodoxy.

An objection is obvious. Is it not a dangerous playing with words to call even this radical Protestantism atheistic and agnostic? Is it not more honest to call the Christian faith a monotheism, and does not this term imply the knowledge of this one God? If I understand the radical theologians well, their answer would run like this: "We do not think that it is accurate to say that the Christian faith is 'a religion,' or 'a monotheism,' because it is misleading to say, 'We believe in God,' 'We know God.' Such sentences are only fragments of confessional utterances, which in their entirety sound: 'God knows us, and therefore we know him'; 'God trusts us, and therefore we trust in him'; 'God places his hope in us, and therefore we hope in him.' The first halves of these sentences are the parts which really count; to leave them out, and to speak of 'our knowledge of God,' distorts the issue." The best way of characterizing the Christian faith according to this interpretation is to say that it is *an atheistic agnosticism with an appendix*: "God knows us and therefore . . ."

G. A RELATED ANTIMETAPHYSICAL POSITION

There are some philosophers who, in regard to the problem of metaphysics, take a position closely related to that set forth in the preceding section. One of them, William James, can be considered (at least in one of the aspects of his philosophy) as a forerunner of present-day analytical philosophy. Others, however, such as Reinhold Niebuhr and Gabriel Marcel, are definitely opposed to modern empiricism. Nevertheless, their thinking is, at least in regard to the problem at hand, much closer to that of analytical philosophers than either they themselves or the analysts are willing to admit. Here follows a short characterization of the position of Marcel.

1. *Gabriel Marcel*

Marcel is a stanch defender of "metaphysics," but the meaning of this term does not coincide with what is meant by the word in this chapter. Roughly speaking, Marcel's claim that a philosophy should be metaphysical means that, according to him, a philosophical account of the world of facts should reckon with the reality of the unseen, of the "Other World." This conviction seems to be far away from a logical empiricist attack upon metaphysics. We should notice, however, that Marcel combines this respect for the Other World with a fierce criticism of what he calls "the spirit of abstraction," and that this spirit is very closely akin to what we have called metaphysics. Marcel discloses that his revulsion toward the spirit of abstraction is one of the deepest roots of his philosophizing.[64]

a) Marcel distinguishes "abstraction as such" from "the *spirit* of abstraction." Abstraction as such is a perfectly legitimate and useful "mental operation to which we must have recourse if we are seeking to achieve a determinate purpose of any sort." It is an indispensable method in science, mathematics, and everyday life. Marcel points out that man cannot even get into contact with the concrete without help of abstraction. "What is given at first" is not the concrete but "a sort of unnamed and unnamable confusion." Therefore: "It is only by going through and beyond the process of scientific abstraction that the concrete can be regrasped and reconquered." [65]

b) Marcel characterizes the *spirit* of abstraction in the following way:

(1) This spirit operates by means of a dualistic procedure. On the one hand, one category is isolated from all other categories and accorded "an arbitrary primacy." There are, for instance, people who

[64] *Man Against Mass Society*, p. 1.
[65] *Ibid.*, pp. 115, 119.

interpret all human problems with the category of the economic. A Marxist interprets artistic creations by means of the economic structure of the period. On the other hand, all other categories are reduced to insignificance.[66]

(2) This procedure is not intellectual in its nature; it is "of the order of the passions." Marcel mentions only one passion, namely, that of resentment. Abstract assertions such as "*This* is nothing other than *that* . . ." are reductions to insignificance based upon resentment.[67]

(3) The abstractionist procedure reveals a mental imperialism. "Equality" is a term which belongs in the realm of mathematics. It "can not be transferred to the realm of beings without becoming a lie." Still, Marcel asserts that "equality" makes some sense in the human realm, namely, in regard to rights and duties. These "must be postulated as equal." Marcel gives in his book several examples of these procedures of "illicit extrapolation," an "illicit process of thinking." [68]

(4) The spirit of abstraction is contrasted with the legitimate procedure of abstraction in science, by accusing this spirit of consisting in a "contempt for the concrete conditions of abstract thinking." [69]

(5) The passions "that underlie the spirit of abstraction" are considered to be "among the most dangerous causes of war." They force people to deny human reality and dignity in their opponents and to replace human beings by abstract entities, such as "*the* Communist, *the* anti-Fascist." [70]

It is scarcely necessary to point out the basic agreement between Marcel's view and the analysis offered in this chapter. The metaphysical jump, pars. (1) and (3); the convictional character of metaphysics, par. (2); the personal (as distinguished from the intellectual) nature of metaphysics, par. (2)—all of these are either clearly indicated or suggested.

[66] *Ibid.*, p. 116.
[67] *Ibid.*, pp. 3, 116.
[68] *Ibid.*, pp. 116, 120, 93, 99, 126.
[69] *Ibid.*, p. 116.
[70] *Ibid.*, p. 117.

PART TWO

The Background of Modern Man's Language Structures

CHAPTER FIVE

MYTH

Primitive and Ancient Man Lived by Means of a Mythical Establishment

INTRODUCTION

Why is the problem of myth so important that we dedicate a whole chapter to its discussion? The answer is that myth is a crucial problem for many philosophers and theologians and for all historians of religion.

In contemporary philosophy, scholars such as Susanne K. Langer and Ernst Cassirer contend for the recognition of myth as a significant philosophical problem. Mrs. Langer, for instance, claims that man possesses two legitimate modes of expressing his experiences. She protests against those philosophers who give their attention exclusively to discursive symbolism (accounting for science, philosophy, analysis, abstraction, and literal truth). The other mode of expression, the non-discursive mode, deserves the serious interest of philosophers as well. This second mode deals with meaningful forms and "accounts for imagination, dream, myth and ritual." [1]

In theology the problem of myth has been made acute by Rudolf Bultmann, with his notion of dymythologizing the Bible, but other theologians also give a significant place to myth in their discussions. The problem of myth in the realm of theology has two aspects: the relationship between the "historical" biblical faith and the "mythical" religions, and the relationship between "historical" and "mythical" elements within the Bible.

In the field of the history of religions scholars had taken it for granted that myth was only a naïve, crude form of science entertained by primitive people, or the product of childish imagination. Since about 1910 some astute minds have asserted that the meaning of the words "myth" and "primitive" required considerable qualification. It is not at all self-evident what myth is.

The problem of myth has been presented to us, not only by the

[1] *Philosophy in a New Key* (Cambridge, Mass.: Harvard University Press, 1942); Pelican ed., 1948; in this edition, p. 116, see also pp. 35, 70-73.

dignified disciplines of philosophy, theology, and history of religions, but also by the not-so-dignified turbulent historical events of our era. The Hitlerite Alfred Rosenberg called his book *The Myth of the Twentieth Century*."[2] Apparently the Nazi leaders felt that the German nation could not "live" if it was not aware of its "myth," the glorious story of the splendid Germanic race with its great past. Perhaps most of the Nazi leaders did not take seriously the myth which they presented to their followers, but the majority of these were very serious indeed, and were ready to die for their myth. Here we are clearly miles away from the idea that myth is primitive science. The myth of the Aryan race and of *Blut und Boden* (blood and soil) expressed an idea that was precious for the believers, the most real, the most profound meaning of life.

However, if the Nazis lived for and by the power of a myth, should we not say the same thing about the Soviet Communists? What life is, and what it is for, are here expressed in the myth of the invincible proletariat which will redeem from oppression and misery not only this specific generation, not only the people of this or that nation, but all future generations and nations.

Further, do only other nations live by the power of myths and not we ourselves? The meaning of life is understood by many Americans in the myth of the bootblack who becomes a millionaire, of the newspaper boy who becomes president. Is not the cowboy hero a mythical figure, who singlehanded destroys white and red scum, rights the wrong, and saves the helpless innocent?

Myth is therefore an extremely important issue. We cannot gain a satisfying understanding, either of ancient or of modern man, without making clear to ourselves what meaning we should attach to the word "myth." Is mythical language convictional language, and if so, what are its characteristics? If myth is more than, or different from, primitive science, can we say that there is such a thing as a mythical way of being man, a mythical way of establishing our existence?

It is impossible to answer all the questions raised here, for the simple reason that an interpretation of myth which is generally accepted by philosophers, theologians, and historians of religion has not yet been formulated. It is my opinion that a profound new interpretation is offered by the most modern among the historians of religion. In this chapter we will try to understand a little of what these scholars say. A satisfying discussion of the problems raised by scholars like Bultmann, Cassirer, and Langer, and a real understanding of the modern "polit-

[2] *Der Mythos des Zwanzigsten Jahrhunderts.*

ical" myths, will be possible only after the findings of modern history of religions have been digested by philosophers, theologians, and political scientists. A thorough discussion between these groups of scholars has not even been started yet. Some simpler problems, such as set forth by the historian Frankfort, and the philosopher Holmer, will be treated shortly. A few remarks will be made about the relationship between mythical and biblical language.

A. THE PRESENT-DAY POPULAR UNDERSTANDING OF MYTH

1. *Interpretations of myth in some encyclopedias*

The meaning of mythical language can be satisfactorily discussed only if we take as our starting point the interpretation of myth which is felt to be self-evident by contemporary thought. We find these widely accepted interpretations in authoritative encyclopedias. The works are quoted in chronological order. The key terms of Eisler (1904) are: myth is the work of the "myth-forming phantasy"; further, myth is "a social product." The *New International Encyclopedia* (1916) calls myth "a form of folklore which sets forth as an historic tale the processes of nature or beliefs concerning cosmogony, religion, custom, tradition." *The Encyclopaedia of Religion and Ethics* (1917) says that most myths are "ætiological," and that they "grew up or were invented to explain certain phenomena, beliefs, customs, and names." *The Encyclopedia Americana* (1920) asserts that "during the pre-scientific ages, the greatest of all virtues was credulity in the . . . beliefs of the mass of one's fellows." It was the time "before the knowledge of the laws of nature came to replace the exercise of the imagination in the explanation of natural phenomena." Webster (1928) uses as key words "invented," and "not verifiable." *The Encyclopaedia Britannica* (1929) offers "based upon misunderstandings," "fancy," and "imagination," while some myths have been "purified of earlier crudities." It distinguishes between "rational and irrational" myths. The rational myths represent the gods as "beautiful and wise," whereas the irrational element "appears to the modern mind as senseless or repellent." *The Shorter Oxford English Dictionary* (1936) characterizes myth as "a purely fictitious narrative." Ferm's encyclopedia (1945) suggests: "fiction," "without understanding," "truth is hardly required"; we should not talk about myth "in terms of truth and error, because it is a stimulus to required behavior." *The American People's Encyclopedia* (1948) combines the usual characteristics (myths "entertain," "explain," "instruct") with new ones, "Myths awe the listener, who perceives in them a world that transcends and governs his own obvious universe." [3]

2. *Summary of the popular interpretation*

The generally accepted interpretation of myth considers it a mental phenomenon which is relegated to four domains of mental life, to wit: the intellectual, the moral, the imaginative, and the social. Furthermore, this interpretation contains strong elements of evaluation.

a) Some of the terms used disclose that myth is taken as an *intellectual* phenomenon: myth is an explanation of practices, of natural phenomena, of names, and of traditions. Also, myth is a kind of instruction. Other terms which relegate myth to this domain, while at the same time *evaluating* it as an unsatisfactory intellectual activity, are: crudities, irrational, senseless, prescientific, misunderstandings, not verifiable.

b) The terms which place myth in the *moral* domain all carry at the same time a negative *evaluation:* repellent (opposed to "wise and beautiful"), credulity, submission to beliefs of others.

c) Some of the terms which put myth in the realm of *imagination* seem to be merely descriptive: fancy, imagination, myth-making fantasy; whereas other terms reveal much more clearly a negative *evaluation:* fiction, fictitious, invented.

d) Terms which point to the *social* area are: neither true nor false but a stimulus to action, a social phenomenon, entertainment.

There is only one expression in all quoted definitions which places myth in the *religious* domain: awe toward a transcendent world. This fact should make us wonder whether the popular interpretation deserves the title "interpretation" at all. It begins by saying: "This phenomenon of myth which is presented to us as belonging to the religious realm actually does not belong there. We must bring it back to another realm." This procedure is highly suspect. It betrays an unwillingness to let the facts speak for themselves. A serious consideration of the nature of mythical language must begin by asking: What did the people who told and believed myths think about these stories? It is highly probable that the popular "interpretation" does not explain myth, but explains it away. This means that this "interpretation" reveals to us more about the views of the interpreters than about myth.

[3] R. Eisler, *Wörterbuch der philosophischen Begriffe* (2nd ed., 1904), *s.v. Mythos; The New International Encyclopedia* (2nd ed., 1916, Vol. XIV), *s.v. "myth"*; J. Hasting's *Encyclopaedia of Religion and Ethics* (1917, Vol. IX), *s.v.* "mythology"; *The Encyclopedia Americana* (1920), *s.v.* "mythology"; Webster's *New International Dictionary of the English Language* (1928), *s.v.* "myth"; *Encyclopaedia Britannica* (14th ed.), *s.v.* "myth and ritual"; *An Encyclopedia of Religion,* ed. Vergilius Ferm (1945), *s.v.* "myth"; *The American People's Encyclopedia* (1948), *s.v.* "mythology."

In the following section we will listen to scholars who have tried to attend to what the primitive and ancient nations tell us about their own myths.

B. THE METHOD OF MODERN HISTORY OF RELIGIONS

1. *Kristensen's method of history of religions*

Kristensen aims at an understanding of the "religious reality" as it is experienced by the believers themselves.[4] Man is moved by what is for him his god; man claims that his god reveals himself in a specific event, and man responds in a specific way and gives the event his interpretation. The nature of his response is expressed in certain myths, teachings, and celebrations. These are, at least partly, at the disposal of the historian, and he will use them to try to fathom their meaning. History of religions therefore does not assert that it is able to tell us who this god is; it wants to make us see what their religious life meant for the believers. They considered it a primary, absolute, infinite, ultimate reality—something which they knew better than anything else. The historian can know this "reality" only approximately.[5]

a) Here follows a more detailed account of the range and the possibilities of the historic method, according to Kristensen. His own tacit assumptions are the greatest enemy of the historian. He is nearly always motivated by the need to orient himself in history. He *wants* to find a historical framework either of a Christian or a rationalistic character, and thus he *does* find such a frame, because he not only describes the phenomena, but instinctively evaluates them and arranges them in a suitable pattern. A scholar who is prejudiced in this way cannot abstain from comparing the phenomena he is studying with norms which he, the scholar, brings with him from his modern (Christian and rational) world. "*This comparison is at the same time an evaluation*," and an arbitrary one for that matter. It measures primitive or ancient data with standards which are foreign to the primitive and ancient world. The result is that the scholar does not penetrate very far into the religious life he studies. What he finds is not a primitive or ancient belief, but pictures of his own twentieth-century problems. He cannot listen to others, he hears himself.

Kristensen stresses the distinction between two types of comparison: first, the above-mentioned comparison between a phenomenon and a

[4] W. B. Kristensen, *Symbool en Werkelijkheid* (Arnhem: Van Loghum Slaterus, 1954). Kristensen, 1867-1953, was professor of history of religions at the University of Leiden, 1901-1937.

[5] *Ibid.*, pp. 14, 29, 91.

norm or ideal, which is detrimental for historical research; second, the comparison between one phenomenon and another, which is indispensable in all scholarship. If one studies a Greek ritual dance, the comparison with a Roman dance is very helpful; a comparison with modern conceptions of dances and religion, which considers dances as light entertainment and religion as a serious business, will lead to an evaluation of the ancient dances as manifestations of a childish and "primitive" mentality and so make an understanding of the phenomenon impossible.[6]

b) Kristensen's denunciation of the scholar's inclination to impose his evaluation upon the phenomena does not mean that he believes that such a thing as a completely neutral historical science is possible. One cannot understand religious reality without "the creative work of our phantasy." "Phantasy does not mean here arbitrariness, or ignoring reality." It means sympathy with the people whose life we try to understand; empathy or the imaginative endeavor to put ourselves mentally in the place of these people; the willingness to give ourselves to the material we study, which is connected with "the willingness and ability to forget ourselves"; the insight which comes with this sympathy and empathy.[7]

c) Even the scholar who would have checked most of his own evaluations, and who would approach the ancient religions with rich empathy and have at his disposal the profound insights of sympathy, would not know the "religious reality" of these nations in the way they knew it themselves. We understand myths only by means of a *symbolic* interpretation. The ancient nations themselves understood their myths and rites in a *direct* way, which is for us inaccessible. In Greece and Crete "the life and fertility of the earth were ascribed to the 'bull of the earth.' This fertility was present in the horns of the bull." We may say that these sacred horns were the symbols of the fertility; "for the ancient nations the horns were its actual carriers." When these religions were in their prime they did not even possess a word for symbol. It is only in later periods of decline that poets and philosophers begin to explain the religion of their forefathers "symbolically." They then always reveal that they do not any longer understand the original meaning.[8]

d) Kristensen claims that whereas the ancient nations did not use symbols they did use figurative speech. Only by means of figurative speech is it possible to signify the divine, superhuman reality. A myth

[6] *Ibid.*, pp. 66 ff.

[7] *Ibid.*, pp. 25, 35, 75 ff.

[8] *Ibid.*, pp. 7-10.

tells us how Chronos sleeps in a cave on the isle of the blessed (in the realm of death) and "dreams the destiny of the world." Kristensen explains: "this destiny, the divine order of life, is a dream, i.e., a trans-empirical reality which is visible only in another world." Human beings can enter this other world "when they fall asleep after a ritual preparation," and dream. In their dream "they can discern the divine order and connection of all that happens; after awakening they can communicate their insights." This was called a dream oracle. "This myth of the sleeping Chronos is no construction of playful phantasy," no poetry or leisure time daydreaming, "but the figurative speech of a profoundly moved thinker." This kind of speech is indispensable, because the divine reality and the relationship between man's life and the cosmic order is ineffable.[9]

e) Kristensen's treatment of the ancient religions has had a revolutionary impact upon historical scholarship. The outcome of his methodical combination of sympathetic, imaginative empathy with being on his guard against modern prejudices has resulted in an interpretation of the religious life of ancient nations which is surprisingly new as well as highly plausible, of unusual depth as well as confirmed by the historical data at our disposal. The study of non-Christian religions has been deeply influenced by him, whether it concerns those of the ancient nations (Kristensen's own special field), those of the old Norwegians, the Eastern Asiatic nations, or the "primitives." His method has been considered of high scholarly standing, not only by men teaching in a theological department, like himself, but also by those teaching humanities. We have to ask how such a conspicuous success was possible, in view of the fact that his predecessors certainly did not lack in technical linguistic scholarship.

The answer to this question is suggested in the beginning of this chapter. Kristensen himself, however, makes several remarks which render the explanation much more specific. He refers not only to the influence of Christian apologetics, which is concentrated upon the defense of its own faith, but points out repeatedly how detrimental the rationalism of the Greek enlightenment has been. The Greek philosophers of the fifth and later centuries, Kristensen says, believed themselves to be spokesmen of a universal wisdom, which had been held true by all nations and all ages. It was therefore impossible for them to assume that there could exist any difference between their own teachings and the beliefs manifested in the old myths. "The truth which these philosophers thought they knew *must* have existed from eternity and

[9] *Ibid.*, pp. 19, 20, 99.

manifested itself in all ages, though in different forms. If they were 'only' interpreted in the right, i.e., symbolic way" and purified from "crudities" and "immoralities," "then it would become clear that the old gods and their myths taught the same truths as the Greek philosophers." The rational and moral ideals of the Greek enlightenment have deeply influenced Western civilization. This is the reason why so many scholars have seen the Greek and other ancient myths through the eyes of Plato and Plutarch, and thus arrived at very unsatisfactory interpretations.[10]

2. *Some examples of Kristensen's interpretation of myths*

We will take as an example Kristensen's interpretation of some myths centered around the god Hermes.

a) Kristensen first mentions the usual interpretation of Hermes as given by modern authors. He is a naughty god, a thief and a deceiver. His naughtiness can be easily understood, for he is the god of trade, "and the ancient merchants could not dispense with deceit and theft in their business." Hermes' immorality merely mirrors the immorality of the primitive Greek society.

b) Kristensen proposes to consider Hermes' theft and deceit as divine and not as human characteristics. Not only the poets but also the believers thought of him as a deceiver. "In Pellene, in eastern Achaia, [stood] an image of Hermes, who was *worshipped* there as *Dolios,* the deceiver." Who was this strange god? Several names under which Hermes was adored manifest his character of a god of the earth (*chthonios, erichthonios, phytalmios*); "he causes life to surge up in the vegetation." He is "the giver of good gifts," "the giver of blessings," for instance, when "he guides the Charites, the three goddesses of the blessings of life, from a cave" to the human world. Hermes brings Kore each spring from the realm of death back to earth. Hermes is therefore a savior, and the step from savior to healer is very small. "To be healed means" to receive life again, "to be resurrected from the dead."

The saving and healing aspects of Hermes point to his power. He is "the god of the word, that is to say, the magical word which signifies divine power and insight." "The insight meant here is that into the Cosmic Order, into the Eternal Life," into the mystery of life and death which rules human existence as well as the cosmos.

c) The deceptive nature of Hermes has to be understood against the background of his saving and life-giving activities. "Hermes has lured man to death by deceit." This is related in the myth of Pandora (she who gives all things). "Prometheus has stolen the divine fire,

[10] *Ibid.*, pp. 8, 9.

the principle of life," and brought it to man. "The gods first punish Prometheus and then man. This is achieved by sending Pandora to the earth." When she is created, "Hermes equips her with deceit and temptation, and guides her to the human domain." "People receive her with joy but soon detect that they are victims of her deceitful nature"; since her arrival they know disaster and death. In the vase which she brought with her all calamities were hidden and came out when it was opened. Only hope remained in it, at the very bottom.

Kristensen tells us that "the vase represents the realm of death." Pandora's gifts are therefore "what is hidden in the netherworld: cosmic Life, which reveals itself in the mystery of vegetation," and in the life which sustains man and earth. Man accepted Pandora's gifts, but forgot that "they are ambiguous." For cosmic life is not just human life, but also implies what we call death, and even resurrection. He who desires divine gifts and accepts them, has to die. He has to take the divine life which he craves, in its entirety; he has to accept not only its blessings, but also the disaster and the death which form an integral part of the total, cosmic life.

The ancient Greeks acknowledged and affirmed the ambiguity of the mystery of cosmic life. They worshiped Hermes, because without his deceit, participation in this life would have been kept from them.

Hermes' theft has a similar meaning. Orestes had fallen into the hands of the Erinyes, after he had murdered his mother. Apollo and Hermes save him from dementia and death. "Apollo cures and purifies him. . . . Hermes brings him back to the realm of life." "The Erinyes are furious. . . . 'You have stolen the murderer from us,' they cry." The meaning of the myth is that "what belongs to death can be released from it only by 'theft.' Resurrection is a theft committed towards death." Hermes' insight signifies his "grasp" of what is "most difficult to obtain: Life hidden in the realm of death." [11]

d) Another important Greek deity was Athena. Her attributes are the serpent, the owl, the "tree of destiny," her status of virgin, the *peplos* she weaves, and her wisdom. The problem is how to make sense out of this series of seemingly unrelated elements.

Kristensen claims that they are more intimately connected than appears at first sight. For instance, both the owl and the serpent reveal Athena as the goddess of the realm of death. The owl announces death by its cries, and the serpent belongs to the netherworld and represents the life of the earth which arises in a mysterious way out of this realm.

[11] W. B. Kristensen, *Verzamelde Bijdragen tot de Kennis der Antieke Godsdiensten* (Amsterdam: Noord-Hollandsche Uitgevers Maatschappij, 1947), pp. 118 ff.

"The destiny which is connected with the tree is determined in the kingdom of death; . . . this destiny is the Law of Life for man and cosmos, and comprises both death and life." This tree is a gift from Athena to her people, the *polis* of Athens. The gift means that "the life which the goddess grants her people is imperishable because it originates in the realm of death."

Athena's most revealing name is *Parthenos,* the virgin. This title had a very specific, sacred meaning in the ancient Greek and Roman religions. The virgin is not opposed to the mother but is identical with her. If a goddess is called a mother, it means that she causes the cosmic life to arise. If she is called a virgin, the divine, mysterious aspect of her activity is emphasized: as a divine being she does not need any outside help to bring forth life. All necessary power is at her own disposal.

Finally, Athena is the goddess of art and wisdom. She is, however, not a patron of the art of Phidias. "Her art is that of creation." Athena "creates Life, cosmic and human Life." "Her art is at the same time her wisdom," for she is not a patron of philosophy or science, but the possessor of insight in the mysteries of life and death.[12]

3. *The nature of myth*

a) Myth does not refer to something imaginary, but to what was reality in the eyes of those who told and believed the myth. That is to say, if we assert that there is no realm of death, and that Athena and Hermes are the figments of the fantasy of the ancient Greeks, we are introducing our own convictions into our research. It is beyond all doubt that their myths expressed the ancients' belief about what really existed, their convictions about the meaning and value of human and cosmic reality. The ancient Greeks noticed the change of the seasons, the rhythm of life and death; they noticed animals, planets, and human communities. "Notice" does not mean here scientific observation, but a consideration guided by convictions. The Greeks "saw" this visible world and an invisible world in a specific way in which both were very real for them. As scholars and philosophers we cannot say at all whether they were mistaken or not. We have only to try to understand what they themselves meant.

b) The myths refer especially to what was for the ancient people *true reality*. In the realm of true reality the nature of life and world, the meaning of human life and of everything else, has been established once and for all. The myths tell that Psyche marries Eros, and Kore marries Hades. Both Eros and Hades are "gods of death and resurrection." These divine, "mythical" marriages are "the proto-type . . . of

[12] Kristensen, *Het Leven uit de Dood* (Haarlem: Bohn, 1949), pp. 188-200.

each human marriage." They tell us what human marriage "really" is and means: marriage is "an initiation into the mystery of death," that is to say, of cosmic life.

Perhaps we may say that the true reality sometimes is approached in temporal, at other times in spatial categories. A temporal category is, for instance, that of the Primary Age. For the ancient Egyptians a victory in war was not so much a military or political "fact" as a rite, a celebration, a repetition of the victory which the gods, in the Primary Age, had won over their enemies. This primary, "mythical" victory made possible the cosmic order of things, cosmic life and therefore also human life. The human victory merely reaffirmed and manifested the "mythical" triumph over the enemies of life and order.

The spatial categories used to designate the true reality are, e.g., the netherworld, the cave, the ocean, the island of the blessed, the western horizon (where the sun sets, and enters the realm of night and death in which the cosmic life has its origin).

c) Mythical language is picture language and story language, simply because it is impossible to speak of true reality in any other way.[13]

4. *The message of myth*

Kristensen's analysis of the nature of myth has thus far made clear that we cannot separate the nature of this language from the message it implies: a belief that the visible world receives its meaning from an invisible Reality. We will try to spell out in more detail some of the major aspects of this message.

a) The conception of *death* occupies a very striking place in all ancient religions. "Death has two aspects, everywhere he appears, in the cosmos or in human life: he is the arch enemy, but at the same time the only complete form of true life." In Egypt "death is first of all the enemy of the gods," just as darkness is the opponent of light. "Each morning the serpent (Apap) is vanquished and bound by the gods . . . at the eastern horizon." This view of death is accompanied by "a dualistic conception of the relationship between life and death. . . . Both elements are independent, they are powers in their own right, though life possesses the greatest power and the highest right." The dualistic conception is, however, never the only one, and is not even the ruling conviction. It is more than balanced by a monistic view: death also means eternal, cosmic life. "Death is in reality the condition of life, of absolute Life." "Death is an element, be it the most important element in the self-revelation of Life. The dualism between life and death is therefore merely an appearance"; death is not really an enemy.

[13] *Symbool en Werkelijkheid*, pp. 7, 13, 14, 18-20.

Kristensen claims that the Egyptians did not try to minimize the tension between the monistic and the dualistic conceptions, to sacrifice one to the other. They knew that they were confronted by a mystery which could not be clearly expressed, without contradictions, in human language and thoughts. Set, the enemy of Osiris, the god of life, is also his brother; he is an evil power, but he is also worshiped.[14]

b) Cosmic life is virtually identical with *cosmic order*. The Egyptian goddess Ma-a-t, corresponding to Themis of the Greeks, means the divine order by means of which world and man exist. Ma-a-t is repeatedly connected with words which mean "truth," "reliability," i.e., that which characterizes the order of life. One text says: "Creator of the world, receive Ma-a-t. Thou livest by her grace. Thou existeth through her and she through Thee. . . . She is the solidity of Thy dwelling."

The cosmic order is many times represented as a cloth, a tapestry, a net. The net "comprehends heaven and earth"; that is to say, there is nothing accidental in what happens anywhere in the universe. Everything has its place in the divine plan (Babylon, Egypt). The woven cloth, either created by a god (Athena) or presented to a deity (Marduk in Babylon), is connected with the gods' victory over the powers of Chaos. Kristensen interprets: "The cosmic Order comprises downfall and ascension." The order also implies "the Law of Life for gods and men"; it is divine justice (Ma-a-t, Themis), which is here "not so much a moral or a legal term as a cosmic, sacred word," meaning "the 'right' way of life for all the universe." [15]

c) This last sentence reveals that the most striking characteristic of the cosmic order, or law of life, is its *supramoral* nature. Kristensen claims that this supramoral element is typical for all ancient religions. We have already met it in the myths of Hermes. The terms "theft" and "deceit" are not terms of moral disapproval; they do not condemn but praise, and they are not moral but religious in character. In an unforgettably vivid, unsurpassably trenchant way it is proclaimed here that the divine order is totally different from the human way. A behavior which would be immoral in human relationships is the highest grace in a god.

This point of view does not mean a slighting of morality in itself. Human beings have received their moral law, and the gods are pleased if they live in accordance with it. The point is that human moral law and human moral behavior do not possess an independent value. This

[14] *Het Leven uit de Dood*, pp. 14 ff.

[15] *Ibid.*, pp. 70 ff.; 81 ff; *Symbool en Werkelijkheid*, pp. 103, 115 ff.

moral law derives its validity and authority from the gods. The gods themselves, however, are not bound to the human moral law. The wisdom and the justice of the gods are beyond the accounting of human judgment.[16]

5. ***Mircea Eliade's treatment of myth***

One of the leading scholars in the field of history of religions is Mircea Eliade, a Rumanian, who has lived in France and England for the last decade. He is very close to Kristensen, both in method and results. We quote from his textbook on history of religions only those characteristics of myth which have not been stressed by Kristensen.[17]

a) One of the contents of the mythical message is the conviction that man mirrors the nature of the cosmos. Innumerable myths of the ancient and also of the primitive religions tell us about the creation of the cosmos from the cosmogonic egg. Eliade relates how myths and rituals in Indonesia and Polynesia express the belief that "man is born from an egg" too. He states that this means that the cosmogony serves as a model for the anthropogony, that the creation of man imitates and repeats that of the cosmos.[18] This conviction points in the direction of the philosophical doctrine of microcosm, the notion that man is a "small cosmos."

b) Eliade makes some remarks concerning the general character of the mythical approach to reality.

(1) The term "mythical" applies not only "to what people *tell* about certain events which took place and about certain persons who lived in the Primary Age, but it refers to everything which is related, directly or indirectly, to those persons and events." Eliade warns us therefore to dissociate ourselves from the notion that myth is exclusively word, fable, story.[19]

(2) We err if we take the terms of mythical language in a profane, modern sense. "A 'woman' in a mythical text or in a rite is not a female of the genus *homo sapiens,* but the embodiment of a 'cosmic principle.' " If, furthermore, gods are described as bisexual, that means that, "in the bosom of divine reality cosmological principles which seem to be mutually exclusive are combined." A spiritual reality is expressed "by means of biological terms." [20] We have to add to Eliade's statement the consideration that according to Kristen-

[16] *Symbool en Werkelijkheid,* pp. 37 ff., 74.
[17] *Traité d'histoire des religions* (Paris: Payot, 1953), pp. 350 ff.
[18] *Ibid.,* p. 353.
[19] *Ibid.,* p. 355.
[20] *Ibid.,* p. 359.

sen's view the ancient nations did not make the distinction between "natural" and "spiritual" which is for us so self-evident. Eliade's expression "biological terms" is therefore misleading. It should be "what seem *for us* to be biological terms." For the rest, his remark is very trenchant. It reminds us of Kristensen's position, that terms such as "theft" and "deceit" may not be taken in their profane or moral sense, but have to be understood as conveying a sacred meaning.

(3) Eliade claims that mythical language possesses a multiple truth. The Polynesians relate how Io, the High God, created the world by his words. A Polynesian of our time explains all the implications of the god's words. The words which Io pronounced to form the universe are also employed "in the rites which must make fertile a sterile matrix." "The words spoken by Io to create the light which vanquished darkness are also employed . . . in the rites which have to heal men from impotence and senility, . . . to cheer up a despondent heart, and to inspire those who have to compose chants." [21] Kristensen would agree; he would say that all mythical notions possess such a multiple meaning. The netherworld *is* also the realm of death, also the realm of the birth of new life, also the hiddenness of spontaneous life. The bull *is* also divine fertility.

c) Eliade has some remarkable things to say about the degradation of myth. He claims that myths can survive "as epics, as ballads, in novels, . . . as superstitions and habits." He considers Ulysses, Parsifal, Faust, and some of Shakespeare's personages as descendants of the mythical heroes, and sees also relationships with the "tests" and sufferings of the young men who had to undergo initiation rites. The isle of the blessed survives in Camoëns' and in Daniel Defoe's creations. This view of Eliade concerning the survival of myth is connected with his thesis that myths represent "archetypes" which are ineradicable.[22] It seems doubtful as to whether Kristensen ever would have lent himself to such far-reaching conclusions.

6. Hidding's anthropological method

K. A. H. Hidding is a disciple of Kristensen. He accepts Kristensen's method but wants to undergird it with an anthropology. His ideas are related to the work of the French philosopher M. Merleau-Ponty.[23]

[21] *Ibid.*, pp. 350, 365.

[22] *Ibid.*, pp. 367-70.

[23] *Mens en Godsdienst* (Delft: Gaade, 1954). Hidding, born in 1902, has been professor of the history of religions at the University of Leiden since 1948. M. Merleau-Ponty, *Phénoménologie de la perception* (Paris: Gallimard, 1945).

a) The foundation of Hidding's anthropology is the thesis that "man can stand in the world in two different ways." First, man can live "as a part of the cosmic reality and participate in it." Second, man can live as a being who considers himself not merely a part of the world but also "differs from it and transcends it in his mind." The first attitude is called the *participating* structure of living, the second one the *objectifying* structure. Participation is oriented toward the body, objectification toward the mind.

b) For the participating structure, "*reality* is alive"; man is surrounded by "many kinds of powers with different qualities." He participates in the mysterious cosmic process which is manifest everywhere—in the vegetation, the heavens, in man's community life, in the animals. "By means of augury, astrology or contemplation, man tries to receive insight into the cosmic events." He has to get acquainted with the powers in order to deal gently with them; without such respectful treatment no man could live.

In the objectifying structure man "is aware of his independence." "The cosmos is not the living, mysterious reality which completely determines his life," but something from which man can dissociate himself and "make it the object of scientific research." Qualities are reduced to quantities.

For the participating structure "*community* is primary to the individual." Traditions, rites, taboos, celebrations, settle and prescribe man's behavior. In the other structure, the individual is primary. Man is free, critical of the world and of himself.

God means something totally different to people living in these two structures. For the first attitude "the Totality of the Cosmos," the cosmic order is divine. The various gods are only aspects of this all-embracing Reality. Or, God is the hidden Power which sustains everything and continually creates and re-creates all things. For the other attitude, the cosmos is not God himself, but his work, and therefore different from him in principle. God is the Wholly Other than his creation and his creatures, and is therefore unknowable by them. If they can speak of him at all, that is because he has revealed himself in a sacred law (Israel), a sacred book (Islam), or a sacred person (Christianity).

Sin is, for the one way of living, "a disturbance of the cosmic Order" by trespasses upon the laws which make human community and cosmic life possible. For the other mentality, the effects of an action are not important but "the motives and intention of the person who acted."

The participating and objectifying structures are not mutually exclusive. Neither an actual person nor an actual religion can live exclusively according to one structure. There are only different emphases.[24]

c) We do not have room enough for a full discussion of the merits and implications of this approach. At this moment two things need to be said. First, Hidding uses the term "objectification" not convictionally, as a term of abuse, but as a means of analyzing human behavior, man's "stand in the world." This procedure differs sharply from that of some contemporary philosophers, such as Berdyaev, who identify objectification with the fall into sin. Second, it must be asked whether objectification means the same thing in the case of the scientist who separates himself from certain elements of reality as objects, and in the case of the deities of Judaism, Islam, and Christianity, who create and maintain a distance toward their creations. It is not impossible that these two kinds of objectification are related, but the differences and the kinship have to be clearly elaborated.

7. The mythical establishment

In the first part of this book we have said that our analysis pertained only to the languages of modern man, of the Western civilization. *Homo loquens, homo convictus* is a characterization, not of man in general, but in the first place of modern man and perhaps also of other men. Do the ideas set forth by Kristensen, Eliade, and Hidding throw some new light on this problem? In other words, can we say that primitive man knows a convictor? Further, does primitive man establish himself as a person in drafting convictional world views?

The following remarks are merely a suggestion. Their tentative character should be emphasized. Our knowledge of primitive man is still too superficial for us to speak in any other way.

a) Prudence seems to require that we speak about man establishing his own existence only in regard to modern man. Perhaps we may say that primitive man does not so much establish his existence as *live in an establishment*. This establishment is characterized by the following traits:

(1) It is mythical; that is to say, the human establishment is supposed to be a replica of the cosmic establishment which was set up in the Primary Age. Hence the human establishment shares the characteristics of the cosmic order: it is unchangeable, total, eternal, etc. Instead of persons establishing their individual existence, the primitive view shows us the gods as having established the existence and order of the whole cosmos, once and for all.

(2) Hence this cosmic establishment should not be questioned. Doubt and criticism would undermine the cosmic order.

[24] Hidding, *op. cit.*, pp. 12-23.

(3) It is an establishment in which, after the cosmos, the group is important, not the individual.

(4) The establishment is a structure ready for man to enter into. This availability is a characteristic of all language structures, but here the convictional world view is self-evident and "natural" for the believer in a nearly complete manner.

b) In contrast with the mythical establishment modernity can be depicted as follows:

(1) There is not one view, but many, and of no view can it be proved beyond doubt that it possesses exclusive right and authority. The realization of this fact came as a great shock to the people of the West. Sometimes it took an era of civil and religious wars before the transfer from one to the other mentality could be made. In this regard Western civilization remained primitive until the seventeenth century.

(2) There are not only many world views, but they are of different kinds, such as convictional and indicative views.

(3) Some convictional views (those which we have called "open") have discarded the desire to offer a picture of the world which is all-embracing. Instead of giving a place to everything in a total Whole, they leave question marks and gaps.

(4) Hence, establishment becomes a highly individual matter. Becoming a person implies a convictional struggle in which doubts, rebellions, decisions, and affirmations play an important role. A person does not merely share the beliefs of his environment. He is responsible, not only for his behavior, but also for his convictions, that is, for what kind of person he is.

(5) There is little in modern man's convictional world view which is self-evident. This world view does not develop naturally, but results from much (convictional) thinking, is influenced by personal and group conflicts, and is partly a response to decisive events in the life of a person, his group, his nation.

(6) Modern man's establishment is therefore always threatened. Other people, other convictions, unforeseen events, may overthrow it. The element of threat is also known in the mythical establishment, but there it is canceled in advance. Death is part and parcel of the cosmic rhythm; demons and titans have already been conquered in the Primary Age.

(7) This means that modern man always takes account of the possibility of a disestablishment of his existence, and the necessity to re-establish it. Actually, in a given person's life the aspects of dises-

tablishment and of re-establishment will seldom be completely absent.

c) This picture of modernity is incomplete. Modern man is possessed by an indomitable yearning for the protective Home which the mythical establishment offered the believers. He resents the characteristics of the modern situation, that is to say, of his own situation, of his own existence. He shrinks from the acknowledgment that there may be many views and even views of a different nature. He is thoroughly tired of questioning, doubts, and self-criticism, and the never-ending struggle to find a more satisfying establishment.

Therefore he listens avidly to the men who present themselves as guides and saviors, offering a world view which is "natural," unquestionable, and comprehensive, and which therefore comes close to the comfortable Home of the mythical establishment. Ontological and theological systems hold out to modern man abodes which are fashioned to re-create the dreamlike quality of a lost paradise.

Perhaps Freud meant something of this kind when he spoke of man's craving for the mother's womb, or for death, or for not-yet-life, where there are no disquieting problems.

Logical empiricism and existentialism are revolutionary movements in philosophy because these schools claim that it is not the task of philosophy to reconstruct a lost paradise by intellectual means.

C. MYTH AND HISTORY

1. *Myth and Bible*

What impact do the views of the modern history of religions have upon our understanding of the Bible? The word "myth" has been widely used in this connection. People have said that "naturally" stories such as those of the Creation, about Adam and Eve, about Abraham, Joseph, and Moses, did not "really" happen but that they were "only" myths. The difficulty with such a statement is that it takes for granted that myth may be opposed to reality. If there is any truth at all in the approach of modern history of religion this is an erroneous supposition. This tacit assumption reveals to us something about the convictional world view of the man who entertains it and leads us away from the understanding which the biblical believers had of their own stories. We have to raise the question in a new way, one which is in tune with the methods of the modern scholars.

a) We are helped by a new approach of some contemporary biblical scholars. G. Ernest Wright and Gerhard von Rad defend the thesis "that the earliest confessions of faith which the Old Testament contains are recitals of the saving acts of God." [25] The title of Wright's book is *God Who Acts,* instead of the customary "God who speaks," because the center of the biblical message is formed by God's acts, whereas the word of God "is the accompaniment of the act." The theology of the Bible is then understood as based upon the *story* of these acts, upon "the confessional recital of the redemptive acts of God in a particular history." In setting forth this thesis the author attacks the characterization of biblical theology as constructing a "system of ideas," as "propositional dogmatics," and "the systematic presentation of abstract propositions or beliefs about God, man and salvation." [26]

b) This thesis of Wright and Von Rad raises the question as to the exact nature of the relationship of mythical language (as discussed in Sec. B) and one of the biblical languages, that of "the earliest confessions of faith." Both languages are story languages; both tell about the saving deeds of God or gods. The problem is to determine where this biblical confessional language and mythical language are similar, and at what points they show fundamental differences. Some of the similarities, besides the story-character already mentioned, are as follows: First both languages are "concrete, poetical, metaphorical, picturesque." These terms are used by G. E. Wright for biblical language,[27] but they apply just as well to mythical language. Second, both languages invite the listener to understand himself and his destiny in the light of the Primary events related by the "story." Wright says: "The worshipper listens to the recital and by means of historical memory and identification he participates, so to speak, in the original events." [28] This reminds us of Kristensen's statement that the ancient Egyptians interpreted their military victories in terms of a victory in the Primary Age.

A basic difference between mythical and biblical language has already shown itself in what is just said. Some words of the quotation from Wright's book do not apply to mythical language, namely, "by means of historical memory." All biblical thinking is dominated by a "historical" conception of God, which will not be found in religions which are not derived from the Bible. This conception carries the conviction about a God who is the directing and driving power behind all history, a God who cannot be understood at all without taking into account his saving activity in the history of men and nations. These "historical" religions are not oriented toward the rhythm of the seasons, and the life of

[25] G. E. Wright, *God Who Acts: Biblical Theology as Recital* (London: SCM Press, 1952), p. 70.

[26] *Ibid.,* pp. 12, 13, 32, 35.

[27] *Ibid.,* p. 32.

[28] *Ibid.,* p. 28.

vegetation; they claim that God cannot be known in that way, but only by accepting the specific revelatory meanings of specific historical events.

However, Eliade makes a remark which should prevent us from asserting too easily a classification of religions into a "historical" and a "natural" group. Especially Christian theologians are wont to claim that the "natural" religions do not have a concept of history at all. This is, at its very best, an imprudent assertion. The ancient religions and those primitive religions of which we possess something which approaches satisfactory understanding, all entertain very definite convictions about history. It would not be correct to say that they think in terms of two dispensations, the Primary Age and the present era, for the mythical time is "eternally present." [29] "The man who celebrates a rite, in a certain sense transcends the profane time, as he does profane space." Myth and rite reintegrate man in a nontemporal age, beyond history. Eliade's most fortunate formulation runs: "Primitive man knows history not in the modern meaning of the word (events which are irreversible and non-repeatable), but as an exemplary history which can repeat itself, either periodically or not, a history which finds its meanings and value in the very repetition itself." [30]

Eliade's remarks seem to be highly plausible and lead us to the following considerations. First, the basic difference between the so-called historical religions and mythical language has to be maintained to a certain extent. Judaism, Christianity, and Islam reckon with historical events in a way which no other religion shares. These events are dated concretely, as the Hegira, A.D. 622; the birth of Christ; the exodus out of Egypt, *circa* eleven centuries B.C. Second, whereas the primitive's profane time is evaluated only lower than the mythical time, the "historical" religions know besides a positive evaluation: the profane time is considered good enough by God to be the receptacle for his sacred acts. This time is therefore no longer merely profane. Third, whereas many modern men who are not Christians are inclined to think of the Christian conception of history as naïve and primitive (how arbitrary, they say, to ascribe decisive meaning to a small number of historical data), Eliade's last remark about the nonrepeatable character of time shows how close the modern and the Christian understanding of time actually are. Fourth, Eliade's discussion points to the fact that the "historical" religions (and this holds especially for Christianity) entertain not one but two conceptions of time. Periodical repetition is, e.g., repre-

[29] Eliade, *op. cit.*, p. 366.
[30] *Ibid.*, pp. 366-67.

sented by the church year, with its seasons of Advent and Lent, and its festivals like Christmas and Easter. The distinction between historical and primitive religions is therefore not clear-cut, and we should beware also of proposing that the distinction between mythical and biblical confessional language is a simple matter.

There is, however, enough difference between these languages so that we should be careful with our terminology. It appears that we are in need of three terms: one, to characterize the story language of biblical confessions; a second, to characterize the story language of the ancient and primitive religions; a third, to use as an over-all term for both of the above, as well as for other languages which possess similar characteristics. Biblical scholars have to decide about the first term, whether recital or kerygmatic language is the best. The obvious term for the story language of the primitive religions is "mythical." The over-all term could be either "story language" or "narrative." "Narrative language" will be used by us to indicate this kind of language, which in many respects differs so much from statemental and propositional language.

2. *Does the language of "historical" religions contain indicative elements?*

We still have to deal with a problem raised by P. L. Holmer (Chap. I, Sec. C-7). Holmer asserts that religious language contains sentences which are cognitive of historical events; furthermore, that belief in the truth of these sentences is not a part of faith itself, but is required as a condition of faith. This view seems to be incompatible with the insights which we have gained in this chapter. The languages of the Hebrew and the Christian faiths certainly contain sentences which refer to historical events, but they belong to "narrative" language. This holds both for the sentences which occur in the Bible and for the sentences repeated at the present time. If a Christian says: "I believe that nearly twenty centuries ago Jesus Christ lived, and died, and rose again," he does not intend to make a cognitive statement, but to repeat the old recital, be it in an abbreviated and flat form. This is not to deny that the sentence has some cognitive implications, but these are not the focus of the believer's interest.

What is required in the Hebrew and Christian faiths is therefore not a belief in the truth of cognitive sentences, but a willingness to repeat the old recital. Such sentences are not primarily cognitive but convictional. The belief in them is not a condition of faith, but an integral part of it.

D. A TYPICAL MISUNDERSTANDING OF MYTH

The implications of the new method in history of religions appear more clearly if we compare this approach with different points of view. We take first, as an illustration of an orientation widespread but out of date, the Penguin edition, *Before Philosophy*, of *The Intellectual Adventure of Ancient Man.* [31]

1. *Frankfort's account of myth*

a) We will not follow the method used elsewhere in this book of first allowing the author to speak for himself and then adding our comments. We suppose that the book is well known, and we start immediately with our discussion. Hereby we refer only to the title, the subtitles, the preface, and ch. i, "Myth and Reality," which are presumably written by H. Frankfort. First, we will try to analyze Frankfort's position, and formulate it in two theses. Second, we will offer an appreciation of the validity of these theses.

Thesis I: Frankfort treats religion as a kind of thought. Frankfort thinks of religion in terms of thought, religious thought. Notice the repetitious use of the term "thought" in expressions such as "mythopoeic thought," "religious or metaphysical thought," "emotional thought," "speculative thought." [32] Notice further the leading role of related terms, such as "intellectual," [33] "problem," [34] "question and answer." [35] Thesis I is not contradicted but affirmed by Frankfort's reference to the I-Thou relationship, for this is called "a mode of cognition." [36]

The key term of the whole discussion of myth and religion is "explanation." [37] A strong emphasis is placed upon the problem of "causality," "asking for causes." [38] Myth is seen by Frankfort as an attempt to "answer" certain "intellectual problems," that is, to answer them, not by means of modern science (which is introduced by the terms "analysis," "conclusions," "universality," "theoretical statement," "justifica-

[31] *The Intellectual Adventure of Ancient Man* (Chicago: University of Chicago Press, 1946). *Before Philosophy: The Intellectual Adventure of Ancient Man, An Essay on Speculative Thought in the Ancient Near East*, by H. and H. A. Frankfort *et al.* (Penguin Books).

[32] *Op. cit.*, pp. 7, 8, 19; subtitle.

[33] *Ibid.*, subtitle, p. 14.

[34] *Ibid.*, pp. 14, 17, 36.

[35] *Ibid.*, p. 17.

[36] *Ibid.*, p. 13.

[37] *Ibid.*, pp. 15, 19, 24, 25, 26, 27, 28, etc.

[38] *Ibid.*, pp. 23-29.

tion before the critical"), but by means of an "explanation" in which the whole man, i.e., also his emotions and imagination, participates.[39]

Thesis II: Frankfort uses the mental structure of modern man as the measure of what is normal, as the standard of evaluation. Frankfort notices that modern man approaches the world in several ways, e.g., the scientific and the speculative. He assumes arbitrarily that the ancients must have striven for these same approaches, and that, if these approaches cannot be found in explicit forms, they must have been implicit in ancient man's dominant attitude to the world, to wit, in religion and myth. "The ancients told myths *instead of* presenting an analysis."[40] The very first sentence of the first chapter begins, "If we look for 'speculative thought' in the documents of the ancients. . . ," and thus reveals the twentieth-century framework in which the religion of people who lived twenty-five centuries ago will be "understood," i.e., forced.

Frankfort takes for granted that ancient man's mental habits must be interpreted as leading up to ours, preparing the way. This is strongly suggested, for instance by the book's title: *Before Philosophy!* This view is a parallel to one still found in some Christian circles, that Plato's philosophy has to be understood as a preparation for the Christian gospel, or that the meaning of the non-Christian religions is to be discerned as a preparation of the heathens for the Christian faith. Frankfort sees the mentality of modern man as the outcome of an evolution, a series of steps manifesting the development of man's thought. Notice "one step farther," "the next step."[41] The development moves into the direction of a decrease of fantasy and an approach to autonomy.[42] Notice further the statement "The Greeks *evolved* critical from mythopoeic thought."[43] The main steps of the progressive series are: religion-speculation-science.

The picture of modern man given by Frankfort shows a hierarchy of elements, which not merely describes but at the same time carries an evaluation:

(1) The highest element is science, i.e., thought purified from non-intellectual elements (emotions, volitions, fantasy) and therefore autonomous. Modern man equals scientific man.[44]

(2) Somewhat lower in value is speculative thought, which has to respect "the sacred precincts of science." It must not trespass on the realm of verifiable fact."[45]

[39] *Ibid.*, pp. 14-16.
[40] *Ibid.*, p. 15. Italics mine.
[41] *Ibid.*, pp. 17, 18.
[42] *Ibid.*, p. 17.
[43] *Ibid.*, p. 8. Italics mine.
[44] *Ibid.*, pp. 12, 14, 30-35.
[45] *Ibid.*, pp. 11-12.

(3) Decidedly lower are emotions and fantasy. See ". . . tainted with fantasy." [46]

(4) Religion, whether Christian or other, does not play a perceptible role in Frankfort's picture of modern man.

b) We will now offer an appreciation of Frankfort's two theses. Both theses are not the outcome of a scholarly attempt to understand ancient man, but are the result of an interpretation of ancient religions which is highly colored by a specific convictional world view, especially by particular convictions about the nature of man and the meaning of history. Kristensen and Eliade disclosed that ancient and primitive man were motivated in their religious life by the mystery of death, longing for salvation, the status of human goodness in relationship to the will of their gods, and the desire to worship other-than-human reality. Frankfort has not seen anything of the like, but is convinced that man, both ancient and modern, is characterized by, first, curiosity, intellectual interest (hence "adventure" in the subtitle); second, the desire to increase his security. Because Frankfort has not been able to keep these convictions in check, because he was not suspicious of them, he read them into ancient man and thus misinterpreted him. He thus found in primitive man merely a more naïve modern man. It is not difficult to understand why this happened. Frankfort's conviction about man is implicit; he is not even aware that his thinking is guided by it; he thinks that his way is self-evidently the right way to appreciate man.

Thesis I further presupposes that the ancient religions are actually no religions at all. Frankfort does not offer any serious discussion of central religious elements like worship, prayer, the conception of salvation. He just takes it for granted that he may discuss religion in terms of mental attitudes, and assert that primitive religion is such an attitude in which the intellectual element is still (!) intermingled with emotional and volitional elements. This procedure is the arbitrary reduction of one thing (religion) to another thing (thought). It does not explain, but explains away. It is not the outcome of a careful, scholarly investigation of the facts at hand, but an assumption unquestioned because unrecognized. This procedure has been dictated by the same implicit convictional world view which we noted above. These convictions which interfere with the scientific process are generally related to rationalism, and, more specifically, to nineteenth-century positivism.

Auguste Comte described the development of man's mind in three stages. In the first stage (religion), man explained natural phenomena by means of supernatural beings; in the second stage (metaphysics), by

[46] *Ibid.*, *p.* 11.

means of invisible entities, such as essence, substance; in the third stage (science), by means of discussion of observable facts. Frankfort is not so critical of the second phase as pure positivists are. He gives a diluted positivistic theology of history. Perhaps it is more accurate to say: Frankfort shares the popularized positivistic theology, which is what people of our period call "common sense." [47]

Frankfort's ch. i reveals to us more about his own mentality than about the mentality of ancient man. It is not so much a scholarly publication about some non-Christian religions, as a convictional utterance, a theology of the popular section of the modern Western world. Actually it is a cryptotheology, because the convictions are presented in the disguise of a nonconvictional, scholarly treatment.

E. THE "METAPHORICAL" CHARACTER OF RELIGIOUS LANGUAGE

The insights gained in this chapter can throw some light upon the problem of metaphor.

1. *The traditional view*

It is usually taken for granted that religious language possesses a metaphorical character. This holds both for Christians and for those who are critical of religious beliefs. It is pointed out that in the Christian language God is referred to with the help of terms such as "Father," "King," "Rock." These terms are not literally true; therefore (so runs the conclusion), they must be metaphors. Let us see what contemporary logic has to say about the term "metaphor."

a) A clear discussion is to be found in Beardsley's *Practical Logic*. He discusses metaphorical statements and metaphorical noun phrases. Since the latter can easily be transformed into the first, we will confine ourselves to the statements. Beardsley claims that "a statement is 'metaphorical' if it has both of the following characteristics: First, it must be *literally* false. That is, the subject cannot possibly have the characteristic *designated* by the secondary term. . . . Second, a metaphorical sentence *may* be . . . true on the level of *connotation*." Beardsley further discusses the concept of "dead metaphor." In this case

> we mean something that was a metaphor but is not any longer. "Spinster" is a "dead metaphor." Once it designated *a person who spins* (man or woman). Then, because most such people were unmarried women, it came to connote

[47] It has to be said that the positivism mentioned here is not the totality of logical positivism, but the elements C-I and C-II discussed in Chap. IV, Sec. E-2.

that characteristic. But when it began to be used very widely in contexts that emphasized this connotation, the connotation became to be so closely linked with the word that *unmarried woman* became the standard meaning, or designation.[48]

b) If the term "metaphor" is used to characterize religious language, sometimes another element of reasoning is connected with that just mentioned. This new element is the distinction between public language and some languages which can be understood only by certain persons. Religious language then belongs to the last group. This distinction is used to explain the "metaphorical" use of terms such as "king" and "rock." The fundamental meaning of these terms is considered to be the literal one, belonging to public language, i.e., understandable for everybody. The metaphorical use, which points to some particular connotations of the term "rock," is supposed to be derived from public language. For instance, the following connotations of "rock" are supposed to play a role in the religious metaphor: permanence, relative immovability, capacity to provide shelter.

2. *Discussion*

a) Indicative language is so widespread, and its "objective" character so much appreciated that many people simply call it "public language." They take this for granted as the self-evident starting point for linguistic discussion. There is a danger in this way of thinking. Indicative language is certainly not public in the sense of being completely objective, not related to a particular group. It pertains undeniably to a specific group; it is the language of educated people in the Western civilization from about 1600 or 1700 until the present. This means that we need to reject any suggestion that indicative language supplies a standard, with which to measure the validity, rank, or plausibility of other languages, in this case, religious language. Such opinions are convictional in character; indeed they are of a type that must be disqualified as metaphysical, i.e., claiming objective authority, while actually inspired by specific convictions about the value of convictional language.

b) Let us proceed to specific examples, and take, e.g., the term "king." It is impossible to understand its religious meaning by starting with a so-called literal meaning. It is better to begin with the convictional meanings of this word. The primitive and ancient nations who knew kings did not consider them in a "literal" way, but were *convinced* that kings were half-gods, representatives of the Highest God, incarnations of such a Highest God, a god in disguise. This was the

[48] (New York: Prentice Hall, 1950), pp. 101, 102.

case in ancient Egypt, in China, among many ancient and primitive nations. In the Hebrew nation the concept was different, but here also "king" was a convictional term. Though the king was considered not as a half-god, but as a human being, he was still closely related to God, still his representative, a man to be anointed as priests were anointed; a man with a specific, divine calling; a man with a religious function.

c) What could be called, inappropriately, the literal meaning of the word "king," e.g., a male sovereign, a monarch, is an abstraction. In the countries of the Western civilization the convictional aspects of the term "king" have been discussed during two or three centuries, have been criticized and, to a large extent, rejected. But this process has not gone as far in one country as in another; in different lands and for different groups of the population the word "king" does not have the same meaning.

The main point to be taken into account is that a philosopher should abstain from evaluating this process of "deconvictionalizing" terms such as "king" and "father." There are people—for instance, romantic theologians—who consider the process as mainly evil. Other men, such as those who adhere to Enlightenment convictions, attach to the process the value of a liberation from bondage. Everybody has a right to his convictions, but they should not enter into a man's philosophy.

d) This means, in regard to terms such as "king" or "father," that there is not one meaning which is self-evidently the right or the fundamental one. In the case of "father" we can say, for instance, that the term has a specific meaning in biological language, another in legal language, another in the moral languages of most Western nations, still others in the confessional languages of various religious groups. We should be very careful in claiming *necessary* connections between these various meanings, though one could probably show that, e.g., the moral notion of "father" shows traces of influences by the Hebrew-Christian conviction about God being our father.

Similar things are true for the term "king." This word has kindred meanings in the legal languages of the constitutional monarchies of some Western European nations. It has other meanings in the political convictions of the same nations, for instance the king being a symbol of the traditional values of such a nation. The term has other meanings again in the religious languages of the various confessional groups of these nations, different again among Roman Catholics, fundamentalists, liberal Protestants, nationalists. Again, it can be shown that traces of the Hebrew-Christian convictions about God's kingship or Christ's rule are not without influence upon the legal and political usages.

None of these usages gives *the* authentic meaning, either in the case of the term "king" or in the case of the term "father."

One of the implications of our discussion is the insight that the traditional use of the term "metaphor" is meaningless in a discussion of the meaning of religious terms.

e) Some philosophers will reject the above argument by claiming that they are not interested in historical but only in logical relationships. Such an objection begs the question, for it has to be asked whether logical analysis can provide a proper approach to convictional language. Our discussion (just as the remarks in Chap. I, Sec. D) implies an argument for the thesis that logical analysis cannot do this. We have to say that this analysis is an appropriate tool for the understanding of indicative language, but that it cannot help us out, either for an elucidation of convictional language, or for the clarification of the relationships between convictional and indicative language.

CHAPTER SIX

COSMOS

Enlightened Man Establishes His Existence by Means of the Greek Cosmos Conviction

A. INTRODUCTION

In order to get a better understanding of the languages spoken in our present-day civilization, we need a more detailed and concrete analysis of the various convictional world views of our age. This more concrete understanding is necessary, not only in view of the problem of convictional language, but also for a better appreciation of other languages. It will be one of the main theses of this chapter, that the languages of science, politics, and most philosophy are dependent upon one specific convictional world view, which will be labeled the "Greek cosmos conviction." In order to show the wide range of this world view, we will first analyze the convictions of a poet and essayist, Ralph Waldo Emerson, who is important as a representative of a modern form of this world view.

1. *The convictional world view of Emerson*

a) The first thing we notice when we read one of Emerson's essays is the fact that he arranges his key terms in two fields; the terms of one group are charged with an outspoken positive evaluation, while the terms of the other carry either a negative or a weak positive evaluation. We take as an example the first essay, "History":

Strongly Positive	Less Positive
thought (3)	fact
laws (4)	fact
first man (4)	epoch . . . kingdom, empire, republic . . . are merely the application
immortal sign (8)	fact
Eternity; own mind (8)	Greece, Palestine, Italy
unity (9)	difference

intrinsic likeness (10)	accidents of appearance
intellect . . . vision of causes (10)	surface differences
life (10)	circumstance
unity of cause (10)	variety of appearance
the soul; genius (11)	time . . . magnitude . . . form
same thought (11)	troops of forms
one moral (11)	twenty fables
spirit . . . alone omnipotent (11)	bruteness and toughness of matter
identity (12)	diversity
center (12)	surface
one man, same character (12)	many acts
very few laws (13)	innumerable variations
divine model (14)	lame copies
true ship (14)	(suggested: actual ship)
eternity (21)	time passing away
truth (22)	the confusion of tradition and the caricature of institutions
metaphysical history of man (28)	the history . . . of the external world [1]

We do not give a full account of the facts if we say that what Emerson offers here are "conceptions" of history, of man, of nature. It is clear that he, by means of these contrasting values, expresses his *convictions* about the meaning of life, the destiny of man, the value and meaning of history. In other words, Emerson offers us a theology, and we may call it a cryptotheology because he is apparently not fully aware that he is presenting a specific set of convictions.

b) The first article of this theology is the belief in a god, called the universal mind. It is "the only and sovereign agent." The man who searches after truth "finds that the poet was no odd fellow who described strange and impossible situations, but that universal man wrote by his pen a confession true for one and true for all." "The universal nature, too strong for the petty nature of the bard, sits on his neck and writes through his hand." [2]

The second article of faith is the conviction that individual man is a small universe. His glory is that he shares in the universal mind. "There is one mind common to all individual men. Every man is an inlet to the same and to all of the same. . . . Who hath access to this universal mind, is a party to all that is or can be done." (The opening sentences of the essay.) "Of the universal mind each individual man is one more

[1] *Essays*, First and Second Series (New York: The Nottingham Society, n.d.), I, 3-32. Figures in parentheses refer to page numbers.

[2] Emerson, *op. cit.*, pp. 3, 24, 27.

incarnation." "It is this universal nature which gives worth to particular men and things." [3]

The doctrine of identity is an implication of the first two convictions. ". . . we *are* Greeks." "A great boy . . . *is* a Greek." "Prometheus *is* the Jesus of the old mythology." [4]

c) Perhaps the most decisive conviction is that which divides both the universe at large and man's small universe into two parts: a core and a surface layer. The core is characterized by such terms as thought, immortal, eternity, unity, spirit, divine, and truth; and the surface, by fact, time, diversity, accident, appearance, variations, many, and matter. Emerson's convictions arrange themselves into a *world view* in the fullest sense of the word. Guided by his convictions he "sees" a universe with a divine core; this core is eternal, unchangeable, true, and real; it is surrounded by a crust which is submitted to time and therefore changes and offers endless variations to the eye which does not penetrate further.

d) With the help of this convictional world view, Emerson establishes his existence. He himself *is* this eternal man, this Greek. It is as this universal man that he encounters the world and interprets his own life.

Emerson is the *enlightened* man, whose light is kindled by the World Light and who in his turn illuminates his world. The enlightened man is man-who-speaks, who by means of his word enlightens the world, confused and darkened by traditions, so that the light of his word can make life transparent. In this luster the hidden center becomes visible in all its glory; it is "brought to light."

The convictional world view with the help of which the enlightened man establishes his existence is called the *Enlightenment*. The Enlightenment is one of the outstanding language structures available to Western man to establish his existence.

2. *The range of this convictional world view*

The preceding paragraph implies the suggestion, which later on we hope to support by evidence, that this world view is not only Emerson's, but has also been, speaking generally, that of the majority of the people of Western civilization since the beginning of the eighteenth century. To the extent that it is one of their basic conditions, it has deeply influenced modern science, modern social and political "thinking," and

[3] *Ibid.*, pp. 4, 5.
[4] *Ibid.*, pp. 19, 21, 24. Italics mine.

several other aspects of modern Western civilization. However, since the First World War, and in some ways since an even earlier date, it has been losing its power over Western man. Several other convictional world views are competing for its place.

3. *The origin of this convictional world view*

A further suggestion says that the origin of this view lies far back, in the age of the great Greek philosophers. It inspired the work of Plato and Aristotle, and that of the "philosophical" schools such as neoplatonism and stoicism. This convictional view has entered the Western world in various forms and at various times (the medieval church, the Renaissance, the Enlightenment), so that it may be called one of the major sources of Western civilization. In this chapter we will first try to trace this conviction in the classical philosophers, and then discuss the forms in which it has influenced the West in our own age.

B. THE GREEK COSMOS CONVICTION

1. *Plato*

a) If we analyze a portion of the *Republic,* we notice how Plato's argument is built upon a series of contrasting terms which carry positive and negative evaluations.[5] We take, for example, a section from Bks. II and III, from 376-E to 399-E. The terms express convictions regarding the state, man, and the cosmos.

I. THE STATE

PLUS	MINUS
1. ***Aspects of ideal state***	1. ***Aspects of bad state***
norms, canons, laws, 383-C	
2. ***Means to reach such a state***	2. ***Elements which block coming of ideal state***
education, corrected (*passim*)	education, traditional (*passim*)
tales true, 376-E	tales false, fictitious, 376-E
supervision, 377-B	chance teachers, 377-B
what passes censorship, 377-C	opinions, 377-B
mold and stamp youth, 377-B	
expunge praises of Hades, 386-D	
simple narration, 394-A, 396-E	imitation, especially of unworthy things 394-A, 396-E

[5] Tr. P. Shorey (Cambridge, Mass.: The Loeb Classical Library, 1953).

3. ***Role of purified religion in education***
attribute the true quality to God, 379-A

3. ***Education endangered by impure religion***
badly portray true nature of gods, 377-E
relate divine revenge, suffering, 378-A
relate divine wars, 378-B
say that God causes evil, 380-B
say that gods change their shapes, 380-D
say that gods deceive us, 381-E

II. MAN

1. ***Ideal man***
a) *civic man*, 379-A
founders of state know patterns
benefit of state supersedes trust, 389-B
b) *guardians*
god-fearing, godlike, 383-C
craftsmen of civic liberty, 395-C

1. ***Dangerous types of man***
poets, 378-E
the multitude, 379-C
women, 388-E

2. ***Virtues***
soul, brave and intelligent and least altered by external affections, 381-A
brave, 386-A
sufficient unto himself, 387-D
self-control, 389-D
obedience, temperance, 390-B
to practice one pursuit only, 394-E
orderly and brave, 399-E

2. ***Vices***
prone to laughter, 388-E
fear death, 386-A
believe in reality of Hades, 386-E
sensitive and soft, 387-C
excited by passions, 390-C
laxity in turpitude, 392-A
imitating a variety of people, 394, 395

3. ***Rule of the mind***
ruler of bodily appetites, 389-E
endurance, 390-D
austere, 398-A

3. ***Rule of passions, pleasure***
acceptance of bribes, greed, 390-D
disposed toward what is merely pleasure, 397-D

III. THE COSMOS

1. ***Real***	1. ***Unreal*** imitation
2. ***What abides*** simple, not departing from your form, 380-D	2. ***What passes*** to be altered by something else, 380-E to be changed by time, 381-A (manifold, variations, changes, 397-C, D)
3. ***Order*** impossible for a god to wish to alter himself, 381-C harmony, 398-D life, speech, and tune must possess same order, 400-A	3. ***Disorder*** polyharmony, 399-D
4. ***The gods, the divine*** good in reality, 379-A simple and true in deed and word, 382-E	4.

b) Just as characteristic for the structure of Plato's "thought" (read: convictions) as the contrasting of positive and negative terms is the grouping together of terms which share the same evaluation. In the section 400-C through 402-C we notice

seemliness, good rhythm, fair diction, and good disposition of the soul.

On the other hand,

unseemliness, bad rhythm, bad diction, and bad disposition of the soul.

Further,

gracelessness, evil rhythm, disharmony, evil speaking, evil temper

are "akin to" each other, in the same way that their opposites are "the symbols and the kin" of each other. Again,

true beauty, grace, and health are guides "to friendship, and to harmony with beautiful reason." Also soberness, courage, liberality, and high-mindedness.

Again,

"there is a coincidence of a beautiful disposition in the soul and corresponding and harmonious beauties of the same type in the bodily form."

Finally,

right love is "a sober and harmonious love of the orderly and the beautiful."

c) The evaluations are applied not only to man, the state, and the cosmos, but are extended to everything thinkable. Rhythm, goodness, and gracefulness, or their opposites, will be found in painting, all craftsmanship, weaving, embroidery, architecture, and the natural bodies of plants and animals.[6] Literally everything participates in the positive or in the negative aspects of the universe. Furthermore, everything belongs to one or more series of "correspondencies," i.e., corresponding values. The universe is a well-ordered structure, in which everything is related to everything else, and occupies its place in the positive or the negative domains of the All.

This convictional view of the All is very trenchantly formulated in another section of the *Republic:* 475-E through 477-A. Plato pictures here two worlds, and two types of men, each corresponding to one of the worlds. World A is fair, honorable, just, and good; world B is base, ugly, unjust, and bad. Man A is a lover of wisdom, capable of apprehending and taking delight in the nature of the beautiful-in-itself. He knows that which *is*. Man B is a lover of spectacles and arts, a man of action. He does not know, but entertains mere opinions, beliefs. In 480-A Plato calls man A: *philosophos,* the lover of wisdom; and man B: *philodoxos,* the lover of what can merely be believed.

d) One more trait has to be added to the picture. It suggests a hierarchy. Plato speaks of the *idea of good* "by reference to which just things and all the rest become beneficial and useful." [7] The knowledge just mentioned of the philosopher should not tempt us to assume that even this man can have adequate knowledge of it. Plato seems to convey to us the notion that, lofty and august, the idea of the good will always remain shrouded in mystery, even for the philosopher. The idea of good is reality par excellence and "you must conceive it as being the cause of knowledge and of truth, in so far as known." [8]

e) One point already mentioned deserves special emphasis. The sec-

[6] *Ibid.*, 400-E, 401-A.
[7] *Ibid.*, 505-A.
[8] *Ibid.*, 508-E.

tion beginning with 376-E discusses education and claims that here censorship of fables is needed. The fable (*muthos*), "taken as a whole, is false, but there is truth in it also." Censorship is needed in order to separate the true from the false element. The false element presents the gods in a way contrary to their true nature: they take revenge, suffer, quarrel, battle, and change their forms. The true element: God is good, "of course." Therefore young people must not learn that "Zeus is the dispenser alike of good and evil to mortals," for God cannot be the cause of all things, but only of the good. God is "simple and true in deed and word." [9]

f) An issue which seems to be different from those we have touched upon up to now is the peculiar role of geometry in Plato's convictional thinking. Geometry was appreciated by Plato, not only for its own sake, but especially for what we could call its revelatory character. What the nature of the really Real is can be understood only through mathematics. Illustration of this thesis can be found all through Plato's work. We refer only to some well-known examples.

In the simile of the line the relationships between the world of appearances and the intelligible world, and between the various forms of knowledge and opinion, are discussed with the help of a geometrical scheme.[10] In the *Gorgias* Plato discusses a group of "arts" and of corresponding "shams" or "flatteries," in the context of a consideration of the relationships between the soul and the body, and of the merits of rhetoric and sophistry.[11] The right way to understand the correspondencies between arts and shams is, according to Plato, to think "after the manner of the geometricians," as follows:

as tiring : gymnastics : : sophistry : legislation

and

as cookery : medicine : : rhetoric : justice

The convictional color of the whole discussion is clearly revealed by a group of invectives used for one of the flatteries: "knavish, false, ignoble, illiberal, working deceitfully."

A very revealing utterance is to be found in another place in the *Gorgias*, where Plato upbraids an opponent with the words "But al-

[9] *Ibid.*, 379-A, -E, 382-E.
[10] *Ibid.*, pp. 509 ff.
[11] In *The Dialogues of Plato*, tr. by B. Jowett (New York: Random House, 1937), I, 465.

though you are a philosopher you seem to me never to have observed that geometrical equality is mighty, both among gods and men." [12]

It is no wonder that the study of mathematics occupies a central place in the education of the philosopher-king. The absolutely certain, unchangeable, and eternal knowledge of mathematics is, for Plato, the model of all knowledge which deserves that name. To this conviction about the nature of knowledge has been added the corresponding conviction that the real, true nature of all that exists is also of such a kind that man can approach it in a mathematical way; in other words, this nature is also mathematical, that is, unchangeable, universally valid, safe from decay and doubts, and highly elevated above the sordid, tangible world.

g) These short remarks on Plato do not pretend to be exhaustive in any way. They certainly do not offer a full picture of Plato's main purpose in the *Republic*, for we have barely mentioned "justice" and all the implications of this term. Our intention was different: to show that Plato's "thinking" was ruled by a group of convictions, which formed a well-ordered whole, a convictional view of man and universe. Further, we do not claim to have offered a complete account of this convictional world view. We have merely tried to demonstrate that even a superficial glance at Plato's work reveals the presence and the important role of such a set of convictions. We do not claim that our remarks are more than an invitation to the classicists among the philosophers to give, in all its depth and all its shades of meaning, a full picture of Plato's convictional world view (which probably has suffered in our schematic presentation).

There is, however, one thing which we may present here as a further suggestion. Are not terms such as epistemology, ethics, cosmology, metaphysics, and ontology misleading? What we have observed leads us to conclude that Plato's view about knowledge and opinion is very much informed by his *convictions* about the nature and destiny of man, about good and evil, about the meaning of life, and about the nature of the universe. Henceforth, we cannot discuss Plato's epistemology without first setting forth his convictional world view. The same thing holds for the other "branches" of his "philosophy." As a consequence, the study of Plato (and of any philosopher) requires three stages:

(1) The investigation of his convictional world view

(2) The setting forth of his epistemology, ethics, logic, ontology, etc.

(3) The consideration of the relationships between his convic-

[12] *Ibid.*, p. 508.

tional world view and his standpoints in the various philosophical disciplines.

It has to be added that what we have called Plato's convictional world view has to be qualified further as an implicit view.

2. *Aristotle*

Aristotle's work is as much dominated by convictions as Plato's and shows the same structure.

a) Throughout the work of Aristotle we find everywhere the arrangement of terms into two groups—one in which the terms carry a positive evaluation, another where the evaluation is either negative or weakly positive. Here follows a double series from *On the Heavens*, Bk. I, chs. ii and iii, 269-a-20 to 270-b-26: [13]

Positive	More or Less Negative
perfect	imperfect
naturally prior	
substance, prior, more divine	the formations we know
nature	the unnatural
continuous and eternal	pass away quickly
beyond, different, separate from the bodies	the bodies that are about us
ungenerated, unalterable	alteration, increase, diminution
unaging, immortal	
nature of the gods, anything divine	

Another place where the same arrangement of terms can be noticed is his *Metaphysics*, Bk. XII, chs. vi and vii, 1071-b to 1072-b:

Positive	More or Less Negative
substance	existing things
unmovable, eternal	physical
movement, continuous, circular	
cause change	undergo change
actuality	potency
without matter, eternal	matter
moves without being moved	
real good	apparent good
produces motion as being loved	move by being moved

b) We find again in Aristotle a second structural element of Platonic convictional thinking, the grouping together of terms charged with the same evaluation. In ch. vii of Bk. XII we notice:

[13] *The Basic Works of Aristotle*, ed. Richard McKeon (New York: Random House, 1941).

something which moves without being moved, being eternal, substance, actuality[14]
exists of necessity, its mode of being is good, a first principle[15]
God, actuality of thought, life, self-dependent, most good, eternal [16]
supreme beauty, goodness, present at the beginning[17]
substance, eternal, unmovable, separate from sensible things, without parts, indivisible, infinite, impassive, unalterable[18]

c) A third element of the structure of Platonic convictional reasoning occupies an important place also in Aristotle's work: the placing of the argument within a geometrical frame. In *On the Heavens* Aristotle reasons as follows: "Now let E stand for the ungenerated, F for the generated, G for the indestructible, and H for the destructible. As for F and H, it has been shown that they are coincident. But when terms stand to one another as they do . . . then E and G must needs be coincident." [19] Aristotle claims that, first, the relationships between the terms of the positive column among themselves, second, the terms of the negative column among themselves, and third, the relationships between the two columns, possess the character of mathematical necessity.

d) In regard to the problem of myth Aristotle assumes a position similar to Plato's. He distinguishes between a "first point" in myth and later additions. The first point is the thought that "the first substances" were "gods." This point is "an inspired utterance," which has been "preserved until the present," while arts and sciences have come and gone. The additions, however, have been formed "with a view to the persuasion of the multitude." [20]

e) Aristotle says that he differs from Plato on several important issues. One of these is the question whether there is anything contrary to Wisdom. Aristotle claims that Plato is obliged to assume that there is something of this contrary nature, and he considers that assumption a weakness. "For there is nothing contrary to that which is primary; for all contraries have matter, and things that have matter exist only potentially." [21]

[14] 1072-a-25.
[15] 1072-b-11.
[16] 1072-b-26.
[17] 1072-b-31.
[18] 1073-a-3-12.
[19] *On the Heavens,* Bk. I, ch. xii, 282-B.
[20] *Metaphysics,* Bk. XII, ch. viii, 1074-b.
[21] *Ibid.,* ch. x, 1075-b-20.

f) Aristotle's convictional thinking is characterized by what could be called the "if-then-therefore" structure. It works as follows:

(1) "If besides sensible things no others exist,

(2) (then) there will be no first principle, no order, no becoming, no heavenly bodies."

(3) (therefore, it is suggested) premise (1) must be denied.

The reasoning is somewhat more complicated, but these three steps are the gist of the matter.[22]

3. *The nature of the Greek cosmos conviction*

a) If we compare Plato's and Aristotle's convictions we are impressed by the extent of their agreement. We may consider that we have encountered one convictional world view, which may have been entertained by the two men in slightly different ways, but which is basically one. Its major tenet seems to have been the conviction that the All consists of two domains: a core, to be evaluated positively; and a surface layer, of less positive or even negative value.

(1) The core is characterized by the following terms: *essential,* whereas what happens in the crust is merely accidental; *one, unity,* as over against many, variety, diversity; *order,* harmony, rhythm, over against disorder; *perfection,* over against imperfection; *necessity,* as opposed to chance; what is naturally *prior,* over against what is later; *self-sufficiency,* as opposed to what is dependent; what is *unchangeable,* over against change; what is *really real,* as opposed to mere appearance; *spirit,* opposed to matter; what is *infinite,* over against the finite.

(2) The core is all three: *good, rational,* and *beautiful.* Perhaps we might say that Plato stressed goodness in this trinity, and Aristotle reason.

(3) The core is *eternal,* lifted out above the processes of time which involve the crust in decay and death; the core is immortal, ungenerated.

(4) The core is the *norm,* that which should rule. To it belong the patterns, e.g., of the "ideal" state.

(5) Man is the universe on a small scale; he is a *microcosmos.* He is "essentially" good, rational, and beautiful. The essential man, related to the cosmic essence, can gain truth and knowledge, whereas the man who is oriented toward what is accidentally fascinating moves in the realm of opinion, error, falsity, and fiction.

[22] *Ibid.,* 1075-b-25 to 34.

It is perhaps helpful to outline, by way of contrast, some of the main aspects of the conviction about the world as held in the New Testament.

(1) The world is *not eternal* (only God is); it has a beginning and an end.

(2) The world is *both good* (created by God) *and evil* (corrupted by sin).

(3) The world is regarded by God to be good enough to be the *scene* of his redemptive activity.

(4) The world, being in the power of sin, has to be redeemed; i.e., it is also the *object* of God's redemption in Christ.

b) We suggest as the name of the Greek convictional world view "the Greek cosmos conviction." What Plato and Aristotle have in common is the belief in a divine cosmos, an Order-Harmony. The most beautiful expression of this conviction is to be found in the *Gorgias,* 508-A, where Socrates says, "And philosophers tell us, Callicles, that communion and friendship and orderliness and temperance and justice bind together heaven and earth and gods and men, and that this universe is therefore called kosmos or order, not disorder or misrule, my friend."

c) The term "*Greek* cosmos conviction" does not imply the assertion that all Greeks shared this conviction. For instance, it does not refer to the convictions of the ancient Greeks of the pre-Homeric period. They also believed in a cosmos, but this belief had quite a different character; it was part of their religion. In referring to this conviction we speak of the ancient, popular religion.

Neither does the term "Greek cosmos conviction" include the convictions of all the Greeks of the classical period.[23] Some groups (for instance, the adherents of the mystery cults) retained the old beliefs, and some individuals, such as the great tragedians, expressed a convictional world view which has more in common with the ancient religion than with the conviction of the classical philosophers.

d) Furthermore, the term "Greek *cosmos* conviction" must not be confused with cosmology or cosmogony. These last terms certainly refer to convictions about the cosmos; they express convictional world views. A cosmology presents such a world view under the guise of a philosophical discipline, employing such terms as time, space, aeons, demiurge, receptacle, one or more heavens; while a cosmogony presents one in the form of a series of stories about the origin of the universe, the key terms being gods, titans, demons, and primary ocean.

[23] Following W. B. Kristensen we distinguish between the *ancient* period of Greek civilization, which reached its height before Homer, and the *classical* period of the fifth and fourth centuries B.C.

The Greek cosmos conviction, however, can be held and has been held by people who did not entertain any cosmology or cosmogony. It seems probable that Socrates shared much of Plato's convictional world view, but that he wanted to avoid any cosmology. In later centuries many people who did not entertain any explicit philosophy, cosmology, or cosmogony, adhered to one form or another of the Greek cosmos conviction.

e) The Greek cosmos *conviction* made Socrates, Plato, and Aristotle into preachers, whether they were fully aware of that fact or not. Sometimes this notion is opposed by saying that Socrates did not set forth a moral or religious doctrine; that he merely brought to light, by means of his maieutic activity, that which his companion in the discussion knew without realizing that he knew it. And of Plato it has been said that he certainly was no preacher, because he spoke haltingly, in dialogues, looking at the issues from all angles, many times not reaching a clear conclusion at all. These objections seem to be based upon a misunderstanding.

Certainly Plato did not intentionally set forth a group of convictions, but these convictions formed the solid foundation of everything he discussed. Whether he examines music or gymnastics, justice or love, the philosopher-king or fables, is not of decisive importance. The thing which counts is that, no matter what the subject, the meaning and value of everything is interpreted in terms of the cosmos conviction.

The same thing is true for the Christian preacher and the Communist preacher; whether the former mentions racial discrimination, forgiveness of sins, or the second coming of Christ, it is always within the framework of the gospel, and he preaches this always, whether he says so explicitly or not; similarly the Communist preacher may argue capitalist disintegration, Western imperialism, or slave labor, but he also always argues on the basis of a specific set of convictions, and, by presupposing them, proclaims them with greater force and persuasion.

The immensely convincing power of Socrates flows largely from the intensity with which he holds his convictions (about the nature of man, the meaning of life, etc.) to be self-evidently true. His opponents always lose out in the debate, not because they are wrong, but first and foremost because they do not share Socrates' convictions about man and life. They entertain another convictional world view; that is to say, they live in another "world," and therefore they do not fit into Socrates' "world." Socrates' seeming abstention from preaching is actually the most subtle and effective preaching possible.

f) We have to qualify the Greek cosmos conviction of the three great classical philosophers as a cryptotheology. It is a theology, because it is a reasoned account of, a searching out of, the implications of a group of convictions. It is a cryptotheology, because the philosophers are only partially (or not at all?) aware of the very specific, "subjective" character of their convictions. They take their convictions either to be self-evident or the necessary outgrowth of right reasoning, or "objectively" defensible on the basis of "evidence" (so Aristotle, *On the Heavens,* Bk. I, ch. iii, 270-b-11, "The mere evidence of the senses is enough to convince us of this").

Because it is hidden from the classical philosophers themselves that they set forth and defend a theology containing a group of very specific convictions, many of their modern interpreters also overlook it. The section with which we opened our discussion of Plato (*The Republic,* Bks. II and III, from 376-E to 399-E) is discussed by Cornford with the help of short introductions, prefaced with titles.[24] They run: "Chapter IX, Primary Education of the Guardian"; "No. 1, Censorship of literature for school use"; "No. 2, The influence of dramatic recitation"; "No. 3, Musical accompaniment and metre." These titles are not wrong, but they are misleading. Education, literature, drama, and music are merely the occasions for developing Plato's theology. The real subject of this section is: education, literature, drama, and music *in the light* of the Greek cosmos conviction.

g) It scarcely has to be demonstrated that this classical cryptotheology is also a metaphysics. The "geometrical" reasoning is the clearest indication of this. By applying the geometrical method, by claiming mathematical necessity for their arguments, Plato and Aristotle show that they take it for granted that one may transfer the characteristics of tautological language to the domain of convictions. The evidence, the logical necessity of a reasoning about a line, has been transferred to considerations about the nature of man's understanding of the All, yes, to the nature of that All itself.

This kind of reasoning strengthens and underlines the *system*-character of this convictional world view. All things—heaven and earth, gods and men—are comprehended within one all-embracing system. It is highly significant that Plato's ode to the cosmos quoted above (*Gorgias,* 508-A) is immediately followed by an appeal to geometry.

h) It is a pity that it is not possible to say very much about the relationship between the Greek cosmos conviction of classical times and

[24] *The Republic of Plato,* tr. F. M. Cornford (London: Oxford University Press, 1941), p. xi.

the popular religion of the ancient period. The reason is, first, a lack of contact between philosophers and historians of religion; second, the fact that the convictional character of the classical philosophy has not been clearly recognized. Because of the difficulty and the virginity of the problem at hand, the following remarks should be considered more as suggestions made hesitantly than as well-established opinions.

Perhaps the best way to indicate the relationship between the ancient Greek religion and the classical Greek cosmos conviction would be to employ the conception of "A in derivation, but non-A in content." For our case, this would mean the assertion that it is highly probable that the cosmos conviction is historically related to the ancient religion, but that the form of the cosmos conviction and especially the content are considerably different from those of the ancient religion. A similar relationship exists between the Christian faith and such convictional world views as the belief in progress and (certain aspects of) Marxism. It is probable that the last two derived from the Christian faith the conviction that the meaning of life has to be talked about in the form of a specific theology of *history;* the interpretation of the meaning of history in the three cases is, however, very different.

In a similar way, the ancient religion and the classical world view both assume that the meaning of life has to be set forth within the framework of an orientation toward the *cosmos*. The interpretation of the cosmos, again, is different. Furthermore, it is highly probable that the classical view is dependent upon the ancient one, in spite of the fact that all classical philosophers were unaware of such a dependence and stressed the differences.

For both world views the cosmos is the All-embracing, of which there is no more adequate rendering in any modern language than Karl Jaspers' *das Umgreifende*. For both views the cosmos is eternal, but here the similarity stops. For the ancient Greeks, the cosmic rhythm embraced all contrasts: life and death, good and bad, victory and defeat. If it were appropriate to use modern terms, we could say that their view was monistic, that their cosmos was a true coincidence of opposites. Using this inappropriate terminology, we might say that the classical philosophers adhered to a dualistic view. Their cosmos was both everything and the core of everything, the really Real, opposed by what was mere appearance. Whereas the cosmic order of the ancients was suprarational and supramoral, the order of the classical philosophers was characterized by the really-good, and the really-reason. The ancient religion affirmed the value of the visible, tangible world; the classical philosophers devaluated it as the realm of change, decay, and unreliability. Finally, whereas the ancient Greeks entertained an overt religion, the classical Greeks hid their convictions behind a "philosophy," offered a cryptotheology, and employed metaphysics.

(1) We may now venture some remarks about the function of the Greek cosmos conviction within the Greek civilization. In the classical period the ancient religion had lost its power over the minds and hearts of most people. It lived on only in small groups (mystery cults) and among such people as the great tragedians. This period may be compared to the Enlightenment of the modern era. Some men, such as Socrates, Plato, and Aristotle, could not possibly live without a powerful, inspiring convictional world view. They felt that there *must* be, in one way or another, a True Reality which supported the pitiful, confused world of tangible things of merely relative value, where norms, laws, and moral rules were changing. Just as geometry showed man unassailable, changeless, absolute truths, so it *must* be possible for a mind trained in this kind of "seeing" to detect the unchanging, unquestionable moral laws and spiritual truths.

In this way, the classical philosophers became the guides of those enlightened Greeks who on the one hand felt far above the old religion with its crude myths, in which the eternal core was not yet peeled out of the accidental crust, and on the other hand dissociated themselves decisively from the cynical relativists who no longer believed at all in anything which was more than relative.

This view of the origin of classical philosophy should not startle anyone. As soon as we have dropped the dangerously naïve, traditional notion that philosophy, religion, and politics are completely different things, and have started to think in terms of convictional language, we notice everywhere phenomena which bear strong resemblance to that which we have seen in Greece. It happens many times that convictions which have taken the form of an overt religion lose their power. Exactly why, it is difficult to say, but the phenomenon occurs. The result is a spiritual vacuum, but such a vacuum does not continue very long, because other convictions rush in to fill it. Sometimes these new convictions also possess the form of an overt religion; at other times the leaders of the new convictional movement call themselves philosophers; and again at other times the vanguard offers its convictions about the meaning of life in the form of a political program. Many Westerners have understood Nazism and Communism in this way. These "movements" were and are much more than political parties; they offer new interpretations about the meaning of life; the fervor of their utterances possesses a "religious" tinge.

Socrates, Plato, and Aristotle philosophized because they wanted to be convinced, to be overcome by a venerable True Reality. Their philosophy was a search for the wisdom which would flow from this True Reality once it was found. These men did not philosophize because they were curious for "explanations," or because they wanted to start a new discipline, because they were dreamers, or because they were critical of the traditions. Some of these elements played a subordinate role in their philosophy, but none of them touches the heart of the matter. They philosophized, i.e., offered convictions, because they could not do anything of lesser value; something of immense importance was at stake—the meaning of life, the nature of the All, the destiny of man, the future of the *polis*. Their basic questions were: How can we live? What may we live for? How can we "think" of the All and man and society in such a way that life is worth living?

In other words, the basic fact from which the classical philosophers started was the *disestablishment* of Greek life. The life of their community, and therewith their own individual lives, were uprooted. The ultimate aim of the philosophizing of these men was therefore to *re-establish* their existence, that is, to find a way in which the communal life could be established again, so that individuals could relate themselves significantly to their community and to the All.

INTERLUDE

Forms of the Greek Cosmos Conviction in the Medieval and Modern Periods

It would take too much space to trace carefully the development of the Greek cosmos conviction in the history of Western civilization. In this book we are interested mainly in the languages spoken by *modern* man. We are, however, not allowed to ignore completely the centuries between Aristotle and our own era. In this interlude we will try to bridge the gap of these more than twenty centuries by offering a short discussion of some of the major forms which the Greek cosmos conviction assumed in the Middle Ages, the Renaissance, and the Enlightenment.[25]

The shortness of the discussion will not influence its clarity too much, since our treatment will be based upon the widely read book by Randall. His discussion of the history of Western thought, in the *Making of the Modern Mind*,[26] amounts largely to what in our termi-

[25] Some other forms have been left out, such as Neoplatonism, Stoicism, Augustinianism.

[26] John Herman Randall, Jr. (rev. ed.; Boston: Houghton Mifflin Co., 1940). Used by permission.

nology can be called a description of the various forms of the Greek cosmos conviction in the West, and of the ways in which one form developed into another. In the following we concentrate upon the three major forms already mentioned. It has to be admitted that the chart does not do justice to all the rich material which Randall supplies. A certain oversimplification was unavoidable.

I. THE GREEK COSMOS CONVICTION IN ITS LATE MEDIEVAL FORM

A. The elements which these forms have in common

1. THE HARMONIOUS WORLD ORDER

a) *the invisible world, the cosmos*
"the intelligible world . . . the realm of imperishable things" (47)

b) *the visible world, the universe*
the universe can be understood (32)
"at the center of this orderly universe lay the earth" (33)
"no growth, no development, no change" (33)
the planets' orbits "had to be circular, inasmuch as they were made by a perfect God and the circle is the most perfect of all figures" (32-33)
"allegory throughout nature" (35)
"the number of planets is necessarily seven" (233)

2. THE NATURE OF AUTHORITY AND CERTAINTY: REASON

authority and certainty are found in reason, embodied in Church and tradition, and represented by saints, fathers, and philosophers (e.g., 24 ff.)
"no truth to seek in nature, but only in the comparison of texts" (233)

3. THE RELATIONSHIP BETWEEN MAN AND THE WORLD ORDER: FAITH

man is "a dweller in these two realms," viz., of ideas and senses (47)
by forsaking the sense realm "man can make himself immortal" (47)
the wise man "should scrutinize every object and event . . . to discover its bearing upon the fundamental purpose of things" (34)
"the aspiration to fulfill the will of God . . . was the cosmic force that made the world go round" (36)

B. Elements particular to this form of the Greek cosmos conviction

1. PURPOSES

"there must be a reason for everything, a purpose it served in the divine scheme" (34)
"The bandbox universe . . . its essential purpose as the scene of the great drama God had prepared" (18)

"the object of investigation [of Thomistic-Aristotelian science] had been the different purposes of objects, the substances or essences of things, their whatness, their qualitative distinctions" (236)

2. HIERARCHY

"a hierarchy of being, qualitatively different, approaching perfection as it receded from the center of the earth" (232)
"the Aristotelian view of Nature as a hierarchy of different types of objects each striving to fulfill its purpose of attaining perfection in its own way" (235)

II. THE GREEK COSMOS CONVICTION IN ITS RENAISSANCE FORM

A. The elements which these forms have in common

1. THE HARMONIOUS WORLD ORDER

a) *The invisible world, the cosmos*

nature is "immutable," "inescapable . . . it is independent of his [God's] decree" (199)
"God was nothing other than that [immutable] order itself" (244)
"to seek some fundamental principles of justice . . . behind and beyond all positive commands and all custom . . . these fundamental principles are easily read into the very structure and reason of the world" (198)

b) *The visible world, the universe*

nature not a hierarchy, but "a great harmonious and mathematically ordered machine" (235)
"Necessity is 'the eternal bond and rule of Nature' " (Leonardo) (235)
"the definite mathematical relations in the world that were revelations of the Divine Spirit" (on Kepler) (236)
"a mechanical order, and . . . amenable to human control" (239)
"the mathematical simplicity and harmony of the cosmos," "an ordered universe" contrasted with "the complex and heterogeneous medieval world" (228, 229)
Copernicus "had greatly extended the boundaries of the universe, but he had not broken them" (230)

2. THE NATURE OF AUTHORITY AND CERTAINTY: REASON

"the old authorities had been found in error . . . even observation and common sense were fallible; only reason operating by mathematical calculation could be trusted" (230)
"those who forsook the authority of the ancients" searched "for a method that would give certain knowledge"; this attitude "sent men to mathematics as the only unshakable knowledge" (220)
"to distrust custom and listen only to reason . . . he resolved to discard all his beliefs that could not pass the test of reason" (on Descartes) (240)

3. THE RELATIONSHIP BETWEEN MAN AND THE WORLD ORDER: FAITH

"a strong faith in the . . . harmony of the cosmos" (228)
"the sublime faith that Nature is an . . . ordered machine" (235)
"modern science was born of a *faith* in the mathematical interpretation of Nature, held long before it had been empirically verified" (235)
"the complete correspondence between algebra and the realm of space—that is, the real world. By algebra man could hope to discover the secrets of the universe" (241)

B. Elements particular to this form of the Greek cosmos conviction

1. THE FUNDAMENTS OF MODERN SCIENCE

"the vision that here, in combining the best in geometrical analysis and algebra, lay the source of all true science" (on Descartes) (241)

III. THE GREEK COSMOS CONVICTION IN ITS ENLIGHTENMENT FORM

A. The elements which these forms have in common

1. THE HARMONIOUS WORLD ORDER

a) *The invisible world, the cosmos*

"the Order of Nature contained an order of natural moral law as well" (365)
"Nature and everything natural were fundamentally good and divine" (370)

b) *The visible world, the universe*

"in such a machine [the harmonious world-machine], time counted for nothing . . . there was no real change" (275)
"the universal order, symbolized henceforth by the law of gravitation, takes on a clear and positive meaning" (260)

2. THE NATURE OF AUTHORITY AND CERTAINTY: REASON

"a guarantee of truth, that 'reason' which was both an individual and a universal authority" (254)
"Newton . . . stamped the mathematical ideal of science, and the identification of the natural with the rational, upon the entire field of thought" (255)
"the new science had not yet led men to give up the . . . Aristotelian ideal of a body of knowledge that could be deductive, universal, and infallible, one great logical system" (261)
"the surest foundation of truth was not . . . sense experience . . . but rather the clear and distinct intuition of geometrical axioms. We *know* intuitively, with absolute certainty" (262)

3. THE RELATIONSHIP BETWEEN MAN AND THE WORLD ORDER: FAITH

"to abolish man-made institutions and allow Nature to function by herself—*laisser-faire*" (277) "the universal order is . . . accessible to the mind" (260)

B. Elements particular to this form of the Greek cosmos conviction

1. HUMANISTIC RELIGION

deism "rejecting revelation entirely, and insisting on the sufficiency of natural and rational religion" (285)
"religion is . . . a science like physics, that is, a system of rational propositions . . . to be tested . . . by the evidence of the human reason" (287)
"religion rends its priestly garb and appears in its divine essence" (384)

2. HUMANISTIC NONRELIGION

"Newtonian science offered a complete explanation of the universe, requiring no further addition whatsoever" (on Holbach) (301)

3. MORALS

"the principles of right and wrong . . . incorporated into the scheme of reason . . . the science of ethics was as independent of any theological or supernatural foundation as any other" science (366)
"the Will of God always and necessarily does determine itself, to choose to act only what is agreeable to Justice, Equity, Goodness, and Truth" (Samuel Clarke) (367)
wickedness is an absurdity, just as it is absurd to disregard in science "the Demonstrable Relations and Properties of Mathematical Figures" (368)

4. "SCIENCE" OF ECONOMY

"eternal, immutable . . . inevitable laws" of economic life (323)
"these laws . . . pertain to the essence of men and things" (323)
"these essential laws . . . the natural laws of the social order" (324)

5. POLITICAL "SCIENCE"

when political theorists "used the adjective 'natural,' they could not help thinking of the harmonious and rational order of divinely ordained laws which Newton had popularized" (340)
"such a government obviously seemed to [the American colonists] natural, rational, and divinely ordained" (345)

6. THE FULL DEVELOPMENT OF THE SCIENCE OF PHYSICS

COMMENTS

1. Most categories used in the table above do not need further explanation; also, the differences between the three forms, shown in this way, will speak for themselves. However, we have to give our reasons for the distinction between cosmos and universe. This distinction is fraught with dangers, since it was not made by the men of the Middle Ages or the Renaissance, but by a person living in the twentieth century.

For cosmos believers, the world order was just one, *the* One, a glorious all-embracing Unity.

The distinction has been made in order to clarify the nature of one of the major differences between the three forms of the Greek cosmos conviction under discussion. Whereas the differences in regard to the conception of the universe are considerable (purpose and hierarchy vs. mathematical and mechanical order), the fundamental belief in the harmonious, good, and intelligible cosmos remains basically unchanged.

2. The Renaissance and Enlightenment forms of the Greek cosmos conviction do not differ on any fundamental points. The major differences are: (1) an elaboration of the implications of the Renaissance convictions in the fields of religion, morals, and political and economic "science" in the Enlightenment period; (2) an unusually heavy emphasis upon morals in the Enlightenment.

3. The chart intentionally stresses, to the extent of overemphasis, the aspects which the various forms of the Greek cosmos conviction have in common. I do not deny the existence of important differences, but assume that the reader is acquainted with Randall's book, and that he remembers expressions such as "the Copernican Revolution" and "the Cartesian Revolution." [27] Whereas Randall strikes a careful balance between permanent and revolutionary elements in the three forms, we are in this book especially interested in the permanent cosmos-structure which holds through in all changes.

4. It is perhaps permissible (if we are aware of the dangers of oversimplification and generalization) to point out the relations between four fundamental modes of cosmos convictions. They are: (1) the cosmos convictions of primitive and ancient civilizations; (2) the Greek cosmos conviction of the classical Enlightenment and the medieval West; (3) the Greek cosmos conviction of the Western Renaissance and Enlightenment; and (4) the Greek cosmos conviction of the modern West. We will compare these modes regarding two points: first, the role of qualities and purposes; second, the role of mathematics.

The result of the comparison is offered in the following chart.[28] In the course of history the element of quality and purpose becomes gradually less concrete, less particular, less awesome, and more abstract, more universal, more nice and kind. At the same time the mathematical element expands its influence; this means more emphasis upon necessity, universality, and absoluteness.

[27] *Ibid.*, pp. 226 ff., 235 ff.

[28] One could argue that modes (2) and (3) actually are subforms of one mode.

FOUR MODES OF COSMOS CONVICTION

Periods of Civilization	Name	Qualities Purposes Hierarchy	Mathematics	Language	Basic Characteristics
1. Primitive and ancient civilization	primitive cosmos conviction	gods, powers		overtly religious	qualities
2. Classical Greece and medieval West	Greek cosmos conviction	*a*) ideas, entelechies	geometric order is exemplary	metaphysical	qualities and mathematics
		b) God, angels, devils, saints	God's and mathematical perfection identical	overtly religious and metaphysical	
3. Renaissance and Enlightenment	Greek cosmos conviction	universe without qualities, but cosmos a moral-rational order	mathematical simplicity of universe	*a*) religious, moral, and metaphysical *b*) moral and metaphysical	qualities and mathematics
4. Modern West	Greek cosmos conviction		universe a mathematical machine	metaphysical	mathematics

C. THE GREEK COSMOS CONVICTION IN THE ENLIGHTENMENT

The Greek cosmos conviction in its Enlightenment form deserves a broader treatment than it received in the Interlude. We will discuss the influence of the cosmos conviction upon the science, the philosophy, the political life, and the church life of the Enlightenment.

1. *Science*

Whitehead rightly points out that we cannot understand the rise of modern science without considering a certain belief in the "Order of Nature."[29] He claims that two factors are involved: First, an interest in brute facts, the "simple immediate facts."[30] Second, an "instinctive conviction in the existence of an *Order of Things*, and, in particular, of an *Order of Nature*."[31] Asking for the source of this conviction, Whitehead refers to "the medieval insistence on the rationality of God, conceived as with the personal energy of Jehovah and with the rationality of a Greek philosopher."[32] We would like to formulate the issue

[29] *Science and the Modern World* (New York: The Macmillan Co., 1946), p. 6.
[30] *Ibid.*, pp. 12, 23.
[31] *Ibid.*, p. 5.
[32] *Ibid.*, p. 18.

somewhat differently. We are certainly dealing with convictions, but it seems probable that the contribution of the Greek cosmos conviction is greater than that of the Hebrew-Christian world view.

a) Empirical science cannot arise without a series of closely related convictions. One is the certainty that the cosmos is a well-ordered whole, of a rational structure. Another is the conviction that man is largely a rational being, whose rationality is of the same order as that of the universe. Without the kinship between the two rationalities it would be unthinkable that man could find a method to gain rational knowledge of the universe. All these convictions have their origin in the Greek cosmos conviction, especially in the doctrine that man is a microcosmos. If in civilizations other than the Western one something like empirical science did not arise, the reason is not to be sought, for instance, in a lesser intellectual endowment, lack of curiosity, love of ease, or other deficiencies, but in the absence of the convictions here discussed.

b) One aspect of the scientific enterprise is the investigation of human documents. This investigation also was promoted by the convictions mentioned above: It is very important and beneficial to gain reliable knowledge about the period in which a document was written, about the person of the author and his purposes in writing. Before long this method of research was applied also to the Holy Scriptures of the Hebrew and the Christian faith, as well as to the religious documents of nonbiblical religions. At the present time nearly all Christian churches not only admit the inescapability of such a procedure, but evaluate it as an integral part of the modern form of faith. The convictional presuppositions of this research represent one of the ways in which convictions that are dependent upon the Greek cosmos belief have entered into the Hebrew-Christian faith.

c) It needs to be stressed that the position defended here is not incompatible with the conception of indicative language. The convictions discussed do not mix with the scientific language itself. These convictions, together with other elements (to be mentioned in Chap. VIII), form the domain of basic assumptions which constitute the foundation of indicative language. They remind us of the fact that indicative language is not an absolute entity, but an utterance of human beings, and since human beings *are* largely their convictions, indicative language is not completely separated from these.

2. *Philosophy*

a) There is scarcely any philosopher belonging to the main historical trend, that which is usually called rationalism or idealism, who is not more or less influenced by the Greek cosmos conviction. Even the representatives of the empirical trend are not completely free from the impact of this conviction. Perhaps David Hume and some existentialists have dissociated themselves most decisively from it.

This is not to say that all rationalist and idealist philosophy can be "explained" completely in terms of the Greek cosmos conviction. But wherever we find deep interest in metaphysics and ontology the influence of the cosmos conviction may be discerned. Further, it seems advisable to investigate a philosophy like Kant's on the basis of the hypothesis that some of his main terms are charged with evaluations pointing back to the Greek cosmos conviction. Whereas terms such as "a priori" and "a posteriori" in Hume's philosophy are used in an analytical way—namely, to characterize types of reasoning—these terms in Kant seem to be charged with a positive or a negative value respectively. Other terms which impress us in the same way are: necessary, universal, and apodictic. Again, whenever in moral philosophy reference is made to absolute norms, principles, or values, the suggestion of a strong influence by the cosmos conviction is plausible.

b) We meet the Greek cosmos conviction even in unexpected places—for example, in the work of Hume. Although Hume's philosophy as a whole is as free from the dominion of this conviction as it is possible for a philosopher, yet in his *Dialogues* it plays a surprising role. When we discussed Hume in Chap. IV, we raised the question as to whether Demea, Philo, and Cleanthes were referring to the same God. We could not follow up the question at that stage of our investigation, but we can do so now, having become acquainted with the Greek cosmos conviction.

Clearly when Cleanthes is referring to God as "the Author of Nature," as a Mind "somewhat similar to the mind of man," he is moving completely within the frame of "thinking" (that is, being convinced) of the Greek cosmos conviction. Cleanthes does not quite make clear whether he is discussing the nature of a god or of the universe. This universe or the mindlike cause of the universe is characterized by "design and intention." Philosophy can prove these characteristics by referring to the order we see around us. God (or universe) and man are so similar that man can understand him (it). The similarity consists largely in rational orderliness. We meet here the convictions about the cosmos and the microcosmos, be it in a very simple form.[33]

It seems that Demea and Philo are referring to the same God. Both

[33] *Hume, Selections,* ed. Charles W. Hendel (New York: Charles Scribner's Sons, 1927), pp. 302, 317.

stress his "incomprehensible nature" and "adorable mysteriousness"; his perfections cannot be understood and it is even profane to try to penetrate to their domain. There are also differences, however. Demea calls God: "Being without restriction, All Being, the Being infinite and universal." Furthermore, Demea claims that we can approach this All Being in our philosophy, that is, by means of "proofs a priori" and "abstract arguments." With these remarks we find ourselves again within the realm of the Greek cosmos conviction. Perhaps we can say that Demea has developed other, more sophisticated implications of this conviction than Cleanthes. Demea's convictional thinking is determined strongly by the "geometrical" aspect of the cosmos conviction. It brings God to the realm of the a priori, the infinite, the universal; and man's reasoning a priori can "see" this God in the realm of the infinite.

Philo, on the contrary, claims that the right approach to God is not by means of philosophy but by worship. He "is more the object of worship in the temple, than of disputation in the schools." [34] Philo's God reminds us, more than the conceptions of the two other disputants, of the Hebrew-Christian notion of God.

We have to ask ourselves what our discussion does to Hume's argument. Hume presents his case as if the three disputants were referring to the same God and as if the problem, therefore, were merely that of establishing the validity of several types of reasoning in demonstrating the nature of this God. Now it appears that each of the three men has a different "conception" (that is, conviction) of God. It is highly probable that each man's position in regard to the validity of the two types of reasoning is dependent on his conviction. Belief in a God such as that of Demea or Cleanthes seems to invite, to imply, the belief that reasoning a priori or a posteriori are valid methods of establishing God's nature. In other words, the Greek cosmos conviction invites metaphysical reasoning.

3. *Politics*

What we call "political ideas" is to a very great extent convictional language. Political language certainly contains indicative elements, and even analytical language (for instance, analysis of terms such as capitalism, socialism, government), but its meaning is largely convictional. Convictions about what is good and bad for the community, about what is good and bad for one's own group, about the "right" ends and means, form the frame for political "thinking."

Political convictions in the Enlightenment period are, for all practical purposes, derived from only two convictional world views, the

[34] *Ibid.*, pp. 300-303, 317.

Hebrew-Christian one and the Greek cosmos view. We will refer only to the latter because we are in this chapter interested only in this conviction and its influence in the modern period.

a) We suggest that capitalism, in its extreme form, cannot be understood at all if we do not consider it as one of the forms in which the Greek cosmos conviction continues to live in our age. Extreme capitalists believe that society possesses the same structure as the universe and individual man, and therefore assume that society consists of a rational and harmonious core and a much less rational and harmonious surface. The surface is apt to show irregularities, such as unemployment and other crises, but for the man who can "see" deeper, these irregularities are "mere appearance." The very life of society depends upon the hidden but powerful core, which is "essentially" orderly and harmonious. Because of its power, this core acts as a healer and redresser of irregularities. It is naïve to expect that artificial measures of a mere human instance, like a government, can deliver society from such a disturbance as unemployment. The hidden but powerful divine order will restore the harmony in the surface layer of society, spontaneously, if it is left alone and allowed to perform its healing activity. At any rate, the hidden harmony will prevail in the end.

We do this convictional world view an injustice if we call an utterance such as, "What is good for G.M. is good for the whole country," a vulgar expression of self-interest, a phrase, a slogan which is not seriously meant. It is the formulation of a strong conviction. This runs as follows: If people assume that there exists a conflict between the interests of big business, and those of farmers, or small business, or workers, or the nation as a whole, they are sadly mistaken. These people look only at the surface of things; one who can "see" deeper will realize that a hidden harmony lies at the root of the universe, and also of society. This harmonious core *guarantees* that the "real" interests of these groups do not conflict. Distrust in the existence and power of the hidden, divine core is an insult to a deity, a lack of "faith." He who appeals to government interference is not merely naïve, but trespasses a cosmic law.[35]

b) Marxism is, in certain of its aspects, another elaboration of the Greek cosmos conviction. If one believes that society possesses the core-crust structure, one can look forward to an era in which the crust will have been peeled off, and only the core will be left. It will shine in its full glory, whereas now its light is hidden by the filth of the crust. A

[35] A similar interpretation of capitalism is offered in Eduard Heimann, *Freedom and Order* (New York: Charles Scribner's Sons, 1947), pp. 244 ff.

difference from capitalism is that the latter thinks in terms of reason and order, while Marxism emphasizes the third element of the Greek cosmos trinity—goodness or justice. In the present dispensation the world is full of injustice and oppression, but in the new era all evil will have fallen away; man's good and reasonable nature will establish itself so completely that there will be no police, no army, no jails, no state, no means of violence and compulsion any more, because man will do the good spontaneously. The divine core will have vanquished the devilish surface layer, once and for all.

What people call the tension between Marx's determinism and his appeal to man to participate in the cosmic struggle is easily understandable in the context of our interpretation. The validity of the term "determinism" has to be questioned. If we ask, not for Marx's explicit presentation of his ideas, but for the convictions hidden behind the explicit formulations, the word "determinism" does not make much sense. Marx is not a cool, detached scholar who defends the hypothesis that in a certain realm of "reality" event B is determined by event A. On the contrary, he is bent on defending the burning conviction that the divine core will and must triumph in the end. Nothing can stop the victorious activity of this god; the defeat of his enemies is inevitable. If one wants to find a comparison for Marxism on this point, Calvin's doctrine of irresistible grace fits better than scientific determinism.

While appeal to voluntary co-operation would be incompatible with determinism in a rational system of thought (such as Marx claims he gives), this appeal goes very well with the belief in an invincible god full of saving power. Let us qualify the foregoing: such a combination of convictions does not seem strange at all to the believers themselves, for instance, to Calvinists and Marxists.

c) It is not the purpose of this section to deal with all the movements in the political life of the Western world which have been influenced or shaped by the Greek cosmos conviction. Therefore we do not take up the question of its contributions to the convictions of democracy, but merely point out that most of these convictions are akin to either the capitalist or the Marxist version of the Greek cosmos conviction. Much of the "idealism" of the Western world is a mild form of Enlightenment utopianism, whereas Marxism is a radical form. In such idealism the violence and the hatred of capitalism are absent, but the main convictional structure is maintained: the belief in a divine core which guarantees the ultimate victory of all that is good and rational. It is the *calling* of any good and rational man, of any person of good will, to assemble all his forces and unite with other men of good will in their efforts to bring about the ideal world.

The above treatment could give rise to the misunderstanding that this idealism is historically derived from Marxism. Actually, both this idealism and Marxism, as well as capitalism, arise from the matrix of the Enlightenment, that is to say, from the Greek cosmos conviction in a modern form.

d) The convictional world view of Marxism, capitalism, and Western idealism are language structures available to Western man for the re-establishment of his life. Marxism is more than a political system, and capitalism more than an economic theory. The popular term which comes closest to doing justice to their real significance is "way of life." Capitalism and Marxism are each a way of establishing life. Man-who-speaks, when employing terms such as "free enterprise," "government interference," and "creeping socialism," or "Western imperialism," "class struggle," and "oppression," re-establishes his existence by claiming the cosmos, revealed in these languages, as his Home. The vehemence of the mutual hatred of capitalists and Communists must be understood on the basis of the fear that the other party may destroy one's Home-world and therewith one's carefully established existence.

4. *The Greek cosmos conviction in the church*

a) The religious liberalism of the nineteenth and twentieth centuries is one of the many combinations of Hebrew-Christian and Greek cosmos convictions in Western civilization. Here follow some examples of liberal theology which show deep-going influence of the Greek cosmos conviction. The illustrations are chosen from three branches of theology—namely, systematic theology, missionary theology, and theology of the social movement.

(1) *Systematic theology*

"Since the intellect can interpret Nature, Nature is *intelligible.* Since Nature is intelligible there must be some *correlation* between its laws or methods and the rational processes in us; since there is this correlation between the intelligible world and the interpretative intellect they must embody *one and the same intelligence*. . . . But this argument admits a further development. The human intellect could *not live* unless embosomed by a universe which was in its constitution and contents as rational as itself. Reason could not live in a world where no reason was. . . . But it signifies one thing more, viz.: that the Intelligence which is embodied in this intelligible Nature is *in kind and quality* one with the intelligence in its interpreter. The Reason that lives in Nature speaks a language that the reason in man can understand and translate" (from Fairbairn, *The Philosophy of the Christian Religion*).

The intelligence which is embodied in this intelligible Nature *is God*. He is immanent in nature. He fills every part of it with His presence; He reveals Himself in every natural force, in every movement and process.[36]

And:

Our modern ways of looking at things make us suppose that the uniformity of natural law expresses most clearly not only the truth and power but also the *beneficence* of God. . . . The *universality* of law, therefore, is to theology only the perfect consistency in the modes of activity of God in carrying out his *immutable* purposes of love. Hence God will always act according to law, —that is, in perfect consistency with his *unchanging* law of love.[37]

I have italicized key terms which indicate clearly the Greek cosmos conviction. Examples: "One and the same intelligence" and "in kind and quality" proclaim the identity between the core of man and the core of the world. The words "is God" show that this core is evaluated by Gladden so positively that it receives divine rank. The term "beneficence" shows that the core is not only rational, but good, one of the main tenets of the Greek cosmos conviction. "Universality," "immutable," and "unchanging" are typical descriptions of the divine aspect of the world, according to the Greek cosmos conviction.

(2) *Missionary theology*

If there were not at the *core* of *all* the creeds a *nucleus* of religious truth, neither Christianity nor any other faith would have anything to build on. *Within* the piety of the common people of *every* land, *encrusted* with *superstition* as it usually is, and weighed down with *vulgar* self-seeking in their bargainings with the gods, there is this *germ*, the *inalienable* religious intuition of the human soul. The God of this intuition is the true God; to this extent universal religion has not to be established, it exists.[38]

The core is indicated by "core," "nucleus," "within," and "germ." The term "encrusted" is heavily charged with evaluations; these show the divine, eternal ("inalienable") character of the core, over against the surface realm of the accidental, which is interpreted as "vulgar," "crust," or "superstition." The terms "all" and "every" proclaim the "universality" of this structure of the world.

[36] Washington Gladden, *Present Day Theology,* 1913, pp. 52, 53.
[37] *Ibid.*, pp. 44, 46.
[38] W. E. Hocking, *Re-thinking Missions* (New York: Harper & Bros., 1932), p. 37.

(3) *Theology of the social movement*

Even the cynical Bismarck found out that there are certain *imponderables* in the universe against which blood and iron are after all impotent. What we are now finding out is that these imponderables are also at the *heart* of the scientific truth. The universe is with the idealist and not against him. At its heart is not the disintegrating force of selfishness, but the *cohesive* force of *good* will, constantly operating to unite and bind humanity together in a larger, truer life.[39]

. . . personality, whose *essence* lies in the making of choices and whose development consists in preferring *moral* satisfactions to material, the *ultimate* to the immediate, the *eternal* to the temporal. . . . The achievement of brotherhood requires the spirit of sacrifice and . . . therein lies the fullest self-realization.[40]

The first quotation voices the cosmos conviction about the world; the second proclaims the corresponding doctrine of man.

b) Turning now to the question about the relationship of Greek cosmos and Hebrew-Christian elements in religious liberalism, we have to admit that this liberalism is not homogeneous. It manifests a variety of ways in which these elements are combined.[41] In some forms of religous liberalism the Greek cosmos elements are predominant, though the Hebrew-Christian elements are never absent. However, in other forms the Hebrew-Christian elements are the decisive ones. What term is the most suitable one to indicate these relationships? Two present themselves:

First, the metaphor "frame." We can say that in Gladden's case the Hebrew-Christian elements are taken up in a Greek cosmos frame. In the case of others—for instance, Rauschenbusch—the relationship is reversed.

Second, the term "multi-determination," which image is perhaps more fitting. Rauschenbusch's convictions about the future are neither purely Hebrew-Christian, nor purely Greek cosmos; they are determined by both world views.

c) Religious liberalism is by no means the only form of modern Christian church life into which the Greek cosmos conviction has penetrated. Roman Catholic and orthodox Protestant theology also have been influenced. We do not discuss these theologies, because such a procedure would lead us outside the Enlightenment period which we are

[39] Harry F. Ward, *The New Social Order* (New York: The Macmillan Co., 1919), p. 105.

[40] Harry F. Ward, *Our Economic Morality and the Ethic of Jesus* (New York: The Macmillan Co., 1929), pp. 321, 315, 316.

[41] Elements of other convictional world views, e.g., empiricism and naturalism, also play a role, but we do not discuss them here.

considering, namely, back to the Middle Ages (Thomas' combination of Aristotelianism and Christianity) and the Post-Reformation period of Protestant orthodoxy. We merely notice that the Greek cosmos conviction also made its influence felt where the explicit "teachings" of the church had a content very different from that of the cosmos belief. This is the case where these teachings are explicitly or implicitly considered to form a set of "truths" about the "true" structure of the All, that is to say, about God, man, the universe, and history. In the more naïve forms of orthodoxy, it was claimed that these "truths" were made known to us by revelation, or were contained in scripture, or were formulated (once and for all in a universally valid form) in the creeds. The Roman Catholic counterpart of this conception of "truths" found its classical formulation in Vincentius a Lerino's definition of traditional truth: *quod ubique, semper, ab omnibus creditum est,* what has been believed everywhere, at all times, and by all people.

D. THE QUALIFICATION OF THE GREEK COSMOS CONVICTION IN THE POST-ENLIGHTENMENT PERIOD

One of the most important events in the history of the last century is the fact that to a large extent the Greek cosmos conviction has lost its powerful grip upon the mind of Western man. This amounts to saying that the modern man is no longer enlightened man. He establishes his life in a way different from the latter. This fact possesses two aspects. First, the way to establish life offered by the Greek cosmos conviction in its Enlightenment form has broken down. This establishment has lost its plausibility, and therewith its hold over modern man's mind. The question as to the reason for this loss of power is difficult to answer. In a satisfactory answer the following elements will figure: certain developments in empirical science; the rise of a new mentality, or perhaps, of new mentalities. One thing, however, is quite clear. Since the end of the nineteenth century (though much more clearly since World War I) we have been witnessing a disestablishment of the language structures of the Enlightenment.

Second, while modern man seems to be sure that the Enlightenment establishment no longer has any meaning for him, he is not at all certain in what way he is now going to re-establish his existence. He tries the ways of Fascism, Nazism, fascistic Communism, nationalism, and sometimes a deepened Christianity.

In this section we will offer a very short sketch of the ways in which this disestablishment and the attempts at re-establishment show themselves in the same areas of our civilization which we discussed in Sec. C.

In some areas we observe a fierce rebellion against the Greek cosmos conviction; in others we notice nothing more than a modest qualification; but nowhere has this world view remained unchallenged.

1. *The qualification of the Greek cosmos conviction in the realm of science*

The modern scientist no longer claims that he in his science can make pronouncements concerning the nature of "reality." Philipp Frank writes: "Two characteristic beliefs of nineteenth-century science broke down during its last decades; these were the belief that all phenomena in nature can be reduced to the laws of mechanics, and the belief that science will eventually reveal the 'truth' about the universe." [42]

a) We cannot here discuss the entire modern theory of science; a short reference to some of its most important aspects must suffice.

(1) Science describes. There is, in principle, no difference in status between so-called laws and other scientific statements.

(2) Science predicts events.

(3) Description and prediction are achieved by means of a set of tools, among which concepts, hypotheses, and theories occupy an important place; these tools do not possess any authority or validity apart from their function as elements of the scientific process.

(4) One of the functions of these tools is to enable the scientist to formulate relevant questions, and, sometimes, to set up experiments.

(5) All scientific statements are provisional; it is expected that the encounter with new facts, or the launching of new hypotheses, will date older formulations and require new ones.

(6) All scientific statements are relative, i.e., related, first, to the spatiotemporal position of the scientist, and, second, to the peculiarities of the scientist's person, his outlook, etc.

(7) The scientist therefore does not "discover" something, for instance, "truths," or "laws" about "reality," which already existed before his research, in eternity, in God's mind. The scientist does not pronounce upon these things, but merely tries to develop tools which for the present are useful for his job of description and prediction.

b) This interpretation of science does not mean that the Greek cosmos conviction has been completely discarded. It has been qualified. Instead of saying: nature possesses a mathematical structure, which is detected by science, and it is therefore proved that the universe *is* rational, the modern scientist makes a proposal. His advice is to assume that nature and man are rational *to a certain extent*, and on the basis of this assumption to try to assemble as many reliable hypotheses as possible.

[42] *Modern Science and Its Philosophy* (Cambridge: Harvard University Press, 1949), p. 4.

The crucial words are: "to a certain extent." They mean to say that the scientist as scientist cannot "know" what nature actually is, but that by assuming the possibility of the rationality of certain of its aspects, certain questions can be formulated and partly answered. In this conception of science, the Greek cosmos conviction is not totally set aside; the new conception would not have been possible without this conviction and the naïve, metaphysical conviction about the achievements of science. The new conception of science is thus no longer hampered by hidden, metaphysical assumptions. [43]

2. *Qualifications of and rebellion against the Greek cosmos conviction in the realm of politics*

a) Some modern political convictions can be contrasted with Marxism, capitalism, and idealistic utopianism as follows: while the latter three world views are explicitly or implicitly based upon the conviction that man, cosmos, and society are *essentially* rational and good, the modern democratic conviction is that man and society are rational *to a certain extent*. According to this conviction men cannot, either by violence or by legislation, erase all evil, everything which is disorderly or unjust, and thus prepare an essentially harmonious society, because man is not exclusively a rational being but is also something else. On the other hand, neither are man and society completely irrational. On this basis, modern Westerners believe that men are able to attempt and should assiduously attempt to eliminate as many disorderly and unjust situations as possible. This moderate conviction is unthinkable without the Greek cosmos conviction; it is a qualification of one of its forms.

b) Other contemporary political convictions are vehemently opposed to the Greek cosmos conviction. This is the case in Nazism, Fascism, and the fascistic form of Marxism which we call Soviet Communism. The Nazi, for instance, saw the world as a field where powerful, vital, instinctive forces are building and destroying nations and civilizations. Man is being ridden by powerful, e.g., racial, instincts.

Man-who-speaks, strangely enough, here openly denies the significance of language. The Nazi established his existence as a true Aryan by renouncing his right to criticize his *Führer*, by giving up his right to form an independent judgment on any important matter. Instead of critical thinking and speaking came the roaring of the mass of "disciplined" followers who in this "language" expressed their surrender to the will of their leader and their veneration for his decisions. In Nazism man-who-speaks established himself as man-who-roars.

[43] This is not to deny that metaphysical assumptions can be connected with this concept of science; but that fact does not invalidate the concept itself.

3. *Rebellion against and qualification of the Greek cosmos conviction in the church*

The most conspicuous rebellion against the Greek cosmos conviction in the church is to be found in the powerful and revolutionary trend in theology which we can best call "Neo-Reformation theology," and which is connected with the names of Karl Barth, Emil Brunner, Friedrich Gogarten, and Reinhold and Richard Niebuhr. This theology is much too complicated and too profound to be made the object of an inevitably limited discussion in this place. We restrict ourselves to a reference to some distinctions made by Reinhold Niebuhr in his *The Self and the Dramas of History*.[44] One of the major themes of the book is the distinction between the two components of Western culture, the Hebraic-Christian and the Hellenic. This last element is very much akin to what we call the Greek cosmos conviction. Niebuhr does not decry the Hellenic approach to life as completely false, or completely incompatible with the Christian faith, but he tries to show how this approach gives a very unsatisfactory account of man's crucial problems. Some of these problems are: "How do I have to understand the self, or rather, myself?" "How do we understand the drama of history?"

Niebuhr characterizes the Hellenic approach as "the Greek concept of the permanent structure in things," in which "eternal structure" the elements of history and drama do not receive their due. The Hellenistic doctrine of man looks for "the root of evil" in the body and "the subrational impulses" of man rather than in pride or *hybris* (this last term refers to the Greek drama which has a different view of man than the one called "Hellenic").[45]

This departure from the Hellenic approach is nothing new in contemporary theology; unusual, at least for the American scene, is Niebuhr's stress upon the ontological reasoning which is inseparable from the Hellenic view. As we have already mentioned in Chap. IV, he connects ontology with "the impulse to falsify the facts [of history] in order to bring them into a comprehensible pattern." [46] Niebuhr's view is very clearly expressed in the following passage:

> It must be noted . . . that the world views which assume the rational intelligibility of the world, without mystery, are not less "religious" because they disavow explicit religious faith. Confidence in a rational order is, as the great rationalist Bradley admits, also a faith. The self, even of a philosopher, is re-

[44] Pp. 75 ff.

[45] *Ibid.*, pp. 77-79.

[46] *Ibid.*, p. 49.

ligious to the degree that the self must commit itself to a system of meaning, even if it has the view that the system is . . . self-explanatory.[47]

4. *The departure from the Greek cosmos conviction in philosophy*

Several leaders of the movements indicated by the terms "pragmatism," "logical empiricism," and "existentialism" have taken leave of the Greek cosmos conviction, at least partially. This thesis scarcely needs to be proved. Some brief remarks will suffice.

a) In the case of the logical empiricists the matter is quite clear. We can observe their break with the cosmos conviction in their conception of the function of philosophy. The entire notion that it is the task of the philosopher to detect the nature of the really Real has been discarded. Other symptoms are: the vehement protest against metaphysical reasoning, the suspicion of everything which looks like a system, the heavy emphasis upon the relativity of cognitive and noncognitive truth.

b) It is also beyond doubt that the existentialist movement wants to withdraw as far as possible from the Greek cosmos conviction. Its protest against the "objectivity of truth," and its suspicion of anything which looks like a system, are clear indications. Gabriel Marcel expresses his loathing for any system by calling one of his books *Homo Viator,* man as a traveler.[48] This view of man is not only connected with Marcel's opposition to those who systematically refuse to accept the "other world," [49] but also with his conviction that one cannot give a systematic account of life in terms of "a purely abstract set of rules," [50] of "man in general," "beauty in general," "liberty in general," and "truth in general." [51] To believe that we live in a well-ordered, static universe is a dangerous, misleading notion, apt to breed complacency. Instead, man is a traveler; he is "required to cut himself a dangerous path across the unsteady blocks of a universe which has collapsed." [52]

c) The determinism which William James combats in "The Dilemma of Determinism" is one of the many forms into which the Greek cosmos conviction developed in the Enlightenment.[53] In the introduction of his essay, James argues that he is dealing with "theories about the world" which give us "subjective satisfaction." [54] The principle of causality

[47] *Ibid.,* p. 62.

[48] *Homo Viator, Introduction to a Metaphysic of Hope,* tr. Emma Craufurd (Chicago: Henry Regnery Co., 1951).

[49] *Ibid.,* p. 153.

[50] *Ibid.,* p. 8.

[51] *Ibid.,* pp. 139, 144.

[52] *Ibid.,* p. 153.

[53] In *Essays in Pragmatism,* ed. Alburey Castell (New York: Hafner Publishing Co., 1952).

[54] The word "theory" here does not mean something purely intellectual. What James has in mind is akin to our term "convictional world view."

is for him not an unassailable principle of science, but "a postulate, an empty name simply covering" the demand for uniformity of sequence, a demand "as subjective and emotional" as any other. It is "an altar to an unknown god." James points out that one of the greatest difficulties of his time is the fact that adherents of this "theory of the world" deny the subjectivity of their demand. They proclaim that other demands, e.g., that for freedom, are subjective, but that "necessity and uniformity are something altogether different." With people who are so completely in the dark about themselves, intelligent discussion is impossible.[55]

The "theory of the world" at which James is aiming his criticism is called by him determinism. Some of the doctrines it "professes" [56] are:

(1) Absolute determinism, i.e., the belief "that those parts of the universe already laid down absolutely appoint and decree what the other parts shall be." This means the belief that the universe is "an absolute unity," "an iron block." [57]

(2) The assertion that necessity and impossibility are "the sole categories of the real." This belief implies the denial of possibilities, for instance, of opportunities for moral action.[58]

(3) The denial that there is anything in the world which deserves to be called unique, because anything unique would not possess "the unconditional property of the whole." [59]

(4) The denial of the existence of variety and plurality.

James goes on to show that this "theory of the world" leads to contradictions (the "dilemma" of the title) which are devastating for so rigid a view of the world. What concerns us here are the following facts. First, James has fully recognized this version of the Greek cosmos conviction for what it is, that is to say, not a set of principles with the status of unquestionable scientific authority, but a "subjective" view of the world. Second (this and the following remark we add to James's discussion of determinism), this nineteenth-century version of the Greek cosmos conviction is a very radical one. The crust has disappeared; science has "proved" that the rational and harmonious core rules the whole universe with absolute power. Third, this version is an emaciated one; the core is reduced to rationality and (rational) order; goodness and beauty have been discarded.

[55] "The Dilemma of Determinism," pp. 38, 39.
[56] This revealing term on p. 40.
[57] "The Dilemma of Determinism," pp. 40, 41.
[58] *Ibid.*, pp. 41, 60.
[59] *Ibid.*, p. 44.

5. *Some contemporary Western convictional world views*

The following diagram represents an analysis of some of the conspicuous world views of our time, and indicates their relationship to the Greek cosmos conviction. In the bottom line, + represents a naïve adherence to one of the modern versions of this conviction; √ represents a qualified acceptance of this conviction; — stands for a vehement rejection of it.

Oversimplification is unavoidable in such a chart. The boxes do not claim to render a complete account of the conviction involved; the entries merely point out some of its main aspects. The vertical columns offer the positions of the respective world views in their most radical form; they are likely to give a one-sided picture. In the column on Soviet Communism only the non-Marxist elements are taken into account. Actually, the world view of Communism is a combination of the view given in this column and that in the column of Marx.

SOME WESTERN CONVICTIONAL WORLD VIEWS

	World Council of Churches	American "Pietism"—Twentieth Century	Extreme—Capitalism
Man	a sinner, who can be redeemed, and may join the communion of saints	an honest workman, who bears the strain of toil; a helpless soul, without refuge in the storms of life; sinful and weary; has to be drawn with cords of love	a rational being, obeying the economic laws, who reaches his destination if left alone
Cosmos	theater of God's redemptive work in Christ, but still ridden by demonic powers	God gives the day for toil, the night for sweet slumber; life is a wild, tempestuous sea, on which individuals are thrown around; but: "tho' destruction walk around us, angel guards from Thee surround us"	a rational cosmos, ruled by eternal, unchangeable principles, in which economic laws are rooted; a harmonious cosmos, in which harmony rises spontaneously from actions of free individuals
Society *a*) law	indispensable rules which make possible civilization and the work of the Church	no drinking, no smoking, no movies, no card playing	unerring economic laws are related to natural law
b) freedom and order	can be realized, though imperfectly, by democratic nations and their governments	none	freedom is the necessary condition of order, which is the inevitable reward of obedience to natural law
c) transformation of society	a demand, in obedience to God's will, who alone can renew and re-create	none	deliberate attempts spoil the healing powers of natural law
Divine elements	God, the Father of our Lord Jesus Christ, who ultimately will establish visibly his full kingship	rest, peace, and joy in the shadow of His wing; the sweetness and tenderness of God's love, manifest in Christ's sacrifice and kindness	the privileged classes, their vested interests
Demonic powers	Satan, who uses men and groups, which are blinded by self-interest, pride, to counteract God's work	the sordid treasures of this vain world; the storms, tempests, billows of life; doubt and fear and things of earth	Communism, socialism, interfering governments, labor unions; "leftist" leaders in whom evil trends are personified
Saving powers	Christ, the Lord of history, who will conquer all demons and establish God's kingdom	Jesus, lover of my soul; warm, sweet, tender, a present help he is; softly and tenderly Jesus is calling: come home!	"free enterprise"; the economic laws, natural law, if allowed to operate "freely"
Eschaton	God's kingdom, which is and will be	the mansions of rest; Beulah Land; perfect love and friendship reign thru all eternity	idealized nineteenth-century society
G.C.C. Elements	√	—	+

	Karl Marx	Democratic Socialism of the Twentieth Century		Soviet Communism
		Radical	Moderate	
Man	in principle rational, good; actually either oppressed and good, or oppressor, clinging to class ideology, evil	see Marx	rational to a certain extent, but apt to be ruled by class and group interests; has to be educated, or led by law, to socially responsible behavior	man is either elite-man, who possesses the answers to all questions, or mass-man, to be pushed or forced for his own good
Cosmos	in principle rational, good; actually battlefield of good and evil powers; moves, via conflicts, inexorably toward complete, rational harmony	see Marx	rational to a certain extent, but spoiled by irrational powers of evil; a gradual progress toward a society with more equality and brotherhood is possible if all men of good will unite	a world of conflicting forces, to be mastered by small, but highly organized body of elite-men, the Party
Society a) law	not expression of eternal natural law, but changing mirrors of class interests of privileged groups	existing laws express present relationships of possession and power; these laws are to be improved gradually by parliamentary means		law is what is prescribed by the Party
b) freedom and order	can be established only in the Good Society (see Eschaton)	are realized already partially in existing society under democratic government and control; have to be defended, with help of bourgeois democrats, against Communists, Fascists, and capitalists		freedom is dependent upon order, established by the Party
c) transformation of society	socialist revolution not merely economic necessity, but the only deed which can save the world	is necessary, but may be performed only if supported by clear majority of the nation, within framework of parliamentary procedure		cannot be performed by mass-man, gradually; results from violent revolution by professional revolutionaries
Divine elements	the forces of history, which cannot be stopped, and most certainly will lead the world to the Good Society	see Marx	none	Russian nation, the Party, the workers, Lenin
Demonic powers	the bourgeoisie, which exploits the wage slaves for its selfish ends, and disregards man's dignity and family life	see Marx	none	Western imperialism, which threatens the world proletariat, the Russians, undeveloped countries
Saving powers	the proletariat, which not only eliminates its own oppressors, but oppression, evil as such, once and for all	see Marx	none	the Russian party, the elite vanguard of both the world proletariat and the Russian people
Eschaton	the Good Society, wherein a New Man does the good spontaneously, which therefore does not need compulsion, government	see Marx	none	the world ruled by the Party, every resistance being eliminated
G.C.C. Elements	+	+	√	−

	Western Capitalist—Bourgeois Democracy—Twentieth Century		Nazi—Fascism
	Radical	*Moderate*	
Man	rational and good in principle; his reason of existence is to transform society into a kingdom of goodness and love	rational to a certain extent, but apt to be ruled by self-interest; has to be educated, or led by law, to socially responsible behavior	a nonrational being, either misled by logos, or ruled by instincts and then immersed in powerful wavelike movements of great races
Cosmos	rational and good in principle; actually battlefield of good and evil powers; moves inexorably toward complete, rational harmony	rational to a certain extent, but spoiled by irrational powers of evil; a gradual progress toward a society with more equality and brotherhood is possible, if all men of good will unite	an irrational, but vehemently alive organism, moved by nonrational powers, instincts, drives
Society			
a) law	See Democratic Socialism		law is what is proclaimed by the exponents of the Race
b) freedom and order	are already partially realized in existing society under democratic government and control; have to be defended (with help of social democrats) against Communists, Fascists, and capitalists		freedom is dependent upon a suprarational order, which has to be enforced by the best race
c) transformation of society	is necessary, and our highest task; has to be performed by means of good will, cooperation, persuasion, rather than by way of conflict		a necessary task, not to be achieved by logos, but by instinct-inspired leadership of the right race
Divine elements	ideas and values, e.g., the Four Freedoms, peace, brotherhood, justice, good will and reason, which guarantee the ultimate victory of the Good	none	the Aryan race, and the nation in which it manifests itself purely: the German nation
Demonic powers	ignorance, selfishness, bigotry, racial and religious prejudice, injustice	none	sick races, which poison Aryan civilization; sick logos-civilization of the West
Saving powers	Great Men, leading other men of good will, and good elements of society, toward victory over egotism and injustice	none	Great Leaders, exponents of the right race
Eschaton	Harmonious World State, without conflicts, based upon brotherhood, equality, liberty	none	the world ruled by the Aryan race, all other races being subjugated
G.C.C. Elements	+	√	—

PART THREE

Language Structures Which Assist Modern Man in Establishing His Existence

CHAPTER SEVEN

MORALS

Moral Language Enables an Establishment in View of Goods and Highest Goods

A. INTRODUCTION

The question which will interest us in Part III is this: "How does modern man establish his existence?" We do not aim at a complete answer. From the many ways in which an establishment is achieved we select only two: the moral way and a Protestant way. Perhaps there are other ways which in the eyes of some people are more characteristically modern, such as the aesthetic, and the political one, or the ways characterized by vital or pragmatic language. Also the modern forms of the Jewish and Roman Catholic faith could have been chosen. I do not, however, possess a knowledge of these ways which is intimate enough to guarantee a satisfying analysis. Yet, it will help to understand modern man and his language situation if we gain a clearer insight into the moral (in this chapter) and a Protestant manner (in Chap. VIII) of establishing one's existence.

There exists a peculiar problem in regard to the subject matter of our present chapter, the moral way of establishing existence. The question must be raised as to whether we can properly speak of "the moral way" of establishing existence. Do people actually establish their lives in a way which is "purely" moral? The quotation marks indicate the peculiarity of the problem: we encounter here an analytical question which can scarcely be formulated satisfactorily because it has usually been covered over by a convictional quarrel. Some people will say immediately—that is, without philosophical reflection—that a "purely" moral establishment is not only possible, and a significant reality, but that it is the only proper manner of establishing one's existence. Other people, just as immediately-convictionally, will claim that a purely "moral" establishment is impossible, because what seems to be "purely" moral is actually dependent upon an overt or hidden religion.

We meet here again the "problem situation." The problem cannot be understood without reference to some bitterly opposed camps of "theologians," without reference to their prejudices and fears, and to the goods at stake. There are mainly two groups, and their identity is clear from what has been said thus far. The first is that of the humanists (in the widest sense). The good at stake here is the dignity and freedom of man. The existence of a "purely" moral language is defended because religion is felt to be an evil power, or at least an arbitrary, tradition-bound institution, from which man should be independent. The other camp consists of Christian theologians who feel that the dignity of their God is endangered as soon as people think that they can establish a good life independent of his will. They think that moral life, truly understood, depends upon faith in God, truly understood. The situation is complicated by the fact that a small contingent of Christian theologians claims that moral language and the language of the Christian faith are natural enemies to each other. These men will shy away from any attempt of linking Christian faith and morals so closely as to suggest that they depend upon or complete each other. This third position (we can scarcely speak of a camp in this case since the view is so unusual in the United States) was given a voice in this book in the ideas of Maurice Pradines presented in Chap. II. Kristensen's work discloses that probably some ancients entertained similar ideas (Chap. V).

The effect of the vehemence of the theological conflicts is that the analytical question about the nature of moral language, especially in view of the problem of the "purity" of this language, has as yet scarcely been raised in a proper way. The main interest of this chapter is an attempt to find a satisfactory formulation for the problem, and to suggest an answer which is free (as free as is humanly possible) from "theological" presuppositions. In order to achieve this purpose we will largely ignore the camp theologies.

The format of this chapter consists of a discussion of the position of three philosophers representing, respectively, the analytical approach (Hospers), the empiricist (Dewey), the existentialist (Marcel). We will propose three questions about these men. First, do they raise the analytical question which we have in mind? (To what extent is it meaningful to say that modern man establishes his existence in speaking morally?) Second, if these philosophers do not raise this question, what are the basic problems which receive their attention? Third, is an answer to our question implied in their discussion of the problems? Finally we are interested in knowing whether the work of these three men throws some light upon the way in which modern man actually establishes his existence.

B. WHAT IS THE MEANING OF MORAL LANGUAGE?

1. *Introduction*

There is an important group of analytical philosophers which does not raise our question explicitly, but whose way of putting the problem of ethics leads us right up to it. According to these men, the problem is: "We notice that people frequently use terms such as 'good,' 'bad,' 'just,' and 'ought,' and we want to know what people mean when they use these terms." Hospers is a representative of this approach.[1]

Before we can go any further, a basic issue has to be decided. As soon as one enters the discussion of moral issues, one meets a peculiar terminological problem. The philosopher notices that not only in everyday language but also in ethical and philosophical studies two terms and their derivations are used, *moral* and *ethical,* many times without a sufficient clarification of their meanings. The usage proposed by two Dutch ethicists, I. J. de Bussy and Nicolaas Westendorp Boerma,[2] is highly suggestive. They point out that in regard to moral issues we have to do with two mental activities different in principle, and suggest that we confine the use of each of the two terms to one of the two activities. Recommendations for our way of life are given by *morals. Ethics* is a science which has the same purpose as all other sciences, namely, to study and explain phenomena which are given to us, in this case moral phenomena. Ethics therefore does not approve or disapprove; it is morally neutral.

I propose to accept the distinction made by de Bussy and Westendorp Boerma, making one qualification. Whereas these scholars called ethics a science, he wants to consider it as a branch of philosophy, to wit, that section of philosophy which analyzes moral language, that is to say, man-speaking-morally. In the terminology of this book: morals is couched in convictional language, ethics in analytical language.

Hence, terms such as "theory" and "explanation" belong to the domain of ethics, and not to that of morals. For instance, an ethical theory attempts to explain what people mean when they use terms such as "good," "just," "duty." On the other hand, terms such as "doctrines," "evaluations," and "interpretations" belong to the realm of morals. A certain confessional group entertains certain moral doctrines, in which

[1] John Hospers, *An Introduction to Philosophical Analysis* (New York: Prentice-Hall, 1953), ch. vii.

[2] Isaac J. de Bussy, 1846-1920, professor of philosophy of religion and ethics, University of Amsterdam, 1892-1916; Nicolaas Westendorp Boerma, 1872-1952, professor in the same fields, University of Amsterdam, 1936-1942.

actions and goods are evaluated and interpreted in the light of the group's convictions.

Actually, we have to distinguish three instead of two languages. Ethics is a *use*-language, in which theories are used to explain the meaning of moral language. Then there are the spontaneous moral judgments, forming a part of people's confessional language. They belong to *is*-language. Finally, moral doctrines are a section of a group's theology, and have to be counted as *employ*-language. We can call the totality of a group's moral doctrines its morals.

From this point of view there exists only one ethics, but there are many morals. There is one ethics because every scholar, no matter what his convictions are, can participate in the analysis of people's moral language. On the other hand, there exist many morals because each confessional group, each theology possesses its own moral doctrines. Only those men who share the convictions of a particular group can participate in the activity of elaborating that group's convictions in regard to human behavior. "Christian ethics" is therefore a contradiction in terms, but we can speak of Christian morals, just as of Moslem, Hindu, stoic, naturalist morals.

2. *Hosper's presentation of the problem*

Hospers claims that the problem of ethics is, "What do ethical terms, such as 'good,' 'ought,' and 'duty' mean?" Or, "We should really ask 'What do we mean (intend) when we use the word?' " [3] In his chapter on "Problems in Ethics" he discusses mainly three theories which try to answer this question.

a) The objectivist theory. Its position is summarized in this sentence: "Since 'X is good' is of the same grammatical form as 'X is round,' it seems natural to believe that goodness is, in these respects, like roundness, and that the word 'good' names an objective property of X just as 'round' does." [4]

b) The subjectivist theory. "According to all subjectivistic theories, when you say of any act that it is right, or a state-of-affairs that it is good, you are not saying that it is good, you are not saying that it has a certain objective property: you are only saying that you (or other persons) have a certain attitude towards X." [5]

c) The emotive theory. Ethical terms do not have a cognitive meaning, but are emotive in their meaning. "Words like 'good,' 'ought,' and

[3] *Op. cit.*, p. 452.
[4] *Ibid.*, p. 455.
[5] *Ibid.*, p. 460.

'duty' have a certain persuasive power which no other words in the language can quite duplicate."[6]

Hospers' chapter consists of a meticulous and thorough discussion of these theories and some other ones which have been derived from them.

3. *Discussion of Hospers' approach*

In part I agree with Hospers' starting point. The problem of ethics is not to determine what a man's behavior *ought* to be, but to ask for the meaning of moral language, for instance, of the term "ought." My objection to Hospers' approach is that, in spite of its appropriate starting point, it remains practically fruitless for ethical analysis. The reason for this is the narrow scope of the investigation. Hospers limits ethics to one question: "Is the moral judgment a function of our intellect or of our emotional life?" He does not raise the question as to the person who makes a moral judgment, and does not seem to be aware of the immensely important role which goods and values play in a man's moral life. That is to say, Hospers isolates the moral judgment from the moral situation, of which persons and goods are elements which one cannot overlook. Thus our fundamental question, "Can we say that modern man establishes his existence in speaking morally?" does not come into view at all. Both Hospers and I ask for the *meaning* of moral language, but we understand this meaning in a different way. I claim that the question about the meaning of a language has not been pressed far enough if this meaning is not related to the way in which man establishes his existence.

In view of these remarks I shall defend, in this section, the following thesis: "An explanation of the meaning of moral judgments cannot be given without reference to the goods and the Highest Good, and to man's desire to establish his existence."

The format of this section will be: (1) a paradigm, (2) goods and Highest Goods, (3) moral language and establishing our existence, (4) some related issues. There will be merely incidental discussion of objectivism, subjectivism, and emotivism, but at the end the points of contact between these theories and the ones set forth in this section will be brought out.

a) *The Paradigm*

The meaning of *goed* (the Dutch equivalent of both "good" and "right," in English) underwent a remarkable change in Holland during the five years of Nazi occupation. During the occupation years, when people said about somebody, "He is good," they meant that he not

[6] *Ibid.*, pp. 471, 475.

only talked against the Nazis but that he actually took his share in the fight against them. Before May, 1940, *goed* was used just as vaguely and sloppily as its equivalent in other Western languages.

b) *Goods and Highest Goods*

(1) The subjectivistic and objectivistic theories are unsatisfactory because they are atomistic. They consider isolated items, e.g., a certain person A and a certain action Bb of a person B. The question they ask is this: "If A calls Bb 'right,' does that mean that A reads 'rightness' from Bb, or does it mean that A expresses his attitude toward Bb?"

Actually, much more is involved than A and Bb. If A means a Dutchman during the occupation and Bb means the action of another Dutchman B, helping a Jewish fugitive C, we can understand the meaning of A calling Bb "right" only if we take into consideration D (the *Wehrmacht*), E (the Nazi secret police), F (Dutch legislation ignoring racial differences), G (Nazi measures, accounting them as decisive), H (concentration camps), etc. In other words, D-Z are just as much part of the situation as A, B, and C.

(2) D-Z are not just some more items added to A, B, and C. All together form a "world." We have to start our interpretation of moral judgments with the recognition of this "world." Human beings live related to individual persons, groups of persons, institutions, material objects used by persons. All these elements of the "world" are meaningful to human beings, and are evaluated by them, either positively or negatively. Many of these elements can be called "goods" or concrete values, e.g., schools, law courts, factories, farms, and railways.

There are various ways of evaluating goods, characterized by terms such as: (1) good, just, coward; (2) harmonious, pretty, ugly; (3) useful, decrepit, handy, etc. In this section we deal with the first evaluation, the moral one.

It is my contention that when people give a moral judgment they have in mind the goods and persons of their "world." An act is evaluated positively if, according to the understanding of the speaker, it promotes, defends, or makes possible the growth of an important good which is threatened. If goods are not particularly important, or not unusually threatened, people do not go out of their way to laud acts promoting them. A called action Bb of his neighbor B "right," because the life and freedom of the Jewish fugitive C is a good, and a threatened good.

Two remarks have to be added: First, the fact that goods are called "concrete" values should not mislead us into considering them exclusively tangible. In goods, tangibles and intangibles are interwoven. "Life and freedom," in the sentence above, do not mean merely biological existence and physical freedom of movement. The expression means certainly bare existence, but also something more, namely, a way of living compatible with human dignity. This illustrates that in an appreciation of a good, convictions about the meaning of life are always implied. The empirical method in ethics does not mean that we are not allowed to refer to these convictions. Never mentioning convictions would amount to the denial of a simple and obvious fact: namely, that human beings always interpret goods guided by specific convictions. In our case "life and freedom" point to convictions typical for people belonging to the Western civilization of the twentieth century.

Second, the act which is judged morally is sometimes considered not only in relation to one particular good—in this case "life and freedom" of the fugitive—but also to the whole "world" to which A and B and the fugitive belong. Loyal Dutchmen called acts such as Bb "right" and men like B "good" also because they were vividly aware that, without such acts and such goods ("life and freedom"), life as they appreciated it could not exist. Without such goods and acts people could still "be alive," e.g., under a totalitarian regime, but could not "live" as Western people meant life to be. In other words, Bb was called "right" because it made possible this Western "world." In ordinary times people scarcely realize that their "world" depends upon their honest, or brave, or just acts to a great extent. It is only in crucial times that people are conscious that their moral judgments have in mind not only the good immediately involved, but also the "world."

It would lead us outside the limits of this section to show that not only moral judgments, but also moral *rules,* cannot be understood without reference to the goods. For the moment it must suffice to make one observation which points in this direction.

During the Nazi occupation members of the Dutch underground stole things (e.g., food ration cards for fugitives from the Nazi terror) and deceived and killed Nazis. The Dutch did not interpret these actions as morally bad—trespasses of unassailable, unchangeable rules, trespasses to be condoned, however, in wartime—neither did they think that moral rules were suspended altogether. The Dutch understood that important goods (e.g., "the life and freedom" of Jews) were threatened to such a degree that they could not be promoted without the suspension, temporarily and on specific occasions, of the moral rules of ordinary times, and the introduction of new rules. It was felt that the *primary* things are not the rules but the goods. Rules exist for the sake of goods, without which life is impossible.

(3) It is not accidental that we have used terms like "view" and "regard" in the preceding pages (namely, "in view of" and "in regard to"). It seems to be appropriate to use the *metaphor of seeing.* The usage of this metaphor in this discussion differs from the usages in both the objectivist and intuitionist theory. The objectivist theory, even if it does not actually use the verb "to see," still suggests that we "read" the goodness from an object or the rightness from an act, in a way similar to our reading the green color from a tree. This usage of the metaphor has to be rejected, because it does not explain in any way the remarkable variety of the reports of this moral reading, which compares unfavorably with the practical unanimity in the reports of physical reading.

The intuitionist theory differs from the latter in that it claims that the object of seeing cannot be revealed by empirical methods. Intuition is a seeing by the "inner eye," and it shows us goodness as a property which no physical eye can detect.[7] This usage of the metaphor has to be rejected because it presupposes a contrast between two types of seeing which is inspired by the Greek cosmos conviction: physical over against mental, that is, a "lower" against a "higher" seeing. Actually, we see with our whole person, so that a separation of mental from physical seeing is out of the question.

The "seeing" meant in this discussion is a consideration of two elements in relationship with each other. A "saw" Bb in relation to the fugitive's life and freedom, even in connection with the whole "world" of loyal Dutchmen. This seeing differs from physical seeing (the usage is therefore metaphorical), but in spite of that it is something about which we can talk in analytical language. It is the same act as the "viewing" in a convictional world view, a seeing guided by specific convictions and evaluations. Other metaphors used in everyday language stress the importance of the "see" metaphors. We can say: "In the light of a specific Western convictional world *view* an act of adultery is *seen* to be damaging to an important good, monogamic marriage, and is therefore called (morally) wrong." The "seeing" meant here is itself convictional, but it can be discussed in nonconvictional, analytical language. Moral judgments are based upon this "seeing." They flow from it.

(4) Since it is evident that "the goods" are indispensable for the

[7] Hospers, *op. cit.*, p. 470.

understanding of "(morally) good," it would be wise to ask whether the concept of *the Highest Good* cannot also help to clarify the meaning of "good." It seems that in the "worlds" of goods, as seen by people guided by particular convictional world views, there are goods which are held to be of decisive importance. In the Nazi "world" it was the Aryan race; in the Communist "world" it is the proletariat, etc. In judging whether an act is right or wrong, or in establishing the relative value of a good, the relationship to such a Highest Good is the final test. A "world" of goods seems to possess a certain structure, the goods are ranged in a certain hierarchy. The Highest Good forms the top of the hierarchy.

A modern term for the Highest Good is "Cause." In crucial times, when important goods are threatened, the people who "see" the threat most clearly assemble around a cause. A free Holland in a free world was the cause for loyal Dutchmen during the occupation years. Acts and goods were "seen," evaluated, in relation to this cause.

Analytical philosophers may hesitate to work with the concept "Highest Good." Their prudence is well founded. The questions raised in connection with the Highest Good are mostly these: "What is *really* our Highest Good?" and "What *ought* we to deem our Highest Good?" These questions cannot be answered by philosophers. The answer depends upon our convictions, our convictional world view. Philosophers should ask another question, one which is too much neglected. It is: "What is *actually* someone's Highest Good?"

Answers to the "really" question are traditionally "God" or "Reason." Such answers are unsatisfactory for two reasons: they naïvely assume the "reality" of nonempirical entities; they are also misleading because they suggest a simplicity which nowhere exists.

In trying to answer the "actually" question we have to deal with these two problems, raised by the unsatisfactory character of the answer to the "really" question. First, if we cannot naïvely refer to God, Christ, Reason, Justice, or Allah, neither can we leave these references out completely. Otherwise we would not be giving a truthful account of the convictions of the people whose moral language we are describing. We have to use the term "intangibles" discussed above, and to refer to "the intangible which is called God," or "the intangible which is called Justice." Second, we have to realize that the Highest Good is not just a single item, but a whole group of items. We can better speak of the *region* of the Highest Good. In Holland during the occupation years this region contained, for the loyal majority of the nation, tangibles such as their own country and intangibles such as God, human dignity, freedom, eternal values, rationality. As was stated before, the distinction between tangibles and intangibles should not be overdone, because most goods are "seen" to be a combination of both.

Two more things may be said in regard to the Highest Good. First, the region of the Highest Good is not a fixed entity. It undergoes changes. Changes in moral judgment follow changes in the Highest Good. During the occupation of Holland several items soared into decisive places of the upper region, such as national freedom, human dignity. As a consequence the moral judgments of the loyal Dutch changed. Before the war it did not mean very much when you said about somebody that he was a courageous man. In 1940 "courageous" suddenly came to be a word of high praise. All goods were in danger of being lost, and especially the highest goods, which make life and its goods possible. Behavior which aimed at their defense was considered of the utmost importance, was called "courageous" or "good."

Second, in such crucial times the region of the Highest Good is "seen" clearly, whereas in ordinary times these highest summits are hidden in the clouds of the (so-called) self-evident and of mores. Hospers notices that if you ask people, "What do you mean by the word 'good'?" they cannot give you a coherent answer.[8] Hospers makes this remark in the discussion of a different problem. The reason that it is quoted here is that Hospers' remark takes for granted that people cannot answer the question about the meaning of "good." That may be the case in the United States in 1958, but it was not at all the case in Holland between 1940 and 1945. "Good" then meant: a man who fights the Nazis. Loyal Dutchmen knew exactly what "good" meant. The reason was the vividness with which they "saw" their Highest Good.

It remains to be seen whether the situation in the United States in 1958 is so different from that in Holland in 1946 as is suggested above. It seems that two groups have been formed in the United States during the last years, within each of which the term "good" receives a meaning opposite to that of the other group. In the first group the word "good" means: "completely free from any contamination by Communism, socialism, and internationalism." The second group is similar to that of the loyal Dutchmen. It consists of the people who "see" through the new Fascism of our time. "Good" means here, first, being anti-Fascist as well as anti-Communist; second, willing to do something about it. Both groups "see" goods, "see"

[8] *Ibid.*, p. 473.

their Highest Good threatened. What a member of one group "sees," one of the other group cannot "see" at all.

In the present discussion the term "Highest Good" has been used instead of the term "convictor." This usage served the purpose of showing the strong connection between morally "good," and the "goods," and the Highest "Good." We have, however, to be aware of the fact that the use of the term "convictor" also has its advantages. It suggests much better than Highest Good its power over a man's life. The convictor is the ultimate point of reference of a man's convictions and his actions. The convictor is that on the basis of which the importance, the meaning, the value, of a man's own life, all his goods, and his world are seen by him.

c) Moral language and establishing our existence

After the preceding remarks aimed at establishing the first part of our main thesis (the impossibility of discussing "good" without reference to "the goods" and the "Highest Good"), in this portion of our discussion we want to show briefly the relevance of this interpretation for the problem of the establishing of man's existence.

(1) We can start our considerations with this problem: *Are morals dependent upon religion?* As was suggested earlier, the issue is very seldom discussed in a philosophical way because the disputants use the answer to this question to defend their particular convictions instead of trying to answer a question of facts. Christians claim that their own morals are founded upon their Christian faith and that Western nonbelievers maintain a system of morals which is largely Christian in origin, while they discard the faith in which their morals are rooted. Non-Christians claim that the fact that so many generations of humanists have lived without any religion proves that morals actually are and should be independent of religion.

I hold that the problem can be rightly understood only if one changes the term "religion" into convictional world views, i.e., the way in which we "see" and interpret the "world" of goods and "view" them in relationship to what we consider the Highest Good. Morals are dependent, not upon religion as such, but upon convictional world views. For both humanists and Christians the fact is that their moral judgments flow from their seeing of the "world" of goods and the Good. The only difference is that humanists refer to their intangibles in nonreligious language, Christians in religious language.

In other words, moral language is an ambiguous term. This language is always a part of a convictional language which implies convictions about the All, a Highest Good, a convictor. Hence the question as to whether one can establish his existence by speaking "purely moral" language is a pseudo problem. If one understands by "purely moral" a language which would refer only to goods and not to a Highest Good, then one entertains a meaningless concept. Moral language, by its very nature, implies a reference to a Highest Good. This thesis will be questioned by those who want to make a case for the self-sufficiency of moral language. The following remarks may not prove the thesis, but perhaps they will enhance its plausibility.

We meet here again the problem of the structure of convictional world views. Some do hold views which have as their center a moral doctrine, but always the view as a whole is more than this doctrine. There live many people in Western Europe and the States who would *not like to commit* themselves as to the meaning of the All, but who are quite certain about the validity and sublimity of the moral law. Other people combine respect for the honest and courageous man with a confession that life as a whole seems *rather senseless* or even absurd to them. A much more old-fashioned point of view combines outspoken moral convictions with a *vague optimism* about life in general. A fourth group contains those who call themselves Christians but confess that what really is important is good moral behavior, whereas "*all those doctrines* about God and Christ" do not mean too much and should not be taken too seriously.

In all these four cases we meet a convictional world view without a "real" convictor. Neither the confessional group, nor the world view as a whole, but the moral aspect of this view has taken over the convictor's position of authority. The convictions about the meaning of life as a whole, however, are always there, respectively, (1) a kind of careful agnosticism, (2) a fundamental pessimism, (3) an optimism without, and (4) one with a divine guarantor. It may even be asked whether we shall not find in all of these cases a remarkable difference between the explicit and the implicit world views. It is not impossible that whereas the *moral* convictions are emphasized in the explicit views, the pessimistic or optimistic convictions about *the All* are decisive in the implicit views. Many times an intense attention to the moral life is the defense which a person assumes as to the horror he feels at his half-avowed admission of the fundamental meaninglessness of life.

Explicitly such a person will establish his existence as that of a decent fellow who defends the dignity of man in an era of Fascism, television, and nationalistic hysterics. Implicitly he may have established himself as a courageous earthling who defies the nonhuman powers which rule the universe by building a life ennobled by moral, aesthetic, and intellectual values.

(2) We should oversimplify the issue, however, if we should say that moral judgments are dependent exclusively upon convictional world views. An important role is played by decisive events, or crucial times, which help to shape the fate of classes, nations, and civilizations. It seems probable that students of history can show us that convictions (moral or otherwise) which seem self-evident in ordinary times can be traced back to clashes of convictions fought out in earlier times. Such clashes led to set convictions which were scarcely challenged until a new time of crisis arrived. These crucial times are not a factor completely independent from convictional world views. These views helped and continue to help people nowadays in the interpretation of fateful events. There thus appears to be mutual influence between convictions and events. These considerations lead to the realization of the importance of the historical point of view for ethical philosophy.

d) *Related issues*

(1) An issue of general importance is that of "*relativism.*" Are we obliged to label the position taken in this discussion in this way? The term is ambiguous. It has at least two meanings. If one understands it to mean that our moral judgments are related to, intimately connected with our country, our civilization, the century in which we live, our convictional world view, then I would emphatically claim the label "relativism" for my point of view. If, however, one understands the term to mean complete arbitrariness, a denial of the abiding values, the term has to be rejected. I do not claim to say anything at all about the existence or nonexistence, the value or nonvalue of any goods and highest goods. Ethical philosophy is not interested in such problems. It does not intend to approve or disapprove of actions or to assert or deny the reality of goods, but it seeks to understand. It analyzes moral language. The term "relativism" as an accusation is also out of place in regard to the various convictional world views and the moral judgments connected with them. All these views are inspired by the awareness of imperishable values to be enhanced, of matters of great importance to be defended. In order to avoid confusion between the two meanings of the term "relativism," the view set forth in this chapter should be called "relational" as distinguished from "relativistic."

(2) The value of an interpretation of the meaning of moral terms is enhanced if the interpretation can throw some light on *the con-*

flicts between moral judgments. We leave out of consideration conflicts related to the cognitive components of moral language. Conflicts which go deeper and may even prove unsolvable have to be understood in reference to decisive convictional world views. If one's convictions were decisively formed by the convictional world view of Nazism, and consequently the Highest Good of one's "world" was the Aryan race, or the glory of the German empire, it was inevitable that one called "good" and "right" persons and actions which served these Highest Goods. People whose convictions are influenced mainly by the convictional world views of the Enlightenment, or one of the various Christian views, will use "good" and "right" in ways which are certainly diametrically opposed to Nazi usage.

e) Concluding remarks

In closing this section we might try to formulate which elements of the *objectivist,* the *subjectivist,* and the *emotivist* theories mentioned by Hospers are pointing in the direction of the interpretation of moral judgments presented in this section.

The subjectivist theory gives account of the fact that moral judgments are related to specific individuals and groups which possess a unique view of goods, persons, and actions.

The objectivist theory recognizes the fact that, for the person who is judging, something of importance is at stake, something which is real for him, a reality other than himself.

The emotivist theory realizes that moral terms possess other than cognitive meaning.

C. MARCEL'S CRYPTOMETAPHYSICS AND CONCRETE ETHICS

Marcel does not present himself as an ethicist. Yet his writings are full of relevant ethical analysis. Marcel does not go along with the analytical distinction between ethics and morals. He calls his realm of discourse: philosophy, or reflection, or secondary reflection, and does not make quite clear what its function actually is. In spite of the resulting vagueness Marcel makes notable contributions to the cause of ethical analysis. First, he entertains the notion of man's establishment. Second, he discusses moral problems in the context of the moral situation, and gives his full attention to its elements of persons and goods.

We intend first to investigate Marcel's analysis of the nature of value; then to set forth his consideration of the nature of man; to continue with a discussion of his moral doctrine; and to finish with an examination of his convictional world view.

1. *Marcel's analysis of the nature of value*

A typical treatment of this issue is to be found in the essays "Value and Immorality," "The Dangerous Situation of Ethical Values," and "Obedience and Fidelity." [9]

a) The first characteristic Marcel gives of values is that they are "incarnate," that is to say embodied, incorporated in something. He refers to "all the embodied values, whether they are incorporated in the life of a family, a school, a hospital, a museum or a church." In stressing this embodiment, Marcel takes his position against an abstract way of referring to values. "We do not consent to die for beauty in general, or even for liberty in general; all that means absolutely nothing. We accept death in order to save our country, or perhaps more truly for our enslaved brothers." (This essay was written in 1943, the time of the Nazi occupation of part of France—the time, too, of the underground resistance.) Speaking of aesthetic values, Marcel introduces an objection: "Is not gracefulness a value for instance?" He answers, "Perhaps the answer is that we establish a category of the graceful and then set it up as a value by virtue of an illusion. What really exist are graceful human beings, there are also works of art that are graceful." [10]

b) The second important characteristic of value is its close relationship to life, to what is real. "It is indeed of the nature of value to take on a special function in relation to life and, as it were, to set its seal upon it." Marcel elaborates this point in a penetrating discussion of unemployment. The unemployed is detached from values because he is "cast away by what is real. . . . It seems to him that life has no more use for him."

To be at work, on the other hand, is to be possessed by the real in such a way that we no longer know exactly whether it is we who are fashioning it, or it which fashions us. . . . It involves the reciprocal movement by which man and reality embrace each other, which is none the less effective in the artist and the scholar than in the artisan, for instance, or the labourer. All that varies is the manner in which the real is present to man or, correlatively, the manner by which man is present to the real.[11]

c) A value is furthermore incorporated in a *cause*. Marcel goes along with Josiah Royce to a large extent. Marcel says:

A cause is neither an individual nor a collection of individuals, nor an abstract principle. A cause is not impersonal, but rather supra-personal; it is a

[9] *Homo Viator*, pp. 135-54, 155-65, 125-34.
[10] *Ibid.*, pp. 162, 143, 144.
[11] *Ibid.*, pp. 141, 145.

particular type of unity which holds together a number of persons within a life which they share. Hence a relationship of a special kind, which we can call loyalty, is established between the individual and the cause. It is not a mystical renunciation, but a fully conscious attachment which presupposes the free subordination of the self to a superior principle.

Marcel departs from Royce when the latter claims that conflict between varying loyalties is the greatest of evils. He quotes Royce as saying, "A cause is good not only for us but for humanity—that is to say, in itself—according to the measure in which it serves the spirit of loyalty." Marcel, whose country is suffering from the S.S. man's loyalty to the Nazi cause, calls Royce's concepts of cause and loyalty "empty." The spirit of loyalty is a "fiction," unless it is clearly qualified which specific cause is meant.[12]

d) Because values are incorporated in causes, they have to be served. Marcel declares that "all life is a *service*." This means that "it is its essential nature to be consecrated to God, or some high purpose such as knowledge or art, etc., or even to some deliberately chosen social end." [13]

e) All through Marcel's work one notion is presented with exceptional force: values are precious and vulnerable. They are always *endangered*. This is the case not only because we live in a world where Fascism and Communism are powerful. Also the nice people, the decent men of good will of the West, undermine values, even if this happens by means of mental attitudes which seem harmless. Marcel mentions in this connection the theology of Karl Barth (which presumably devaluates our values by an undue stress upon revelation) and a certain type of "undiluted sociology" (which kills values by a merely statistical treatment).[14]

f) Hence, value is related to the willingness to take risks for its sake, to *courage*, to "a *sacrifice* which is at least possible." The context in which Marcel makes these remarks is a salute of honor to the underground resistance in his beloved France.[15]

g) Marcel suggests, finally, a structure in the realm of values. "Value is . . . only authentic when something incommensurable is not only granted but established, something beside which all the rest, at least for the time being, sinks into non-existence; all the rest, including myself, that is." [16]

[12] *Ibid.*, pp. 155, 156.
[13] *Ibid.*, pp. 126, 141.
[14] *Ibid.*, p. 161.
[15] *Ibid.*, p. 143.
[16] *Ibid.*, pp. 140, 25.

2. *Marcel's conception of the nature of man*

a) The central concept used by Marcel to characterize man is *act*. (Marcel follows here the phenomenological method of Edmund Husserl.) Man is not a thing, an object, which is merely there, but he establishes himself in an act. He is not an object, the fixed characteristics or faculties of which one can list and record in a catalog. On the contrary, we have to describe the *possibilities* which man can choose, in which he can establish himself by means of an act.[17]

b) Marcel discusses several of these possibilities (for instance, in regard to the problem of death, we have to ask by what kind of act a human being encounters death). We concentrate our attention upon two possibilities which Marcel discusses amply: to establish the self as an *ego* or as a *person*.

About the *ego* Marcel says:

> It is very instructive to give a careful account of the act which establishes what I call myself, the act, for instance, by which I attract attention of others so that they may praise me, maybe, or blame me, but at all events that they notice me. In every case I *produce* myself, in the etymological sense of the word, that is to say I put myself forward.

Being a *person* is connected with assuming responsibility. This way of living implies acknowledging the reality of other persons, that is to say, admitting that they are important for their own sake. For the ego another individual is merely a mirror of its own greatness. Being a person, however, means to be engaged in work, to participate in the community with other real persons, to be directed toward reality and to be absorbed in it.

The most trenchant term used by Marcel in this connection is "availability." A person is available when he can give himself to any opportunity which offers itself; or perhaps it is better to say that a person can "transform circumstances into opportunities." In this way a person participates in the shaping of his own destiny; he creates his own self. This term "creation" is not meant arrogantly by Marcel. He uses the notion of "creative fidelity" and claims that "that which is essential in the creator is the act by which he places himself at the disposal of" what is real.

[17] It has to be noticed that Marcel shares this approach with Kierkegaard and Heidegger. The latter describes the possibilities of an authentic way of living and an inauthentic way; Kierkegaard pictures the aesthetic, the ethical, the religious ways of living.

Marcel sums up by saying:

The personality is only realized in the act by which it tends to become incarnate (in a book, for instance, or an action or in a complete life), but at the same time it is of its very essence never to fix itself or crystallize itself finally in this particular incarnation.[18]

c) Marcel's discussion of the ego and the person possesses unusual implications for ethics. He warns us not to identify ego with badness and a person with goodness. "The truth is much more that [personality] controls the existence of a world where there is good and evil." "The ego, so long as it remains shut up within itself, . . . the prisoner of its own feelings . . . desires . . . anxiety . . . , is really beyond the reach of evil as well as of good. It literally has not yet awakened to reality." Many people live their lives in this unreal dreamworld of the ego. "There is no doubt that direct judgment cannot be applied to such beings." Marcel goes on to say that "each of us, in a considerable part of his life . . . is still unawakened, that is to say that he moves on the margin of reality like a sleepwalker." [19]

3. Some elements of Marcel's convictional world view

The above remarks, taken in themselves, give of Marcel's work a picture which is so incomplete that it tends toward distortion. The fact is that Marcel's analysis of value and of man is always offered within a framework of very outspoken and definite convictions. We will first try to indicate some of the most decisive of these convictions, and then to discuss the relationship between Marcel's analysis and his convictions.

a) Marcel is a Christian, but does not consider himself to be a theologian. As a Roman Catholic he feels that he has to leave explicit discussions of the faith to professional theologians. What Marcel offers is, by his own designation, philosophy (also reflection, or secondary reflection), and this leads to the borders of faith, points to it, suggests it.

As a consequence Marcel's work shows mostly the following structure: in the first part of an essay (which is sometimes the largest part) a philosophical analysis prevails, studded with references to his faith. Toward the end of the essay Marcel reasons on the basis of his own convictions, although he does not offer explicit statements of his faith but works with suggestions.

b) First, we notice suggestions about *God,* such as "the Absolute" (in the very last sentence of an essay), "the absolute Thou!" When analyzing fidelity, Marcel says, "Fidelity can never be unconditional,

[18] *Homo Viator,* pp. 14, 15, 20-26, 143.
[19] *Ibid.,* p. 22.

except when it is Faith" (on the next to the last page of an article). After analyzing the notion of personality, he claims that it cannot be understood without reference to a "supra-personal reality." Probably he means the God of the Christian faith, for he goes on to contrast this suprapersonal reality with its "rivals," which he also calls "caricatures," and "idols," and which he contends have led to "the incredibly false religions so prevalent, alas, in our time" (two pages from the end of an essay).[20]

c) Extremely vague are the references to "*the other world*." We suspect that it is the kingdom of God of which the New Testament speaks, but we are not sure, for it is also called "a world more firmly established in Being," which expression could point to a Greek conception of invisible reality. When Marcel speaks this convictional language, he does not employ "value" as a technical ethical term but says that it is "the mirror wherein it is given us to discern . . . the real face of our destiny. . . . What it shows us certainly reaches its full development in another world." Marcel himself sees it to be the major characteristic of his philosophy that he, in contrast to nearly all contemporary philosophers, makes "the other world the axis of our life." Elsewhere Marcel speaks of "the order in which any true values find their expression," and mentions truth and justice. On each occasion the statements are made at the end of an essay.[21]

d) Marcel's convictions are very markedly expressed in utterances such as these: "If death is the ultimate reality, value is annihilated in mere *scandal*, reality is pierced to the heart." "In a world of scandal . . . where what is best and highest was at the mercy of blind forces . . . there would not perhaps be a single value which was not in danger of appearing ludicrous and suspect." [22]

e) Marcel's conviction about *man* is that he is a traveler, *homo viator*.

Perhaps a stable order can only be established if man is acutely aware of his condition as a traveller, that is to say, if he perpetually reminds himself that he is required to cut himself a dangerous path across the unsteady blocks of a universe which has collapsed and seems to be crumbling in every direction. This path leads to a world more firmly established in Being, a world whose changing and uncertain gleams are all that we can discern here below.[23]

f) Speaking convictionally about values and virtues, Marcel claims that they are "*natural*." It is not easy to see exactly what is meant by

[20] *Ibid.*, pp. 26, 133, 134, 147.
[21] *Ibid.*, pp. 153, 27.
[22] *Ibid.*, pp. 152, 153.
[23] *Ibid.*, pp. 153, 154.

this word. He refers to "the natural foundations" on which were built the beliefs in "the order which frames our existence," but claims that he does not want to resuscitate "natural religion." These beliefs, connected with respect for life, he calls "pre-christian," and "peri-christian." Marcel feels that our civilization will perish if we cannot "put this peri-christian piety in our relations to life at the basis of ethics." This leads him to a concrete proposal. What we need is moral renewal, and this is possible only in small communities, which are "centres of examples," or "nuclei of life." [24]

4. Discussion of Marcel's method

a) On the basis of our analytical approach, we have to object to the structure of Marcel's work. It consists of two elements, an analytical and a convictional one, which are related in a way that is unacceptable. This is not to deny, however, that each of these two elements, if taken in isolation, has a meaning and validity of its own. This holds not only for the analytical element. As philosophers we cannot quarrel with the convictions which any person entertains. It lies outside the range of a philosopher's competence to question the validity of Marcel's convictions. What we do reject, however, is the method of suggesting that specific convictions, in this case those of Marcel, are supported by, made plausible by, authenticated by, the analysis which preceded them in the essay. What Marcel says about value and its relationship to sacrifice and courage, or about man's two possibilities to establish himself as an ego or as a person, holds for a Protestant just as well as for a Roman Catholic, for an atheist as well as for a Jew, or a Moslem. Marcel's convictions, on the contrary, are *completely* acceptable only to certain liberal Roman Catholics, whereas many other Christians may agree with *part* of them, and only to a certain extent. Agreement with Marcel's convictions, however, depends upon one's own convictions, and not upon the validity of the analysis. Marcel's procedure to assume tacitly that his convictions are based upon his analysis represents a peculiar form of metaphysics: the tacit assumption is illegitimate and confusing. Marcel would have done well if he had written two kinds of essays: one in which he would deal exclusively with problems of ethical analysis; a second kind in which he would have started with the confession that he is a Roman Catholic, and in which he should have developed his evaluations of man, society, and values on the basis of his specific form of liberal Catholicism.

b) The situation is, however, more complicated than has been suggested. We must emphasize that analytical and convictional languages

[24] *Ibid.*, pp. 161-64.

are languages *sui generis,* which therefore need to be clearly distinguished; but we must also stress the fact that these two languages are related. We meet here a problem which is parallel to that raised in Chap. I, where we discussed the relationship between convictional and indicative language. There we said that this relationship can be heuristic; that is to say, convictional language can sometimes inform indicative thinking, stimulate it, destroy clogs which prevent a clear indicative view.

The same applies to the relationship between Marcel's convictions and his analysis. There is, despite casual first impressions to the contrary, a real relationship, but it is heuristic rather than intrinsic. Marcel's convictions are those of a liberal Roman Catholic. Such a man, living in the confused and desperate France of the war and the postwar years, is haunted by the following convictional questions: How can we live in this situation of ours, live honorably, live with *personal* dignity? How can we maintain such a personal life without being swallowed up by mass movements, by techniques, hatreds, utopian systems, illusions, and the *empty words* of Communists and other political formations? These convictional questions stimulate analytical questions, such as:

(1) What is a person?

(2) What is a value?

Analytical thinking, prompted by convictional questions of this type, enabled him to see (analytically):

(1) A *person* is not a thing given; a definite act is required, an act in which a man establishes himself as a person.

(2) A value is not indicated by terms such as "love," "beauty," because such terms are *empty words;* value is part of what is real, part of life: a family, a farm, a painting, a school.

It is not necessary to share Marcel's convictions in order to agree with such analytical insights regarding person and value.[25]

c) It would be a misunderstanding of Marcel if we considered him to be just another metaphysician (see our discussion of the spirit of abstraction in Chap. IV). The antimetaphysical tendencies in his work are perhaps just as strong as the hidden metaphysical assumptions. First, though Marcel employs the term "metaphysics" charged with a heavy positive evaluation (meaning something like the belief in a higher world), he knows very well the illegitimate use of language which we disqualify with the help of the same term "metaphysics." When discussing Fichte's idealism he denounces his claim to deduce the empirical self from the transcendental self. "To apply methods of deduc-

[25] Marcel gives a similar account of the heuristic relationship between his convictions and his analysis in *The Philosophy of Existence,* pp. 29 and 30.

tion in such a realm is arbitrary and even false. . . . It is the unlawful transposition into the metaphysical order of a requirement which only has value and meaning in certain definite departments of scientific thought." [26]

Second, Marcel is guided by a very strong sense of the necessity to avoid a system. He does not want to write books which, in a well-ordered series of chapters, offer a well-rounded picture of life, of the universe, or even of philosophical problems. He considers a man who aspires after such harmonious presentations to be a fool, blinded by arrogance. Hence, most of his books are a collection of articles, addresses, and essays. In his major work, *The Mystery of Being* (the Gifford Lectures of 1949-50), he regrets being under the necessity of presenting his thoughts in a systematic form. Systematic exposition "always runs the risk of profoundly altering the nature of the truths [the philosopher] has discovered." The most he can do is to "retrace the movement of my thought." [27]

Third, Marcel's work possesses a quality which it is extremely difficult to define exactly, but which certainly demonstrates a strong antimetaphysical tendency. Perhaps the term which best expresses this quality is "both-and-thinking," as opposed to "either-or-thinking." Marcel displays it more in his analytical than in his convictional passages. He uses a certain term, discusses its advantages, and then partly takes back what he has said by pointing out some disadvantages, and proposing another term. So he uses, both in the Gifford lectures and in *Homo Viator,* terms like "travel," "movement of thought," "itinerary," "journey," to indicate the nature of his philosophizing. In an essay which forms part of *Homo Viator,* "Value and Immortality," he claims, however, that "we must regard the image of a journey as misleading." [28]

The work of systematizers evokes in us the picture of a large diagram or chart, with series of boxes for definite periods of history, definite forms of religion, types of anxiety, etc. Marcel's work, on the contrary, suggests the image of a map without boundaries, with winding roads indicated here and there which do not always lead to a certain point of arrival, and which furthermore branch off in several sidepaths.

Because Marcel's method offers a weird combination of antimetaphysical tendencies and a metaphysical jump from an ethical analysis to a specific convictional position, we have to call it "cryptometaphysics." The ethical analysis, if taken separately, can be called "concrete ethics."

[26] *Homo Viator,* p. 136.

[27] Gabriel Marcel, *Reflection and Mystery,* tr. G. S. Fraser (*The Mystery of Being,* Vol. I [Chicago: Henry Regnery Co., 1951]), pp. 2, vii.

[28] P. 135.

d) Summary

(1) Marcel does not confine the function of philosophy to analysis, as do Hospers and other analysts.

(2) Hence, Marcel mingles the convictional and analytical approaches and thus cannot avoid a metaphysical jump.

(3) Still Marcel makes two very significant contributions to ethical analysis. He draws our attention to the notion that man establishes his existence, and he shows that ethical analysis has to reckon with embodied values, concrete goods, "life," and "reality," though it must be clear to us that the last two terms have to be protected against metaphysical misuse.

(4) Marcel does not raise our primary question, "Can man establish his existence in speaking morally?" Instead of this analytical question he asks a convictional one, "Can man establish his existence satisfactorily without taking recourse to the 'Higher World'?" The preoccupation with his convictions prevents Marcel from seeing the possibility and the significance of the analytical question.

D. DEWEY'S EXPERIMENTAL MORALS AND RATIONAL ETHICS

We will discuss Dewey's treatment of ethical and moral problems by setting forth, first, Dewey's frame of reference, that is to say, his account of man and history; second, his ethical theory; third, his moral doctrine. This exposition of Dewey's thought will be followed by some critical remarks. The texts to be analyzed are "Reconstruction in Moral Conceptions," which is ch. vii of his *Reconstruction in Philosophy,* and "The Construction of Good," which is ch. x of *The Quest for Certainty*."[29]

1. *Dewey's frame of reference: an account of man and history*

The basic presupposition of Dewey's treatment of ethics and morals is the thesis that both ethical theory and moral doctrine have to be understood as man's response to his situation. Ethics, e.g., has to be taken, not only as a philosophical discipline, but in the first place as a way in which human beings react to the situation in which they find themselves as individuals and as members of the community. Furthermore, individual and community have to be understood in their historical context. This is to say that, according to Dewey, ethics and morals have to be interpreted against the background of the specific problems of a specific civilization in a specific period of history. We may say that Dewey's method is both historical-cultural and "anthropological."

[29] John Dewey, *Reconstruction in Philosophy* (enl. ed.; New York: Mentor Press, 1950); *The Quest for Certainty* (New York: Minton, Balch & Co., 1929).

a) In order to understand the problems of modern ethics and morals, we have to consider, according to Dewey, three periods of the Western civilization: the age of the classical Greeks, the Middle Ages, and the modern period.

The "situation" of the *Greeks* is characterized by the fading away of religion and the collapse of custom. The men whom we usually call ethical philosophers are better characterized as leaders of the community. Socrates and Plato realized that the conduct of life presupposes a foundation. They saw that in their time religion and custom no longer supplied a foundation which possessed vitality and power, and they proclaimed that therefore another basis had to be looked for. The heart of their ethical philosophy consisted in the claim that we do not have to make wild guesses, or to construct a foundation in an arbitrary way, because it is already there: it is to be found in reason. This notion implies the conviction that reason has always been the real, the true, the actual foundation of the regulation of conduct, but that this fact was masked by the naïve, uncritical beliefs of the religious period.[30]

b) Dewey places ethical and moral problems, not only in a historical-cultural frame, but also in an "anthropological" context. He claims that we have to *know what kind of being man is* before we can understand his moral reaction to his specific "situation." We have to consider Dewey's anthropological conceptions before we can continue his historical-cultural analysis.

(1) If custom breaks down, man loses his certainty. If the authority of rules, laws, customs, is no longer self-evident, man no longer has solid ground under his feet. He begins to feel uncertain, and the increased insecurity releases the "quest for certainty."

(2) Insecure man seems to be strongly attracted by the notion of fixed laws, fixed goods, fixed ends. Human beings, made timorous by the fact that their goods are changing and imperfect, are apparently hypnotized by the idea of unchanging, perfect, unquestionable goods, of ends which possess a reassuring finality, of laws which are perfectly reliable because they are ultimate and supreme.

(3) Hence, insecure man is liable to be hypnotized by the notion of two realms of being, a higher and a lower. This notion is one of the main tools of religion in the period of unchallenged customs, when the religious leaders dispelled feelings of insecurity by means of the reassuring picture of a higher world, the inhabitants of which benevolently guided the destinies of men. In an age of increasing feelings of insecurity the "philosophical" leaders retain the notion

[30] *Reconstruction*, pp. 131, 39.

of the higher world, but change the gods for the powers of reason and goodness.[31]

c) Dewey claims that the peculiar response of insecure man to a certainty-crisis finds its "classical" expression in Greek ethical theory. The classical philosophers offered to their contemporaries who were searching for a reliable stronghold a "belief in a bounded, ordered cosmos, wherein rest is higher than motion." According to this view human conduct can be guided by laws which are trustworthy because they are universally valid and because they participate in and express the hidden but essential cosmic order.[32]

d) We take up again the thread of Dewey's cultural analysis. The second period which is decisive for the undertaking of the modern moral situation is that of the *Middle Ages*. The system of the Roman Catholic Church satisfied the craving for certainty of insecure man by offering him universal rules and necessary truths, supported by the authority of a powerful God, and embodied in the institution of an impressive church. Our *present situation* (in the modern period) is brought about by the breaking up of the medieval system under the impact of modern science. The implications, consequences, and applications of science resulted in effecting a breach between man's most powerful concerns: his concern about the world, the here and now, and his concern about values and purposes. This latter concern had been expressed and largely remained expressed in beliefs in an ultimate reality which could not any longer be made to tally with a scientific attitude.[33]

e) The *problem confronting modern man* is that of restoring the integration between these two concerns. Dewey is convinced that this problem can be solved; there are, however, serious difficulties to be overcome. A solution is suggested by modern science, which has given an example of integration in its experimental procedure. This solution combines knowing and doing. "Philosophy is called upon" to effect the integration between knowing, doing, and believing, between theory and practice, between the scientific attitude and "the beliefs about values and purposes." The difficulty mentioned is that philosophy in its present form is not well prepared for this task of guiding a process of integration. Dewey holds that philosophers are either in the grasp of the idealist Greek approach, believing in the existence of a superior and an inferior order of being, or they adhere to a traditional empiricism which is marred by a deficient interpretation of the nature of values.[34]

[31] *Quest for Certainty*, p. 254; *Reconstruction in Philosophy*, p. 131.
[32] *Reconstruction*, p. 132.
[33] *Quest for Certainty*, pp. 254, 255.
[34] *Ibid.*, pp. 255, 256.

f) The *shortcomings of the idealistic response* to man's insecurity are for Dewey self-evident. He is so deeply convinced of the illusory character of the belief in a Higher Realm that he does not even take the trouble to argue against this illusion. He seems to think that his historical and "anthropological" account in itself is a disqualification of "transcendental Absolutism." What Dewey attacks explicitly, by means of arguments, are not the illusionary idealistic convictions themselves, but merely some implications which have not been sufficiently noticed. They are:

(1) The encouragement of an uncritical acceptance of traditional opinions and attitudes. If values, truths, and rules are fixed, and universally valid, they are thought to be above questioning. Actually, many "truths" are prejudices; many "values" are unjust situations. Idealism therefore tends to confirm prejudices and injustices instead of criticizing them. If critical inquiry is discouraged, self-interest takes its place along with class interest in determining human behavior.[35]

(2) The division of ends and goods into intrinsic and instrumental ones, the first supposed to possess a worth in themselves, the second deriving their significance only from the intrinsic goods they are designed to serve. A tragic consequence of this theoretical, and therefore seemingly harmless, distinction is the chasm created in the actual living conditions between religious and aesthetic goods (so-called intrinsic) and the "material" goods of everyday life (so-called instrumental). This divorce led to a loss of vitality of the ideal, intrinsic goods; they lost much of their power and are now considered by many people to be merely a luxury. The material goods of economic life were deprived of close contact with the other goods, and this accounts largely for "the obnoxious materialism and brutality of our economic life." To sum up: Dewey shows the devastating influence of thinking in terms of high-low, and suggests the healing power of integration.[36]

(3) The distinction between moral goods and natural goods. Dewey sees no reason why we should make a distinction between the virtues, as the truly moral goods, and mere natural goods like "health, economic security, art and science." Everything that "contributes to the amelioration of existing ills" deserves the name of "good." Again, it is a matter of integration. The root of the evil lies "in the separation of natural and moral science. When physics, chemistry, biology,

[35] *Ibid.*, p. 265.
[36] *Reconstruction*, pp. 137, 138; *Quest for Certainty*, pp. 269, 271.

medicine, contribute to the detection of concrete human woes and to the development of plans for remedying them . . . they become moral: they become part of the apparatus of moral inquiry or science." [37]

g) Dewey, though an empiricist, is very critical of *the ethical theory of traditional empiricism* and its moral implications. His main objections are:

(1) The usual empiricism fails to discriminate between the enjoyed and the enjoy*able*. In this failure the empiricists forget that to say that a thing is enjoyed is to make a statement of fact; whereas to say that it is enjoyable is to give a value judgment. Morals has to do with the latter. Moral judgments are characterized by words which end on "able," "worthy," "ful," such as advisable, blameworthy, wonderful. Words such as "blamed," "advised" are portions of reports of facts, not of moral judgments. The danger inherent in this lack of discrimination is that reports about facts suggest something which possesses finality. The usual empiricist theory, therefore, encourages an acceptance of existing enjoyments. To declare, however, that certain things are enjoyable, satisfactory, honorable, points to the future, asks for action, contains a promise, namely that these things "will do."

Another danger of the theory described is that it does not distinguish between what is a value by accident and those values which have been inquired into and tested by thinking and action—and which therefore *deserve* our adherence, and have a *right* to claim our attention.[38]

(2) The usual empiricism is just as guilty of "antecedentism" as idealism is. Dewey has in mind the widespread habit of people to consider good, valuable, or true, that which conforms to an antecedent reality. In religion this attitude is expressed in the conception of revelation which discloses the nature of the antecedent reality; further in the proclamation of the life of one person as an exemplary life, to which all later generations should conform; again, in reliance upon institutions which endow past experiences with the aura of authority. In idealist philosophy we find the same attitude in the assumption that what is good has to be understood in terms of reference to universal, eternal moral laws, rooted in Ultimate Reality. Dewey claims that empiricism, in spite of the fact that it seems to differ basically from religion and idealism, in that it disclaims belief

[37] *Reconstruction*, pp. 138, 139.
[38] *Quest for Certainty*, pp. 260-65.

in any invisible Higher World, yet must be blamed for a similar slavery to an antecedent authority. "The theory in question holds down value to objects *antecedently* enjoyed." This dependence upon the past is an implication of the lack of discrimination between the enjoyed and the enjoyable, discussed above.[39]

(3) Because of its one-sidedness, the prevalent empiricism keeps alive the idealistic misinterpretation of moral problems. In the same way as one-sided empiricism in epistemology "evokes, by way of reaction, the transcendental theory of *a priori* ideas," so ethical empiricism "automatically calls forth the assertion that there are values eternally in Being that are the standards of all judgments and the obligatory ends of all action." [40]

2. ***Dewey's ethical theory***

a) Dewey's ethics offers an analysis of the "moral situation." He tries to see all aspects of this situation and the ways they interact and are related.

(1) The first element of the situation consists of goods and ends. We notice a plurality of goods and ends. People speak of a Highest Good, but if there is one such good, nobody can make clear what it is; everybody who uses this notion means something different by it. If we take a look, not at theories, but at life as it is actually lived, we can only say that human beings are interested in a great variety of goods and ends, which moreover are changing and moving and highly individualized. [41]

(2) Other elements of the moral situation are principles, laws, criteria, standards. These are not fixed entities, but intellectual instruments, and as such they are continually being tested, changed, or confirmed. The recognition of their hypothetical character will cure the inclination to present them as final and unquestionable. There is "something strange in the fact that men should consider loyalty to 'laws,' principles, standards, ideals to be an inherent virtue." "A moral law, like a law in physics, is not something to swear by and stick to at all hazards; it is a formula of the way to respond when specified conditions present themselves." [42]

(3) It has to be seen that not only goods and ends, laws and standards, are always specific; the same thing has to be said about

[39] *Ibid.*, pp. 258, 272, 275.
[40] *Ibid.*, p. 263.
[41] *Reconstruction*, p. 132.
[42] *Quest for Certainty*, p. 277.

actions. Because the goods in view of which we act are individualized and unique, so our actions are always specific, concrete, and individualized.[43]

(4) The aforesaid implies some notions about the nature of the moral judgment. Because man does not seek and cannot seek goods in general—such as health in general, learning in general, or justice in general—but wants to attain the health of his child, or a degree in dentistry, his judgments as to ways to act also refer to specific cases. The "moral situation" is always the specific situation of a specific human being who wants to live in a specific way. Mr. A., who is concerned about the health of his wife, wants "to live healthily"—for instance, to go and live in California. Mr. B., who is caught up in a racial situation, wants "to live justly"—for instance, by refusing to sign a restrictive covenant. The expressions "to live healthily" and "to live justly" reveal that the key terms of moral judgments are adverbs and not nouns. Nouns such as "health" or "justice" suggest static entities. Adverbs, like "healthily" or "justly," "are modifiers of action in special cases." [44]

(5) A central category of Dewey's account of the moral situation is "life." Goods and ends are not separate from a man's life, but significant aspects of the way he lives. Dewey claims that there actually exist people who pursue goods as ends which are apart, separate, distinct, but he thinks that they are fanatics. "A man who aims at health as a distinct end becomes a valetudinarian, or fanatic, or a mechanical performer of exercises or an athlete so one-sided that his pursuit of bodily development injures his heart." "The endeavor to realize a so-called end" in the case of the ordinary man does "temper and color all other activities." What we are talking about when we speak morally is a unity—man's life, or his way of living—and this implies all man's activities, all the goods and ends with which man's whole personality is concerned.[45]

(6) Dewey places special emphasis upon the role of intelligence. Since ends and goods are in each case different, the aid of intelligence is required in order to recognize the merits of each specific situation, and this same aid is necessary to decide upon the specific action needed. This appreciation of the role of intelligence has two aspects: first, the awareness of the importance of the role; second, the realization of the interrelatedness of the intellectual and the value elements.

[43] *Reconstruction,* p. 135.
[44] *Ibid.*
[45] *Ibid.*

Both aspects appear clearly when Dewey gives a short summary of the "moral situation." He lists five elements of this situation, but prefaces his analysis with the remark that his position means the transference of "the weight and burden of morality to intelligence." The elements are:

(*a*) The presence of conflicting desires and alternative apparent goods.

(*b*) An inquiry into the situation: observation of the details, analysis of the situation into its divers factors, clarification of what is obscure, tracing the consequences of the various modes of action, etc.

(*c*) The presence of moral traits which either endanger the inquiry (moral failures like bias, absence of sympathy) or make it possible (sympathy, sensitiveness, balance of interests).

(*d*) Judgment and choice.

(*e*) Based upon the foregoing, overt action.[46]

3. *Philosophy as the guide to a better life: experimental morals*

Dewey solves the problem of reintegrating knowing, doing, and believing, by assigning to philosophy the task of giving leadership to man's moral enterprise. This enterprise should be performed intentionally, critically, by the method of trying, testing, forming new hypotheses, asking advice of scientists; and has to be contrasted with attitudes of the past, which were characterized by the lack of any clear method, uncritical reliance upon customs and traditions, and suspicion or disdain for mere science. The moral enterprise of the future is one of intelligent experimenting.

a) Dewey lists several facets of the experimental method in the moral enterprise:

(1) It cannot be stressed enough that inquiry and discovery will occupy a place of the highest honor. If one thinks in terms of generalities, bad consequences of certain actions will not be investigated and explained, but ascribed to man's perversity or to fate. For the new approach "mistakes . . . are lessons in wrong methods of using intelligence, and instructions as to a better course in the future."

(2) The recognition of the uniqueness of a situation means the admission that each situation has its own ultimate and final good. If a person is seriously ill, his health becomes the ultimate good for him and his family. It is supreme in this specific case, and not merely instrumental, as the theory of fixed ends would have it.

[46] *Reconstruction*, pp. 132, 133.

(3) The new experimental morals will do away with Phariseeism. Dewey means by Phariseeism not so much deliberate hypocrisy as the conviction that everybody, without regard for his particular situation, has to be judged with the same fixed standard. What is important for the experimental way of looking is the consideration as to whether a person is moving in the right direction, and by means of intelligent investigation we will be able to notice whether a person moves forward or backward.

(4) This means that growth is more important than result. What counts, what constitutes the "aim of living," is not "perfection as a final goal, but the everenduring process of perfecting, maturing, refining." [47]

b) The new experimental method contains definite ideas about the purpose of life.

(1) This purpose is connected much more with happiness than with possession. Traditional approaches thought too much in terms of health, wealth, learning, and the like, as goods to be possessed. There is, however, no happiness in possession. It "is found only in success, . . . getting forward, moving in advance . . . the overcoming of obstacles, the elimination of sources of defect and ill." Worthy happiness is further characterized by "esthetic sensitiveness . . . renewal of spirit . . . purification of emotion."

(2) The purpose of life is also the setting free of all man's capacities and possibilities. It would be misleading, however, to interpret this notion in a "subjectivistic" way. Dewey warns emphatically against the tendency to think of growth and happiness only in terms of the individual. This leads to the idea that we have to change, not the world, but ourselves; that is, it leads to "the other-worldliness found in religions . . . [and] in estheticism." Change in the self is not an end in itself, but "a means to alteration, through action, of objective conditions." [48]

4. *Discussion of Dewey's method*

a) Though it cannot be denied that Dewey is closely related to the empirical trend in philosophy, he disregards the fundamental problem which is a starting point for so many empiricists and analysts, and which we formulated by claiming that ethical analytical language and moral convictional language should be clearly distinguished. The reason for Dewey's disregard lies in the fact that he adheres to a conception of

[47] *Ibid.*, pp. 139-41, 145-47.
[48] *Reconstruction*, pp. 143-47; *Quest for Certainty*, p. 275.

philosophy as a guide to life, set forth by the Greek cosmos conviction, but rejected by most empiricists and analysts. This position of Dewey leads to a remarkable inconsistency in all his work, because on other points (e.g., the mind-body dualism) he is vehemently opposed to the Greek cosmos conviction.

b) However, Dewey has made significant contributions to the cause of ethical analysis. Thus, he offers what is really a situational analysis of moral problems. He demonstrates that we cannot understand them without taking into account concrete goods, "life," historical and cultural dimensions, and above all, man himself. Dewey stresses especially the influence of man's intellectual activity on his moral life.

c) One of the main characteristics of Dewey's work is, however, the fact that these truly ethical studies are seldom presented separately but nearly always within the context of a specific moral doctrine.[49] The setting forth and the defense of his own doctrine of morals is so important for Dewey that he cannot take the time to dedicate a book, or even a chapter, exclusively to ethical problems, but offers essays in which analytical ethics and convictional morals are closely interwoven. The analysis is immediately used to defend his own morals, or to attack rival moral doctrines. The failure to keep ethical problems and moral convictions apart results in a considerable confusion. In this way Dewey tacitly assumes that his ethical analysis validates his moral convictions, and therefore makes a metaphysical jump. Dewey's mistake is the same as that made by Marcel, whereas Hospers carefully confines himself to ethical analysis. What Dewey gains, in comparison with Hospers, in the scope of his field of problems, he loses in clearness in regard to the aim of his discussions.

d) We have to say that Dewey's work is made up of both analytical and convictional language. The latter predominates; hence Dewey offers a theology. Since the convictions are presented as a philosophy, we have to speak of a cryptotheology. This leads us to the question as to the main elements of the body of convictions which this cryptotheology wants to defend.

(1) Its most conspicuous aspect is its vehement rejection of some of the major convictions of the Greek cosmos conviction. In this regard Dewey belongs decidedly to the Post-Enlightenment period. Peirce and James and the logical empiricists are with him on this point.

(2) There is, however (as was mentioned before), one major

[49] The exception is John Dewey, *Theory of Valuation* (*International Encyclopedia of Unified Science*, Vol. II, No. 4 [Chicago: University of Chicago Press, 1939]).

Greek conviction which is kept by Dewey, namely, his conviction that philosophy should be a guide for life. While the word "savior" may be too strong for Dewey's case, it is certain that he sees philosophy as the pilot which must lead mankind, if there is to be a better future. In this regard Dewey is still an Enlightenment man. The logical empiricists are not with him here.

(3) Closely related is the very high place which is assigned to science and inquiry in Dewey's scale of values. It seems plausible that inquiry, clear distinctions, and a weighing of consequences play an important role in the making of our moral decisions. But Dewey demands something much more significant for science and intellectual activity, namely, the admission that they carry "the weight and burden" of morality. This view implies an overestimation of the intellect and an underestimation of values, convictions, and moral preferences. Dewey would certainly reject this criticism by insisting that the intellect has contributed its share in the formation of convictions and moral preferences. This is not to be denied. The issue is, however, a different one. Dewey forgets that criticism in the realm of convictions cannot be considered to be exclusively, not even mainly, a matter of the intellect.

However, in following the traditional terminology of "intellect" as opposed to something else which would be free from thinking (moral sympathies?) we fall into the language trap mentioned in Chap. III. There we pleaded for an omission of terms such as "reason" and "critical faculties." [50]

Moral language is a "giving account of" people's behavior, including their language, and especially of *our* behavior, *our* speaking. This "giving account of" is never a matter of "the intellect" as an isolated faculty or mental function, but always an activity in which the whole person participates, a weighing and considering of the various aspects of the moral situation which is inspired by, guided by, our convictions, that is, by our deepest motivating center.

This critique of Dewey implies the assertion that he, in his attempt to elevate the intellect, loses sight of the uniqueness of moral, i.e., of convictional language. He comes close to identifying the experimental procedures in science with those in moral life.

In his raising of science and the intellect to apex positions in his scale of values, Dewey belongs to the Enlightenment. Here, too, the logical empiricists are with him.

(4) Other values high in the hierarchy are: tolerance, justice,

[50] See Chap. III, Sec. C-2-*c*.

sympathy, freedom, the last-named understood as freedom from the authoritarianism of unquestioned traditions, customs, institutions, traditional philosophy, and the church. Dewey is a strong opponent of prejudices, but we have to ask whether he is not prejudiced in matters of religion. It is not my purpose to defend my own kind of Christianity; I should then leave the field of analysis and be guilty of cryptotheology. It is even necessary to say that Christianity taken empirically has lived largely by the belief in the existence of two realms, just as Dewey has pointed out.

Dewey is prejudiced, however, in regard to the old, pre-Homeric religion. This religion, just as all other ancient and primitive religions, lived by convictions of a different kind. They were more monistic than dualistic. The relationship between the ancient Greek religion and the classical philosophy is much more complicated than Dewey's naïve analysis suggests. If Dewey had sought for a more genuine understanding of that popular religion, he would have realized that there is more to religion in its relationship to morality, culture, and science than the mere supporting of moral and social structures by persuasive pronouncements about a Higher World.

e) When discussing the moral situation, Dewey relates man only to goods, not to a Highest Good; that is to say, he does not see how important the relationship is between man-who-speaks-morally and that which he assumes to be his Highest Good. The reason for this oversight is that Dewey, at least on this issue, is so caught up in the power of his own convictions, that he cannot analyze clearly. In his own (explicit) convictional world view there is no place for a Highest Good; hence Dewey neglects to ask the analytical question whether we can understand man's moral life without reference to what is *for him* his Highest Good. Dewey thinks that he has discarded the whole issue of the Highest Good, if he points out that nobody has been able to establish beyond reasonable doubt what that so-called Highest Good "really" consists in. Thus Dewey does not see at all that in regard to this Good we know not only the (convictional) "really" question but also an (analytical) "actually" problem.

Because of this position Dewey has not raised our primary question, "Can man establish his existence in speaking morally?" However, in his ethics, as it is influenced by his convictions regarding the Highest Good, the position is implied that our question has to be answered in the affirmative: Man establishes his existence without reference to anything other than his goods.

f) It should be noted that there is some affinity between Dewey's position and the existentialist account of man. Since "existentialism" is a vague term, the following remarks are short and tentative. The affinity shows up:

(1) Where Dewey stresses the importance of the feeling of insecurity, and man's response to it, for the understanding of man as a moral being.

(2) Where Dewey speaks in terms of the unique situation and emphasizes again and again the uniqueness of goods, principles, decisions, and actions.

(3) Where Dewey transfers the attention from "goods in general" to man's life, his specific way of living.

E. CONCLUDING REMARKS

The answer which a person gives to the question of how man establishes his existence is closely related to that person's view of the "world." Both Dewey's and Marcel's ideas about man's establishment depend upon an outspoken conviction about the nature and the value of the "world."

We can say that, for people who adhere to the popularized form of ontology traditional in Western civilization, the "world" looks like a place safely fenced in: a solid basis, protected by a heavenly vault. At the apex of the structure a Deity is located (a God, an Idea, Being) which supports and guarantees the existence, enduring strength, and fundamental goodness of the whole structure.

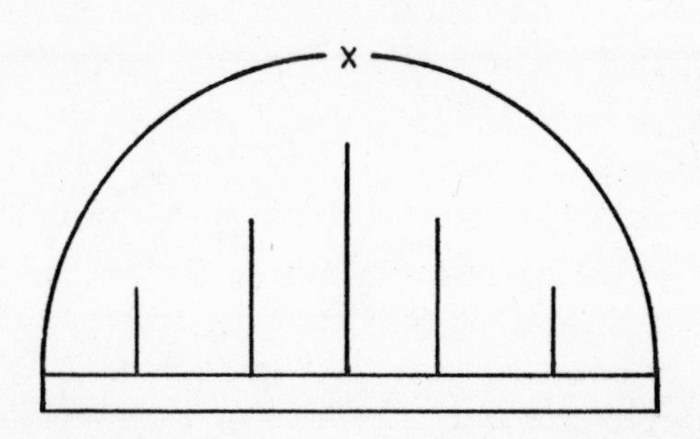

Dewey's picture of the "world" differs from the popular ontological one, but the difference is not so decisive as it would seem to be. The vault of heaven is no longer there, but the solid foundation remains. To say it more accurately, life itself and the solid foundation coincide. Now a qualification must be made: whereas the basis in the popular ontological structure is static, in Dewey's picture it is moving forward, since life itself is on the move. This life basis, and also its movement forward, are good, just as growth is good. This goodness is guaranteed, not, as in the case of popular ontology, by a divine guarantor outside life, but by the nature of life itself.

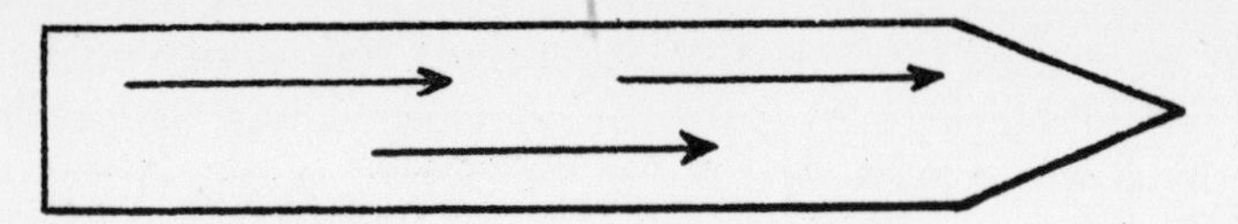

Marcel's picture of the "world" is quite different. Here both the vault of heaven and the solid basis have disappeared. The "world" has collapsed. No reliable and good foundation upon which we can build a comfortable life exists at all. The "world" has fallen into ruins. Marcel's picture is, however, not completely desolate. The "world" is full of concrete goods. Yet their existence is not self-evident, not guaranteed beyond question. The goods are threatened by man himself because of his foolishness, his power of self-destruction, and especially because of his desire to ignore and deny the "reality" and significance of the Higher World.

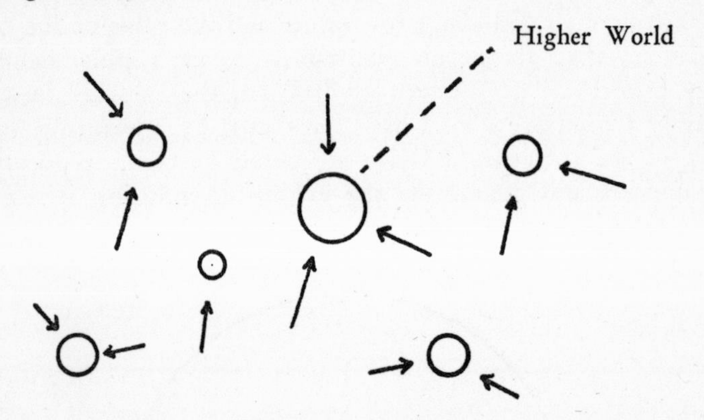

As analytical philosophers we are not in the position to agree or disagree with any of these three convictional pictures of the "world," nor should we try to construct our own picture. Our task is merely to understand such pictures and to make clear their relationships with the convictions of the persons involved. Such pictures are part of the tacit assumptions which determine, to a very large extent, the tone of a "philosophy" (read: theology). It is our task to bring them into the open.

The above considerations throw some light upon our primary question, "Can man establish his existence in speaking morally?" A large segment of the people living within the boundaries of Western civilization agree with Dewey's picture of the "world," whether they adhere to the other elements of his philosophy or not. Such people will claim that a "purely moral" establishment of life is possible. There *is* no vault of heaven; we cannot speak of a Highest Good. The notion of a "purely moral" establishment is a conviction, implied in and demanded by a convictional world view such as that of Dewey.

Marcel gives a more complicated answer: man tries to establish his existence without regard to the Higher World, but in this way he destroys life, civilization, and himself. A firm and good establishment is possible only if one fully recognizes this Higher World. In our eyes both Marcel's and Dewey's answers are convictional in nature and therefore leave open the analytical question.

The analytical answer to our primary question points out that the term "purely moral" is ambiguous. Every man adheres to a Highest Good of one kind or another, whether he admits this fact or not. His moral language is therefore not "purely moral," if one is to understand this term to mean a language without reference to anything other than his goods. A Highest Good is always involved, is even the decisive, inspiring element of moral language. People who want to establish their existence in speaking only morally are often men who are not fully aware of the nature of their Highest Good. In this case we meet again a convictional world view without a "real" convictor. His place is taken by the world view, in this particular instance a view of a highly moral character.

CHAPTER EIGHT

THE CHURCH

Modern Christians Establish Their Existence with the Help of Several Church Languages

A. INTRODUCTION

One may ask: "In what way, in which language structure, does the Christian establish his existence?" The answer could be: "He achieves that by means of the language of faith." This, however, is far too simple an approach to the matter.

First of all, *the* Christian does not exist. Even the concept of "*the* modern Christian" is much too dangerous a generality. Roman Catholics establish their existence in a manner very different from Protestants, for the church, Mary, and the saints play a decisive role. Even among Protestants we must distinguish various groups. We select for our investigation those Protestants whose denominations co-operate in the World Council of Churches. These Protestants are distinguished not only from Roman Catholics, but also from Unitarians, Universalists, and Fundamentalists, as well as from some non-Protestant groups which participate in the World Council, such as the Orthodox (sometimes called Greek Orthodox) and some of the Anglicans.

Secondly, we cannot very well speak of *the* language of faith. For it likewise does not exist. There is rather a group of languages spoken by particular groups within the Christian churches. Some of these languages are: (1) the language spoken by the biblical authors, (2) the language employed by the present-day theologians, (3) the language peculiar to the theologians of the past (all three convictional in character), (4) the language used by modern scholars who ask scientific questions (indicative in character, such as in biblical archaeology and textual criticism), (5) the languages of worship, of prayer, and yet others. The picture is even more complex: these languages are variously interrelated, depending upon the particular community of churches within which they are spoken. This chapter will offer an analysis of these and similar languages.

It is unavoidable that many readers will be dissatisfied by this procedure, for they will want to know more: How does such a modern

Christian, granted that the above-mentioned languages are spoken in his community, actually establish his existence, in relationship to God, to Christ, to the Church, to the world, and to himself; and how does he establish his existence in relation to his understanding of salvation, sin, the new life, and predestination?

I do not feel capable of fulfilling these desires. I am too much involved in the Christian faith to provide an analytical discussion. If I should try to answer such questions I should bring forth nothing more than a convictional account of the aforementioned relations, instead of a philosophical analysis.

The reader ought to expect a clear-cut answer only if he asks not for an analytical but for a convictional account. Several contemporary theologians offer their convictional interpretations of how a Christian establishes and ought to establish his existence. The reader should compare the convictional interpretations offered by different theological schools. He might also read the accounts of the modern Christian's establishment by non-Christian theologians.[1]

Therefore, I shall avoid the question of how modern Christians establish their existence, in relationship to God, to Christ, to the world, etc., and restrict my analysis to those language structures in regard to which it is easier to preserve the analytical attitude.

B. THE FUNCTION OF BIBLICAL THEOLOGY

1. *The three branches of theology*

In discussing the character and the functions of the languages in question, we should start with the language which is called "biblical theology." In Chap. I we mentioned briefly the problem of language change. We will now consider it in greater detail as applied to Christian theology.

a) We have to distinguish the intentional change achieved in scientific language from the change accomplished by theology. The coinage of new terms, and especially the formation of new hypotheses and theories, are continually causing alterations in the languages of the various sciences. The changes in the confessional languages of Christian churches brought about by their theological activities are of another kind. If a church wants to improve its language it turns to certain documents. When people speak about a "Luther-renaissance" they do not mean only the growing interest in scholarly research in Luther's works, but primarily the awareness that one's way of speaking about God and

[1] See Bibliography.

Christ will benefit if one allows his language to be enriched by Luther's language. The discipline which strives to achieve such improvements is the branch of theology which can be called *historical theology*. Another branch of theology is *discursive theology*. It is the field of those scholars who believe that they can enrich their language, especially when they speak about man and his plight, if they enter into a discussion with Kierkegaard, Freud, and Marx. Much more important than these two aspects of theology is that which is called *biblical theology*.[2] Theologians think that their convictions about God, man's plight, and salvation can be corrected and deepened with the help of the language of Calvin and Schleiermacher, of Nietzsche and Heidegger, because they believe that the thought and the language of these men did not develop without the help of the Holy Spirit. How much more must they welcome a confrontation with those other documents, which are called the Bible, which they believe contain the records of God's revelation in the prophetic and apostolic ages. The primary responsibility of the theologian is always biblical theology.

b) The confessional language of the church has been improved, for example, in the following ways. Rather than holding Jesus up as "our example" or claiming that he was "the greatest man who ever lived," the biblical theologian has urged the church to acknowledge him as "Savior," "Lord," and "King." Such slogans as "We will build the Kingdom" should give way to the recognition that "God will bring his kingdom in his time; let us beseech him to use us and our churches as his instruments." Another proposal may be to speak about salvation, not only in terms of the *lutron* (the ransom paid for salvation), but also in terms of the *einai en christō* (being in Christ).

2. *The existential position of the biblical theologian*

About one thing we must be clear, the temporal location of the biblical theologians is in the twentieth century, and not A.D. 30 or 50. They are not contemporaries of Jesus or of Paul, and they should not pretend to be. Their way of thinking and speaking about God, and man, and history, is determined by the fact that they are modern Protestant Americans or Europeans. Their convictions are influenced by Augustine and Francis, by Descartes and Kant, by the Renaissance and the Industrial Revolution, by the Crusades and the American Civil War. They

[2] It should be noticed that the term "biblical theology" is used in a variety of ways. Some, for instance, do not designate by this term an aspect of the discipline of theology, as is done above, but a certain orientation of that whole discipline. These scholars speak of biblical theology in order to voice their convictions that theology ought to be oriented toward the Bible, and not to something like "experience."

cannot free themselves from these influences. If they could, they would no longer be themselves. Throughout the whole process of returning to the Bible in order that their language may be corrected by the language of the Bible, they remain located in their own time and space.

3. *The elements of choice and evaluation in biblical theology*

The process of improving the language of the church in the light of scripture is more complex than one might suppose at first glance. The theologians do not change their language simply because they find out that the Bible speaks a different language from their own. The correction which takes place is not a mechanical one, for the theologians are not completely passive. On the contrary, there is one aspect of the process which may be described as their *choice*. They prefer, for instance, Paul's way of speaking about God to James's way, and the language of Luke to that of Esther. Sometimes they even explicitly reject a particular biblical writer's way of speaking about God and man, as in Exod. 4, the language concerning the staff and the snake.

Therefore it is simply not true that in every case in which their language differs from biblical language, they automatically give up theirs and accept the biblical one. In spite of the fact that the theologian approaches the Bible with the desire to be corrected in his beliefs and his language, he *evaluates* the language of the Bible. In these evaluations he is guided by his convictions, that is to say, the convictions which he shares with his church. We should notice that these convictions, this language, is just the very language which is in need of improvement.

This means, naturally, that there is a very real possibility for nothing at all to happen; as when the theologian reads the Bible, but hears only his own language. In fact, this happens all the time. There are churches which have been reading their own doctrines into the Bible for decades and centuries. Nothing happens, no correction takes place, they move in a closed circle. The circle can be broken only if there is a real willingness to change one's language, that is, for theologians to admit that their old way of speaking about God and salvation is not infallible. From the standpoint of philosophy we may say no more than this: the theologian evaluates the Bible according to his own lights, i.e., the lights of his church; but he hopes that in dealing with the Bible these lights may be purified.

4. *Special helps for the biblical theologian*

The churches which we have in mind claim that the biblical theologian who takes seriously his task of improving the confessional language of the church, needs special tools, namely, facility in the original languages of the Bible, biblical archaeology, textual criticism, etc. The term "tool" is inadequate to express clearly the relationship between biblical theology and biblical research. Strictly speaking, a tool is "the instrument by which something is effected or accomplished" (Webster), and it is in accordance with this notion that the churches which we discuss assert that theologians cannot perform their task adequately without using the tools of biblical research. But at the same time this research is much more than a tool; it comprises a series of disciplines, each with its own methods, and it is considered the responsibility of the theologian to take into account the various findings of these disciplines. In the following sections we will undertake the examination of the complex relationships between biblical theology and biblical research. This relationship—or more accurately, the way in which a specific group of Christians interpret it—is of particular significance; for it is one of the aspects of the relationship between convictional and indicative language.

C. THE FUNCTION OF BIBLICAL RESEARCH

1. *Biblical research functions within the context of the churches*

"Biblical research," just like the term "biblical theology," is an abbreviation. We mean by this term the critical-historical studies of the Old and the New Testaments as carried on in church-sponsored seminaries and divinity schools. There is a basic difference between biblical research in this sense and what can be taught in the general courses in religion at Columbia University. The biblical studies we have in mind have as their deepest purpose the service of their churches.[3]

2. *This biblical research is not neutral but tries to be as unbiased as possible*

a) It is clear that we cannot call this research "neutral," for no science or research floats in the air, free and undetached. All sciences and studies serve particular communities, to further the material or spiritual well-being of institutions and nations. Yet there is behind the ideal of neutrality a very important assumption: it is both desirable and possible to *approach religious data in an unbiased way*. This assumption is a significant characteristic of the type of Christianity which we have in mind. It is a conviction which distinguishes it from the "Bible colleges" in America, some of the good old orthodox Calvinist churches in Holland, and fundamentalist groups in other countries such as England and

[3] This is not to say that general courses in religion of this type would *not* possess such a deeper purpose. Also these courses and studies have to be understood from the context in which they function. Only in this case it is more difficult to indicate this context. It is not an easily identifiable entity such as a group of churches, but something virtually indefinable, such as a particular section or aspect of Western civilization.

Germany. This conviction distinguishes this "ecumenical" kind of Christianity also from many non-Christian religions, except some branches of Judaism. At the same time the ideal of unbiased research associates these churches with many non-Christians of the Western civilization. This is actually not one but two convictions.

The first is the conviction that it is *possible* to get reliable knowledge about our universe by unbiased investigation. To this universe belong not only stars, trees, and insects, but also customs, moral systems, and religions. As has been shown in Chap. VI, this conviction has its roots in the Greek world; it has been sustained by the scholastics, and further developed by the Renaissance and the Enlightenment. Modern science dealt in the beginning almost exclusively with physical objects. Only gradually did it dawn upon the Western world that this conviction implied that it is also possible to gain reliable knowledge about moral and religious data, even about Christianity.

Second, there is the conviction that it is not only possible but very *desirable* to attain this reliable knowledge. In regard to Christianity this conviction became strong and stable only in the nineteenth century.

b) The type of church which has accepted the scientific standards of excellence is convinced that the work of theology can be carried on only when the biblical and other theological studies may exercise their full freedom, i.e., when they are allowed to follow their own methods. The spokesmen of these churches are convinced that no church, no dogma, no confession, should prescribe for the biblical scholar what he should find. This "should" is also expressed by saying that the man of biblical research should be as unbiased as possible. There are considerable differences between this formulation and the formula which is often used: "Science should be neutral." In the first place, the word "should" is here an indication that we ought to focus our attention on the scientist, and not on the science. We cannot direct a moral demand to research, but we can say that the student who performs the research should satisfy this demand (namely, being unbiased); otherwise, he is not a good scientist. In the second place, our standpoint of directing a demand to the man of biblical research is more cautious. It does not claim that it is possible to be completely neutral, but it asserts that to a certain degree it is possible to bracket our prejudices, our preferences, and even our deepest convictions.

3. *The "Christian scholar"*

There now appears above the horizon the problem of the Christian scholar. Many people say, "It is not only almost impossible to be unbiased but it is highly undesirable. Being a Christian is a prerequisite for the biblical scholar. If he is not a Christian he cannot understand what the Bible is talking about." This opinion contains a half-truth. The term "Christian scholar" is every bit as misleading as "neutral science," but at the same time it is the indication of an important problem.

a) Nobody is simply a "Christian." One must be either an Orthodox or a Roman Catholic or a Protestant Christian. Nobody is just a Protestant Christian. People belong either to the Lutheran or to the Calvinistic, to the Methodist or the Baptist tradition. Nobody is just a Protestant of the Calvinistic tradition. People's convictions, their languages, are formed under influence of Kierkegaard and Heidegger, or of Schleiermacher and Ritschl, or of Freud and Jaspers. Even when unaware of it, everyone is more or less influenced by Nietzsche, Dostoevsky, Freud, and Barth; and everyone is affected very deeply by the language of Plato and Aristotle. All scholars use terms such as "essential," "form" and "content," "autonomy" and "heteronomy," "subconscious" and "father-image."

To say that a particular man is a "Christian" scholar is therefore a very incomplete and inaccurate, even misleading, description of his mental make-up. Let us confine ourselves to one example. Let us assume that a particular man is a Protestant of the Calvinistic tradition, more especially of the Congregational group; further that he has been formed most by Plato, Aristotle, Kant, and Marx. Now we turn back to the study of the Bible. It may be that our Kantian Congregationalist is well equipped to understand certain aspects of the New Testament, but it is just as certain that he will be blind to other aspects. The same thing is true for a Kierkegaardian Presbyterian, and for a Platonizing Episcopalian. There is only this difference, that the blind spots of a Kierkegaardian are different from the blind spots of a Platonist.

For this reason Christian scholars ought to be suspicious of their own convictions, and strive to be as unbiased as possible. If they do not know that categories such as "essential" and "accidental" are much more likely to confuse their understanding of Jesus' message than to clarify it, they are uncritical scholars. However, they ought to be aware that they are in danger of being duped, not only by Aristotelian, Kantian, Freudian, and Heideggerian language, but also by their denominational language. Scholars are most vulnerable to distraction when they assume that they can be simply "Christians." Often a scholar may be *helped* by the fact that he was reared as a Lutheran or as a Calvinist, but as often his specific outlook will be a *hindrance* to a deeper understanding of the Bible. For centuries Lutheran and Calvinist leaders quite naïvely read their own convictions into the Bible. For example, they forced the Old Testament into a christological scheme which was largely postbiblical in its origin. Their Christian faith thus prevented their reception of more than the traditionally accepted interpretations of the Bible.

b) Real progress in biblical study became possible only from the moment that Christian scholars learned to distrust their own convictions, and wanted to know, not what Methodists or Episcopalians would *like* Paul to have taught, but what Paul actually taught. Real research is possible only when Christian scholars openly admit that Isaiah, Luke, Paul, and even Jesus can endorse convictions which are not only alien to all that we believe, but which we cannot take over in our body of convictions, in our language. Johannes Weiss and Albert Schweitzer realized how exceedingly important is the eschatological element in Jesus' convictions, and this fact remains true, whether we like it or not. Jesus thought largely in eschatological terms, yet not one Christian church or individual Christian living in the twentieth century who thinks "eschatologically," thinks in exactly the same terms as Jesus did.

4. *Research as an "ascetic" enterprise*

From time to time the conception of the scientific attitude presented here is opposed as being too idealistic. "Can scholars actually rise to such an angelic height of lofty detachment?" This skepticism rests upon a misunderstanding. First, the foregoing discussion does not pretend to include all the motives for scientific research. Had that been intended, a variety of very "human" factors would have wanted mention, e.g., personal ambition, the desire to outdo one's colleagues in scholarly output, etc. Second, the scientist is not an angel who may rise far above petty prejudices, sympathies, and antipathies into the pure, clear air of scholarly labor. His attitude is not so much superhuman as subhuman. Our prejudices are joined to our preferences, our deepest convictions; and these convictions, our beliefs, are we ourselves. We *are* what we live for, what we fight for, what we die for. To say that we should be as unbiased as possible, that we should be suspicious of our own preferences, means therefore that we have to give up that which is most characteristic in us. Scientific work is a kind of "ascetic" exercise.

To get back to our present topic, biblical scholars study the Bible in a scientific way in order to serve the theological work of their church; that is to say, they try to detach themselves from their convictions in order to correct, to deepen, to enrich these convictions. They prefer "research as unbiased as possible" to "Christian scholarship" for the sake of a better Christian theology.

D. THE CONCEPTIONS OF TRUTH IN BIBLICAL THEOLOGY AND IN BIBLICAL RESEARCH

1. *The conception of truth of biblical research*

a) We can clarify the differences and the relations between biblical theology and biblical research by asking for the meaning of the terms "truth" and "decision" in both languages. In both cases these terms are abbreviations which we may use only if we are fully aware of what they stand for. What is the "truth" about a certain biblical passage in terms of research?

Let us assume that it is a passage over which New Testament students have been divided for decades. At this moment, however, there exists a considerable amount of agreement among recognized scholars. The majority of the leading scholars all over the world agrees that theory A, which was defended mainly in Germany during the nineties, has many more arguments against it than in its favor. This majority admits, however, that the view B, which was developed in the thirties under the leadership of some British scholars, has many arguments in its favor and only a few against it. The majority of scholars also agrees on the relative merits of theories C and D, launched by Americans and Swedes in the forties. What is now the "truth" about this passage? To the analytical philosopher it is no less than the whole picture in which figure: first, the majority of the recognized scholars; second, the year 1958; and third, the relationships between theories A, B, C, and D. Some elements of this analytical conception of truth must be developed:

(1) Truth is *relative*. There is no absolute truth. What is generally accepted as the most plausible explanation of a group of facts, is relative to the century in which we live, and to the personal characteristics and background of the scholars who set forth the theory.

(2) It is *hypothetical*. Each theory is only an attempt to explain certain phenomena, a tool in the process of understanding. This tool may be more or less useful. New data may turn up, for which the old theory may not give a satisfactory explanation. In this case scholars will set up a new hypothesis, with which they will try to cover both the old and the new facts.

(3) It is *revisable*. There is no final, ultimate truth. There are no eternal laws and unchangeable formulations of scientific truth. Even laws possess the hypothetical character which belongs to all theories and explanations. Therefore they are all revisable. A better knowledge of the koine or of the Aramaic, the detection of hitherto unknown manuscripts of Genesis or proto-Luke, may throw new light on quite a number of problems, and change our ideas about the Hebrew repre-

sentation of the world, or the position of the Jerusalem congregation in the early church.

b) There is an element of decision in this process of searching for truth. When a scholar reads a paper on a topic such as "The disciples of John the Baptist," he sets forth the standpoint of the majority of the leading scholars, the position of one or two divergent groups, and concludes with some arguments for a view of his own. He decides in favor of this new view, and his personal characteristics and those of his church play a significant role in the decision he reaches. His church, for instance, is the Presbyterian; as an individual he has a strong preference for Heidegger.

So far the new theory of our scholar is only an unattested hypothesis. If he writes an article about it, his theory may be discussed in other journals, and perhaps also in books. Should many authorities on the subject support the new view, it becomes a well-founded theory. Not all of these authorities, however, are Presbyterians, and only a few have submitted to the allurement of Heidegger. It is probable that the new theory, in the course of the discussions, has been changed somewhat and has lost most of its one-sidedness. When the majority of leading scholars considers the new theory a valuable scientific tool, their decision is much less colored by Presbyterian and Heideggerian elements than was the decision of the originator of the theory. The elements of personal preference and conditioning have been checked, controlled, and reduced to their right proportions. We can now give a fourth characteristic of scientific truth:

(4) It is *intersubjective*. No product of scientific investigation may be called objective, because the subjective element can never be completely expelled. However, it is not necessary for a theory to remain purely subjective. At the end of the process of scientific research and criticism, it can be raised to the intersubjective level.

2. *The conception of truth of biblical theology*

In the language of biblical theology the terms "truth" and "decision" have quite other meanings than in biblical research. Here the so-called subjective elements should not be checked and controlled, but are the basis of each decision, of all truth. "True" here means: "true according to one's lights." This type of truth cannot be demonstrated. That Jesus Christ is "the Son of God," and not "the greatest man who ever lived," cannot be proved or disproved, either by logical reasoning or by empirical evidence. It is an appraisal, an evaluation.

This does not mean that "reason" has nothing to do with it. On the contrary, the theologian "employs" his language, and this implies that he "employs" his intelligence. For instance, he employs his thinking if he wishes to make clear to himself and others what "Son of God" means. Again, he employs his "reason" if he shows the implications of such theological convictions for practical life, i.e., their deeper "reasonableness." The bases of these convictions, however, are not of reason-character but of evaluation-character. Evaluations cannot be reduced to anything else, be it ideas or emotions. They are *sui generis.*

We can give the following characteristics of theological truth:

(1) Truth is *given,* in contrast with scientific truth which has to be searched for, which is therefore hypothetical. The truth given to people in their convictions, by their convictor, has to be unfolded. They have to think out the implications of these convictions for their behavior. In confronting the convictions with their sources they have to be enriched, deepened.

(2) Theological truth is *relative,* just as is scientific truth, to historical and geographical elements and to the personal character of the scholars, but above all to the insights and convictions received by the particular church of which the theologians form the vanguard. Whereas the relativity of the scientific truth is canceled out by its intersubjectivity, the relativity of theological truth becomes clearer as the specific character of this truth is more convincingly elaborated.

(3) Theological truth is, like scientific truth, not final and ultimate, but *revisable.* People revise their theological language, however, not on the basis of new facts and new theories, but by the force of new insights, in the sense of deepened convictions.

3. *Exegesis and interpretation*[4]

In view of the basic differences between the languages of biblical research and biblical theology, it would be proper if the scholars of the churches with which we are concerned would use the term "exegesis" in connection with only one of these disciplines. Perhaps it would be best if they reserved "exegesis" for biblical research and used "interpretation" for biblical theology. A problem of exegesis is formulated in the following way: "How did Jesus think about his relationship to God?" Answer: "According to some Swiss professors, passage *a* in Matthew, chapter *b,* shows that it is probable that . . ."

A problem of theological interpretation is formulated: "How do *we* have to think about Jesus' relationship to the Father?" The answer would run: "According to the lights of our church we are led to believe that . . ." A more correct answer would be: "According to the

[4] Our discussion will not refer to the specific positions taken by scholars such as Bultmann and Barth in the argument about exegesis.

lights of our church, and taking into account the achievements of biblical research, we are led to believe . . ."

The bases for such a belief, however, are never the achievements of biblical research, but always "the lights of our church," which lead us to prefer Paul to James, or the Apocalypse to John. Biblical research never comes further than the statement that Paul believed this and that, and that James believed such and such; but it can never tell anyone which of these two is right. Who is "right" for a specific group of believers—that is something which these believers have to decide for themselves, on the basis of the light granted them. If they prefer Paul, they take a certain *risk,* because no one can prove that his beliefs are more true. Theological interpretation is always based on one's own light, i.e., on one's own faith.

If we accept this terminology, the term "theological exegesis" is a contradiction in terms. Theological activity has to be sharply distinguished from scientific activity. The first can never replace the latter. Each has its own task, its own method, its own right. One's theology will be better served by an independent than by an enslaved biblical research.

E. CRYPTOTHEOLOGICAL LANGUAGES

1. *Cryptotheology in biblical research*

We still have to take account of certain phenomena in the field of biblical studies which have not been covered by our discussion of biblical theology and biblical research. There are, for instance, some utterances which have something in common with both fields. We find books and articles which claim to produce biblical research and which certainly offer scientific theories, but which unmistakably show also signs of affinity with biblical theology, for instance, the publications of the Tübingen school.

There were in the nineteenth century many scholars who professed to produce neutral, objective science, which they rated much higher than the prejudiced products of the prescientific period. Actually, their publications contained, besides some valuable scientific explanations, a defense of, and an attempt to clarify and improve, a certain convictional world view, namely, that of a Hegelian version of Christianity. This second purpose, however, this theological activity for the sake of the Hegelian-Christian world view, was not openly acknowledged; and perhaps these theologians were not clearly aware of it themselves. Therefore, we say that such publications contain both indicative, scientific language, and cryptotheological language.

It is necessary to stress the point that we as philosophers have no quarrel with this Hegelian-Christian world view as such, but only with the confusion of languages. Each publication of a biblical scholar should move exclusively in the field of research, or exclusively in the theological field. If a biblical man wants to discuss both kinds of problems in one volume, he should deal with them in two separate parts of the book. A good example is Hans Windisch's *Der Sinn der Bergpredigt.*

Even the most conscientious scholar has to be continually aware of the temptation of seeing only those truths which are compatible with his own convictional world view, that is to say, of offering a cryptotheological instead of a scientific treatise. Probably no work of research is completely free from theological elements. As long as the man of research is aware of this fact and seeks a check against it by asking for criticism by scholars of different denominations and world views, we refer to him as a scientist and to his work as science; he lives up to the moral requirement of the scientist, to try to be as unbiased as possible.

2. *Cryptotheology in theological publications*

There is cryptotheological language, not only in scientific publications, but also in theological ones. The authors of such works openly confess that their purpose is not research, but the defense of the Christian faith. However, it is for outsiders very clear that the convictions which these men wish to defend and clarify, are not only partly Christian, but also heavily influenced by particular world views which have little to do with biblical ideas. We refer to publications by the leaders of Neo-Calvinistic groups, of Fundamentalists, and of certain Roman Catholic authors. It is not only the Hegelian world view, but also these other hidden views which have hindered people from admitting highly probable theories and explanations, which did not comply with their particular world view, as scientific truth.

Certain churches disqualify the whole science of biology, and a view of Gen. 1 which would take into account modern biological and geological theories; their disqualifications resting neither on the basis of scientific arguments, nor on purely religious grounds, but on the force of a convictional world view which combines biblical elements, seventeenth-century theology, and obsolete scientific theories about man and nature. Perhaps the basic notion of this type of cryptotheologians is the conviction that, because they themselves are honest and convinced Christians, and the biblical authors deserve the same words of praise, these authors must think and believe exactly as they themselves think and believe.

F. THE RELATIONSHIP BETWEEN THE AFOREMENTIONED AND SOME OTHER CHURCH LANGUAGES

1. *The language of revelation*

a) Christian believers refer to something which they could call a language, namely, God's revelation. They could replace and actually do replace a sentence such as "God reveals himself to us in Christ," by the sentence "God speaks to us in Christ." Revelation, as conceived by Christians, is clearly understood as a kind of language, spoken by God to man, or to specific men or nations.

If we refer in this chapter to "the language of revelation," we do not mean to imply an assertion of the reality of revelation, or a witness to its "truth" or importance. What takes place is something quite different; first, as philosophers who are interested in language we try to analyze various observable languages spoken by a certain group of Christians; second, we notice that these languages point back to an intangible, an unobservable (namely, revelation); third, this intangible, or more correctly, the intangible as presented in the tangible account given by believers, shows typical language characteristics.

It is possible for us as philosophers to study, not this language itself, for revelation is not a datum at our disposal, but to investigate the *account* which these believers give of this language-like unobservable. Questions as to whether this language is or has been actually spoken, and as to its value and validity, or as to the reality of its speaker, lie outside the range of a philosopher's competence and interest. The only thing in which he is interested is that this "language" means something to the believer.

b) It is scarcely necessary to collect evidence that revelation is a language for the Christian believer. He refers to Jesus as the *Logos,* the "Word" of God. Not only are the words spoken by Jesus of Nazareth considered to be part of this Word, but it is claimed that God spoke to man by means of Jesus' entire life, his actions and his birth and death included. Further, many sermons have themes such as "God speaks to us in history," or "in the events of our daily lives."

c) It seems that all other languages spoken in Christian churches, as far as the believers are concerned, are responses to this one specific language. We therefore cannot understand these other languages in their meaning for those who speak them, if we do not try to understand what this "first" language means to them. They call the words of the Bible "the record of revelation," and claim that their faith, i.e., their faith language, is a response to what God has "said" to them.

2. *Confusion of languages*

a) In the life of the Christian church we find a phenomenon which is a close parallel to the problem of metaphysics in philosophy. In the Christian community first the liberals, and later the adherents of Neo-Reformation theology, have accused other groups, namely, orthodox Protestants and Roman Catholics, of what amounts to confusion of languages. The background to this accusation is the age-old protest by the liberals that the orthodox unduly ascribed divine authority to the creedal formulations of the church. A parallel accusation was that of bibliolatry, that is to say, of their elevating the Bible to the rank of an unquestionable statement of divine truth.

We can translate these quarrels into modern terminology by stating that, according to liberals, the Christian church knows various languages, each with a character of its own, each with its own kind of truth, authority, and validity; and that the orthodox caused confusion by not taking these differences into consideration.

b) The liberals and the Neo-Reformation theologians (who in this matter are the heirs of the liberals without always acknowledging it) claim that we have to count at least the following Christian languages:

(1) The language of revelation.
(2) The language of the biblical authors.
(3) The language of the church creeds.
(4) The confessional language of the present churches.
(5) The language of present-day theology.
(6) The language of present-day biblical research.
(7) The personal language of faith of individual Christians.

We will try to analyze some of these languages and see wherein the differences exist.

3. *Language categories*

A language, or more accurately, a language situation, gives rise to a series of questions. Attempts to answer them enable us to track down several language categories. Some of them we have met already in Chap. I. We will illustrate each category by references to one or two of the above-mentioned seven Christian languages.

a) The first category is simply that of the *communicator*. Who is it that speaks this language? On the basis of this category alone it is possible to make a fundamental distinction between the language of revelation and all the other Christian languages: one is thought to be spoken by God, the others by human beings. Even the language of scripture is human language, at least to Christian understanding. It is the Moslems, not the Christians, who assume that their scriptures were written by God himself.

b) The next question which suggests itself is: To whom is this language directed? or, Who is the *communicatee?* This category does not offer many problems for most of the Christian languages. In regard to confessional language it has to be said that, for the churches concerned, this language is directed in the first place to God, then to members of the group itself, and also to outsiders.

c) Similarly, we have to ask for the *content* of the communication. It would take several chapters to give a complete survey of all problems involved, for the language of revelation alone. What follows are merely a few sketchy remarks.

There was a time when theologians asserted that God communicated "truths" about himself, about man, about the world. Nowadays most theologians would say that God communicates himself; "God gives himself in Christ." It seems we have to say that this content also comprises God's blessings, and a certain understanding of his will for man and the world.

We should not be surprised at the turn which the problem of the content of communication takes. In the languages which are the usual objects of research for most analytical philosophers, such as those of mathematics, empirical science, and logic, not many questions arise as to the content. The "what" which the communicator communicates to the communicatee consists of: information, theories, objections to theories; that is to say, the "what" is clearly expressed in the sentences used. As soon, however, as we get away from the cognitive languages, from the *use*-languages, the picture changes. Word and language form only a part of the communication.

If a son leaves for the army, especially in the case of war, his parents on taking leave of him communicate much more than the content of the words they speak, taken in their strict meaning. This "more" is also present in many cases of moral approval or disapproval. This is not to say that the words are superfluous, or even insignificant. It means that of the total communication, part is discursive, part is nondiscursive. Philosophy, as I see it, does better to confine itself to an analysis of the discursive aspects of communication. In other words, philosophy is part of a larger group of disciplines, which study all the utterances of man, in all their various facets. To this group belong psychology and those disciplines which study symbols, arts, etc.

It is not difficult to understand why Christians of all denominations have claimed that it is impossible to give an exact verbal account of the content of the language of revelation. It may be questioned whether it is possible at all to translate nondiscursive communication into discourse, in the case of human language just as much as in the case of the language of revelation.

d) Further, it makes sense to ask for the *means* of communication. This is the question of the "how" of communication, as distinguished from the "what." It is again an important problem in the language of revelation. The biblical authors and Christian believers have offered several answers, such as: dreams, the inspired words of prophets, and specific events. Most Christians will claim that *the* means used by God are his "Word," Christ, and the Holy Spirit.

e) If we ask for the *purpose* of a communication, it appears that on some occasions it is appropriate to distinguish between an immediate and a basic purpose. The immediate purpose of the language of biblical research, for instance, is to gain reliable information about biblical documents. It would be insufficient to stop here. We have to take account also of a farther reaching purpose of biblical research, namely, to serve the church, especially its theological activity. It can be argued that all scientific languages have two similar purposes: the immediate one, to gain reliable information about animals, metals, stars, human beings, and instruments; the basic one, to serve mankind in its attempts to arrange for a comfortable and "decent" life on this planet.

f) In the same way we have to ask the question about the *community* in such a manner that there is room for different aspects of the question. Language always functions within a certain community. It is understood by the members of this community and not by outsiders. The language of chemistry is understood by the trained chemist only. Biblical scholars publish their technical work in journals and books meant only for other scholars. We can call the community of these scholars the "immediate community." Biblical research is done, however, not only for the sake of other scholars but in view of a more "basic" community, which is a denomination, or a group of denominations; and here perhaps some Christians will speak of "the church of Christ."

There is even a third kind of community, which we could call the "presupposed community." A discipline such as modern biblical research presupposes the whole Western world, with its scientific interest, its scientific tools, and its appreciation of critical thinking. The language of the biblical authors, on the other hand, presupposes a quite different civilization. The difference in presupposed community is a complicating factor in the relationship between the various languages which play a role in the Christian faith.

g) We could use the term *character* to indicate whether a language is convictional, indicative, or tautological, etc. We conclude that all languages which function within the realm of the Christian faith are convictional in character, with the exception of biblical research, which is indicative.

h) An exceedingly difficult matter is the type of *truth* of a language. Though this is an important category, it is not one which is among the first to be discussed. The type of truth of a language depends upon its purpose, its content, and its means of communication. It makes a difference whether a language is a clearly delimited kind of communication, wherein the nondiscursive element is either absent or plays a subordinate role, or whether we have to do with a language which is an aspect of a communication with important nondiscursive elements.

In the first case (for instance, cognitive language) the characteristics of the type of truth can be more or less clearly stated. In the latter case the question can be put whether we should speak only of the truth of a language or also of the authority on which it depends.

This is not to deny that there is any truth in nondiscursive communication. So it makes sense to say that there is truth in a painting of Rembrandt or of Van Gogh. No Christian will consent to the thesis that one cannot speak of the truth of the language of revelation, but it is clear that what is meant here is very different from the kind of truth of empirical science. Truth in this language of revelation, and therefore also in the convictional languages related to it, depends upon the authority of the convictor. It is probable that we are dealing here, not with one category, but with a group of interrelated categories.

i) We enter now upon a group of categories which form the *basis* of a language. First, we can speak of *basic presuppositions*. We have already met some of them in Chaps. I and VI when we discussed the convictional basis of indicative language. We claimed that this language, though itself free from convictions, was based upon the convictions that it is possible to gain reliable knowledge of the external world, that this knowledge is very valuable, etc.

Whereas these convictions constitute the basis of all empirical sciences, they assume a specific form for each particular science. Something like biblical research was not possible at all before Christians assumed that the Bible "is" not only the record of revelation, but "is" also a set of human documents about which it makes sense to ask scientific questions. Those Christians who object to this "higher criticism," not only disagree with the results of this research, but they cannot share its underlying convictions. The vehemence of fundamentalist opposition to modern biblical scholarship derives primarily from convictions which conflict with these underlying assumptions.

It is not only indicative language which is built upon convictional presuppositions. For instance, the activity of the theological vanguard is founded upon the assumption of the insufficiency of the confessional language of the group.

j) A second group of categories which belong to the basis of a language is formed by the *requirements for the communicator*. These categories also are convictional in character. For a biblical scholar there are, first, moral requirements, such as, to be as unbiased as possible. To this group belongs also the willingness to give ear to what can be learned from the "heathen" religions, referred to in the Old Testament. Second, intellectual requirements, such as empathy, which is the mental versatility necessary to understand people of other times and civilizations. Finally, requirements which we might call "spiritual," though this is a much misused word. What is meant is being congenial with the Hebrew faith and with the Christian faith.

That whole section of the empirical sciences which sometimes is called the humanities is based upon a similar set of requirements. These languages cannot function well if these requirements are not taken seriously. If the communicators trespass upon them, the outcome is not so much science as a mixture of science and cryptotheology.

The accompanying diagram does not claim to offer a final account of the languages in question. It is more a stimulus for further analysis. The words contained in the boxes are at the very best a short indication of the field of problems involved, and at worst a proof of the unsatisfactory status of the discussion on a particular point. If terms are placed between brackets, it means that they are not satisfying, but that clearer concepts are not yet available.

G. THEOLOGY, PHILOSOPHY, AND PHILOSOPHY OF RELIGION

1. *The old situation*

a) According to the traditional conception of philosophy, this discipline had a normative role. For philosophy of religion, this meant a theological function. This notion was worked out in different ways.

(1) Philosophy of religion could be a branch of theology, namely, that section which took up the conversation with the non-Christian world. Philosophy of religion was then sometimes called apologetics, especially if the aspect of the defense of the own faith was stressed. This was the usual position of traditional Protestants. The term "apologetics" was dropped if the defensive attitude was changed into one of welcoming the contributions of modern civilization. In this latter

CATEGORIES	REVELATION	BIBLICAL AUTHORS	CONFESSIONAL LANGUAGE
Communicator	God	Prophets and Apostles	Individual members Denomination
Communicatee	Chosen-nation prophets	All mankind	God Other believers All men
Content	God himself His blessings Images Evaluations	Records of revelation	Praises Thanksgivings Confessions
Means	Dreams Prophets Events God's Word the Holy Spirit	Books	Church services Testimonies Hymns Creeds
Purpose (immediate)	Salvation	To witness to revelation	To profess Christian faith
Purpose (basic)		To serve God and man	
Community (immediate)	That between God and man	God and his people	God and his church
Community (basic)			
Community (presupposed)		Eastern civilization	Western civilization
Character	Convictional	Convictional	Convictional
Truth	[Has to be testified to by the Holy Spirit]	Can be understood by believers only	Relative [given]
Presuppositions	God's love	God's pleasure to use human beings as tools	The assumption that God has to be worshiped
Requirements for communicator		Faith Obedience to God	Intellectual — understanding of Christian faith Moral — obedience to God Spiritual — belief

CATEGORIES	BIBLICAL THEOLOGY	BIBLICAL SCIENCE
Communicator	Theologians	Scientists
Communicatee	Own denomination Other denominations	Scientists Theologians
Content	Evaluations of biblical doctrines	Exegesis of biblical records
Means	Scholarly publications	Scientific publications
Purpose (immediate)	To improve confessional language	To clarify meaning of biblical records
Purpose (basic)	[To serve church]	To serve the theological activity
Community (immediate)	Denomination	Group of biblical scientists
Community (basic)	*Communio sanctorum*	Denomination
Community (presupposed)	Western civilization	Western civilization
Character	Convictional	Indicative
Truth	Relative [given] [subjective]	Relative Hypothetical Intersubjective
Presuppositions	The assumption that confessional language needs improvement	The assumption that scientific approach to Bible is possible and worth while
Requirements for communicator	Intellectual: empathy Moral: ecumenicity Spiritual: openness to God	Intellectual: empathy Moral: as unbiased as possible Spiritual: congeniality to the Christian faith

case the less traditional Protestants felt that contact with modern science, philosophy, and art would strengthen their own attitude of emancipation from traditional, authoritarian, dogmatical theology. Philosophy of religion was seen as the guide on the path of enlightenment and freedom. This view was usually taken by liberal Protestants.

(2) Philosophy of religion could be conceived as a preparation for theology. It was considered as a discipline which could guide the believer to some truths but not to all truths, especially not "saving" truths. Philosophy and philosophy of religion had to be supplemented by theology, in the sense that they had to receive their guiding principles from that discipline, and therefore to be judged by it. In its purest form this point of view is taken by Roman Catholic scholars,

though less sharply marked forms can be met in Protestant circles too.

(3) Philosophy of religion could be conceived as the heir of traditional theology. Those who took this stand saw this theology as a narrow-minded enterprise, biased because it based itself upon the truth of only one "religion." Philosophy of religion, on the contrary, looked for a broader basis, and earned thereby respectability in the eyes of modern men. It took into account not only the "truths" of the biblical religions, but also those of non-Christian religions; truths acceptable not only to Hebrews and Christians but also to men of other beliefs. It believed that God had given truths not only to priests but to men of science, to poets, philosophers, and other wise men.

This view implied the belief that if the philosopher of religion worked on the various "experiences" of all these groups and men, he could by means of a process of criticism and purification decide upon the relative value of each "experience" and in this way build a system of truths which was in a certain sense universal (namely, over against the traditional theology which was "one-sided" in starting point, method, and outcome) and definitely intellectually respectable.

This position has been taken by several American liberal Protestants. It can be detected in the educational policies in church-sponsored colleges, where usually the main subjects taught in the "Department of Bible and Religion" are Bible, and philosophy of religion, but not theology.

b) The older concept of philosophy of religion as a normative discipline can also be seen in the arrangements in the teaching schedules in Protestant seminaries, where philosophy of religion is coupled with *Christian* ethics as a group of disciplines taught by one man. Christian ethics means here a doctrine of moral teachings for the lives of individuals and communities. The philosopher of religion is thus not supposed to be a philosopher, but a theologian; he has to give, not philosophical ethics, but Christian morals.

c) It is not too far-fetched to connect this view of the function of philosophy of religion with the Greek cosmos conviction. All philosophy, and therefore also philosophy of religion, has the task to penetrate to the core of things, to set aside what is unessential, and to bring to the fore that which is universally true, valuable, and beautiful.

2. *The proposed situation*

a) If one starts from the notion that the function of philosophy is not normative but analytical, the relationship between philosophy of religion and the other theological disciplines changes entirely. Philosophy of religion is no longer conceived as a kind of theology; it is an independent discipline. It is more correct to say that, instead of the one traditional philosophy of religion, two disciplines have to be set up:

(1) *Philosophy of religion proper,* which is a branch of philosophy, an analytical discipline which investigates religious language and other convictional languages.

(2) *Discursive theology,* a branch of theology, a convictional discipline which, in the name of the church, enters into discussion with the world outside that church.

The first of these disciplines is the field within which the present treatise wishes to move.

b) In the seminaries of the churches which we have in mind, the function of theology has not yet been completely clarified, but we can say that the following understanding is growing. Theology is the central discipline; as such it is closely related to the other major disciplines. This relationship possesses the character of challenge and response. Within theology we can distinguish not so much various branches as different aspects: biblical, historical, moral, and discursive theology. These aspects are all of them clearly theological; that is to say, the theologian who moves in them starts on all occasions from the convictions of his group. For the right performances of his task (the improvement of the confessional language of his group), the theologian needs to be challenged by the findings of the other theological and several nontheological disciplines. At the same time the theologian asks questions of these other disciplines, which they may or may not be able to answer.

biblical theology (convictional) — biblical research (indicative)
historical theology (convictional) — historical research (indicative)
moral theology (convictional) — philosophical ethics (analytical)
discursive theology (convictional) — philosophy of religion (analytical) and also: philosophy, arts, and several sciences, such as psychology, sociology, economics, political science

An example may give us some insight into the theological process. If the churches feel the need of teaching more clearly what a Christian approach to the problem of property consists in, the theologian consults biblical research (What do the Old and the New Testament teach about the value of property in God's eyes?), historical research (teachings and attitudes of church fathers, the medieval church, the Reformers, recent movements), ethics (Which factors are involved in a "moral situation" like this one?), philosophy of religion (Which convictional world views determine the attitudes of present-day Westerners, including church members, toward property?), and last but not least, the sciences of economics, sociology, and politics.

H. FINAL REMARKS

The analysis offered in this chapter needs supplementation for several reasons. The obvious one is that the present investigation must be corrected by people who fulfill two requirements: first, that of being an insider in the same group of churches; second, that of understanding what it means to analyze one's own set of language relationships while abstaining from the defense of a specific convictional language.

a) Our insight into the relationships of different languages will, however, be deepened considerably if the present analysis is paralleled by investigations of similar relationships in other confessional groups, such as present-day Jewish, Roman Catholic, Anglo-Catholic, and Greek Orthodox groups. Such a comparison is not complete if another kind of confessional groups is not also drawn into it: those of the naturalists, the humanists, the French existentialists, the Communists, the Fascists. The difficulty of inaugurating discussion with this last kind of confessional groups is that some of them are so much more loosely organized than the churches. Yet it is possible to ask the question as to the manner in which convictional, analytical, and indicative languages are *actually* related in these groups.

Another comparison which needs to be made is that with some of the confessional groups outside the Western civilization. Which kind of languages can be distinguished here? What are their actual relationships? Can these languages be compared at all with those which we know in Western civilization? Do civilizations exist where only one language is spoken?

b) Before we can be satisfied with our information about the kinds of relationships between various languages, a quite different type of question has to be asked. In the foregoing we had in mind the actual relationships between languages within a number of confessional groups. For each of these groups we can ask the question, What is the relationship between the analytical account of the actual character of the set of language relationships and the *self-interpretation* of this character by the leading agencies of the group? It can, for instance, be argued that it is highly probable that an analysis will show that in the Roman Catholic group something will exist which is a parallel of the vanguard activity of improving the confessional language which we noticed in the group of ecumenically minded Protestants. The question which we raise now is: How much weight does the official Roman Catholic theology give to this improving activity? Is it possible for this theology to admit fully all the characteristics of this activity, in view, for instance, of its doctrine of truth (truth is that *quod ubique, semper, et ab omnibus creditum est*)?

It will be very instructive and interesting to compare for each confessional group the analytical account of its languages with the account which is inspired by its convictional self-interpretation. In this way we will receive some insight into how clearly a group understands itself.

POSTSCRIPT

Is not this book a defense through philosophical means of just another convictional world view? Is not therefore the ideal of a completely neutral analysis a naïve illusion?

Let us summarize the possible relations between convictional and analytical language:

1. An analysis (just as a scientific theory) can be basically nothing but a *rationalization* of a specific convictional world view.

2. Specific convictions can function as a *heuristic* principle of the analytical activity; in this case they inform the analysis, without interfering with it.

3. Convictions can block the analysis; the philosopher is *prevented from seeing* certain things analytically, because he cannot dissociate himself from his convictions.

4. The analytical approach is *compatible with* certain convictional world views, and incompatible with others.

5. A philosopher can be *attached* to a specific analysis in a very personal way, so that it seems to him that his worth stands or falls with this analysis—hence the language in which he defends the analysis is ablaze with convictional colors.

Only points 4 and 5 require further discussion. The last remark holds for the scientist as well as for the philosopher. A chemist (or philosopher) can attack another scholar who doubts the value of a hypothesis (or analysis) dear to his heart in language shot through with moral judgments. It is, however, not at all necessary that this strong attachment influence the validity of the hypothesis or the analysis.

Again, the scientific as well as the analytical approach is compatible with only a limited number of convictional world views. This fact may not lead us to question the worth of these approaches. When modern geology and biology are incompatible with a certain type of fundamentalism, this fact does not give us the right to disqualify these sciences.

It is highly probable that each philosophical work participates in all five relations mentioned. The contrast is not between publications which do, and others which do not participate, but between works which are intensely, and others which are merely superficially, influenced by some of these relations. We cannot but expect that books which set forth new analyses are influenced more deeply in this respect than works which keep to the beaten paths. On the other hand, it is not impossible that a new analysis, to a certain extent, is free from respectable, age-old prejudices which have beset philosophy for many centuries.

Philosophical analysis as understood in this work is compatible with some forms of Protestantism (Neo-Reformation theology, a certain kind of reconstructed liberalism), perhaps a liberal Catholicism, some form of Anglicanism, and several kinds of humanism, whereas it is incompatible with fundamentalism, orthodoxy, older liberalism, and all forms of metaphysics, Communism, Fascism, and other totalitarianisms.

BIBLIOGRAPHY

The following bibliography is offered with considerable hesitation. Each student is in danger of reading too much and thinking too little. If one section of this book should commend itself especially to the reader, he should not begin with reading more about this particular topic, but first of all reconsider his own thinking on the subject. A bibliography tempts the student to extend his reading and to postpone his own philosophizing. (There is one exception, the problem of myth, in which a thorough study of the sources is a condition of better thinking.)

Since a bibliography is unavoidable, I have compiled one, but I have omitted secondary sources insofar as possible. The next best thing to doing your own thinking is to study original philosophers. Nice and good books *about* logical positivism, Heidegger, Plato, and Hume should be avoided. If a student reads "good books about" his mind will be cluttered up by the questions which Professor A. and Professor B. direct to Aristotle and Sartre, and he will never get to the point where he asks these philosophers his own questions.

If a student feels that he cannot understand one of these original thinkers, and is aware of the temptation of surrendering to a "good book about," he can protect himself against intellectual laziness by means of the following procedure: he should ask himself of which leading philosophers in the past this philosopher reminds him, and start to study these predecessors. For instance, if one wants to understand Heidegger, he should read Husserl, Nietzsche, and Kierkegaard. The understanding of Tillich is greatly enhanced by the study of Schelling, Boehme, Eckhart, and Plotinus. Few pages in philosophy are so revealing as Windelband's account of Jakob Boehme's thought. Windelband gives here in one page a masterful summary of Tillich's ontology.[1]

INTRODUCTION

1. The revolutionary change in philosophy since the 1920's

a) Analytical philosophy

Carnap, Rudolf. *Introduction to Semantics.* Cambridge, Mass.: Harvard University Press, 1942.

Moore, George E. *Principia Ethica.* New York: Cambridge University Press, 1954.

———. *Some Main Problems of Philosophy.* New York: The Macmillan Co., 1953.

Russell, Bertrand. "The Philosophy of Logical Atomism," *The Monist,* XXVIII, 495-527; XXIX, 32-63, 190-222, 345-80.

Von Mises, Richard. *Positivism.* Tr. Jerry Bernstein and Roger G. Newton. Cambridge, Mass.: Harvard University Press, 1951.

Wittgenstein, Ludwig. *Philosophical Investigations.* Tr. G. E. M. Anscombe. New York: The Macmillan Co., 1953.

———. *Tractatus Logico-Philosophicus.* New York: Harcourt, Brace & Co., 1922.

[1] Wilhelm Windelband, *Geschichte der Philosophie* (2nd ed.; Tübingen and Leipzig: J. C. B. Mohr, 1900), p. 307.

b) Existentialist philosophy

Heidegger, Martin. *Holzwege.* Frankfurt am Main: Vittorio Klostermann, 1952.

———. *Sein und Zeit.* Tübingen: Neomarius Verlag, 1949.

Marcel, Gabriel. *Homo Viator.* Tr. Emma Craufurd. Chicago: Henry Regnery Co., 1951.

———. *Reflection and Mystery.* Tr. C. S. Fraser. Chicago: Henry Regnery Co., 1950.

Sartre, Jean Paul. *Being and Nothingness.* Tr. Hazel E. Barnes. New York: Philosophical Library, 1956.

2. The preparation of the change

Hume, David. *A Treatise of Human Nature.* Ed. L. A. Selby-Bigge. New York: Oxford University Press, 1941.

Husserl, Edmund. *Ideas: General Introduction to Pure Phenomenology.* New York: The Macmillan Co., 1956.

———. *Logische Untersuchungen.* Halle a. S.: Niemeyer, 1900-1901.

Kierkegaard, Sören. *Concluding Unscientific Postscript.* Tr. D. F. Swenson and W. Lowrie. Princeton, N.J.: Princeton University Press, 1941.

———. *Philosophical Fragments.* Tr. D. F. Swenson. Princeton, N.J.: Princeton University Press, 1936.

3. About analytical philosophy

a) General

Von Aster, Ernst. *Die Philosophie der Gegenwart.* Leiden: Sijthoff, 1935.

b) Roman Catholic

Copleston, F. C. *Contemporary Philosophy: Studies of Logical Positivism and Existentialism.* Westminster, Md.: Newman Press, 1956.

c) Protestant

Zuurdeeg, Willem F. *A Research into the Consequences of the Vienna Circle Philosophy for Ethics.* Utrecht: Kemink & Zoon, 1946.

4. Oxford school of philosophical theology in "linguistic" style

Flew, Antony, and Macintyre, Alasdair, eds. *New Essays in Philosophical Theology.* New York: The Macmillan Co., 1956.

Hick, John. *Faith and Knowledge: A Modern Introduction to the Problem of Religious Knowledge.* Ithaca, N.Y.: Cornell University Press, 1957.

Ramsey, Ian T. *Religious Language: An Empirical Placing of Theological Phrases.* London: SCM Press, 1957.

The Socratic, No. 5: *Contemporary Philosophy and Christian Faith.* New York: Philosophical Library, 1952.

5. What is analysis?

Black, Max, ed. *Philosophical Analysis.* Ithaca, N.Y.: Cornell University Press, 1950.

Feigl, Herbert, and Sellars, Wilfrid, eds. *Readings in Philosophical Analysis.* New York: Appleton-Century-Crofts, 1949.

Russell, Bertrand. *The Analysis of Mind.* New York: The Macmillan Co., 1921.

Schlick, Moritz. *Gesammelte Aufsätze.* Vienna, 1938.

6. What is language?

Carnap, Rudolf. *The Logical Syntax of Language.* Tr. Amethe Smeaton. New York: Harcourt Brace & Co., 1937.

Cassirer, Ernst. *Language and Myth.* Tr. Susanne K. Langer. New York: Harper & Bros., 1946.

———. *Philosophy of Symbolic Forms.* 3 vols. Tr. Ralph Manheim. New Haven, Conn.: Yale University Press, 1953.

Gusdorf, Georges. *La Parole.* Paris: Presses universitaires de France, 1953.

Langer, Susanne K. *Philosophy in a New Key.* New York: Pelican Books, 1948.

Morris, Charles W. *Signs, Language and Behavior.* New York: Prentice-Hall, 1946.

Ogden, C. K., and Richards, I. A. *The Meaning of Meaning.* 5th ed. New York: Harcourt Brace & Co., 1930.

7. Philosophies of religion in traditional style

Brightman, Edgar S. *A Philosophy of Religion.* New York: Prentice-Hall, 1940.

Tennant, F. R. *Philosophical Theology.* 2 vols. New York: The Macmillan Co., 1928-30.

Thompson, Samuel M. *A Modern Philosophy of Religion.* Chicago: Henry Regnery Co., 1955.

CHAPTER ONE CONVICTION

1. On conviction

Kant, Immanuel. *Critique of Pure Reason,* 2nd ed. rev. Tr. F. Max Mueller. New York: The Macmillan Co., 1949. Pt. II, ch. ii, sec. 3, "Of Trowing, Knowing, and Believing."

Newman, J. H. *The Grammar of Assent.* Ed. Charles F. Harrold. New York: Longmans, Green & Co., 1947.

2. On Gusdorf

Gusdorf, Georges. *La découverte de soi.* Paris: Presses universitaires de France, 1948.

———. *L'expérience humaine du sacrifice.* Paris: Presses universitaires de France, 1948.

———. *Mémoire et personne.* Paris: Presses universitaires de France, 1951.

———. *Mythe et métaphysique.* Paris: Flammarion, 1953.

———. *Traité de l'existence morale.* Paris: Colin, 1949.

CHAPTER TWO POWER

1. Lebensphilosophie

Bergson, Henri. *Creative Evolution.* Tr. Arthur Mitchell. New York: Modern Library, 1944.

Dilthey, Wilhelm. *The Essence of Philosophy.* Tr. Stephen A. and William T. Emery. Chapel Hill: University of North Carolina Press, 1954.

Eucken, Rudolf. *Collected Essays.* Ed. and tr. M. Booth. London: Fisher Unwin, 1914.

2. Freud

Freud, Sigmund. *The Future of an Illusion.* Tr. W. D. Robson-Scott. New York: Liveright Publishing Corp., 1949.

———. *Moses and Monotheism.* Tr. Katherine Jones. New York. Vintage Books, 1955.

3. The relationship between religion and morality

Bergson, Henri. *The Two Sources of Morality and Religion.* Tr. R. Ashley Audra and Cloudesley Brereton. New York: Henry Holt & Co., 1935.

Garnett, A. Campbell. *Religion and the Moral Life.* New York: Ronald Press, 1955.

4. On fanaticism

Sartre, Jean Paul. *Anti-Semite and Jew.* Tr. George J. Becker. New York: Schocken Books, 1948.

CHAPTER THREE WORLD VIEWS

1. About Heidegger

Biemel, W. *Le concept de Monde chez Heidegger.* Louvain/Paris, 1950.

Macquarrie, John. *An Existentialist Theology: A Comparison of Heidegger and Bultmann.* New York: The Macmillan Co., 1955.

2. On world views

Buber, Martin. *The Eclipse of God.* New York: Harper & Bros., 1952.

Tillich, Paul. *The Dynamics of Faith.* New York: Harper & Bros., 1957.

3. On the primitive world

See bibliography to Chap. V.

CHAPTER FOUR METAPHYSICS

1. On Hume

Hendel, Charles W. *Studies in the Philosophy of David Hume.* Princeton, N.J.: Princeton University Press, 1925.

2. On logical positivism

Kraft, Viktor. *Der Wiener Kreis, Der Ursprung des Neopositivismus.* Wien: Springer, 1950.

See bibliography to Introduction.

3. On metaphysics

Bergmann, Gustav. *The Metaphysics of Logical Positivism.* New York: Longmans, Green & Co., 1954.

Smart, J. J. C. "Metaphysics, Logic and Theology," *New Essays in Philosophical Theology.* Ed. Antony Flew and Alasdair Macintyre. New York: The Macmillan Co., 1955.

4. On Whitehead

Ely, S. L. *The Religious Availability of Whitehead's God.* Madison: University of Wisconsin Press, 1942.

Whitehead, Alfred N. *Process and Reality.* New York: The Macmillan Co., 1929.

5. On Tillich

Boehme, Jakob. *The Aurora.* Tr. J. Sparrow. London: Watkins, 1914.

Tillich, Paul. *Biblical Religion and the Search for Ultimate Reality.* The University of Chicago Press, 1955.

CHAPTER FIVE MYTH

1. Modern history of religions

Eliade, Mircea. *Images et symboles.* Paris: Gallimard, 1952.

———. *Traité de l'histoire des religions.* Paris: Payot, 1949.

2. On myth

Cassirer, Ernst. *Phliosophy of Symbolic Forms.* Vol. II: *Mythical Thought.* Tr. Ralph Manheim. New Haven, Conn.: Yale University Press, 1955.

Eliade, Mircea. *Le mythe de l'éternal retour.* Paris: Gallimard, 1949.

Gusdorf, Georges. *Mythe et métaphysique.* Paris: Flammarion, 1953.

Otto, Walter F. *Die Gestalt und das Sein.* Düsseldorf: Diederichs, 1955.

3. On Bultmann

Bultmann, Rudolf. *Kerygma and Myth.* Ed. H. W. Bartsch. Tr. Reginald H. Fuller. New York: The Macmillan Co., 1954.

Hepburn, R. W. "Demythologizing and the Problem of Validity," *New Essays in Philosophical Theology.* Ed. Antony Flew and Alasdair Macintyre. New York: The Macmillan Co., 1955.

CHAPTER SIX COSMOS

1. On Plato

Cornford, F. M. *Plato and Parmenides.* New York: Humanities Press, 1951.

———. *Plato's Cosmology.* New York: Humanities Press, 1952.

———. *Plato's Theory of Knowledge.* New York: Humanities Press, 1951.

2. On the Greek cosmos conviction

Bultmann, Rudolf. "The Understanding of Man and the World in the New Testament and in the Greek World," *Essays: Philosophical and Theological.* Tr. James C. G. Greig. New York: The Macmillan Co., 1955.

3. The relationship between Greek religion and Greek philosophy

Cornford, F. M. *Principium Sapientiae.* New York: Cambridge University Press, 1952.

4. The Enlightenment

Hoffmann, H. *Aufklärung* in R.G.G., 2nd ed.
Randall, J. H., Jr. *The Making of the Modern Mind.* Rev. ed. Boston: Houghton Mifflin Co., 1940.
Shaw, Ch. G. *Enlightenment* in E.R.E.

a) The Enlightenment in philosophy

Cassirer, Ernst. *The Philosophy of the Enlightenment.* Tr. F. C. A. Koelln and J. P. Pettegrove. Princeton, N.J: Princeton University Press, 1951.
Descartes, René. *Meditations on the First Philosophy.* 13th ed. Tr. John Veitch. 1902.
Kant, Immanuel. "Was heisst Aufklärung?" in *Berliner Monatschrift,* December, 1784.
Leibnitz. See Latta, R. *The Monadology and Other Philosophical Writings.* Oxford, 1898.

b) Enlightenment in the church

Cherbury, Herbert of. *De veritate.* London, 1627.
Locke, John. *The Reasonableness of Christianity.* 1695.

c) Enlightenment in science

Newton, Sir Isaac. *The Mathematical Principles of Natural Philosophy.* London, 1803.

d) Enlightenment in politics

Locke, John. *Two Treatises of Government.* Ed. Thomas I. Cook. New York: Hafner Publishing Co., 1947.
Montesquieu, Charles L. de Secondat, Baron de. *The Spirit of the Laws.* 2 vols. Tr. Th. Nugent and J. V. Prichard. Bohn, 1896-97.

5. The Post-Enlightenment

a) Post-Enlightenment in philosophy

See the bibliography to Introduction.

b) Post-Enlightenment in the church

Barth, Karl. *Church Dogmatics.* New York: Charles Scribner's Sons, 1956.
Otto, Rudolf. *The Idea of the Holy.* Rev. ed. Tr. J. W. Harvey. New York: Oxford University Press, 1936.
Schleiermacher, Friedrich E. D. *On Religion.* Tr. John Oman. New York: Frederick Ungar Publishing Co., 1955.

c) Post-Enlightenment in science

Frank, Philipp. *Modern Science and Its Philosophy.* Cambridge, Mass.: Harvard University Press, 1949.
Russell, Bertrand. *The Scientific Outlook.* New York: W. W. Norton & Co., 1931.
Whitehead, Alfred N. *Science and the Modern World.* New York: The Macmillan Co., 1946.

d) Post-Enlightenment in politics

Carr, E. H. *The Twenty Years' Crisis, 1919-1939.* New York: The Macmillan Co., 1940.
Heimann, Eduard. *History of Economic Doctrines.* New York: Oxford University Press, 1945.
Kennan, George F. *Realities of American Foreign Policy.* Princeton, N.J.: Princeton University Press, 1954.

Morgenthau, Hans J. *Politics Among Nations.* New York: Alfred A. Knopf, 1948.
———. *Scientific Man vs. Power Politics.* The University of Chicago Press, 1946.

CHAPTER SEVEN MORALS

1. Analytical ethics

Schlick, Moritz. *Problems of Ethics.* Tr. David Rynin. New York: Prentice-Hall, 1939.
Sellars, Wilfrid, and Hospers, John, eds. *Readings in Ethical Theory.* New York: Appleton-Century-Crofts, 1952.
Stevenson, Charles L. *Ethics and Language.* New Haven, Conn.: Yale University Press, 1945.
Von Mises, Richard. *Positivism.* Tr. Jerry Bernstein and Roger G. Newton. Cambridge, Mass.: Harvard University Press, 1951.

2. On Marcel

Marcel, Gabriel. *The Decline of Wisdom.* London: The Harvill Press, 1954.
———. *Homo Viator.* Tr. Emma Craufurd. Chicago: Henry Regnery Co., 1951.
———. *Man Against Mass Society.* Tr. G. S. Fraser. Chicago: Henry Regnery Co., 1952.
———. *The Mystery of Being.* 2 vols. Vol. I tr. G. S. Fraser; Vol. II tr. R. Hague. Chicago: Henry Regnery Co., 1951.
———. *The Philosophy of Existence.* Tr. Manya Harari. New York: Philosophical Library, 1949.

CHAPTER EIGHT THE CHURCH

1. On exegesis

Barth, Karl. *Church Dogmatics,* Vol. I, Pt. II. Tr. G. T. Thomson and Harold Knight. Charles Scribner's Sons, 1956.
Bultmann, Rudolf. "The Problem of Hermeneutics," *Essays: Philosophical and Theological.* Tr. James C. G. Greig. New York: The Macmillan Co., 1955.

2. Convictional interpretations of the Christian faith by Christians

a) Roman Catholic

Maritain, Jacques. *True Humanism.* Tr. Margot Adamson. New York: Charles Scribner's Sons, 1938.

b) Protestant

Barth, Karl. *Dogmatics in Outline.* Tr. G. T. Thomson. New York: Philosophical Library, 1949.
Niebuhr, H. Richard. *Christ and Culture.* New York: Harper & Bros., 1951.
Niebuhr, Reinhold. *The Self and the Dramas of History.* New York: Charles Scribner's Sons, 1955.

INDEX